Dark Tourism and Place Identity

Dark Tourism, including visitation to places such as murder sites, battlefields and cemeteries is a growing phenomenon, as well as an emergent area of scholarly interest. Despite this interest, the intersecting domains of dark tourism and place identity have been largely overlooked in the academic literature and this book aims to fill this void.

The three main themes of visitor motivation, destination management and place interpretation are addressed in this book from both a demand and supply perspective by examining a variety of case studies from around the world. This edited volume takes the dark tourism discussion to another level by reinforcing the critical intersecting domains of dark tourism and place identity and, in particular, highlighting the importance of understanding this connection for visitors and destination managers.

Written by leading academics in the area, this stimulating volume of 19 chapters will be valuable reading for postgraduate and advanced undergraduate students in a range of discipline areas; researchers and academics interested in dark tourism; and other interested stakeholders including those in the tourism industry, government bodies and community groups.

Leanne White is a Senior Lecturer in Marketing in the College of Business at Victoria University in Melbourne, Australia.

Elspeth Frew is an Associate Professor in Tourism Management in the Department of Marketing, Tourism and Hospitality at La Trobe University in Melbourne, Australia.

Contemporary Geographies of Leisure, Tourism and Mobility

Series Editor: C. Michael Hall

Professor at the Department of Management, College of Business and Economics, University of Canterbury, Christchurch, New Zealand

The aim of this series is to explore and communicate the intersections and relationships between leisure, tourism and human mobility within the social sciences.

It will incorporate both traditional and new perspectives on leisure and tourism from contemporary geography, e.g. notions of identity, representation and culture, while also providing for perspectives from cognate areas such as anthropology, cultural studies, gastronomy and food studies, marketing, policy studies and political economy, regional and urban planning, and sociology, within the development of an integrated field of leisure and tourism studies.

Also, increasingly, tourism and leisure are regarded as steps in a continuum of human mobility. Inclusion of mobility in the series offers the prospect to examine the relationship between tourism and migration, the sojourner, educational travel, and second home and retirement travel phenomena.

The series comprises two strands:

Contemporary Geographies of Leisure, Tourism and Mobility aims to address the needs of students and academics, and the titles will be published in hardback and paperback. Titles include:

1. **The Moralisation of Tourism**
   Sun, sand . . . and saving the world?
   Jim Butcher

2. **The Ethics of Tourism Development**
   Mick Smith and Rosaleen Duffy

3. **Tourism in the Caribbean**
   Trends, development, prospects
   Edited by David Timothy Duval

4. **Qualitative Research in Tourism**
   Ontologies, epistemologies and methodologies
   Edited by Jenny Phillimore and Lisa Goodson

5. **The Media and the Tourist Imagination**
   Converging cultures
   Edited by David Crouch, Rhona Jackson and Felix Thompson

6. **Tourism and Global Environmental Change**
   Ecological, social, economic and political interrelationships
   Edited by Stefan Gössling and C. Michael Hall

7. **Cultural Heritage of Tourism in the Developing World**
   Edited by Dallen J. Timothy and Gyan Nyaupane

8. **Understanding and Managing Tourism Impacts**
   An integrated approach
   C. Michael Hall and Alan Lew

9. **An Introduction to Visual Research Methods in Tourism**
   Edited by Tijana Rakic and Donna Chambers

10. **Tourism and Climate Change**
    Impacts, adaptation and mitigation
    C. Michael Hall, Stefan Gössling and Daniel Scott

Routledge Studies in Contemporary Geographies of Leisure, Tourism and Mobility is a forum for innovative new research intended for research students and academics, and the titles will be available in hardback only. Titles include:

1. **Living with Tourism**
   Negotiating identities in a Turkish village
   Hazel Tucker

2. **Tourism, Diasporas and Space**
   Edited by Tim Coles and Dallen J. Timothy

3. **Tourism and Postcolonialism**
   Contested discourses, identities and representations
   Edited by C. Michael Hall and Hazel Tucker

4. **Tourism, Religion and Spiritual Journeys**
   Edited by Dallen J. Timothy and Daniel H. Olsen

5. **China's Outbound Tourism**
   Wolfgang Georg Arlt

6. **Tourism, Power and Space**
   Edited by Andrew Church and Tim Coles

7. **Tourism, Ethnic Diversity and the City**
   Edited by Jan Rath

8. **Ecotourism, NGOs and Development**
   A critical analysis
   Jim Butcher

9. **Tourism and the Consumption of Wildlife**
   Hunting, shooting and sport fishing
   Edited by Brent Lovelock

10. **Tourism, Creativity and Development**
    Edited by Greg Richards and Julie Wilson

11. **Tourism at the Grassroots**
    Villagers and visitors in the Asia-Pacific
    Edited by John Connell and Barbara Rugendyke

12. **Tourism and Innovation**
    Michael Hall and Allan Williams

13. **World Tourism Cities**
    Developing tourism off the beaten track
    Edited by Robert Maitland and Peter Newman

14. **Tourism and National Parks**
    International perspectives on development, histories and change
    Edited by Warwick Frost and C. Michael Hall

15. **Tourism, Performance and the Everyday**
    Consuming the Orient
    Michael Haldrup and Jonas Larsen

16. **Tourism and Change in Polar Regions**
    Climate, environments and experiences
    Edited by C. Michael Hall and Jarkko Saarinen

17. **Fieldwork in Tourism**
    Methods, issues and reflections
    Edited by C. Michael Hall

18. **Tourism and India**
    A critical introduction
    Kevin Hannam and Anya Diekmann

19. **Political Economy of Tourism**
    A critical perspective
    Edited by Jan Mosedale

20. **Volunteer Tourism**
    Theoretical frameworks and practical applications
    Edited by Angela Benson

21. **The Study of Tourism**
    Past trends and future directions
    Richard Sharpley

22. **Children's and Families' Holiday Experience**
    Neil Carr

23. **Tourism and National Identifies**
    An international perspective
    Edited by Elspeth Frew and Leanne White

24. **Tourism and Agriculture**
    New geographies of consumption, production and rural restructuring
    Edited by Rebecca Torres and Janet Momsen

25. **Tourism in China**
    Policy and development since 1949
    David Airey and King Chong

26. **Real Tourism**
    Practice, care, and politics in contemporary travel culture
    Edited by Claudio Minca and Tim Oakes

27. **Last Chance Tourism**
    Adapting tourism opportunities in a changing world
    Edited by Raynald Harvey Lemelin, Jackie Dawson and Emma Stewart

28. **Tourism and Animal Ethics**
    David A. Fennell

29. **Actor Network Theory and Tourism**
    Ontologies, methodologies and performances
    Edited by René van der Duim, Gunnar Thór Jóhannesson and Carina Ren

30. **Liminal Landscapes**
    Travel, experience and spaces in-between
    Edited by Hazel Andrews and Les Roberts

31. **Tourism in Brazil**
    Environment, management and segments
    Edited by Gui Lohmann and Dianne Dredge

32. **Slum Tourism**
    Edited by Fabian Frenzel, Malte Steinbrink and Ko Koens

33. **Medical Tourism**
    Edited by C. Michael Hall

34. **Tourism and War**
    Edited by Richard Butler and Wantanee Suntikul

35. **Sexuality, Women and Tourism**
    Cross border desires through contemporary travel
    Susan Frohlick

36. **Adventure Tourism**
    Steve Taylor, Peter Varley and Tony Johnson

37. **Dark Tourism and Place Identity**
    Managing and interpreting dark places
    Leanne White and Elspeth Frew

38. **Backpacker Tourism and Economic Development**
    Perspectives from the less developed world
    Mark P. Hampton

39. **Peace through Tourism**
    Promoting human security through international citizenship
    Edited by Lynda-ann Blanchard and Freya Higgins-Desbiolles

Forthcoming:

Gender and Tourism
Social, cultural and spatial perspectives
Cara Atchinson

Scuba Diving Tourism
Kay Dimmcock and Ghazali Musa

Travel, Tourism and Green Growth
Min Jiang, Terry DeLacy and Geoffrey Lipman

Contested Spatialities, Lifestyle Migration and Residential Tourism
Michael Janoschka and Heiko Haas

Research Volunteer Tourism
Volunteer voices
Angela Benson

Dark Tourism and Place Identity

Managing and interpreting dark places

Edited by
Leanne White and Elspeth Frew

LONDON AND NEW YORK

First published 2013
by Routledge
2 Park Square, Milton Park, Abingdon, Oxon OX14 4RN

Simultaneously published in the USA and Canada
by Routledge
711 Third Avenue, New York, NY 10017

Routledge is an imprint of the Taylor & Francis Group, an informa business

© 2013 Leanne White and Elspeth Frew

The right of Leanne White and Elspeth Frew to be identified as the authors of the editorial material, and of the authors for their individual chapters, has been asserted in accordance with sections 77 and 78 of the Copyright, Designs and Patents Act 1988.

All rights reserved. No part of this book may be reprinted or reproduced or utilised in any form or by any electronic, mechanical, or other means, now known or hereafter invented, including photocopying and recording, or in any information storage or retrieval system, without permission in writing from the publishers.

Trademark notice: Product or corporate names may be trademarks or registered trademarks, and are used only for identification and explanation without intent to infringe.

British Library Cataloguing in Publication Data
A catalogue record for this book is available from the British Library

Library of Congress Cataloging in Publication Data
White, Leanne.
Dark tourism and place identity: managing and interpreting dark places / Leanne White and Elspeth Frew.
p. cm.
Includes bibliographical references and index.
1. Tourism-Psychological aspects. 2. Geographical perception. 3. Place attachment. I. Frew, Elspeth. II. Title.
G155.A1.W46 2013
910.68-dc23
2012032164

ISBN: 978-0-415-80965-8 (hbk)
ISBN: 978-0-203-13490-0 (ebk)

Typeset in Times New Roman
by Book Now Ltd, London

Contents

List of figures	xiii
List of tables	xv
Notes on contributors	xvii
Acknowledgements	xxiii

1 **Exploring dark tourism and place identity**   1
ELSPETH FREW AND LEANNE WHITE

PART I
Visitor motivation   11

2 **The Père-Lachaise Cemetery: between dark tourism and heterotopic consumption**   13
STÉPHANIE TOUSSAINT AND ALAIN DECROP

3 **African Americans at sites of darkness: roots-seeking, diasporic identities and place making**   28
LINDA LELO AND TAZIM JAMAL

4 **Place identity or place identities: the Memorial to the Victims of the Nanjing Massacre, China**   46
WEI DU, DAVID LITTELJOHN AND JOHN LENNON

5 **The contribution of dark tourism to place identity in Northern Ireland**   60
MARIA TERESA SIMONE-CHARTERIS, STEPHEN W. BOYD AND AMY BURNS

x Contents

6 Dark tourism, heterotopias and post-apocalyptic
   places: the case of Chernobyl   79
   PHILIP R. STONE

PART II
Destination management   95

7 Pagan tourism and the management of
   ancient sites in Cornwall   97
   CHANTAL LAWS

8 Soviet tourism in the Baltic states: remembrance
   versus nostalgia – just different shades of dark?   115
   BRENT MCKENZIE

9 Turning the negative around: the case of Taupo,
   New Zealand   129
   ALEX MORALES

10 Commemorating and commodifying the
   Rwandan genocide: memorial sites in a
   politically difficult context   142
   PETER HOHENHAUS

11 Dark tourism and place identity in French Guiana   156
   OLIVIER DEHOORNE AND LEE JOLLIFFE

12 Place identities in the Normandy landscape
   of war: touring the Canadian sites of memory   167
   GEOFFREY R. BIRD

PART III
Place interpretation   187

13 Holocaust tourism in a post-Holocaust Europe:
   Anne Frank and Auschwitz   189
   KIMBERLEY PARTEE ALLAR

14 Dark detours: celebrity car crash deaths
   and trajectories of place   202
   GARY BEST

15 **Marvellous, murderous and macabre Melbourne: taking a walk on the dark side** 217
LEANNE WHITE

16 **War and ideological conflict: prisoner of war camps as a tourist experience in South Korea** 236
EUN-JUNG KANG AND TIMOTHY J. LEE

17 **Dark tourism in the Top End: commemorating the bombing of Darwin** 248
ELSPETH FREW

18 **Darkness beyond memory: the battlefields at Culloden and Little Bighorn** 264
PAUL WILLARD, CLARE LADE AND WARWICK FROST

19 **Beyond the dark side: research directions for dark tourism** 276
LEANNE WHITE AND ELSPETH FREW

Index 283

Figures

1.1	The three themed sections of this book	2
2.1	Mano Solo's tomb and tributes (singer)	20
2.2	Touching Kardec's mausoleum	22
2.3	Objects at the souvenir shop near the Père-Lachaise Cemetery	24
3.1	Life-size wax figures (engaged in a funerary ceremony)	38
4.1	The sign displays that 300,000 lives were lost at Nanjing	51
4.2	Candles are lit for 'Hundreds of Thousands'	53
4.3	The peace bell stands as a symbol of friendship	55
4.4	Four key influences on the construction of place identity	57
5.1	Mural of Bobby Sands on Belfast's Republican Falls Road	67
5.2	Museum of Free Derry	68
6.1	A dark tourism cylinder: a conceptual model showing the dark tourism experience within a heterotopian framework	90
7.1	Mên an Tol monument, West Penwith	106
7.2	A 'Cloutie' tree at Madron Holy Well, marking the way to the original well head and showing the difficult access	107
7.3	CASPN signage at Madron Holy Well	109
8.1	Soviet World War II Memorial, Antakalnis Cemetery, Vilnius, Lithuania	117
8.2	Soviet World War II Memorial, Estonian Defence Forces Cemetery, Tallinn, Estonia	118
8.3	Soviet World War II Memorial, Pokrov Cemetery, Riga, Latvia	119
10.1	Display of victims' skulls at Gisozi Genocide Memorial, Kigali	147
12.1	Flags and anthems: local commemoration on 6 June 2008 at Basly	173
12.2	Gravestone of Trooper Morton, Beny-sur-Mer, Canadian Military Cemetery	176
12.3	Abbaye d'Ardenne: site of Canadian executions	178
12.4	Flags, poppies and crosses left behind at the Abbaye d'Ardenne	179
13.1	A dark tour passes under the well-known gates of Auschwitz	196

Figures

15.1	Crime tour guide Alex explains the plaques at the Victoria Police Memorial	221
15.2	The Russell Street Police Headquarters and its striking Art Deco architectural style	223
15.3	The Hoddle Street Massacre occurred near Julian Knight's home (the large building on the left)	224
15.4	The main entrance of the Melbourne General Cemetery was built in the 1930s	227
15.5	Cemetery tour guide Jan enlightens us on the life and times of Sir Samuel Gillott	229
15.6	The simple grave and repaired headstone of Melbourne's famous ghost – Federici	231
15.7	Melbourne's popular laneways such as Hosier Lane are known for creative graffiti	232
15.8	Ghost tour guide Matt tells us the story of Federici	233
17.1	Depiction of the expansion of the Japanese Empire at the Defence of Darwin Experience	250
17.2	The interactive table depicting the bombing of Darwin at the Defence of Darwin Experience	251
17.3	Depiction of the impact of air raids on Darwin civilians	253
17.4	Contrasting Australian and Japanese uniforms at the Darwin Military Museum	255
17.5	The original brass air mail postal slot from the bombed Darwin Post Office at the Darwin Aviation Heritage Centre	258
17.6	Blood-soaked life jacket at the Defence of Darwin Experience	261

Tables

3.1	Visitor arrivals at Elmina Castle: 2002–2004	31
3.2	US sites of African American heritage	32
3.3	Blacks in New Amsterdam	34
5.1	Total visitor figures and revenue: select years between 1974 and 1989	65
5.2	Visitors to Northern Ireland and revenue generated (1995–2009)	66
8.1	Selected examples of dark sites in Estonia, Latvia and Lithuania	123
10.1	Overview of the six national genocide memorial sites in Rwanda	149
11.1	Dark tourism sites listed in French Guiana	161

Contributors

Gary Best lectures in cultural tourism, festival and event management and gastronomy at La Trobe University, Melbourne, Australia. His research interests are diverse but tend to focus on tourism and the media; travel writing; distinctive cultural interactions in touristic contexts; automotive history, heritage and culture and the means by which all of the above operate in popular culture. He has published on the media/tourism dynamic; on being Japanese in three Australian film landscapes; on film-induced tourism; on identifying, exploring and understanding diversity through specific cultural interactions; and on writing the American road. He has also discussed cultural tourism on both Australian and US radio.

Geoffrey R. Bird is an Associate Professor at the School of Tourism and Hospitality Management at Royal Roads University in Victoria, BC, Canada. He completed a PhD in 2011 at the University of Brighton, UK, where he studied the relationship between tourism, remembrance and landscapes of war. In addition to teaching for the past 12 years, Geoff has a wide range of tourism-related experience in government, consulting and the private sector, both in Canada and overseas. His research interests relate to his work history and include dark tourism, heritage experiences, poverty alleviation through community tourism, tourism policy and tourism product development.

Stephen W. Boyd is Professor of Tourism at the University of Ulster, Northern Ireland. His research interests focus on heritage and cultural tourism, World Heritage Sites and national parks and how communities engage in the development of tourism. He is working closely on research projects with his graduate students on event tourism, food tourism and political tourism.

Amy Burns completed her Bachelor of Science in Nutritional Sciences at University College, Cork, Northern Ireland and her doctorate in the School of Biomedical Sciences at the University of Ulster, Northern Ireland. She is a Lecturer in the Ulster Business School, and has published widely on aspects of nutrition and consumer issues.

Alain Decrop is Dean of the Faculty of Economics, Social Sciences and Business Administration at the University of Namur, Belgium. Professor Decrop is a member of the Center for Research on Consumers and Marketing Strategy within the Louvain School of Management group. He holds master degrees in modern history and economics, and a PhD in business administration. His research interests include consumer decision making and behaviour, qualitative interpretive methods and leisure marketing. He is the author of *Vacation Decision Making* and co-editor of the *Handbook of Tourist Behavior*. His other works have appeared in a number of books and academic journals.

Olivier Dehoorne works at the Université des Antilles et de la Guyane based in Martinique where he coordinates the Masters programme with a specialty in tourism. He is a member of CEREGMIA – Centre d'Etude et de Recherche en Economie, Gestion, Modélisation et Informatique Appliquée. His research, based on the discipline of geography, relates to tourism development in the French territories in the Caribbean.

Wei Du has recently gained her doctoral degree in tourism at Glasgow Caledonian University, UK. Her research focuses on tourism motivation for visiting dark tourism sites via a case study of the Nanjing Massacre Memorial. She studied at Bedfordshire University, UK for her undergraduate degree in Advertising and Marketing Communications.

Elspeth Frew is an Associate Professor in Tourism Management in the Department of Marketing, Tourism and Hospitality at La Trobe University in Melbourne, Australia. Elspeth's research interest is in cultural tourism, with a particular focus on dark tourism and festival management. Elspeth has published several articles in the area of dark tourism, most recently in the *International Journal of Heritage Studies*. The paper considered the contemporary commemoration and interpretation of the 1996 Port Arthur massacre. She has also conducted research into the relationship between the media and tourism management. Consequently, Elspeth's research is often inter-disciplinary since she considers aspects of tourism within the frameworks of psychology, media studies, anthropology and sociology.

Warwick Frost is an Associate Professor in the Department of Marketing, Tourism and Hospitality at La Trobe University, Melbourne, Australia. He is the co-author (with Jennifer Laing) of *Books and Travel: Inspirations, Quests and Transformations* and *Commemorative Events: Identity, Memory, Conflict*. He is an editor of the Routledge Advances in Events Research book series and a member of the editorial board of *The Journal of Heritage Tourism*. Warwick is a convenor of the biennial International Tourism and Media conference series. His current research includes explorers and adventure travellers, and tourism and media in the American West.

Peter Hohenhaus is originally from the field of language and linguistics. In this he holds a PhD, has published widely, held lecturer positions at the UK universities of Nottingham and Bradford and also taught and researched in Germany. In more recent years he has moved into the field of dark tourism studies – and the relevant practice. In connection with this he has developed and runs www.dark-tourism.com, a comprehensive online resource on the practice of dark tourism. He has personally visited and investigated hundreds of dark tourism sites in virtually all corners of the world.

Tazim Jamal is an Associate Professor in Recreation, Park and Tourism Sciences at Texas A&M University, College Station, Texas, USA. She specializes in sustainable tourism, with a strong focus on collaborative planning and community-based tourism development. In this context, she also addresses critical and methodological issues related to cultural heritage, human–environmental relations and destination management. She conducts research locally in Texas plus internationally in diverse community and destination settings. She is an editorial board member of several peer-reviewed journals and is the co-editor of *The Sage Handbook of Tourism Studies*.

Lee Jolliffe is Professor of Hospitality and Tourism at the University of New Brunswick, Canada. Her teaching and research interests focus on heritage and culinary tourism. She is the editor of *Tea and Tourism, Tourists, Traditions and Transformations, Coffee Culture, Destinations and Tourism, Sugar Heritage and Tourism in Transition* and co-editor with Michael Conlin of *Mining Heritage and Tourism: A Global Synthesis*. Lee is an editorial board member of a number of journals including *Annals of Tourism Research, International Journal of Contemporary Hospitality Management* and *Tourism – An International Interdisciplinary Journal*.

Eun-Jung Kang is a Lecturer in Tourism Management at the Jeju National University, South Korea. She recently completed her doctoral research in visitor studies at the University of Queensland, Australia and holds a Masters degree in Tourism Management from the same institution. Her interests include: visitor studies in dark tourism sites; cultural heritage tourism; small island tourism development; and the meetings, incentives, conferences and exhibitions (MICE) industry. She has published many refereed journal articles including one on dark tourism experience in *Tourism Management*. She is currently involved with several research projects in small island tourism development and MICE.

Clare Lade is a Lecturer in Tourism and Hospitality in the Department of Marketing, Tourism and Hospitality at La Trobe University, Melbourne, Australia. She completed her PhD in regional tourism development, concentrating on network development and competitiveness through business cluster theory along Australia's Murray River. Clare has previous experience working with local communities and industry associations in regional Victoria and has successfully carried out numerous research projects within these regions in recent years. Her primary research interests include regional tourism development, marketing of regional festivals and events, and dark tourism.

Chantal Laws is a Senior Lecturer in the School of Leisure at the University of Gloucestershire in the United Kingdom, where she teaches events, festival and heritage management. Chantal's research interests focus on cultural experiencescapes and liminal events and she regularly presents and publishes work on these topics. Chantal has previous professional experience in the cultural industries and a lifelong interest in the heritage and archaeology of Cornwall.

Timothy J. Lee is Professor of Tourism and Hospitality Management at the Ritsumeikan Asia Pacific University, Japan. He has successfully supervised six PhD research students in tourism studies. His research interests include medical/wellness/health tourism, ethnic identity issues in the tourism industry, cultural heritage tourism and tourism developments that incorporate East Asian values. He has published more than 70 research articles in academic journals and conferences including in *Annals of Tourism Research*. He is a member of the editorial board of five leading academic journals including *Tourism Management* and *Tourism Analysis*.

Linda Lelo is an Assistant Professor of Hospitality and Tourism in the Division of Business and Technology at Wiley College, Marshall, Texas, USA. Her dissertation work looked at the experiences of African American visitors to slavery-related sites and the representation of slavery at these sites. Her research interests include: dark tourism, slavery tourism, tourism in Africa and black travellers.

John Lennon is Head of Department of Management and Director of the Moffat Centre for Travel and Tourism Business Development. It is the UK's largest university-based tourism consultancy and research centre, and is responsible for international consumer and market research and business consultancy. With its profits, the centre funds scholarships for students wishing to study travel and tourism. Professor Lennon has undertaken over 550 tourism projects in over 40 countries. He is a Policy Advisor to Visit Scotland, a Non-Executive Director of Historic Scotland and the author of five books and over 100 articles and reports on the travel and tourism industry.

David Litteljohn recently retired from a full-time career in tourism, travel and hospitality, most recently at Glasgow Caledonian University, UK. Professor Litteljohn is a graduate of Strathclyde University and the University of Manchester, both UK. David worked in tourism and policy development for a government enterprise agency in Scotland and later lectured at Huddersfield and Edinburgh Napier Universities. He regularly works in Europe and Asia, and his research spans market developments in hospitality, strategic management applications to hospitality and the internationalization of hotels and tourism markets. Past research projects include work for hotel chains, national tourist boards, government enterprise companies and merchant banks.

Brent McKenzie, PhD Griffith University, is an Associate Professor in the Department of Marketing and Consumer Studies at the University of Guelph, in Ontario, Canada. Brent has a special interest in the countries of the former Soviet Union, in particular the Baltic States of Estonia, Latvia and Lithuania. He has engaged in extensive research fieldwork, and conducted a number of workshops and presentations in these countries. He has also presented numerous research papers at North American and international conferences, and published his work in a number of academic and practitioner journals.

Alex Morales is a Masters candidate in the Department of Tourism at the University of Otago in New Zealand. Her research interests include destination image, crime, effects of crime in tourism and tourism information management. Her research focuses on the portrayal of crime against the international tourist in New Zealand's media.

Kimberly Partee Allar is a student in the PhD programme of Holocaust and Genocide Studies at Clark University in the United States. Her research interests include exploring how the impact of physical place, post-war crime trials and the media in particular influence the perception and creation of history. She is currently in the beginning stages of her dissertation research titled, 'Lessons in Terror and Death: Comparative Studies in the Training of Holocaust Perpetrators', which focuses on the methodological, psychological and ideological training of concentration camp guards from 1933 to 1945, taking into account gender, age and ethnicity.

Maria Teresa Simone-Charteris is a PhD student in the Department of Hospitality and Tourism Management at the University of Ulster, Northern Ireland. She is researching the potential interconnections between religious and political tourism in Northern Ireland. Her research interests include cultural heritage tourism, pilgrimage and religious tourism, food and wine tours and festivals, dark tourism, political tourism, peace and reconciliation through tourism, and sustainable tourism planning and development.

Philip R. Stone is Executive Director of the Institute for Dark Tourism Research (iDTR) at the University of Central Lancashire (UK). Philip, who has a PhD in Thanatology, has published extensively in the area of dark tourism, including being co-author/editor of books such as *The Darker Side of Travel: The Theory and Practice of Dark Tourism, Tourist Experience: Contemporary Perspectives* and *The Contemporary Tourist Experience: Concepts and Consequences*.

Stephanie Toussaint is a Research and Teaching Assistant at the Louvain School of Management (Université Catholique de Louvain in Mons, Belgium). She is currently working on her doctoral thesis and teaching marketing classes. Her research interests focus on various aspects of sacred and profane consumption, with an emphasis on space, place and contexts of consumption within the consumer culture theory perspective. Stephanie has worked in several research fields and favours the ethnographic approach. She is a member of the Center for Research on Consumers and Marketing Strategy in Belgium.

Leanne White is a Senior Lecturer in Marketing in the College of Business at Victoria University in Melbourne, Australia. Her research interests include: national identity, Australian popular culture, advertising, commercial nationalism, destination marketing and cultural tourism. Leanne's doctoral thesis examined manifestations of official nationalism and commercial nationalism at the

Sydney 2000 Olympic Games. She is the author of more than 35 book chapters and refereed journal articles, and co-editor of another Routledge volume in this series: *Tourism and National Identities: An International Perspective* (2011). Leanne is a reviewer for several academic journals, and a member of professional associations in marketing, tourism and sport.

Paul Willard is an Associate Lecturer in the Department of Marketing, Tourism and Hospitality at La Trobe University, Melbourne, Australia. His research interests include heritage tourism, experiential marketing, and visitor motivation and satisfaction. He is currently studying for his PhD on experiential tourism at battlefield sites.

Acknowledgements

We hope that you will be energized and engaged by the diverse international cases of dark tourism and place identity explored in this edited volume. As editors of this collaborative international body of work, we are delighted that from the tremendous collegial work of scholars around the globe, we have produced a volume that advances the academic debate surrounding dark tourism and place identity. All contributors have combined an applied approach with solid academic and critical analysis. We would like to thank the authors who made this book possible. They have been wonderful to work with, extremely responsive to our many emails and always highly cooperative.

On a personal level, we are grateful for the immeasurable support from our friends and families. Leanne would particularly like to thank Clarke Stevenson for his ongoing support and understanding, while Elspeth would like to thank Pat, Zoe and Callum Figgis for their inspiration and encouragement.

This book would not have been possible without a period of research leave from our respective universities – Victoria University and La Trobe University. We are thankful to our employers for these sabbaticals as they provided the opportunity to focus on this book, along with a range of other publications.

We would like to thank our publisher Routledge, along with the wider production team involved in seeing this book come to fruition. In particular, we thank Emma Travis, Carol Barber, Joanna Green, Emily Davies and Richard Cook.

This book builds upon our earlier Routledge volume *Tourism and National Identities: An International Perspective* (2011) by narrowing the focus of the tourism analysis to dark tourism (acknowledging that the definition of dark is wide-ranging) while, at the same time, broadening the discussion of identity to encompass the wider notion of place.

While this book is a reference text aimed principally at the academic market, it will hopefully provide interesting reading to anyone who has taken a walk on the dark side – whether they knew it at the time or not. This book is designed to address the void that currently exists in the discursive (and occasionally inexplicable) space where dark tourism and place identity meet.

All photographs in the book were taken by the contributors themselves.

Leanne White
Victoria University, Australia

Elspeth Frew
La Trobe University, Australia

1 Exploring dark tourism and place identity

Elspeth Frew and Leanne White

Understanding the dark places

This chapter provides a brief theoretical background to dark tourism and place identity, and then provides an overview of the sections of the book and the chapters. Chapters 2 to 18 then investigate case studies from around the world exploring dark tourism and place identity issues. To consider various aspects of dark tourism, the book uses case studies from the following countries: Australia, the Baltic States, Canada, France, French Guiana, the Netherlands, New Zealand, Poland, Rwanda, South Korea, the United Kingdom and the United States. The book is divided into three sections: visitor motivation, destination management and place interpretation (see Figure 1.1).

This edited volume provides a significant study of the motivation, destination management and place interpretation of international contemporary and historic sites associated with death, disaster and atrocity and their association with tourism. The book also explores the associated issues relating to marketing, management and interpretation of such contemporary and historic sites. As such, the book examines the physical and intangible legacies of historic and contemporary dark tourism sites around the world, and advances an understanding of how these sites are managed to allow visitors to respect the victims, and, at the same time, to avoid the glorification of the event associated with the site. Thus, this book explores the contribution such sites make to place identity.

The intersecting domains of dark tourism and place identity have been largely overlooked in the academic literature to date and this complex relationship between the two domains (and indeed, the multifaceted strategies used to define that relationship) is a subject worthy of further attention. By understanding dark tourist sites through the lens of place identity, the tourist may develop a deeper appreciation of the destination. Thus, this edited volume provides a composite model for discussing place identity and dark tourism that advances current understanding of these two areas.

2 *Elspeth Frew and Leanne White*

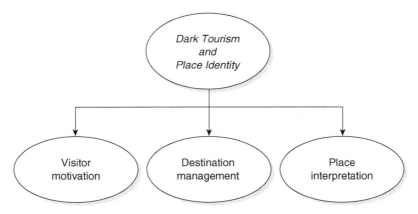

Figure 1.1 The three themed sections of this book

Dark tourism

Visitation to places such as murder sites, battlefields and cemeteries, is often referred to as 'dark tourism' (Lennon and Foley 2000). Such sites represent a range of events such as natural and accidental disasters, broad group atrocities, wars, large-scale killings or massacres and genocide (Tunbridge and Ashworth 1996). Although dark tourism is not a new phenomenon, there has been a recent emerging scholarly interest in researching and analysing dark tourism (see, for example, Sharpley and Stone 2009) and dark tourism has been recognized as a growing phenomenon in the twenty-first century, from both a demand and supply perspective (namely, the motives of visitors to sites and the provision of on-site interpretation and visitor facilities).

Since national events such as wars, national catastrophes, assassinations and massacres are experiences of shared grief that can help knit generations together (Frow 2000), memorials commemorating a tragic period in a nation's history can also reflect aspects of a nation's identity (Cooke 2000; Nanda 2004; Rivera 2008). Thus, this book takes the opportunity to investigate death sites and the development of national and place identity particularly because visiting such a site in one's own nation is, "to worship at the altar of collective identity" and because the sites can reflect a "commitment to the values and goals of the nation" (Hogan 2009: 205). Recent studies in tourism have considered the role of heritage attractions in helping create a national identity (see, for example, Palmer 2005; Pretes 2003). Tourists receive messages sent to them by the creators of the sites they visit, and these sites of significance, presented as aspects of a national heritage, help to shape a common national identity, or "imagined community" among a diverse population (Pretes 2003). Each of these attractions can help disseminate "national guiding fictions", and promote a discourse of national inclusion and a shared past (Pretes 2003). A shared identity is often an official goal of countries comprised of many different cultures particularly where there exists a common urge to create a national identity to overcome diversity and difference within the nation-state. In particular, monuments represent something shared by all citizens, helping to popularize a hegemonic nationalist message of inclusion (Pretes 2003).

Research into dark tourism has already identified a range of motives for visiting such sites. Some individuals wish to indulge their curiosity and fascination with thanatological concerns (i.e., the study of death and its related phenomena) in a socially acceptable environment that provides them with an opportunity to construct their own contemplation of mortality (Stone and Sharpley 2008). However, some visitors are motivated to visit for ghoulish titillation, and to be entertained (Wilson 2004). The modern day interest in celebrity, famous places and the development of communication that produces images of violence, war and tragedy, may support an individual's desire to visit such death sites (Lennon and Mitchell 2007). From a supply side perspective, recent research has considered the interpretation at museums and memorials that deal with sensitive issues (Beech 2000; Miles 2002; Wight and Lennon 2007), the commemoration of war crime victims (Rivera 2008) and, from a contemporary perspective, the most appropriate way to interpret Ground Zero in Manhattan (Gutman 2009; Lisle 2004; Sturken 2007; Tumarkin 2005). This swift transformation from murderous site to tourist site is not unusual, as places of death routinely transmute into places for visitors, and appear on ever-new tourist itineraries as part of the performance of dark tourism (Urry 2004). Tours of historic sites where death has occurred are often considered more acceptable places to interpret than the locations of more recent tragedies. Buildings associated with horrific or tragic events from contemporary times may be demolished, and replaced with a neutral park or other place of remembrance to stem an unacceptable level of public interest (Lennon and Mitchell 2007). Thus, from a supply side perspective, the significance of this book is in the recognition that sites associated with violent death need to be sensitively interpreted to ensure tourists show respect for the victims and avoid glorifying the perpetrator(s) of the crime.

Memorials built to commemorate war, regimes of terror or institutionalized violence reflect society's need to honour the memories of those who have died. Memorials operate as a reminder of the experience of others and the importance of ongoing vigilance on behalf of the nation (Manderson 2008). However, since heritage has been described as the deliberate selection from the past to satisfy present needs and demands (Ashworth 2008), difficulties can arise when selecting the most appropriate aspects of heritage to commemorate and interpret. The term 'dissonant heritage' has been used when particular groups or stakeholders believe that the heritage of atrocity has become distorted, displaced or disinherited (Sharpley 2009). The factors that determine whether an event is selected and subsequently remembered reflects the scale and uniqueness of the event; the ease of identification of the observer with that event, including its currency and its memorability in terms of recordability, contemporary relevance and usability. With the passage of time, some sensitive sites (such as concentration camps or sites of atomic bomb explosions) have developed international significance and have been declared

World Heritage sites (Uzzell 1989). When considering how to manage these sites, questions arise about who has the responsibility to make such decisions: the actual owners of the site, the survivors and families of the victims, the local community or the broader national or international community. These significant questions are addressed in this book.

Understanding such sites may help planners and destination managers develop a better understanding of the most appropriate way to commemorate sites associated with incidents of accidental or violent death. In addition, the respectful development and interpretation of sites associated with death and atrocity will encourage site managers to create places where family, friends and interested visitors can pay respect to the dead, allow visitors to understand the tragedy and to value the site. From a social and cultural perspective, the examination of these sites provides a better understanding of the complex connections between people, events and places, including appropriate interpretation at a sensitive visitor site. In addition, the respectful interpretation of these dark tourism sites may assist in creating a place where visitors can pay their respects to those that have died, and better understand past events within the context of the site and indeed the nation.

Tourism is fundamentally important to many economies and communities. Thus, from a tourism management perspective, the strategic development of dark tourism sites may have the potential to enhance a region economically and socially, and to create high levels of post-trip satisfaction among visitors, repeat visits and positive word of mouth recommendation. In addition, benefits to an individual nation will be achieved by better understanding the multi-faceted and complex connections between people and places, including appropriate interpretation at sensitive visitor sites. Thus, this book provides a systematic investigation of the key components and distinguishing features of this type of dark tourism around the world, to document its presence and to locate it more explicitly in the general tourism system.

About this book

Part I: visitor motivation

Chapter 2

This chapter by Toussaint and Decrop offers an interpretive analysis of the Père-Lachaise Cemetery, a major symbolic and tourist destination in Paris, where individuals visit the memorials and particular tombs, to meditate or mourn. Based on interviews and observations, the chapter describes the visitors' profile and shows that they are driven by touristic, spiritual and relational motives, and, for some of them, by fanatic mysticism. The authors note that going to a sacred place, such as a cemetery, or having a meaningful experience there may give a sacred meaning to the visit and suggest that the Père-Lachaise Cemetery may be considered as a heterotopia, a space set apart from everyday life that conveys deeper meanings to thanatourists.

Chapter 3

In their chapter Lelo and Jamal consider the phenomenon of slavery tourism, which includes visits to places and sites related to the Transatlantic Slave Trade. This phenomenon has a geographic scope including the Caribbean, Europe, North and South America, and destinations include plantations, castles and forts, burial grounds and museums. A large number of African Americans in the US undertake travels throughout the African diaspora in search of personal identity and belonging (roots-seeking), or simply to satisfy a degree of curiosity about their ancestral homeland and historical origin ('heritage' tourists). This chapter provides an exploration of this phenomenon, drawing on primary data as well as secondary literature related to the slave castles on the West African coast, and sites of slavery in the US. Included in the US part of the study is the African Burial Ground National Monument, a former cemetery for enslaved Africans who lived in New York (New Amsterdam) during the seventeenth and eighteenth centuries that is visited by a large number of African Americans today.

Chapter 4

In their chapter Du, Litteljohn and Lennon focus on the different meanings of place for different social groups by drawing on a major study of tourism motivation for visiting the Memorial to the Victims of the Nanjing Massacre. The Nanjing Massacre was an atrocity on a major scale perpetrated by Japanese soldiers in 1937, where arguably up to 300,000 Chinese civilians and military personnel were systematically massacred. However, the historical narrative of this event is highly controversial and has been the subject of much acrimony between Chinese and Japanese commentators. The memorial is now well established and achieves around one million visitors per year. The chapter considers the diverse motivations of different social and cultural groups of visitors and explores the contexts from which different readings of the memorial have arisen. The chapter illustrates contrasting narratives and ideological impacts on interpretation and understanding.

Chapter 5

In their chapter, Simone-Charteris, Boyd and Burns explore undesirable and atrocity heritage and reflect that in some cases and in specific destinations, dark tourism can be considered as an example of this type of heritage. The chapter examines murals in Northern Ireland and other dark/political tourism attractions, which are part of the wider culture of the two main communities. The chapter reports on a survey of visitors to various attractions in Northern Ireland and semi-structured interviews of public and private sector organizations to explore the contribution of dark/political tourism to place identity. The chapter investigates the motivations that inspire visitors to visit dark/political tourism attractions, and considers the views of tourism organizations and bodies within the Province on the management, interpretation and promotion of sites associated with death and atrocity.

6   *Elspeth Frew and Leanne White*

Chapter 6

In his chapter Stone uses the case study of the world's worst nuclear accident at the Chernobyl Nuclear Power Plant in the Ukrainian Soviet Socialist Republic (now Ukraine), and explains that, despite there being health and safety concerns, illegal visitor tours to Chernobyl have flourished over the past decade and the area has become a destination associated with dark tourism. He examines how a place of industrial death and disaster conveys broader political narratives and identity, including that the politics of the past are interfaced with the present, and that the utopian ideals of the former Soviet Union are exposed within the ruins of a dark tourism place.

Part II: destination management

Chapter 7

The chapter by Laws considers pagan tourism and the management of ancient historic sites in Cornwall, UK. The chapter focuses on the ancient pre-Christian heritage of the West Penwith area of Cornwall, which is designated as an Area of Outstanding Natural Beauty and recognized by ICOMOS (the United Nation's International Council for Monuments and Sites). The chapter uses the case study of the establishment and development of the Cornish Ancient Sites Protection Network, which actively promotes and supports the needs of niche users as well as mainstream tourism visitors. The case study illustrates how the dark tourism phenomenon can be harnessed to promote year-round sustainable access that respects the identity of the living, sacred place within the framework of a contemporary heritage tourism industry.

Chapter 8

In his chapter McKenzie focuses on Soviet tourism in the Baltic States of Estonia, Latvia and Lithuania and explains that each country worked at developing a museum and special exhibits to bring to light their shared experiences under the Communist system. A constant theme throughout these exhibits was to communicate to the outside world the harsh and often brutal oppression placed upon many of the citizens of these countries. The chapter considers the motivations and perceptions of those that offer, support/do not support or frequent such attractions. The chapter reflects on the implications of the findings to the promotion/suppression of such tourist experiences and suggests that this relevance may extend beyond the Baltic States to countries with similar shared histories.

Chapter 9

The chapter by Morales focuses on a murdered Scottish backpacker in Taupo, New Zealand. This case study considers the media representation of violent crime in New Zealand and examines how this community interpreted and managed a violent event. In this case, it brought the community together to work on ways to

Exploring dark tourism and place identity 7

prevent future violent offences. The chapter explains how the event changed the town and how community spirit and collaborative work helped provide a positive legacy to a dark event.

Chapter 10

The chapter by Hohenhaus examines contemporary Rwanda as a place where many people visit at least one of the genocide memorials. He notes that these sites range from visible underdevelopment to highly developed, modern multimedia exhibitions. The chapter examines the current situation and developments in Rwanda's commemoration and commodification of the genocide in the context of place identity, both with regard to internal preservation of memory (and education of the next generation) and representation to foreign tourists.

Chapter 11

In their chapter, Dehoorne and Jolliffe consider dark tourism and place identity in French Guiana from both historical and literary sources. They identify dark history sites as components of the tourism product of the territory. They examine the policy setting of French Guiana that might have influenced the development of dark tourism and examine current and future directions of dark tourism sites in both the tourism product and sense of national identity. In so doing, they consider how dark tourism sites contribute to place identity and conclude that the patrimonial inheritance of the penal colony has not yet been recognized, and tourism developments are currently random.

Chapter 12

The chapter by Bird used the example of the Canadian sector in Normandy where the D-Day Landings of 6 June 1944 took place to examine the relationship between what is remembered, forgotten and silenced in a landscape of war. The chapter explores sense of place, heritage dissonance and the meanings co-constructed by Canadian visitors and battlefield tour guides, including visitor participation in commemorative practices. The chapter demonstrates the complexity of the context, conflicts and contributions of the tourism–remembrance relationship.

Part III: place interpretation

Chapter 13

The chapter by Partee Allar considers two different places where people became victims of the Holocaust in Europe. The first place is the Anne Frank House in Amsterdam and the second is the concentration and extermination centre of Auschwitz–Birkenau in Poland, with both places being visited by millions of people each year. The chapter examines how these places have evolved over the past 60 years into iconic sites and universal images that represent the Holocaust.

8   *Elspeth Frew and Leanne White*

The author also reflects on the debates and controversies surrounding their development.

Chapter 14

The chapter by Best considers the dangerous intersection of a number of dimensions, namely, fame and fandom, the lure of automobility, the finality of fatal car crashes or accidents and the interest in such locations and sites. He provides four examples of death sites that have become popular dark tourism destinations and notes that such visitation sometimes occurs when there is no tangible evidence of the event and no formal acknowledgement in the form of memorialization.

Chapter 15

The chapter by White examines three dark tours in Melbourne, Australia. The chapter explores dark tourism and place identity in a combined manner as the dark experience is often simultaneously consumed with the tourism experience in an inseparable way. For the local or visitor seeking an escape from the more predictable Melbourne tours, the dark tourism experience is an increasingly popular option, which often sheds new light on little-known aspects of the city.

Chapter 16

The chapter by Kang and Lee considers the prisoner of war (POW) camps on Geoje Island, South Korea. The site can be considered as representative of the Korean War and presents three main themes: the memorial tower for refugees, POW camps and the Peace Park. The chapter identifies the characteristics of the site, which significantly differ from other war attractions and also suggests factors that lead some dark tourism sites to become customer-friendly, famous tourist attractions.

Chapter 17

The chapter by Frew concentrates on the commemoration of the war-time bombing of Darwin and considers the local on-site interpretation of the event within the context of dark tourism. The three museum sites and the outdoor settings provide much evidence of a variety of techniques to interpret the bombing and associated killing of over 250 civilians and military. The chapter in particular highlights the illustrative examples of the bombing of the Darwin Post Office and the story of a captured Japanese airman to demonstrate the on-site interpretation. The chapter reflects on how such interpretation needs to be managed to ensure the public receive an appropriate exposure to the topic balanced with reflective, respectful commemoration of those who died.

Chapter 18

The chapter by Willard, Lade and Frost considers the battlefields of Culloden in Scotland and Little Bighorn in the United States. Although both battles were fought so long ago that they are well beyond the memory of people today, their attraction continues as they represent sites that mark the extinguishment of traditional (though romanticized) cultures. The chapter considers how interpretation is effectively constructed, particularly the use of story-based (or thematic) interpretation and compares the two sites from the perspective of interpretation and experience provided to visitors, who may or may not have direct heritage connections.

Conclusion

Chapter 19

In the concluding chapter White and Frew summarize the book's contents and main themes by contrasting the chapter contents. The chapter also suggests future research themes and topics, linking to key models and theories from dark tourism and place identity.

Visits to sites of significance play an important part in a nation's self image and place identity. Thus, this book provides a range of case studies to illustrate various aspects of dark tourism and place identity through the lenses of visitor motivation, destination management and place interpretation.

References

Ashworth, G.J. (2008) 'The Memorialization of Violence and Tragedy: Human Trauma as Heritage', in B. Graham and P. Howard (eds) *The Ashgate Research Companion to Heritage and Identity*, Aldershot, Hampshire: Ashgate Publishing Ltd, pp. 231–244.

Beech, J. (2000) 'The Enigma of Holocaust Sites as Tourist Attractions: The Case of Buchenwald', *Managing Leisure*, 5: 29–41.

Cooke, S. (2000) 'Negotiating Memory and Identity: The Hyde Park Holocaust Memorial, London', *Journal of Historical Geography*, 26: 449–465.

Frow, J. (2000) 'In the Penal Colony', *Journal of Australian Studies*, 24(64): 1–13.

Gutman, Y. (2009) 'Where Do We Go from Here: The Pasts, Presents and Futures of Ground Zero', *Memory Studies*, 2(1): 55–70.

Hogan, J. (2009) *Gender, Race and National Identity: Nations of Flesh and Blood*, New York: Routledge.

Lennon, J. and Foley, M. (2000) *Dark Tourism: The Attraction of Death and Disaster*, London: Continuum.

Lennon, J. and Mitchell, M. (2007) 'Dark Tourism: The Role of Sites of Death in Tourism', in M. Mitchell (ed.) *Remember Me: Constructing Immortality. Beliefs on Immortality, Life and Death*, New York: Routledge.

Lisle, D. (2004) 'Gazing at Ground Zero: Tourism, Voyeurism and Spectacle', *Journal for Cultural Research*, 8(1): 3–21.

Manderson, L. (2008) 'Acts of Remembrance: The Power of Memorial and the Healing of Indigenous Australia', *Adler Museum Bulletin*, 34(2): 5–19.

Miles, W.F.S. (2002) 'Auschwitz: Museum Interpretation and Darker Tourism', *Annals of Tourism Research*, 29(4): 1175–1178.

Nanda, S. (2004) 'South African Museums and the Creation of a New National Identity', *American Anthropologist*, 106: 379–385.

Palmer, C. (2005) 'An Ethnography of Englishness: Experiencing Identity through Tourism', *Annals of Tourism Research*, 32(1): 7–27.

Pretes, M. (2003) 'Tourism and Nationalism', *Annals of Tourism Research*, 30(1): 125–142.

Rivera, L.A. (2008) 'Managing "Spoiled" National Identity: War, Tourism, and Memory in Croatia', *American Sociological Review*, 73: 613–634.

Sharpley, R. (2009) 'Shedding Light on Dark Tourism: An Introduction', in R. Sharpley and P.R. Stone (eds) *The Darker Side of Travel: The Theory and Practice of Dark Tourism*, Bristol: Channel View Publications, pp. 3–22.

Sharpley, R. and Stone, P.R. (2009) (eds) *The Darker Side of Travel: The Theory and Practice of Dark Tourism*, Bristol: Channel View Publications.

Stone, P. and Sharpley, R. (2008) 'Consuming Dark Tourism: A Thanalogical Perspective', *Annals of Tourism Research*, 35(2): 574–595.

Sturken, M. (2007) *Tourists of History: Memory, Kitsch, and Consumerism from Oklahoma City to Ground Zero*, Durham: Duke University Press.

Tumarkin, M. (2005) *Traumascapes: The Power and Fate of Places Transformed by Tragedy*, Carlton: Melbourne University Press.

Tunbridge, J.E. and Ashworth, G.J. (1996) *Dissonant Heritage: The Management of the Past as a Resource in Conflict*, Chichester, West Sussex: John Wiley and Sons.

Urry, J. (2004) 'Death in Venice', in M. Sheller and J. Urry (eds) *Tourism Mobilities: Places to Play, Places in Play*, London: Routledge, pp. 205–215.

Uzzell, D.L. (1989) 'The Hot Interpretation of War and Conflict', in D.L. Uzzell (ed.) *Heritage Interpretation, Vol. 1: The Natural and Built Environment*, London: Belhaven, pp. 33–47.

Wight, A.C. and Lennon, J.J. (2007) 'Selective Interpretation and Eclectic Human Heritage in Lithuania', *Tourism Management*, 28: 519–529.

Wilson, J.Z. (2004) 'Dark Tourism and the Celebrity Prisoner: Front and Back Regions in Representations of an Australian Historical Prison', *Journal of Australian Studies*, 82: 171–173.

Part I
Visitor motivation

2 The Père-Lachaise Cemetery

Between dark tourism and heterotopic consumption

Stéphanie Toussaint and Alain Decrop

Introduction

Each year on November 1st (All Saints Day), candles light up the Père-Lachaise Cemetery and flowers bloom everywhere. Surprisingly, few people still have family members buried in this green and peaceful place. Today, the Père-Lachaise Cemetery is recognized as a major tourist destination in Paris. The spot is especially visited for its famous 'residents' such as La Fontaine (fabulist), Molière (playwright and actor), Delacroix (artist), Chopin (composer and pianist), Edith Piaf (singer), Jim Morrison (singer), Oscar Wilde (writer and poet) and Allan Kardec (founder of the spiritualism movement). But the location is also valued as a place for relaxation, as a hill on which to go for walks, or as an art museum in the open air. Many people visit the Père-Lachaise to learn about memorials and particular tombs, to enjoy transcending experiences, and to have the opportunity to meditate or to mourn.

Since it opened its gates in the early 1800s, the Père-Lachaise Cemetery in Paris has always been a very special location. Designed with a garden-like appearance by the famous French architect Alexandre Theodore Brongniart, the cemetery launched what might be described as its first marketing campaign in 1817. At that time, the cemetery was not attractive and was considered by most of Paris' citizens as too far from the city centre (as it was built on a hill outside the city for public health reasons). Its attractiveness really became established when the authorities decided to move in Molière's and La Fontaine's remains. In the same year, the cemetery received the relics of Heloise and Abelard, two famous medieval lovers, whose arrival was widely covered by the media. This gave rise to a keen interest in luxury gravestones and people competing with each other in order to be buried next to the most famous figures (de Valverde and Hughes 2007).

Travelling to memorials or graveyards, and pilgrimages to the resting place of celebrities (Seaton 1996; Sharpley 2009) represents a category of dark tourism activities. Generally speaking, dark tourism may be considered as a behavioural phenomenon, defined by the traveller's motives rather than the features of the attraction itself (Seaton 1996; Sharpley 2009). In this chapter, we refer to dark tourism as "the act of travel to sites associated with death, suffering and the seemingly macabre" (Stone 2006: 146). As the ultimate destination of any human being, a cemetery is usually assumed to be a dark place. Therefore, the Père-Lachaise Cemetery may be considered as a black spot (Rojek 1993; 1997). A black spot generally refers to the marker of a death site or to disaster or memorable death sites.

As a cemetery, the Père-Lachaise possesses the usual properties of the sacred and may be considered as a *heterotopia* (Foucault 1967), that is 'a place out of space and time', defined by its own principles and a transitional (liminal) zone within its surrounding walls. Place identity is thus key to the interpretation of the Père-Lachaise Cemetery as it "offers a sense of mental proximity and feeling of belonging" (Blom 2000: 30).

This chapter raises three questions surrounding dark tourism and place identity regarding the famous cemetery of Père-Lachaise: Why do people visit 'dark' sacred places, such as famous graveyards? What are the perceptions, meanings and processes associated with the visit? How does the dialectic between the profane and sacred in postmodern consumption find its expression in the case of the Père-Lachaise? Three theoretical frameworks are useful to address these research questions: place identity and attachment, heterotopia, and the sacred in postmodern consumption. The following sections present such frameworks.

Place identity, heterotopia and the sacred in dark tourism

Place identity and attachment

According to Relph (1976: 46), "our experiences of places are direct, complete and often unconscious". Referencing Albert Camus's writings (1965), the author presents three major components of the identity of places: the static physical settings, the activities and the meanings or symbols. The meanings of a place may stem from the physical setting and the activities, but still belong to the realm of experiences. Meanings can change from one object to the other and, for any given object, they may vary from one individual to the other. Moreover, the feelings and identity associated with a specific place will be determined by the context (social, economic and cultural) in which people live. Thus, identity is based both on the object and the individual, and on the global culture to which they belong (Blom 2000).

'Space' and 'place' are not synonyms but belong to different perceptual categories (Borghini and Zaghi 2006). 'Space' is changing, moving and is no one's property. In contrast, 'place' is more or less stable, absolute, occupied and provides the possibility to experience sensations related to the area. A place is thus a tried and consumed space. Debenedetti (2004: 7) defines place attachment as "an affective and positive bound between an individual (or a group) and its physical environment". Low and Altman (1992: 5–6) maintain that "place refers to space that has been given meaning through personal, group or cultural processes", and that place attachment "implies that the primary target of affective bonding of people is to environmental settings themselves". The analysis of "dark resting places" (Stone 2006) focuses on cemeteries as potential objects of dark tourism.

In this contemporary perspective, the cemetery is more like a romanticized "urban regeneration tool" (Stone 2006: 154), which poetically confronts dark and possibly mysterious corners of the city with supposedly real authentic life experiences (Crawshaw and Urry 1997: 179). This last dimension refers to the place's ability to provide a positive, entertaining experience to the individual (Pearce 2005), induced by the esthetical dimension of the environment (Filser 2002). It is not surprising then that the Père-Lachaise "attracts over two millions visitors a year, and beyond its primary function of internment, [remains] the largest park in Paris and [continues to evolve] into an open air museum and pantheon garden" (Stone 2006: 155). Tours of the cemetery take place at special dates related to its residents, such as birth- or death-day, or at any other occasion during the year.

Heterotopia

Literally meaning 'other places', the concept of heterotopia (Foucault 1967) is "a rich concept that describes a world off-center with respect to normal or everyday spaces, one that possesses multiple, fragmented or even incompatible meanings" (Dehaene and De Cauter 2008). Heterotopian spaces turn out to be collective or shared spaces allowing overlaps within surrounding borders. They are "simultaneously mythic and real contestations of the space in which we live" (Foucault translated by Dehaene and De Cauter 2008: 17). Heterotopias rely on six principles. First, there is not a single culture without heterotopias:

> in all civilization, [those] real and effective places are a sort of counter-emplacement, a sort of realized utopias in which the real emplacements... are simultaneously represented, contested and inverted; a kind of places that are outside all places, even though they are actually localizable.
> (Foucault translated by Dehaene and De Cauter 2008: 17)

Second, each heterotopia may appear, evolve and disappear in the course of time. Across centuries, the cemetery has become "the 'other city' where each family possesses its dark dwelling" (Foucault translated by Dehaene and De Cauter 2008: 19). Third, the heterotopia has "the power to juxtapose in a single real place several spaces, several emplacements that are themselves incompatible" (Foucault translated by Dehaene and De Cauter 2008: 19). As a consequence, different meanings may stem from the experiences lived in such a place.

The fourth principle relies on the space–time continuum. Indeed, the heterotopia makes sense when individuals completely disconnect with their daily life. The cemetery is once again a remarkable heterotopia by definition, since it historically blends several eras. Moreover, the graveyard reveals itself as a strong heterotopian place since it begins with death and defines a new time: the time of perpetuity and eternity. The fifth principle assumes "a system of opening and closing that both isolate [heterotopias] and make them penetrable" (Foucault translated by Dehaene and De Cauter 2008: 21). The interior space of the heterotopia may not be specifically public or private, sacred or profane, but rather "heterotopian" (Foucault translated by Dehaene and De Cauter 2008: 16). One cannot enter the heterotopia as if it was a mundane place, and visitors are often expected to follow rituals while being there. Such rituals help to maintain the distinction between inside and outside the heterotopia. The sixth principle highlights the function that heterotopias have in relation to the surrounding space. Their role is to create a space of illusion or a place of compensation: as perfect and bright as our world is harsh and superficial.

The sacred and the profane in postmodern consumption

In their *Consumer Behavior Odyssey*, Russell Belk, Melanie Wallendorf and John Sherry Jr. (1989) carried out a wide and detailed analysis of contemporary consumption phenomena in various settings. Parts of their findings involve symbolic and sacred consumption. The authors argue that the consumption of products and activities with symbolic and/or sacred value can be approached from places prone to the dialectic between the sacred and the profane. Indeed, "consumption implies more than the means by which people meet their everyday needs. Consumption can become a vehicle of transcendent experience; that is, consumer behavior exhibits certain aspects of the sacred" (Belk, Wallendorf and Sherry 1989: 2).

Generally speaking, the sacred refers to religions and to entities that inspire an absolute respect. In contrast, the profane characterizes 'what is not sacred'. Etymologically, both dimensions are in opposition: 'sacred' stands for what is separated and confined (in Latin, *sancire* means to bound, to surround and to sanctify), whereas 'profane' implies what is outside the preserved surrounding wall (*pro-fanum*) (Dumas 2005). Profane is also used to describe the uninitiated individual who is novice to a ritual or to its practice. Belonging to the sacred sphere implies that one must be used to a religion, to follow its rites and to worship the sacred with the highest respect. According to Dumas (2005), the sacred does not belong by itself to the substance of objects or places but it exists with reference to some faith, even unconsciously. Beyond the etymological opposition between sacred and profane, the term 'sacred' may also refer to the enigmatic, the unverifiable and the unattainable. Traditionally, religion organizes the sacred authority. However, the decline of the sacred (or at least of its formalism) does not automatically imply its disappearance or the loss of personal transcendence. For Belk *et al.* (1989: 2), "religion is one, but not the only, context in which the concept of sacred is operant". According to Eliade (1965), sacred power can manifest itself as different from the profane. Consequently, any object may, at a particular moment and/or in a particular place, manifest its sacredness.

In search of meaning and of a break with his/her everyday life, the postmodern consumer is looking for the sacred. "Released from everything and from all" (Decrop 2008: 86), s/he is eclectic, hedonist, nomadic and in quest of authenticity and nature. Boundaries between sacred and profane are shifting, since the consumer transposes the sacred to new entities. "Potentially sacred consumer domains, like potentially sacred religious domains, fall into six major categories: places, times, tangible things, intangibles, persons and experiences" (Belk *et al.*

1989: 9). Nowadays, individuals are looking for the essence of the sacred in what is traditionally regarded as secular. Art and music (Belk *et al.* 1989) but also tourism illustrate such sacralization of the secular.

Places such as natural sites often express an eruption of the sacred, which gives rise to a separation between the space as a whole and a qualitatively different territory: the *hierophany* (Eliade 1965: 29). Sacred objects reveal themselves to us as another (supernatural) order of things. Other places are connected to the holy by the occurrence of extraordinary events that contaminate the space with magic. One such example is the Miracles in Lourdes, France. In addition, sites such as churches, sanctuaries and to some extent cemeteries, take their sacredness from particular activities. Such places constitute, according to Eliade (1965: 26), "breaks into the homogeneity of the space". The sacred can be experienced through events as well, and to be in a sacred place or to have a sacred experience already contributes to the sacredness (think of pilgrimages, even towards a profane or secular destination such as Disneyland). Sacred and profane poles seem to mix through a more permeable border (Belk *et al.* 1989; Arnould, Price and Zinkhan 2004). According to some authors, the sacredness in consumption is mainly lived through experiences rather than through tangible objects (Arnould *et al.* 2004: 130). Such experiences reflect "the various modes through which a person knows and constructs a reality" (Tuan 1977: 8). For example, museums, like holy places, impose singular codes and contain specific types of architecture.

An entity may reach a sacred status through various processes: rituals, pilgrimages, quintessence, gift-giving, collecting, inheritance and external sanction (Belk *et al.* 1989). "[Except for] quintessence and external sanction, these sacralizing processes are enacted purposefully by consumers in an effort to create meaning in their life" (Belk *et al.* 1989: 21). Four categories of actions help to maintain an entity's sacred character (Belk *et al.* 1989; Hetzel 2002). Separation is the first category, as the sacred and the secular have to be clearly and permanently separated. Second, rites and rituals support sacredness and avoid contamination of the profane; third, inheritance may ensure the continuity of the sacred and finally, objectification (i.e., tangibilized contamination through objects) may preserve the experience (for example, 'immortalizing' a journey by pictures or bringing a souvenir home). Nevertheless, secularization of the sacred is threatening when meanings become associated with the kitsch or are decontextualized. The kitsch threatens the sacred because of its intrinsic inauthenticity, whereas decontextualization takes elements out of their space–time conditions (Belk *et al.* 1989).

Methodology of the ethnographic study

The questions of the motives and meanings related to the visiting experience of the Père-Lachaise have been investigated through an interpretive qualitative approach. Two types of informants were recruited for this ethnographic study, in accordance with Lennon and Foley's (1999) typology of dark places, i.e., spiritual and tourist visitors. The first type is made of travellers who are looking for thoughts, experiences, bereavements or personal memories of places or events they are emotionally, spiritually or physically bound to. The second type is comprised of people who visit places related to death, tragedies or disasters in order to be entertained or thrilled during their touristic experience. Ten open-ended interviews were carried out with informants. Discussions were conducted in the Père-Lachaise Cemetery itself, while people were visiting the site. Because of the fear it generates, the sacred may be a taboo topic that individuals prefer to avoid. Therefore, we discussed the subjects of death, evil and emptiness by using facilitation techniques. Most of the interviews were recorded or filmed with participants' authorization. We used a semi-structured interview with open-ended questions and several pictures as a visual support (such as alleged profane and sacred places). In addition, we conducted a series of non-participant observation sessions, observing visitors and their surroundings and accompanying some of them during their tour. This resulted in substantive field notes, pictures and films. The collected data was analysed through thematic inductive analysis based on the principles of grounded theory (Glaser and Strauss 1967; Strauss and Corbin 1990), which helps to generate theoretical propositions from the field through a systematic coding of the data.

Visitors' motives and sacred properties at the Père-Lachaise Cemetery

In this section, we briefly examine visitors' motives and we look over six sacred features of the Père-Lachaise Cemetery. First, we deal with heterotopias and temporal hierophany. Second, we examine commitment, sacrifices and rituals. The third distinctive element concerns *communitas* (Turner 1969), ecstasy and 'flow' experiences (Csikszentmihalyi 1997). Fourth, we discuss contamination and objectification. The fifth motive is about myth, mystery and kratophany. Finally, we end this section with a discussion of the opposition between the sacred and the profane.

The primary drivers to the Père-Lachaise Cemetery are personal, spiritual or relational motives related to the location itself (promenade, history, architecture and celebrities) and to the Père-Lachaise's residents. Most visitors are attracted to the cemetery by its famous inhabitants, the architecture and the overall infrastructure. The harmony between the nature and sepulchres offers a peaceful and pleasing place to go for a walk. One interviewee describes the Père-Lachaise as "the best place to read the daily newspaper". The cemetery is portrayed by many informants as an open-air museum, rich in architectural styles. The graveyard is well known and has acquired the unofficial title of the most famous cemetery in the world: "But the Père-Lachaise, by its nature, is a tourist destination! . . . It's more a tourist destination than a cemetery, there aren't so many people that still have family here" (Marc, 37; with a friend).

Both poetic and romantic, the fabulous cemetery looks like a "history book, a book of art" (Martine, 57). For some individuals, the artistic and cultural features of the place even offset its dark side. Beyond curiosity, the visit to the Père-Lachaise Cemetery is akin to a pilgrimage or is close to a waking dream. Going to the cemetery, experiencing it and contemplating it with one's own eyes is an expression of the "need to verify that [one is] at a specific place that is known to others" (Blom 2000: 32). The individual's commitment is critical in order to reach a required level of intensity in the experience. Some fans we met in front of Jim Morrison's grave gave us indications of proper behaviour that must be enacted when visiting the place: "to spend time, to look at the grave, to come back at least five times a year... These are all behaviours associated with being a 'true fan'" (Gianluca, 17).

Cemetery of cemeteries, the East Cemetery (as the Père-Lachaise is also known to locals) nevertheless remains a place to be in-tune with oneself, to commune with others or to pray for people that have passed away. The graveyard appears to be a pretext for meeting others because it promotes social interaction. For some informants, visits are prone to create links and to share their passion of "the man and his work" (Gianluca, 17, talking about Jim Morrison) with each other. Building on Durkheim (1915), Eliade (1965) and Belk *et al.* (1989), we now focus on the properties of sacredness and how these properties reveal themselves at the Père-Lachaise Cemetery.

Heterotopias and temporal hierophany

Places where the sacred power manifests are perceived by visitors as breaks in usual space–time boundaries. Foucault (1967) has qualified such breaks as heterotopias. Heterotopias are generally the seat of momentary and extraordinary consumer experiences that are part of individuals' existence. In the case of the Père-Lachaise Cemetery, the spatial hierophany is often confused with the temporal one: sacred time is thus revealed within a sacred place. For the time of their visit, informants are living a transcending experience, in a different place than the surrounding environment, such as illustrated by this quotation:

> When I'm here, I feel like I am swimming in the ocean without seeing anyone, but only, you know, looking at the clouds, looking at the graves, looking at how this was, looking at the pictures and so on... These are my feelings. There's nothing else I'm looking for.
>
> (Appolonne, 78)

The cemetery is filled with divine qualities and is described by many as iconic, out of time and out of the surrounding world: it is "a dream", "a magical place". The Père-Lachaise heterotopia is a special and magnificent place, a powerful entity where people feel good and where daily life and anxiety are left aside.

Commitment, sacrifices and rituals

The emotional attachment to the sacred object is a major dimension of our informants' identity. Their commitment translates materially in a series of presents and tributes they make during the visit such as candles, flowers and notes (Figure 2.1). These offerings or 'sacrifices' establish a link with the sacred realm, keeping it

Figure 2.1 Mano Solo's tomb and tributes (singer)

going physically and mentally after the tour. This powerful link is illustrated by Marco's statement:

> M.: It's important to leave a note, a personal message.
> Interviewer: Did you leave something?
> M.: A cigarette. With 'Marco e Georgia. Per Jim' written on it... We are leaving a sign, in order to let him know we were here.
>
> (Marco, 21; with his girlfriend Georgia)

Gift giving is also a good indication of the high commitment towards the sacred entity such as illustrated by the cigarette 'offered' to Jim Morrison. Such a self-enhancement act reinforces the individual's role in the consumption experience and towards others, and is the individual's way of marking the environment. As to sacrifices, rituals prepare the sacred union and avoid the destructive power of kratophany while maintaining the mystery of the sacred entity. Rituals mentioned by informants include visits at predefined periods (one example is Jim Morrison's birthday), or communing with the deceased via prayer.

Communitas, *ecstasy and flow experiences*

Heterotopias constitute ephemeral places of socialization wherein consumers can share transcending consumption experiences of sacred objects, referring to Turner's (1969) idea of *communitas*. *Communitas* is a "social antistructure that frees participants from their normal social roles and statuses and instead engages them in a transcending camaraderie of status equality" (as cited in Belk *et al*. 1989: 7). "This is most likely to occur when the individual is in a 'liminal' or threshold state betwixt and between two statuses, such as may occur on religious pilgrimages" (Belk *et al*. 1989: 7).

The notion of *communitas* is akin to the Durkheimian *collective effervescence* (Stone 2009: 60); that is, "the construction of new moral orders mediated by collectivities of embodied individuals who are emotionally engaged with their social world". In the Père-Lachaise Cemetery, we observed such phenomena in front of the most visited graves, where the audience behaves as one (such as at Morrison, Kardec, Chopin and Trintignant's tombs). The community effect can also be akin to a physical recognition, which allows authenticating an individual as a member of the 'tribe' (Cova and Cova 2001): people will use their external appearance in order to claim their membership to the community. For example, we met people in and outside the cemetery wearing T-shirts depicting the face of Jim Morrison. This behaviour helps the individual to be identified as a fan of the singer and to be associated with his value system. Sometimes, experiences of the sacred are exacerbated, resulting in 'flow' experiences (Csikszentmihalyi 1997) and ecstatic behaviours through which visitors feel as though being in direct connection with the holy. In the Père-Lachaise, we met a follower of Kardec's spiritualistic thought and she told us that she had received the 'light and the perfume' after coming back from her pilgrimage. With these words, she referred to the after-life existence and to Kardec's ability to help people connect with 'the other world'.

Contamination and objectification

Being in a sacred place contributes to the contamination of the sacred. Being in the cemetery and touching some graves enables tourists to catch elements of the sacred and to better benefit from its properties. For example, the mausoleum of Oscar Wilde is covered with pink/red lipstick marks left by visitors' kisses, whereas Kardec's tomb is polished by visitors' strokes (see Figure 2.2). Such meaningful spots function as healers, and reinforce the feeling of the sacred power. Filled with the 'holy spirit', the individual feels stronger and better. Beyond contamination, objectification enables tourists to bring the experience back home. Souvenirs, pictures, maps or even postcards tangibilize the sacred and are often put together as relics or collections in shrines in the profane/home environment. Myths and rituals help maintain their holy character (Belk *et al*. 1989). Moreover,

Figure 2.2 Touching Kardec's mausoleum

objectification is important to share the experience with the people outside, and may even constitute a vehicle for the sacred. As an informant told us, bringing home a postcard or a book from the cemetery can help visitors to share their experience with relatives or friends. Therefore, these possessions safeguard the link with the original sacred place.

Myths, mystery and kratophany

The search for salvation within heterotopias is a major dimension emerging from our discussions. According to most of our informants, death is no longer considered as a poetic or peaceful element but rather as an incontrovertible destination. Belk, Wallendorf and Sherry (1989: 16) account for quintessential places by consumers' desire for authenticity. The more natural, real or authentic the place is perceived as being, the more it will be considered as a holy place. When asked to compare the Père-Lachaise with one season and one of the four elements, informants mentioned each of the four elements. 'Fire' refers to the crossing over from life to death, 'water' to darkness and the uneven landscape, 'air' is used to describe the immateriality of the place and 'earth' to illustrate the initial function of the cemetery. Which location, if not the heterotopia itself, can unify the four elements in a single place? Given the meanings, the perceptions and the comparisons the visitors expressed, we may argue that the Père-Lachaise offers a holy and holistic environment. Finally, myths and legends contribute in giving visitors thrilling feelings. The visit of the cemetery has been compared to a hunt for a treasure ground, with its tortuous paths and numerous dark corners, such as illustrated by the following words of a Chinese tourist:

> Interviewer: What do you feel when you walk here [in the cemetery]? Does this place have any special meaning for you?
> C.: Actually at the beginning we only wanted to buy the map [of the cemetery], and then she said to me, 'Oh don't you think it's like an adventure? Because you don't know where the treasure is, you have to search for it with the map ... '.
>
> (Chu, 26; with her friend Chung)

Opposition of the sacred and the profane

The opposition between the sacred and the profane can easily be observed when exiting the Père-Lachaise's Metro station. The cemetery's surrounding wall marks the hierophany's border. Even within the hierophany itself, 'the ordinary' threatens to desacralize the cemetery as some people touch and walk on tombs or disturb the quietness of the place. For many informants, inscriptions, graffiti and damage caused to the area are offensive and should be punishable. Indeed, rules must be strictly followed within the sacred area of the hierophany. The sacred is elegant, prestigious and perfect. It therefore deserves sufficient protection to avoid any secular (de-)contamination. Indeed, some elements may threaten the sacred nature of the cemetery. Our analyses highlight a series of such disruptive elements. For example, money is often seen as degrading the sacred and demystifying heterotopias. However, dedicated guided tours and the development of nearby souvenir shops (see Figure 2.3) were sometimes perceived as legitimate. For instance, this was the case for an informant who purchased a book in order to stay connected with the cemetery and engage in private prayer from a distance.

The role of money in the Père-Lachaise Cemetery is therefore caught between conveying and degrading sacred power. From a dark tourism perspective, commercial activities are rather accepted, as they are part of the visiting experience. In public places, the commercial side does not disturb the visitors very much. Respect for death and touristic activities are well accepted. Nevertheless, commoditized products such as mugs and magnets raise the question of authenticity and rarity of the sacred, as these products are accessible, abundant and superficial. The link

Figure 2.3 Objects at the souvenir shop near the Père-Lachaise Cemetery

between authenticity and uniqueness is subtle but clear as they both embody the values of originality and identity. Finally, excessive crowds and commoditization of the Père-Lachaise experience may reduce the sacred aspects of the cemetery. A Chinese informant told us of her disappointment about the guided tours, the groups and the "mass" of people packing the place on November 1st. The 'dramatization' of the cemetery can lead to disenchantment and has the potential to destroy the hierophany. For some individuals, however, the Père-Lanchaise was never a heterotopia. For these individuals, it is simply a way to get from point A to point B in Paris. As the cemetery is 44 acres, people cross it in order to reach one of the nearby Metro stations or neighbouring streets rather than going around it.

Conclusion

Sacred places, heterotopias, cemeteries and dark tourism: in the battle to attract tourists to new attractions, to address the postmodern demand of travellers and citizens in search of transcending experiences, there is definitely a new and increasing potential to enhance the identity of special places. Blom (2000: 35) highlights future tourism as possibly:

> marked not only by a growing desire to get to know environments where the focus is on the physical, material symbols in close symbiosis with

consumption-related attractions, but also by a search for identification where the emphasis is on the social environments and existential proximity.

Blom (2000: 35)

This chapter informed the relationship between dark tourism and sacred consumption, in the context of the famous Père-Lachaise Cemetery, valued for its mausoleums, architecture and well-known residents. We suggested that the place is a heterotopia (Foucault 1967), as it meets its basic principles and provides a valuable background in the study of the blurred sacred–profane dialectic. While the profane dark touristic offering is paradoxically opposed to the holy, we have shown how cemeteries can address the postmodern concern for re-sacralization and are continuously triggering consumers' interest. The physical settings, the activities but also the meanings visitors give to the place lie at the core of their experience. With its historical, cultural and commemorative ethos, the cemetery fulfils an 'edutainment' function. Its artistic and aesthetical characteristics contribute to make it a quintessential place, preserving the sacred in a secular era.

The Père-Lachaise appears to be prone to marketing activities and to dark tourism, since its very opening two centuries ago. Nevertheless, such a secular positioning of the cemetery does not undermine its sacred qualities. Visitors' sayings and behaviours at the Parisian cemetery emphasize a series of conducts and rituals, which clearly highlight properties of the sacred. Rituals are a powerful means of reinforcing the heterotopia. The emotional commitment of the individuals is communicated through tangible signs, such as flowers, candles and notes, or food offered to celebrities and loved ones. These behaviours make the experience more personal and allow visitors to leave their (sometimes only temporarily) mark on the cemetery (Holt 1995; Ladwein 2002; Low and Altman 1992). Such a personal touch makes consumers actors of their heterotopian experiences. Our findings also support the concept of the Turnerian *communitas* and its transcendental dimension within contemporary spaces, as well as the Durkheimian *collective effervescence* (Stone 2009: 60). Finally, the contention that hierophanies and heterotopias break the space–time continuum in the postmodern era is in line with Kopitoff (1986, quoted by Arnould 2004: 52) for whom the sacred and the profane can be viewed as poles of a spatial and temporal continuum. For consumers, 'absolutely different' places provide opportunities for self–place identification: heterotopias and fortiori dark tourism places are therefore centres of symbolic and sacred consumption.

References

Arnould, E.J. (2004) 'Special Session Summary: Beyond the Sacred–Profane Dichotomy in Consumer Research', in B.E. Kahn and M.F. Luce (eds) *Advances in Consumer Research*, Valdosta, GA: Association for Consumer Research, *31*(1): 52–55.

Arnould, E.J., Price, L. and Zinkhan, G.M. (2004) *Consumers*, 2nd edn, New York: McGraw-Hill.

Belk, R.W., Wallendorf, M. and Sherry, J.F, Jr. (1989) 'The Sacred and the Profane in Consumer Behaviour: Theodicy on the Odyssey', *Journal of Consumer Research*, *16* (June): 1–38.

Belk, R.W., Wallendorf, M. and Sherry, J.F., Jr. (1991) 'The Sacred and the Profane in Consumer Behaviour: Theodicy on the Odyssey', in R.W. Belk (ed.) *Highways and Buyways: Naturalistic Research from the Consumer Behaviour Odyssey*, Provo, UT: Association for Consumer Research.

Blom, T. (2000) 'Morbid Tourism: A Postmodern Market Niche with an Example from Althorp', *Norwegian Journal of Geography*, 54(1): 29–36.

Borghini, S. and Zaghi, K. (2006) 'Marketplace and Attachment: A Journey Through Ordinary and Extraordinary Consumer Experiences', Proceedings of the 34th European Marketing Academy Conference, Athens, Greece.

Cova, V. and Cova, B. (2001) *Alternatives Marketing: Réponses Marketing aux Evolutions Récentes des Consommateurs*, Paris: Dunod.

Crawshaw, C. and Urry, J. (1997) 'Tourism and the Photographic Eye', in C. Rojek and J. Urry (eds) *Touring Cultures: Transformations of Travel and Theory*, London: Routledge.

Csikszentmihalyi, M. (1997) *Finding Flow: The Psychology of Engagement with Everyday Life*, 1st edn, New York: Basics Books.

de Valverde, J. and Hughes H. (2007) *Le Cimetière du Père-Lachaise: Promenades au Fil du Temps*, Renner: Itinéraires de Découvertes, Editions Ouest-France.

Debenedetti, A. (2004) 'L'Attachement au lieu de service: Etat de l'art, Perspectives et Voies de Recherche', *Cahier DMSP, 338*, Paris: Université Paris-Dauphine.

Decrop, A. (2008) 'Les paradoxes du consommateur postmoderne', *Reflets et Perspectives de la Vie Economique, XLVII*(2): 85–93, Wavre: De Boeck Université.

Dehaene, M. and De Cauter, L. (eds) (2008) *Heterotopia and the City: Public Space in a Postcivil Society*, New York: Routledge.

Dumas, A. (2005) 'Sacré', *Encyclopédie Thématique Universalis*, 9: 6991–6996.

Durkheim, E. ([1915] 1991) *Les Formes Elémentaires de la Vie Religieuse*, Paris: Librairie Générale Française.

Eliade, M. ([1957] 1965) *The Sacred and the Profane: The Nature of Religion*, trans. Williard R. Trask, Chicago: University of Chicago.

Filser, M. (2002) 'Le Marketing de la Production d'Expériences: Statut Théorique et Implication Managériale', *Décisions Marketing*, 28: 13–22.

Foucault, M. (1967) 'Dits et Ecrits 1984: Des Espaces Autres', Conference at the Cercle d'études architecturales, March 1967, in *Architecture, Mouvement, Continuité* (1984), 5: 46–49.

Foucault, M. (2001) 'Des Espaces Autres', in M. Foucault with D. Defert, F. Ewald and J. Lagrange (eds) *Dits et Ecrits II: 1976–1988*, Quatro, Paris: Gallimard.

Foucault, M. (2009) 'Les Heterotopies', in M. Foucault, *Le Corps Utopique suivi des Hétérotopies*, Paris: Nouvelles Editions Lignes.

Glaser, B. and Strauss, A. (1967) *The Discovery of Grounded Theory: Strategies for Qualitative Research*, Chicago: Aldine.

Hetzel, P. (2002) *Planète Conso: Marketing Expérientiel et Nouveaux Univers de Consommation*, Paris: Edition d'Organisation.

Holt, D.B. (1992) 'Examining the Descriptive Value of "Ritual" in Consumer Behavior: A View from the Field', in J.F Sherry and B. Sternthal (eds) *Advances in Consumer Research*, Provo, UT: Association for Consumer Research, 19: 213–218.

Holt, D.B. (1995) 'How Consumer Consume: A Typology of Consumption Practices', *Journal of Consumer Research*, 22(1): 1–16.

Ladwein, R. (2002) 'Voyage à Tikidad: De l'Accès à l'Expérience de Consommation', *Décisions Marketing*, 28: 53–63.

Lennon, J. and Foley, M. (1999) 'Interpretation of the Unimaginable: The US Holocaust Memorial Museum, Washington, DC', *Journal of Travel Research*, *38*(1): 46–50.

Lennon, J.J. and Foley, M. (2000) *Dark Tourism: The Attraction of Death and Disaster*, London: Continuum.

Low, S.M. and Altman, I. (1992) 'Place Attachment: A Conceptual Inquiry', in I. Altman and S.M. Low (eds) *Place Attachment*, New York: Plenum Press.

Pearce, P.L. (2005) 'Tourist Behaviour: Themes and Conceptual Schemes', *Aspects of Tourism*, *27*, Clevedon, England: Channel View Publications.

Relph, E. (1976) *Place and Placelessness*, London: Pion.

Rojek, C. (1993) *Ways of Escape*, Basingstoke: Macmillan.

Rojek, C. (1997) 'Indexing, Dragging and the Social Construction of Tourist Sights', in C. Rojek and J. Urry (eds) *Touring Cultures: Transformations of Travel and Theory*, London: Routledge.

Seaton, A.V. (1996) 'Guided by the Dark: From Thanatopsis to Thanatourism', *International Journal of Heritage Studies*, *2*(4): 234–244.

Sharpley, R. (2009) 'Shedding Light on Dark Tourism: An Introduction', in R. Sharpley and P.R. Stone (eds) *The Darker Side of Travel: The Theory and Practices of Dark Tourism*, Bristol: Channel View Publications.

Stone, P.R. (2006) 'A Dark Tourism Spectrum: Towards a Typology of Death and Macabre Related Tourist Sites, Attractions and Exhibitions', *Tourism: An Interdisciplinary International Journal*, *52*(2): 145–160.

Stone, P.R. (2009) 'Dark Tourism: Morality and New Moral Spaces', in R. Sharpley and P.R. Stone (eds) *The Darker Side of Travel: The Theory and Practices of Dark Tourism*, Bristol: Channel View Publications.

Stone, P.R and Sharpley, R. (2008) 'Consuming Dark Tourism: A Thanatological Perspective', *Annals of Tourism Research*, *35*(2): 574–595.

Strauss, A. and Corbin, J. (1990) *Basics of Qualitative Research: Grounded Theory Procedures and Techniques*, Newbury Park, CA: Sage Publications.

Tuan, Y.-F. (1977) *Space and Place: The Perspective of Experience*, London: University of Minnesota Press.

Turner, V. (1969) *The Ritual Process: Structure and Anti-Structure*, London: Aldine Transaction.

3 African Americans at sites of darkness

Roots-seeking, diasporic identities and place making

Linda Lelo and Tazim Jamal

Introduction

Research within the field of tourism studies has only recently started to look at the phenomenon of slavery tourism, particularly in relation to the transatlantic slave trade (see Butler, Carter and Dwyer 2008; Buzinde 2007; Buzinde and Santos 2009; Modlin 2008). The geographic scope of this phenomenon is extensive, and includes the Caribbean, Europe, and North and South America (among others), with 'dark' sites ranging from plantations, castles and forts, to burial grounds and museums. This chapter focuses on African Americans in the United States, who are increasingly engaging in travel throughout the African diaspora seeking to explore their ancestral homeland and their cultural heritage. As the chapter illustrates, their motivations are diverse. Destinations such as Ghana and the sites of Elmina and Cape Coast Castles are particular favourites on the West African coast, attracting roots-seeking tourists in addition to casual or scientific visitors. In contrast to this complex, diasporic type of cross-Atlantic travel is travel to sites displaying enslavement history within the country of residence. In the US, former plantation homes in the South are popular sites of visitation. A careful excavation of the relationship between tourism, place and identity for this diasporic population is lacking, however, with the exception of a few studies (see Bruner 1996; Finley 2004; Pinho 2008; Timothy and Teye 2004). The chapter commences to address this lacuna, drawing on secondary literature related to the slave castles on the West African coast, as well as primary data on the African Burial Ground National Monument (henceforth ABG in this chapter), a former cemetery for enslaved Africans who lived in New York (New Amsterdam) during the seventeenth and eighteenth centuries and visited by a sizeable number of African Americans today.

Dark tourism and diasporic travels

The notion of 'dark tourism' is broad and diffusive, encompassing travel to sites associated with death and disaster, such as assassinations and environmental catastrophes, as well as places of atrocity and suffering, like genocides, and even ghettos and slums. Definitions and debates abound, ranging from the appropriateness of labelling some tourism forms as 'dark' to defining it by demand or supply-oriented perspectives (see Lennon and Foley 2000 for a comprehensive discussion of 'dark tourism'; Rojek 1993, on 'Black Spots'; Stone and Sharpley 2008; Sharpley and Stone 2009). Seaton (1996; 2009) offers a consumption-driven, behavioural perspective called 'thanatourism'. Based on a thanatopsis tradition, thanatourism refers to travel motivated by the desire for actual or symbolic encounters with death (including, but not limited to, violent death). While Seaton's term describes a demand-driven activity, this chapter explores both demand and supply sides of a 'dark' phenomenon that is highly challenging to place identity and politics at all levels: African American tourists engaging with African enslavement history at local and global sites.

Slavery tourism includes visits to places such as plantations, slave castles and forts, burial grounds, and museums that are related to the transatlantic slave trade, which encompassed the Caribbean, Europe, and North and South America. Research on African American visitors and US tourism experience is scarce (Butler, Carter and Brunn 2002; Philipp 1994; Pinho 2008), with only a mere handful of studies addressing slavery tourism. A few concentrated on former slave plantations (see Butler, Carter and Dwyer 2008; Buzinde 2007; Buzinde and Santos 2009; Modlin 2008), while others addressed the roots-seeking behaviours of this diasporic population (see Austin 1999; Bruner 1996; Finley 2004; Pinho 2008; Timothy and Teye 2004). The experiences and motivations of African American travellers in the African diaspora vary greatly; some, for instance, seek cultural identity and belonging (roots-seeking), while others are motivated to satisfy curiosity about their ancestral homeland and historical origin. Ghana and the historic and popular Elmina and Cape Coast Castles have attracted both regional and overseas visitors, including President Barack Obama and his family in July 2009 (Bomani2007 2009). In addition to such cross-Atlantic travel are regional and local forms of travel within the diasporic home of the dispossessed group, such as to former plantation homes in the South (which are visited by Anglo Americans as well as African Americans). Not surprisingly, motivations to travel to such places seem to vary significantly, though both are enslavement-related sites – one located in the everyday home world of the US, and the other in an 'imagined' past and ancestral homeland. Careful excavation of the relationship between place and self is currently lacking, with the exception of a few studies such as those mentioned above. This chapter uses primary and secondary data to explore slavery tourism overseas and in the US. Drawing on secondary information sources, the chapter commences with a look at the highly visited World Heritage Site of Elmina Castle, a former slave castle in Ghana, where enslaved Africans were held before being taken to the Americas. This is followed by an empirical case study of the ABG, a former cemetery for enslaved and freed Africans in New York during the seventeenth and eighteenth centuries.

Roots tourism in Ghana: "conscientious remembrance" and Sankofa

Since the 1950s, many African Americans have been attracted to the African continent and to Ghana in particular. One reason is Ghana's highly publicized independence in 1957, as the first sub-Saharan country to make this move. Additionally, travels from the US were encouraged by development-related motives: Ghana's first president, Kwame Nkrumah, was very involved in the Pan-African Movement, which encouraged solidarity between blacks in the US and blacks in Africa through the travel of African American professionals to help build the new nation of West Africa in the 1960s (Holsey 2004). Moreover, in the 1970s and 1980s the media played an important role in African Americans' desire to visit Africa. Based on Alex Hailey's book, the film *Roots* (also a television miniseries broadcast in 1977), and the film *Beloved* (Toni Morrison's 1987 novel) recreated the history of slavery in the Americans' imagination and accelerated the flow of tourists to West Africa (Finley 2004; Holsey 2004; Pinho 2008; Reed 2004).

Ghana gained international recognition for its unique heritage when UNESCO designated Elmina Castle as a World Heritage Monument in 1972 (Finley 2004). Elmina Castle was built and named São Jorge da Mina (St George of the Mine) by the Portuguese in 1482. Under Portuguese rule, Elmina was primarily used for trading with other African states and for protection from other Europeans (Bruner 1996). Goods such as gold, ivory, pepper and sugar were stocked in the fortress. After multiple military attempts, the Dutch seized Elmina in 1637 with the help of some local African allies and enlarged the castle. As their predecessors had done, the Dutch used the castle as a holding fort for enslaved Africans until 1814, when the transatlantic slave trade was banned by Great Britain and the Netherlands (Gocking 2005). The last European occupants of Elmina were the British, who took control in 1872 (Bruner 1996; Gocking 2005). Throughout its history, Elmina was used for multiple functions: it served as a storage structure, a holding fortification for enslaved Africans, a prison, a secondary school, the office of the Ghana Education Service, the District Assembly, a police training academy and, finally, a tourist attraction (Bruner 1996; Richards 2005). Today, as the oldest standing European-built structure in sub-Saharan Africa, Elmina Castle is the most visited of these castles because of its historical and cultural significance (Teye 1988).

Tourism in Ghana contributed to nearly 25 per cent of West Africa's tourism revenue in 2000 (WTO 2005). It represented the fourth-largest source of foreign exchange earnings (estimated at US$650 million) by 2005 and contributed approximately 5 per cent to the country's GDP (Ministry of Tourism and Diasporan Relations 2006). The average length of stay of tourists grew slowly from 9.5 in 2000 to 10.6 nights in 2005 (2006 data were not reported). By 2006, the largest percentage of visitors arrived to see friends and relatives (25 per cent) and for business purposes (22 per cent) (Ghana Tourist Board 2007). The Ghana Tourist Board (2007) reported 428,533 tourist arrivals and $836.09 million in receipts in 2005, which rose to 497,129 tourist arrivals and $986.80 million in 2006. The top generating markets by nationality were the US, Nigeria, the UK, the Ivory Coast and Germany (Ghana Tourist Board 2007).

Data on African American tourists is quite scarce, and information has to be drawn from diverse sources to piece together insights on the regional and transnational travels of this diasporic population. Other than high interest in visiting African countries as possible vacation destinations, Goodrich's (1985: 28) previous research has shown no major differences between the vacation destination choices made by African Americans and other Americans. In that way, many African American tourists visit Ghana for its historic legacy and to seek meaning, healing, guidance and cultural identification (Christie and Crompton 2001). Roots-seekers attempt to reconnect with their African cultural traditions and familial roots, often tracing genealogical and ancestral ties to the places where the African American experience and the African diaspora began (Pinho 2008: 72). Visiting Africa is not simply a vacation but a unique spiritual journey, a pilgrimage (Austin 1999 cited in Timothy and Teye 2004; see also Reed 2004). On-site reenactments, libations, prayers, songs and dances, offer visitors performative opportunities to feel more connected to each other and to the ancestral land. "Through the Door of No Return – The Return", for instance, reenacts the capture of Africans and the return of their descendants to Africa (Bruner 1996).

In 2003, about 27,000 tourists arrived in Ghana from the Americas, of which around 10,000 were African Americans (Mensah 2004). Between 2005 and 2006, arrivals from the US reached 60,592 (Ghana Tourist Board 2007). The African American tourist market is a lucrative niche market and seems to hold the greatest growth potential in terms of arrivals and receipts (Mensah 2004). In 1993, Elmina Castle received 17,091 visitors, of which 67 per cent were Ghanaian residents, 12.5 were Europeans and 12.3 North Americans (Bruner 1996). As Table 3.1 shows, more recent statistics indicate that close to 50,000 people have visited Elmina Castle; about 23 per cent of these are non-Ghanaian residents. African American tourists to Ghana tend to use specialized travel agencies catering to their specific needs and many prefer to travel with other black tourists through what, for many, is a highly emotional journey (Pinho 2008). Bruner (1996) indicated that most African American visitors to Ghana are class-privileged, with more leisure time to travel and more education.

'Sankofa' is an *Akan* (Ghanaian) word meaning 'go back and take it', or in other words, it expresses the necessity to look back to the past in order to move forward. Roots-seeking African American visitors to slavery-related sites such as Elmina practise Sankofa through place identification and existential search, actively appropriating the past into the present, or making "contemporary use of the past" as Graham, Ashworth and Tunbridge (2000: 2) put it. Through this experiential relationship with Elmina, they strive to make sense of present reality as US 'subjects' and attempt to reclaim cultural identity and a sense of belonging long

Table 3.1 Visitor arrivals at Elmina Castle: 2002–2004

Year	Total arrivals	Ghanaian arrivals	Ghanaian total arrivals (%)
2002	44,658	32,565	73
2003	39,478	28,395	72
2004	49,286	37,898	77

Source: Ghana Tourist Board (2005)

denied to them through slavery and dislocation (see DeGruy-Leary 2005; Latif and Latif 1994; Shipler 1997; and Thompson-Miller and Feagin 2007, on post-traumatic stress syndrome among the African diaspora in the US).

Such transnational journeys within the diaspora may help to facilitate well-being and "existential authenticity" (Cohen 1979), but what if such travels of origins and beginnings are not affordable or perhaps even conceivable? What acts or journeys might better situate a dislocated population in "in-between" (Bhabha 1994) diasporic spaces in the 'new world'? Slavery heritage sites are not only important for Sankofa; they are also political and moral spaces that help in the task of *conscientious remembrance* nationally and globally. Discussing the importance of US sites of slavery heritage, Linenthal notes that "conscientious remembrance is more than a necessary expansion of the nation's narrative; it is an act of moral engagement, a declaration that there are other American lives too long forgotten that count" (Linenthal 2006: 224 cited in Rice 2009: 246). The case of the ABG in New York illustrates the existential, political and moral significance of sites like the ABG to the national narrative of US history and heritage.

Slavery tourism in the US: sites of significance and belonging

Of the 38.9 million African American residents in the US, only a small fraction engages in transnational travel to Africa; only 10,000 visited Ghana in 2003 (Mensah 2004). Statistics on heritage-related travel by African American visitors within the US are unfortunately scant. Personal fieldwork estimates in 2010 indicate that about a third of the visitors observed at the ABG were black. Table 3.2 presents the number of visitors at five different US sites related to African American heritage, including the Civil Rights Movement and slavery.

Table 3.2 US sites of African American heritage

Sites	National Civil Rights Museum	Martin Luther King, Jr. National Memorial	The Martin Luther King, Jr., National Historic Site	Cane River Creole National Historical Park (Magnolia and Oakland Plantations)	African Burial Ground National Monument
Location	Memphis, TN	Washington DC	Atlanta, GA	Vacherie, LA	New York City, NY
Operating entity	Private	National Park Service	National Park Service	National Park Service	National Park Service
Number of visitors	220,000 (in 2010)	2,235,536 (in 2011)	666,482 (in 2011)	26,382 (4,197 at Magnolia Plantation) (in 2011)	108,585 (in 2011)

Sites related to the civil rights movement, such as the newly inaugurated Martin Luther King, Jr. National Memorial in Washington DC or the Martin Luther King, Jr., National Historic Site in Atlanta, received a significant number of visitors in 2011. These two sites reflect on the life, death and accomplishments of Dr Martin Luther King, Jr. and the legacy of the Civil Rights Movement of the 1950s. The Martin Luther King, Jr., National Historic Site is particularly important as it incorporates several structures of significance in the life of the Civil Rights leader, including his birth home, Ebenezer Baptist Church where he pastored and his tomb. These places have the mission:

> to preserve, protect and interpret for the benefit, inspiration and education of present and future generations the places where Martin Luther King, Jr. was born, where he lived, worked, and worshiped, and where he is buried, while also interpreting the life experiences and significance of one of the most influential African Americans in the 20th century.
>
> (NPS 2006)

Former plantation homes located primarily in the South are also popular sites of visitation, albeit mostly by Anglo Americans. Scholarly observations indicate that very few black tourists engage in plantation tourism, and those seeking their own family history often tend to find this missing in the sites' narratives (Butler, Carter and Dwyer 2008; Buzinde 2007; Thompson 2000). Where the lives of enslaved Africans living and working on the plantations are acknowledged, they tend to be 'dark' stories overshadowed by those of their white owners (see Butler 2001; Buzinde 2007; Buzinde and Santos 2009; Eichstedt and Small 2002; Modlin 2008). Shipler (1997) postulated that while white visitors enjoy hearing about the architecture and opulence of the plantation house, black visitors wish to make sense of their own heritage. In a rare study of visitors to Laura Plantation, a historic Creole property located in Vacherie, Louisiana, Butler, Carter and Dwyer (2008) found that whites were more interested than other groups in the dominant discourses of architecture, civil war, furnishing, landscape and heritage. Black visitors were not necessarily more interested in enslavement narratives than other visitor groups. They especially did not seem to desire visiting slavery sites that portrayed shame and atrocity primarily, and may have been more attracted to sites depicting a more positive image of slavery. The development and representation of slavery tourism sites can be quite controversial and challenging due to historically entrenched dominant discourses and lack of understanding of black preferences (see Sharpley 2008).

As early emerging research indicates, 'dark' histories are highly political – how these sites are represented and 'produced' greatly influence not only visitor experience, understanding, cultural identification and social well-being, but also national identification – how the nation-state is produced and imagined by its citizens and residents (Anderson 1991). The roles played by the enslaved towards local, regional and national development have typically tended to be underrepresented as well, as Dann and Seaton (2001) noted (see also Rice 2009). The case of the ABG offers valuable insights into the crucial role played by Africans during early Dutch and British colonial settlement that led to the development of present day New York. In contrast to the sanitized interpretations of southern plantation sites noted above, the ABG attempts to present an Afro-centric view of the history of 'New Amsterdam', where more than a third of the population was comprised of enslaved Africans in 1638. Aside from the political tensions and conflicts surrounding this site, the case shows that African American visitors to the ABG have a variety of motivations, experiences and perceptions of the representation of slavery.

Case study: the African Burial Ground National Monument

History of the African Burial Ground National Monument

Protected and managed by the National Parks Service (NPS), the ABG marks a graveyard for freed and enslaved Africans that can be traced back to the colonial history of New York City. The first group of 11 Africans arrived at the newly established Dutch colony of New Amsterdam in 1626 (Hansen and McGowan 1998). Owned by the Dutch West India Company, it is believed that these Africans were Atlantic Creoles with a parentage of European men and African women, indicated by names such as Simon Congo or John D'Angola (Berlin 2003). These early Africans were used as farmers and workers to build New Amsterdam and started families as the Dutch settlers brought in African women. They developed livelihoods, owning land and expanding their farms (about 30 farms at that time) to form what was then called 'The Land of the Blacks', spanning an area from today's Chinatown up to Greenwich Village (Berlin and Harris 2005). Table 3.3 shows the growth of the enslaved African population in the colony from 11 to 300 between 1627 and 1664; the British took over New Amsterdam in 1664, renamed it New York, and ruled over the city until the end of the American Revolution.

While the African population continued to grow during this period, they were no longer granted burial rights at Trinity Church (the first church established within the city of New Amsterdam) under British law. So from 1690 onwards, African New Yorkers buried their dead outside the city limits in "a place for outcasts and dumping ground for the refuse from the nearby pottery kilns, where

Table 3.3 Blacks in New Amsterdam

Date	Total population	Free blacks	Enslaved blacks	Percentage of population enslaved
1627	300	0	11	4%
1638	300	0	100	33%
1664	1,500	75	300	20%

Sources: Hodges (1999) and Berlin (1998)

ceramics were manufactured" (Hansen and McGowan 1998: 34). The 'Negros Buriel Ground', as it was referred to in the 1754 Maerschalk Plan, closed in 1796 and was covered with landfill as the city expanded.

During pre-construction tests in 1991 of the Ted Weiss Federal Building in Lower Manhattan, workers discovered human remains that were traced to the historic ABG. Of the estimated 15,000 to 20,000 burials identified in that area, 419 were excavated, of which more than 40 per cent were of children under the age of 12 (NPS 2009). The General Service Administration (GSA), an independent governmental agency mandated to construct, manage and preserve government buildings, had to deal with this new discovery (see below for more on the ensuing conflict). In 1993, the site was designated a National Historic Landmark and selected as a national monument in 2006. The ABG is located in Lower Manhattan and comprises an outdoor memorial inaugurated in 2007, a commemorative art gallery and a visitor centre that opened in 2010, driven by an effort to enhance visitors' experience and the quality of the interpretive work. The visitor centre includes four exhibit areas, a 40-person theatre for the screening of a short documentary, a library/research room and a gift shop. The outdoor memorial is comprised of seven mounds that denote the location under which the exhumed human remains were reinterred in 2003; a granite Ancestral Libation Chamber, whose structure was inspired by slave ships crossing the Atlantic Ocean from Africa to the New World; the Circle of the Diaspora, where the map of the world with the African continent at its centre is engraved on the ground; two water streams; and different spiritual symbols engraved on the black granite wall surrounding the Circle of the Diaspora.

Conflicted beginnings

The process of development of the ABG was long and complex as it involved different agencies and groups with a variety of interests and preferences, including the African American community in New York City (also referred to as the African descendant community in this chapter), the GSA, the NPS, Congress and Senate members, as well as various community-based organizations. Community activism was manifested through a number of coalitions of artists, architects, religious leaders, lawyers and journalists, among others. Numerous African American individuals and organizations in New York City became involved in the development of the ABG soon after the discovery of human remains in 1991; local and area-based residents were outraged when they heard that the GSA planned to go forward with the exhuming of the graves in order to pursue the construction of a 34-storey federal office building and an adjacent pavilion. To the African American community in New York City, the burial ground was a cemetery, a sacred ground where ancestors were laid to rest in peace. The GSA demonstrated unwillingness to stop excavations, and for that, the community relentlessly organized meetings, protests and vigils at the site. Furthermore, the GSA did not respect the federal mandate to consult and include the community, upon the discovery of the African cemetery. Added to these frictions was the fact that delays by the GSA prevented the reburial of the excavated remains from occurring until October 2003, although set to be reinterred by 2000 (Blakey 2010).

Twenty-seven black visitors aged 20 to 80 years were interviewed in July and August 2010; several interviews involved a second follow-up discussion. The in-depth interviews focused on the relational aspect between experience and the objects of experience (the ABG and items related to it, including tour narratives, exhibit displays and on-site documentary) and attempted to shed light on the perception of slavery from the victimizing side and the uplifting side. Eighteen of the 27 participants were females and nine were males. Among the women, nine were under the age of 50 (six were under 30 and three were between 31 and 50) and nine were older. Five men were under 50 (one was under 30, four were between 31 and 50) and four were over 50. Their occupations included students, journalists, professors, ministers and managers. All participants were African American, with the exception of one Franco-Cameroonian woman, a Canadian woman and a Trinidadian British–American man. All participants lived in New York; however, one shared residency between Trinidad, the UK and the US (New York), and some participants were originally from other states: Minnesota, Ohio, Georgia, Pennsylvania and California. Interviews were held in participants' residences, in coffee shops, restaurants and churches around New York City and lasted an average of one to two hours.

These participants generally fell into three broad categories: the 'curious visitor', the 'serious visitor' who engages in repeat visits (see Kim and Jamal 2007), and the 'guardians' who were involved in the development and management of the site (for example, local resident protestors and volunteers). A major challenge in the recruitment of participants was the inability to solicit visitors on site for potential interviews in accordance with NPS policies. Hence participants were recruited through other means, including recommendations from park rangers, direct encounters with potential participants outside of the park, as well as via a call for participants sent through email distribution lists (or listservs) associated with Africana Studies departments and/or cultural events in New York City (five participants). A call for participants posted at churches, libraries, restaurants, museums, cultural centres and other public places frequented by African Americans generated several more respondents.

Twelve of the 27 study participants were involved in these protests and spoke of the GSA's arrogance and insensitivity towards both ancestors and descendents. They protested with determination and clear purpose to protect what they considered to be part of their African heritage. For many, the ABG represents the achievement of years of struggle against the GSA, and shows a national recognition of the significant contributions of enslaved Africans to the development of New York and the nation.

Differing interpretations

After the excavation of 419 burials, the scientific analysis of the remains was appointed to a team of researchers at Howard University in Washington DC. This work started in 1993 and ended in 2003, when the remains were brought back to

New York City for a ceremonial reburial. The team of researchers hired by the GSA to work on this 10-year process included scholars from diverse institutions and disciplines such as physical anthropology, history, biology and archaeology (however, the degree of their participation in developing the interpretive work shown on site was unclear). In the 20-minute documentary, viewers follow a young enslaved girl who attends the funeral of her father and her infant cousin on the outskirts of the city. The narrator speaks about the lives of Africans in early New York and explains the process starting from the rediscovery of the ABG until the completion of the new visitor centre in 2010. However, this 20-minute documentary and the impressive life-size wax figures at the centre of the exhibit area were perceived to be overly dramatic by a few historians among the respondents. Though not pleased about the cinematic effects employed in the documentary, the visual reproduction of history through wax replicas and an 'edutaining' film (that is both educational and entertaining) was acknowledged by a few respondents to be useful in helping visitors imagine what New York was like under slavery and to make it resonate more easily than dry facts.

Another participant expressed strong feelings about the 'static' and painful nature of the site's indoor exhibits (mostly the wax figures) and contrasted this to the freedom of the outdoor memorial area. For her, the wax figures do not portray the sense of life and humanity of enslaved Africans; rather, they denote a docility or victimization of Africans. As an artist, she perceived the wax figures to be too still and lifeless, and too typically white in the way slavery was depicted (such as Africans in pain, suffering, being beaten and abused). It prevented moving on, to "open up to freedom" and fun, as one participant explained. By contrast, the outdoor memorial, with its water streams, seven mounds, granite Ancestral Libation Chamber and Circle of the Diaspora, fostered such feelings of liberty and joy, she felt.

An interesting source of conflict lies in differing scientific and popular interpretations, in this case between the team of historians (including academics) and participant beliefs with regard to the use and representation of the land where the park exists. One vocal participant, Sylvia, felt that the ABG was really a "dumping ground" because Africans were not buried with any human dignity, but thrown there, adjacent to garbage. Historical accounts report that the burial ground was near pottery kilns where ceramics were manufactured and was indeed a dumping ground, but for discarded pottery, not for humans (Hansen and McGowan 1998). During their tour narrative, the NPS rangers presented the ground as sacred, testifying that Africans were buried properly and with dignity, contrary to some local beliefs (like Sylvia's above, who felt that bodies had been dumped there). However, they did not mention that the land had also been used as a dump for pottery refuse, and it would be fair to ask whether this omission is part of a sanitization strategy from the NPS (along with the clean, well-dressed wax figures).

Participatory engagement and production of pride

Production and representation at the ABG is geared towards illustrating the existence and practice of slavery in New York. The main themes presented at the indoor (visitor centre) and outdoor (memorial) spaces of the site relate to a) the contributions of the enslaved Africans; b) the resistance and rebellion of enslaved Africans; c) the community's involvement in the development of the site; and d) the brutality of slavery. The exhibits, stories, brochures, documentary and tours offer visitors an opportunity to understand how Africans dwelled, worked and resisted their colonial masters. Entrance to the ABG is free and visitors can either book a ranger-led tour or wander around the site on their own. Guided tours take between 30 and 90 minutes depending on the parts of the site covered (visitor centre, outdoor memorial and/or commemorative art gallery). At the time of the fieldwork, the ABG had 11 rangers, of whom eight were black, two were white and one was Hispanic. All rangers were New York residents. During tours of the indoor and outdoor areas, park rangers inform visitors that the renowned Broadway Avenue used to be a narrow path *broadened* by enslaved Africans. They also tell them that Wall Street got its name from a wall once built by enslaved Africans to protect the city from Native Americans. There are no physical reenactments at the ABG but the 20-minute documentary played in the theatre illustrates the daily activities of enslaved New Yorkers, including caring for children, running errands, building constructions and burying their loved ones. In addition, life-size wax figures resembling some of the characters in the film stand in the middle of the visitor centre, in a scene representing a funerary ceremony featured in the documentary; although their clothes are perhaps too pristine for the hard servitude they engaged in, as various respondents noted (see Figure 3.1).

Figure 3.1 Life-size wax figures (engaged in a funerary ceremony)

The scene shown in the above image is intended to invite the visitor to feel personally and emotionally part of the funeral ceremony; the wax figures, engaged in their tasks, are accompanied by sound effects in the background. Just as many African American visitors at slavery sites in Ghana experienced mixed feelings (saddened by the cruelty and tribulations imposed by enslavement but proud that their ancestors survived and overcame immense adversity), the ABG study participants also experienced mixed feelings. Danielle, quoted below, expressed her sadness about what had been done to her ancestors, and her pride in their significant contribution to the foundation of the nation. Many said they hoped that African American visitors to the ABG could emerge with strength and pride for who they are and where their ancestors came from:

> some sadness when you think about what the ancestors went through, no question about that... anger, resentment, but you know I don't want to get into bitterness. On the other hand... a sense of pride because they did leave a legacy. It may have taken years to find it, but they did leave a legacy behind us. So it's like mixed feelings with the African Burial Ground.
> (Danielle, black female participant in her 60s)

Secular and sacred meanings of place

The main reasons cited for visiting the ABG relate to connecting to the past, spiritual engagement, paying homage and respect to ancestors, learning and teaching. For a few respondents, the motivation was entirely secular, and based on curiosity. One participant explained that she had visited a variety of black heritage sites including slavery-related ones, and described how special it was for her to visit these sites as her parents had instilled in their children the importance of understanding their heritage. Several participants interviewed were educators and had visited the ABG with their students, who ranged from elementary school pupils to college students. Natasha, a historian and retired professor, explained that most of her students were uninformed about the history of enslavement that grounds New York and gained their rudimentary understanding from having watched *Roots*. Their trip to the ABG filled in a missing segment of their US history lessons.

For other participants, the ABG was a place for spiritual connection, reflection and homage. Some stated that they went to the ABG on a regular basis to communicate with their African ancestors, and to pray and remember, as more than one participant put it. Through these communications, they felt they received solace and even answers to their questions, as the two female participants below explained:

> I go there, I meditate... in relation to what I do and my connection to the ancestors, with all this, I am not saying history, but well, everything that might have happened, there's maybe an answer. It's a place of answers, or of questioning.
> (Wanda, black female participant in her 40s)

[L]ike sometimes you have stuff built up in you and then when you see it [the ABG] you got a place to release it. Even if 'stuff' are going crazy at the office you can come here and just be with the ancestors and, talk to them, and they listen. You do not actually want to get anyone to answer you back but you just want to get that out and let them know.

(Fiona, black female participant in her 60s)

African American visitors to the ABG thus engaged in multiple acts that facilitate connecting to the past – through acts of spirituality and acts of homage, invoking ancestral relationships through performative acts in various indoor and outdoor spaces at the ABG (for example, libations, prayers and depositing flowers and fruits). Like the roots-seeking tourists to Elmina Castle, they, too, are practising what Sankofa calls for: a return to the past to claim it, to establish connection with it and to develop a sense of rootedness to place – New York and the US (their current residence) in relation to the historic and ancestral space of the ABG.

Coming home to the ABG and New York: reconciling past/present

The notion of homecoming is central to roots tourism, as Elmina Castle represents to many of its diasporic black visitors. Home is a place of reference, a place of comfort, and a place one can always go back to when lost or when tired. Many participants interviewed in the study commented that they do not have a precise place to call home because they do not know where their ancestors came from. For a number of study participants, the ABG was also a place they felt at 'home'. For instance, six of the 27 participants volunteered on site, undertaking tasks such as greeting and guiding daily visitors, and ushering during special events. For these volunteers, the site is the closest place they can get to Africa and their ancestors – to some, it is where they feel connected and most at home. An emotional 62-year-old participant explained that she did not know where in Africa her ancestors originated from, and volunteering at the ABG helps fill that gap because of the connection she feels to the site:

because [of] that connection. Like, you know our ancestors are from Africa but you can't directly trace your roots because of slavery and the other 'stuff' that was done.... And it's like we have no connection, so if you don't know where you come from, to me, I feel empty. A part of me is empty without that knowledge but here [at the ABG], I feel still sad but happy. The ancestors are here.

(Fiona, black female participant in her 60s)

These volunteers shared that it was important for them to be part of the development of the ABG. Three explained that the sense of responsibility they felt towards the site pushed them to volunteer. As one said, he felt it was his duty to protect the ancestors from any possible desecration of their resting place; this refers to the early conflicts, where the African American community in New York City perceived that the human remains of their African ancestors were highly disrespected due to the unethical manner in which they were exhumed, manipulated and stored since their discovery in 1991. Some of them clearly approached volunteering as a calling, a direct instruction from the ancestors as Sam said: "I realized that I was charged by the ancestors to be here, if not physically, at least certainly to be honouring them."

Unlike many other sites of black heritage that are located outside of urban areas (such as Cane River Creole National Historical Park in Louisiana or Booker T. Washington National Monument in Virginia), the ABG is located within the dynamic centre of a large metropolis. In the heart of the administrative district of New York City, close to City Hall and Ground Zero, it is accessible by multiple reliable modes of transportation. Unlike cross-Atlantic journeys to the diasporic homeland, a visit to the ABG entails merely the cost of a subway or bus ride and it is highly accessible to regionally based visitors to New York. In diverse ways, the material presence of the ABG and its powerful story has changed the space, meaning and 'being' of New York to its African American community. While much further study is required, it is suggested that sites of enslavement like the ABG that contain archaeological evidence of almost 400 years of African presence and their contributions towards building the nascent country, offer significant opportunities for facilitating cultural identification and belonging, a home (in the nation-state) away from home (Africa) for its diasporic descendants. The ABG also challenges textbook portrayals of more recent beginnings through harsh plantation slavery in the nineteenth century, which most African Americans learn about at school and believe to be their sole legacy.

Slavery tourism: emancipatory journeys and pedagogic opportunities

Slavery tourism operates on a continuum of darkness, where dark history is illuminated by the everyday life traditions and cultural practices of the Africans who journeyed into the 'New World'. Close to four centuries of African presence in the US raise important considerations in terms of the ethno-politics of place identity and national identity. The government is entrusted with the difficult task of history conservation and interpretation, and wields tremendous power and authority in mediating public understandings (citizens and visitors) of African presence in the US and participation in nation building. How well did government agencies represent the important educational role of the ABG in revealing the roots of New York and those who toiled and tilled the land that eventually bore its iconic bounty?

While participants interviewed seemed satisfied overall with the representation and interpretation of the ABG, it could be argued that the site's pedagogic potential is not yet quite fulfilled. One of the missions of the ABG is to provide relevant research that "contributes to the reframing of the public's knowledge of slavery and the African experience in the United States, and of the history of New York" (NPS 2005: 36). Moreover, "educators will be encouraged to use the burial ground as a tool for learning and teaching through a carefully planned educational program for many grade levels and for traditional and nontraditional learners" (NPS 2005: 57). It could be argued that the site should educate people not only on the existence and prevalence of slavery in New York from 1626 to 1827 but also on the diverse forms of resistance and resilience implemented by enslaved Africans, their significant contributions to the development of New York and the legacy of slavery that the city holds. The ABG indeed tells this story by means of various interpretive information produced on site (brochures, documentary, tour narratives), but offsetting some of the harshness and brutality of enslavement reality with clean clothes and well-fed 'happy' looking wax dwellers (hence the critique of sanitization noted earlier). Furthermore, the ABG could do more to show visitors the social rituals, customs and cultural values and practices of the Africans who inhabited and toiled US soil three to four centuries ago. Little is shown of the artistic, religious and other cultural traditions brought by the early Africans: their everyday lives curiously devoid of emotional expression and social practices. The opportunity to shift a long-held ideological perspective of US slavery as a nineteenth-century phenomenon in the South towards better recognizing a much longer history of seventeenth- and eighteenth-century slavery in the North remains more or less implicit.

Conclusion

The ABG is a site of cultural and heritage significance for African Americans and for blacks in the wider diaspora. It is a 'third space' in which diasporic visitors may explore identities and relationships with place and past, resisting hegemonic and dominant discourses (see Wearing, Stevenson and Young 2010). But it is also a public place that belongs to all Americans; as a national monument, it presents an opportunity for all citizens and publics to learn about New York's role and involvement in the transatlantic slave trade and its reliance on both enslaved and free Africans. The site holds strong potential to facilitate a wider understanding and dissemination of the relevance of enslaved Africans and the ABG to the history of New York City and the US. Its transnational and layered colonial histories also offer an opportunity to provide understanding of the scale and scope of slavery: its local as well as its regional, national and global manifestations. This is not an easy task. Place identity is highly contextual and deeply historical; it is also highly political. A local–global view is needed to understand the role of 'dark' sites transnationally such as in roots-seeking travel to Ghana, and domestically in the production of the local (New York) and the nation-state (US).

Further research is needed to provide a better understanding of motivations to visit slavery-related sites such as plantations, museums or burial grounds, and to understand the diverse experiences and benefits African Americans seek when they engage in slavery tourism. Sites of slavery heritage should be aware of the heterogeneity of African Americans, who may visit these sites for diverse reasons ranging from a search for meaning, paying homage or seeking learning and knowledge. Like Butler, Carter and Dwyer's (2008) study of southern plantations in the US, Singer's (2008) study of black youth showed they were not interested in the suffering instigated on Africans, and more inclined toward understanding ways of resistance, as well as the significant contributions made by Africans to the nation, and the legacy of slavery in contemporary America. Better representation of the long presence of enslaved Africans and their roles as significant contributors to the development of New York City and the New World may be far more engaging to young New Yorkers and African American visitors than focusing on the 'dark' side of African American cultural heritage in the US.

References

Anderson, B. (1991) *Imagined Communities: Reflections on the Origin and Spread of Nationalism*, London: Verso.
Austin, N.K. (1999) 'Tourism and the transatlantic slave trade: Some issues and reflections', in P.U.C. Dieke (ed.) *The Political Economy of Tourism Development in Africa*, New York: Cognizant Communications.
Berlin, I. (1998) *Many Thousands Gone: The First Two Centuries of Slavery in Northern America*, Cambridge, MA: Harvard University Press.
Berlin, I. (2003) *Generations of Captivity: A History of African-American Slaves*, Cambridge, MA: The Belknap Press of Harvard University Press.
Berlin, I. and Harris, L. (2005) *Slavery in New York*, New York: New York Press.
Bhabha, H. (1994) *The Location of Culture*, London: Routledge.
Blakey, M.L. (2010) 'African Burial Ground Project: Paradigm for cooperation?' *Museum International*, 62: 61–68.
Bomani2007 (2009) *President Obama in Ghana at the Cape Coast Dungeons*. Available at http://www.youtube.com/watch?v = 0gmDoon_yC0&feature = related (accessed 25 January 2012).
Bruner, E.M. (1996) 'Tourism in Ghana: The Representation of Slavery and the Return of the Black Diaspora', *American Anthropologist*, 98(2): 290–304.
Butler, D.L. (2001) 'Whitewashing Plantations: The Commodification of a Slave-free Antebellum South', *International Journal of Hospitality and Tourism Administration*, 2(3/4): 159–171.
Butler, D.L., Carter, P.L. and Brunn, S.D. (2002) 'Travails and Survival', *Annals of Tourism Research*, 29(4): 1022–1035.
Butler, D.L., Carter, P.L. and Dwyer, O.J. (2008) 'Imagining Plantations: Slavery, Dominant Narratives, and the Foreign Born', *Southeastern Geographer*, 48(3): 288–302.
Buzinde, C. (2007) 'Representational Politics of Plantation Heritage Tourism: The Contemporary Plantation as a Social Imaginary', in C. McCarthy, A. Durham, L. Engel, M. Giardina, A. Filmer and M. Malagreca (eds) *Globalizing Cultural Studies: Ethnographic Interventions in Theory, Method, and Policy*, New York: Peter Lang Pub Inc.
Buzinde, C. and Santos, C. (2009) 'Interpreting Slavery Tourism', *Annals of Tourism Research*, 36(3): 439–458.
Christie, I. and Crompton, D. (2001) 'Tourism in Africa', *Africa Region Working Paper Series No. 12*, Washington DC: The World Bank.
Cohen, E. (1979) 'A Phenomenology of Tourist Experience', *The Journal of the British Sociological Association*, 13: 179–201.
Dann, G. and Seaton, A. (eds) (2001) *Slavery, Contested Heritage and Thanatourism*, Binghamton, NY: Haworth Hospitality Press.
Degruy-Leary, J. (2005) *Post-traumatic Slave Syndrome: America's Legacy of Enduring Injury and Healing*, Milwaukee, WI: Uptone Press.
Duval, D. (2003) 'When Hosts Become Guests: Return Visits and Diasporic Identities in a Commonwealth Eastern Caribbean Community', *Current Issues in Tourism*, 6: 267–308.

Duval, D. (2004) 'Conceptualizing Return Visits: A Transnational Perspective', in T. Coles and D. Timothy (eds) *Tourism, Diasporas and Space*, London: Routledge.

Ebron, P. (1999) 'Tourists as Pilgrims: Commercial Fashioning of Transatlantic Politics', *American Ethnologist, 26*: 910–932.

Eichstedt, J. and Small, S. (2002) *Representations of Slavery: Race and Ideology in Southern Plantation Museums*, Washington DC: Smithsonian Institute Press.

Finley, C. (2004) 'Authenticating Dungeons, Whitewashing Castles: The Former Sites of the Slave Trade on the Ghanaian Coast', in D. Lasansky and B. McLaren (eds) *Architecture and Tourism: Perception, Performance and Place*, London: Berg.

Ghana Tourist Board (2005) *Domestic Tourism Statistics*. Available at http://www.touringghana.com/documents/Facts_&Figures/DOMESTIC%20TOURISM%202002-2004.pdf (accessed 31 January 2012).

Ghana Tourist Board (2007) *Tourism Statistical Fact Sheet on Ghana*. Available at http://www.touringghana.com/documents/Facts_&Figures/Tourism_Statistical_FactSheet_070316.pdf (accessed 31 January 2012).

Gocking, R.S. (2005) *The History of Ghana*, Westport, CT: Greenwood Press.

Goodrich, J.N. (1985) 'Black American Tourists: Some Research Findings', *Journal of Travel Research, 24*(2): 27–28.

Graham, B.J., Ashworth, G.J. and Tunbridge, J.E. (2000) *A Geography of Heritage: Power, Culture, and Economy*, London: Arnold.

Hansen, J. and McGowan, G. (1998) *Breaking Ground, Breaking Silence: The Story of New York's African Burial Ground*, New York: Henry Holt.

Hodges, G.R. (1999) *Root and Branch: African Americans in New York and East Jersey, 1613–1863*, Chapel Hill, NC: University of North Carolina Press.

Holsey, B. (2004) 'Transatlantic Dreaming: Slavery, Tourism, and Diasporic Encounters', in F. Markowitz and A. Stefansson (eds) *Homecomings: Unsettling Paths of Return*, Oxford, UK: Lexington Books.

Kim, H. and Jamal, T. (2007) 'Touristic Quest for Existential Authenticity', *Annals of Tourism Research, 34*: 181–201.

Latif, N. and Latif, S (1994) *Slavery: The African American Psychic Trauma*, Chicago: Latif.

Lennon, J. and Foley, M. (2000) *Dark Tourism: The Attraction of Death and Disaster*, London: Continuum.

Linenthal, E.T. (2006) 'Epilogue: Reflections', in J.O. Horton and L.E. Horton (eds) *Slavery and Public History: The Tough Stuff of American Memory*, New York: The New Press.

Mensah, I. (2004) *Marketing Ghana as a Mecca for the African-American Tourist*. Available at http://www.ghanaweb.com/GhanaHomePage/features/artikel.php?ID=59447 (accessed 31 January 2012).

Ministry of Tourism and Diasporan Relations (2006) *National Tourism Policy*, Ghana: Ministry of Tourism and Diasporan Relations.

Modlin, E.A. (2008) 'Tales Told on the Tour: Mythic Representations of Slavery by Docents at North Carolina Plantation Museums', *Southeastern Geographer, 48*(3): 265–287.

National Park Service (2005) *Draft Management Recommendations for the African Burial Ground*. Available at http://www.africanburialground.gov/ABG_FinalReports.htm (accessed 14 August 2011).

National Park Service (2006) *Martin Luther King, Jr. National Historic Site 5-Year Strategic Plan*. Available at http://www.nps.gov/malu/parkmgmt/upload/MALU_Strategic_Plan_2011.pdf (accessed 31 January 2012).

National Park Service (2009) *General Management Plan Newsletter 2 – Fall 2009*. Available at http://www.nps.gov/afbg/parkmgmt/upload/AFBG%20NEWSLETTER%20web_final.pdf (accessed 22 March 2010).
Philipp, S.F. (1994) 'Race and Tourism Choice: A Legacy of Discrimination?' *Annals of Tourism Research*, 21: 479–488.
Pinho, P. (2008) 'African-American Roots Tourism in Brazil', *Latin American Perspectives*, 35(3): 70–86.
Reed, A. (2004) 'Sankofa Site: Cape Coast Castle and its Museum as Markers of Memory', *Museum Anthropology*, 1(2): 13–23.
Rice, A. (2009) 'Museums, Memorials and Plantation Houses in the Black Atlantic: Slavery and the Development of Dark Tourism', in R. Sharpley and P. Stone (eds) *The Darker Side of Travel: The Theory and Practice of Dark Tourism*, Bristol, UK: Channel View Publications.
Richards, S. (2005) 'What Is to Be Remembered?: Tourism to Ghana's Slave Castle-dungeons', *Theatre Journal*, 57: 617–637.
Rojek, C. (1993) *Ways of Escape*, Basingtoke: MacMillan.
Seaton, T. (1996) 'Guided by the Dark: From Thanatopsis to Thanatourism', *International Journal of Heritage Studies*, 2(4): 234–244.
Seaton, T. (2009) 'Thanatourism and its Discontents: An Appraisal of a Decade's Work with some Future Issues and Directions', in T. Jamal and M. Robinson (eds) *The Sage Handbook of Tourism Studies*, London: Sage.
Sharpley, R. (2008) 'Dark Tourism and Political Ideology: Towards a Governance Model', in R. Sharpley and P. Stone (eds) *The Darker Side of Travel: The Theory and Practice of Dark Tourism*, Bristol, UK: Channel View Publications.
Sharpley, R. and Stone, P. (2009) *The Darker Side of Travel: The Theory and Practice of Dark Tourism*, Bristol, UK: Channel View Publications.
Shipler, D. (1997) *A Country of Strangers: Blacks and Whites in America*, New York: Knopf.
Singer, A. (2008) *New York and Slavery: Time to Teach the Truth*, Albany, NY: State University of New York Press.
Stone, P. and Sharpley, R. (2008) 'Consuming Dark Tourism: A Thanatological Perspective', *Annals of Tourism Research*, 35(2): 574–595.
Teye, V.B. (1988) 'Coups d'etat and African Tourism: A Study of Ghana', *Annals of Tourism Research*, 15: 329–356.
Thompson, G. (2000) *Reaping What Was Sown on the Old Plantation*. Available at http://www.nytimes.com/library/national/race/062200thompson-plantation.html#about (accessed 11 February 2009).
Thompson-Miller, R. and Feagin, J.R. (2007) 'The Reality and Impact of Legal Segregation in the United States', in H. Vera and J.R. Feagin (eds) *Handbook of the Sociology of Racial and Ethnic Relations*, New York: Springer.
Timothy, D.J. and Teye, V.B. (2004) 'American Children of the African Diaspora: Journeys to the Motherland', in T. Coles and D.J. Timothy (eds) *Tourism, Diasporas and Space*, London: Routledge.
Wearing, S., Stevenson, D. and Young, T. (2010) *Tourist Cultures: Identity, Place and Traveller*, London: Sage.
World Tourism Organization (2005) *International Tourist Arrivals and Tourism Receipts by Country*. Available at http://www.world-tourism.org/cgi-bin/infoshop.storefront/EN/product/1380-1 (accessed 11 September 2009).

4 Place identity or place identities

The Memorial to the Victims of the Nanjing Massacre, China

Wei Du, David Litteljohn and John Lennon

Introduction

The Nanjing Massacre refers to an atrocity that took place from 13 December 1937 until the end of January 1938 in Nanking (now Nanjing), the then capital of the Republic of China (1912–49). Arguably up to 300,000 Chinese civilians and military personnel were systematically massacred by Imperial Japanese soldiers during these six weeks. Women of all ages were raped and killed in a brutal manner while much of the city was looted and burnt. This left a long shadow in the relationship between China and Japan and gave the site of the Nanjing Massacre an iconic and dark historic resonance for both countries.

The year 2012 was the 40th anniversary of the normalization of diplomatic relations between the People's Republic of China (PRC) and Japan. Yet, this element of their shared past is contested, and controversy over the Nanjing Massacre in 1937 continues to haunt relations between the two countries. For example, Takashi Kawamura, mayor of Nagoya, Japan, announced to a high-level Chinese official from Nanjing, "It is true that a considerable number of people died in the course of battle. However, such a thing as the so-called Nanjing Massacre is unlikely to have taken place" (Armstrong 2012). These remarks immediately attracted fierce reactions from groups across China. Notably, the staff of the memorial wrote a public letter expressing their strongest protest over the Japanese mayor's remark (Zhu 2012). In Sino-Japanese relations, the public discourse surrounding the memorial is not confined to the historical accuracy of the Nanjing Massacre. The significance of the memorial is evidenced by the fact that annual visits have exceeded three million. This intimates the presence of a dark tourism heritage site in a non-Western contemporary context.

A number of interesting terms such as Rojek's (1993) 'black spots', Tunbridge and Ashworth's (1996) 'dissonant heritage', Foley and Lennon's (1996) 'dark tourism' and Seaton's (1996) 'thanatourism' were proposed in academic discourse during the period 1993–96. These labels are used to conceptualize visits to places associated with death and disaster, for example atrocity sites such as the Auschwitz–Birkenau complex at Oświęcim in Poland; places linked to the death of famous people, such as the Sixth Floor Museum, Dallas, Texas, where Lee Harvey Oswald allegedly fired the shot that killed US President John F. Kennedy;

and war memorials including the USS Arizona Memorial, located at Pearl Harbor, in Hawaii.

It is not intended here to provide a comprehensive list of categories for such places (see Stone and Sharpley 2008; Seaton 2009 for contrasting documentation and categorization), but to illustrate a further addition to the diversity of sites that can be categorized within the phenomenon of dark tourism. Given this diversity, it is not surprising that academics have suggested a variety of motives with reference to specific categories of sites. For example, Dann (1998) proposed several factors including the fear of phantoms, the search for novelty, nostalgia, the celebration of crime and deviance and basic bloodlust (cited in Stone and Sharpley 2008: 576). Tarlow (2005) later included spiritual experience based on a sense of humanity and offering a pretext for explaining current political conditions and contexts.

While a number of productive discussions regarding possible motives have been generated by commentators as to why visitors go to dark tourism sites, a fundamental question remains: What are the deeper, more powerful motivations for this form of tourism? Indeed, it has been suggested that motivation has not been effectively researched (Stone 2006; Stone and Sharpley 2008; Sharpley and Stone 2009) yet they have to date provided no definitive motivational research.

The theme of death has been a popular element in considering motivation for this form of tourism. As a result, they treat death-related travel as a niche area, focusing on the role played by confronting death in the tourist experience. For example, Seaton (1996: 236) originally defined thanatourism as: "travel to a location wholly, or partially, motivated by the desire for actual or symbolic encounters with death, particularly, but not exclusively, violent death". Later, Seaton and Lennon (2004) elaborate the theme of death into two major categories – *Schadenfreude* and the contemplation of death – suggesting them as two potential motivational features: *Schadenfreude*, as they explain, refers to "secret pleasure in witnessing the misfortune of others", something that they consider part of the intrinsic psychological nature of human beings (Seaton and Lennon 2004: 68–69); and seeking to contemplate death, which according to Stone and Sharpley (2008: 579), means confronting, understanding and accepting death.

An alternative theme in tourist motivation has emerged, which is suggested by those who see dark tourism as a continuation and development of existing forms of tourism such as heritage tourism (Tunbridge and Ashworth 1996). Slade (2003: 793) states in his discussion of visits to battlefields at Gallipoli, "most Australians and New Zealanders who visit Gallipoli are engaged, to some extent, in a journey of discovering who they are, where they came from, and what the meanings of their nations might be in the modern world".

Slade's argument lacks any empirical evidence to support it, but his idea has identified the kind of 'long-term project' tourists may be engaged in by their visits to Gallipoli: that being the creation of collective memory. According to Halbwachs (1968), collective memory refers to: "those memories of a shared past that are retained by members of a group, class, or nation" (cited in Paez *et al.* 1997: 150). Furthermore, shared memories "give existence meaning, purpose and value", which constitutes an integral part of identity (Lowenthal 1985: 41). The contribution to the development of identity can be another theme of motivation in relation to dark tourism sites. Moreover, this sense of identity as a meaningful state of mind becomes possible to interpret when it is related to collective remembering, the 'long-term project' that the tourists are involved in.

The majority of the contributions to this broad field suggest complexities of historical analysis tempered by contemporary contexts. In order to deepen understanding of visits to dark sites, the concept of place identity can be a useful theoretical lens as it applies concepts of human–environment relationships to the studies of self identity (Proshansky 1978). In particular, as highlighted in the introduction of this book, the process involved in attributing a particular identity to a place is driven by the goals of different actors (Huigen and Meijering 2005). Where conflict between these goals exists, a unified place identity is difficult to achieve. Thus, contested identities are possible, illuminating the dynamic characteristics involved in the construction of place identity and three layers embedded in this concept: physical, chronological and social dimension.

The case of the Memorial to the Victims of the Nanjing Massacre

A case analysis of the Memorial to the Victims of the Nanjing Massacre, Nanjing, PRC, based on fieldwork between 2006 and 2011 will be used to illustrate this phenomenon. The study was initially developed to provide the first major Asian analysis of dark tourism motivation. The study gained insight and understanding of differences existing among predominately Asian visitors' motivations and underlying influences based on a site located in a non-Western social context. The memorial was an immediate and obvious choice due to its increasing popularity, with over three million visits annually and the controversial motives surrounding its context and interpretation.

The memorial was built by the Nanjing government and opened to the public in 1985. Nanjing city is located along the Yangtze River that flows from the west to the east and intersects with the major railway line that goes from the north to the south (www.nanjing.gov.cn). This makes the location of the city strategically important for gaining political and military power, which made the city the capital for ten dynasties in the past, including the Republic of China (1912–49). Nanjing city has a population of over 6.4 million and is a well-known tourist destination for both domestic and inbound tourism markets. According to the most recent data released by the National Bureau of Statistics in China (National Bureau of Statistics of China n.d.), Nanjing city attracted over 4.7 million overseas visitors and over 80 million domestic visits in 2010. In spite of such popularity among tourists, the memorial does not lie within the main sightseeing routes that the city government tries to promote (Nanjing City Government n.d.). The location chosen for the memorial was Jiang Dong Gate in the west part of Nanjing, one of many execution and burial sites in the city. There is public transport and it takes about an hour to arrive at the site from the city centre. The majority of visitors come via their own transport.

The memorial was renovated and enlarged twice – between 1994 and 1995, and between 2006 and 2007. As a result of the two expansions, the total size of the memorial has been enlarged from 28,000 to 74,000 square metres and the methods of display and interpretation of the history of the event have become more diversified. For example, besides the exhibition hall and the original graveyard, survivors' footprints are now displayed, having been embedded in a copper passage during the first expansion. There are also plans to renovate and upgrade the exhibition hall through introducing interactive technological equipment in order to recreate the situation of Nanjing in 1937. The aim is to provide visitors with a living experience of the event. As well as the memorial's physical presence, its official website also operates in both Chinese and English.

A mixed-methods approach was undertaken, involving both a survey of 795 respondents and a qualitative element involving more than 50 in-depth interviews and data collection among visitors and major stakeholders at the site. This involved tour guides employed by the memorial and memorial management. This allowed for a vital opportunity to explore, in depth, their thoughts and their construction of meaning attributed to this contested place.

Importantly, the research included an element of direct observation and involvement with visitors through covert observation undertaken by one of the authors in the role of tour guide over a period of four months. As well as facilitating access to visitors, the process of guide training involved an on-site, one month programme. During this process, detailed knowledge about the site was gained, which will be explored in the discussions below. Furthermore, undertaking the role of tour guide provided access to almost 1,000 visitors to the site, from a range of nationalities over a four-month period. This fieldwork provided a detailed analysis of quantitative data on visitor motivation conducted at a dark tourism site and provided a unique insight into this iconic Chinese memorial and its contemporary and historical context. The qualitative findings will be the primary source of data used in this exploration. Further analysis of quantitative data can be located in Du (2012).

Context: understanding the Nanjing Massacre

Conviction for crimes against humanity is not confined to any specific political state or people who may have suffered from these horrific acts (Falk 2002). However, nation-states have become formidable and defensive in the face of intensifying globalization and often seek favourable positioning and global perceptions in the world order (Falk 2002). Accordingly, it is virtually impossible to evoke the memory of any major atrocity, including this focus on the Nanjing Massacre, without considering political implications.

Unlike Germany post 1945, the memory of the Nanjing Massacre was not commentated through trials of the perpetrators (Yoshida 2002). Furthermore, the revolutionary events in China post 1945 meant that recriminations and the atonement for this massacre were simply not a priority. In the aftermath of Japan's defeat, a four-year civil war between Guomingdang or Kuomintang (the Nationalist party) and Gongchandang (The Communist's party) followed. With the defeat of

Guomingdang, the People's Republic of China (PRC) was established by Gongchandang and led by Mao Zedong in 1949. During the period of reconstruction of the PRC, the Nanjing Massacre had been a minor issue for the emergent leaders. At this early stage of the new PRC, the site of the Nanjing Massacre had limited importance, possibly also because it had produced no communist heroes (Buruma 2002).

In the 1970s this perspective changed. It is ironic to note that the change was not instigated in China, but was catalyzed by schoolteachers in Japan. They raised questions about the absence of accounts of the Asia-Pacific War (1931–45) in official Japanese history books, which led to an attempt by many historians to clarify Japan's role as aggressor (Tokushi 2002: 88; Yoshida 2002: 162–163). This gradual awakening of public consciousness to darker episodes in Japan's national history met strong resistance from extreme conservative groups in Japan. Such groups utilize the memory of the atomic attacks against Hiroshima and Nagasaki at the end of World War II, to emphasize Japan's role as a victim of a vicious crime, planned and executed by the USA (Falk 2002: 13; Yoshida 2002: 164). Consequently, conservative revisionists contest that: "Japan should have a national history that its nationals can be proud of, but current history textbooks...have been eroding national pride among the Japanese youth" (Yoshida 2002: 160).

As Lowenthal (1985: 63) noted, "the past not only aids and delights; it also threatens and diminishes us". Clearly the issue of selective and contrasting histories is being confronted. This theme in museum development and interpretation of such sites has been explored before. Lennon and Smith (2004) compared contrasting approaches to Jewish and Roma mass extermination in the museums of Terezin and non-commemorations of Roma atrocities at Lety, in the Czech Republic. Similarly, the selectivity of attention given to the commemoration of the Lithuania Jewish Holocaust was considered by Wight and Lennon (2007). This phenomenon is not unique. The historical interpretation of sites such as the Nanjing Massacre will inevitably be the subject of debate. History is never an objective recall of the past, but is rather selective (Schouten 1995). The past is revisited and viewed from the present, and in so doing multiple constructions of the past are proposed and contested (Crang 1994). In the case of Nanjing, when some Japanese historians sought to reassess the war responsibilities of Japan and assert the Nanjing Massacre as part of national history, a total denial of the existence of the event was the key response made by some Japanese conservative groups. When faced with a reassessment of their national history there was a strong conservative faction in Japan that eschewed the existence of the massacre. Denial, rather than explanation or moderation of the nature of the atrocity, was the response offered. Vanguard figures among these conservatives who were able to gain coverage in the public domain for their perspective included Tanaka Masaaki, an ex-journalist and Ishihara Shintaro, a former mayor of Tokoyo who simply denied the Nanjing Massacre ever took place (Buruma 2002). The authenticity of the site and its quantification of the numbers of those executed in the massacre are also disputed. A figure of 300,000 given by the Chinese historians is highlighted at the site (see Figure 4.1).

Figure 4.1 The sign displays that 300,000 lives were lost at Nanjing

In contrast, a review of history textbooks used in Japan's middle schools found that the number of victims provided by six different texts used in schools ranged from 100,000 to 300,000 (Tokushi 2002). It is interesting to note that the issues surrounding Nanjing raised by the conservative factions did in turn lead to wider debates in Japan about this contested period of their past and their shared history with China. Indeed, a number of liberal commentators warned of hidden political agendas being pursued by ultra conservatives with a view to revising the postwar constitution of Japan (Tokushi 2002). The debate and controversy in Japan was in turn reported in the Chinese media and led to discussions of the meaning of this humiliation and its contemporary place in Chinese history. This debate, which occurred from 1972 until 1979, coincided with the Chinese leader Deng Xiaoping's policies aimed at reforming China's economy. As a result of implementing Deng's policy, China created a new context for its global position. As a consequence, China's relationships with Japan and America changed from an ideological adversary to a close trading partner (Falk 2002). Within China this type of change in foreign policy relationships has helped to create a receptive mood for relatively peaceful reflection upon the Chinese suffering endured during the Japanese invasion and occupation of 1937 to 1945 (Falk 2002). When media reports on the Japanese revisionist debates about the Nanjing Massacre were publicized in China, they had a major impact upon Chinese public opinion.

In particular, attitudes of denial were perceived as a serious attack on China's reputation and history. This resulted in subsequent defensive actions by the Chinese government. The most important response was to commemorate the Nanjing Massacre in the form of investing in a major memorial. The construction of the memorial received wide support from both the Chinese government and the public. Deng Xiaoping, as leader of the nation, even inscribed the memorial's title plate.

Once the development of the Memorial to the Victims of the Nanjing Massacre commenced, relevant documents and relics of the massacre were collected and archived in preparation for the opening in 1995. However, controversy over the scale and extent of the Nanjing Massacre remains. Moreover, as China's economic significance has increased, Sino-Japanese relations have become more complex. Japan has seen its manufacturing importance eroded by China, and China has become perhaps the most significant world economic power next to the US. This background provided the setting for both the original development and the recent major reinvestment in the memorial in 2006–07.

Place identities: paradoxes or dilemmas

The Memorial to the Victims of the Nanjing Massacre was originally built to provide objective historical evidence to counter any revisionist views expressed by Japanese conservative groups and others, and to provide a memorial for commemoration of those executed. However, a variety of 'identities' have been created for the site and these can be categorized as opposite but complementary interpretation contexts that reveal much about how this place is identified as a visitors' site but also as a heritage element of the Chinese psyche.

Site of national humiliation

The initial evaluation might suggest that it was irrational to promote the memorial in relation to the discourse of national humiliation. Naturally, such a designation could produce negative impacts on national pride, particularly as Chinese society places such emphasis on the value of 'face'. The concept of face is a Chinese cultural concept, which refers to a kind of prestige accumulated by a means of personal effort (Hu 1944: 45). Indeed, the Nanjing Massacre is exhibited with the following title: "Nanjing 1937 is our Nation's Humiliation, which ought to be never forgotten." Notably, one of the key monuments displayed at the outdoor area consists of a replica of Nanjing's destroyed city wall combined with another wall shaped like a Japanese sword resting diagonally. Its edge is coloured red to represent blood on the blade of the sword. The interpretation of this monument provided by the memorial guides offers the following perspective: "When it rains in Nanjing and rainwater drips down from the red edge of the wall, it looks as if blood is still dripping."

The theme of 'catastrophe and slaughter' is vividly interpreted, which is reinforced with a series of sculptures of captured men, raped women and body parts scattered around the fractured wall. This interpretive theme reaches its narrative conclusion with a sculpture of women in pain and representations of a dead tree on

Figure 4.2 Candles are lit for 'Hundreds of Thousands'

grey pebbles symbolizing human bones and referencing the human remains buried underneath. This symbol is a representation of massacre that portrays Chinese nationals as victims, which the nation and its government failed to protect. The message of national humiliation is reinforced repeatedly by the narrative of the guides. In the case of the 'Hundreds of Thousands Graveyard' (see Figure 4.2), guides highlight that the youngest victim was only three years old and over ten layers of bodies were discovered in the mass graves.

In interview analysis conducted on over 50 visitors, the following representative views were recorded, which give at least an indication of the qualitative responses collected. It is notable that in undertaking the quantitative research, these findings were overwhelmingly reinforced (Du 2012). It is important to note the feeling of humiliation was found to be particularly present among many Chinese visitors (who constitute over 60 per cent of visitors to the site). As one respondent, (female, over 60 years) stated:

> Today's visit brings back all my memories of the past. It is so vivid that I can smell the blood around me again. Young people must come here. They need to understand... what it means to be invaded. The government was weak. The country was weak. And what happened?... Our people suffered this terrible, terrible consequence.

Similarly, another respondent (male, 25–39 years) stated, "What happened in Nanjing in 1937 is our country's humiliation. It would be humiliating for all the Chinese to see the same thing happen again... simply because we did not remember it."

The message of national humiliation is the overwhelming response from Chinese nationals and the construction of interpretation graphically and symbolically uses the analogy of a blade upon the Chinese heart in the manner of the Chinese character 'ren' (忍). This signifies that no matter how much pain is caused by remembering events like the Nanjing Massacre, the Chinese people will never forget. This belief is reflected in the saying of Confucius who stated: "only if the nation has a sense of humiliation can it be courageous" (Callahan 2007: 5). On the surface, this Confucian idea sounds paradoxical and illogical. In comparison, some commemoration practices in Western societies will exemplify positive and heroic memories to become part of national heritage while defeats and other negative aspects are often downplayed or in some cases ignored. However, in the Chinese consciousness, it is perfectly natural to stress a sentiment such as a nation's humiliation. A possible contributory factor towards this type of attitude could be the Chinese dominant psyche characterized by self-criticism and the quest for self-improvement (Nisbett 2003). In this sense, the personal is transferred to the national consciousness.

In activating public consciousness regarding the Nanjing Massacre a progressive and ambitious perspective develops in society, such as building and developing an image of China as a self-confident and strong global power. The portrayal of defeat is used to justify and help understand current Chinese foreign policy and its relations with Japan over disputed territories. China moves from a defeated nation to a prominent economic and political world leader. Place is identified with the historicism of defeat in order to galvanize a new confidence and self belief. The contested elements (most notably with China's geographical neighbour Japan) are used as a context for territorial ambitions in the South China Sea.

Site of war resistance

The other primary interpretation of the site is via promoting the memorial in relation to the theme of war resistance, which is subtler than the theme of national humiliation. This is of course partially ideological, since no nationalist heroes were involved. A number of names of senior officers who provided resistance to the Japanese troops, and attempted to prevent them from entering the city of Nanjing, are mentioned in the main exhibition hall. However, the level of detail about these nationalist soldiers' sacrifice provided at the memorial is not comparable to the contributions made by the Communist Party in the later defeat of Japan. This selective interpretation of Nanjing, its defeat, occupation and liberation provokes different visitors' reactions. For example, by nationality, some Chinese visitors did not pick up the narrative of resistance at all. As one guide at the memorial recalled, "Chinese visitors asked questions like: 'why didn't we fight back? Why were we so obedient... just letting them do whatever they wanted... without any resistance? Where was our leadership?'" The omission of reading or understanding detailed content of interpretation by visitors is rare. Full analysis or understanding of context would be unusual. In contrast, the substantive national group of Japanese visitors (the third largest nationality who visit the site), offered a perspective that was similarly constructed around positive self perceptions. Japanese visitors did not relate to factors immediately relevant to the position in Nanjing and mainland China but rather, as a representative visitor noted: "Japan's defeat was due to the atomic bombs." The importance here of Japan as the victim and the harmed nation dominates other emotions that might have been expressed at the site.

Since the memorial was built almost 50 years after the massacre, Chinese visitors have only recently had a commemorative site to vent their grievances for the pain and suffering experienced in the past. Strong and intense emotions of sadness and resentment were shown by most of the Chinese visitors interviewed, particularly when they stood in the front of the Hundreds of Thousands Graveyard. The emotions displayed by Chinese visitors were very strong. Indeed, some of the Chinese visitors simply could not accept the monuments that are dedicated to friendship between Chinese and Japanese, such as the peace bell (see Figure 4.3) visited at the beginning of a standard tour.

Figure 4.3 The peace bell stands as a symbol of friendship

Understanding place identities in Nanjing

This chapter set out to explore the concept of place identity from the perspective of dark tourism sties. In order to accomplish this aim, three particular aspects of place identity – its social construction, and its evolving and contested nature – have been the focus. In the process of constructing identities for the Memorial to the Victims of the Nanjing Massacre, a number of stakeholders have been identified in this research. As shown in Figure 4.4, these groups are important in the construction of the constitution of place identity.

The most powerful group is the local government under the control of central government. They aim to help maintain a unified Chinese national identity with an emphasis on pride, continuity and distinctiveness (through investment in the physical monument and its interpretation). The other key influential group is the Chinese state media organizations, subject to the control and censorship of the government (Tang and Iyengar 2011), which aims to contribute to building the notion of Chinese characteristics such as unity and self belief. Other groups include staff working at the memorial, who are in some cases trained to provide different messages for different groups. Japanese right wing factions who wish to protect Japanese national identity are another key group. Finally, non-governmental organizations in Japan such as the China–Japan Society, who aim to achieve full reconciliation with the Chinese people, were identified.

As a consequence, historical interpretation is ambiguous and selective and frequently in conflict in such a location. Moreover, in this context the history of Nanjing is critical to its place identity. As Huigen and Meijering (2005: 21) noted: "Conflicts contribute to the conservation of place identity and the stronger the conflicts are, the more difficult for the place identity to change." Place identity does not seem to be derived from the changes in physical settings or conflicts, but rather, endless interactions among different stakeholder groups striving to achieve their independent goals.

Conclusion

There are three dimensions that are embedded in the concept of place identity of this site: physical, chronological and social. A fuller understanding of this concept cannot be achieved without considering these three dimensions. More importantly, this chapter has attempted to illustrate the use of place identity as a valuable tool in exposing dynamic influences that are critical in gaining an in-depth understanding of dark tourism sites. As highlighted in this chapter, these dynamic influences could be political, historical, social or cultural. Hence, although guided tours are organized in as orderly a way as possible, when viewing the visits to the memorial via the lens of place identity, a picture of a 'battlefield' emerges with various stakeholders trying to achieve their goals that are frequently conflicting.

It should also be noted that the wider empirical study carried out in a non-Western context not only has contributed to a theoretical understanding of place

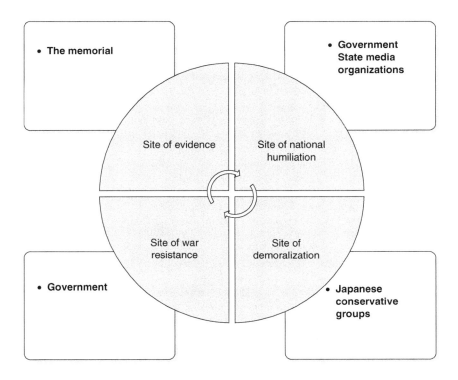

Figure 4.4 Four key influences on the construction of place identity

identity related to the field of dark tourism but also provided fresh perspectives that are distinctively Chinese in the context of Nanjing. It highlighted factors such as cultural influences, which are often overlooked in the studies of tourism motivation carried out in the Western context. Furthermore, it reinforces that a full understanding of the psychology of motivation for visiting dark tourism sites cannot be achieved without considering the social and historical context.

Sites such as Nanjing are important in developing collective memory at a national level. Interpretation and guidance are major factors in the construction of Chineseness. The moral complexity surrounding the selective interpretation reaffirms the importance of place identity in the context of a nation's dark history. As Shiranshi Shinichiro, from the China–Japan Society, succinctly summarized: "The true significance of the memorial lies in a stark contrast of interpreting Nanjing Massacre between Japan and China." Indeed, this highlights intertwined relationships within the physical, chronological and social layers embedded to the concept of place identity.

References

Armstrong, P. (2012) 02/23/2012-last update, *Fury over Japanese Politician's Nanjing Massacre Denial*. Available at http://articles.cnn.com/2012-02-23/asia/world_asia_china-nanjing-row_1_nanjing-massacre-japanese-troops-japanese-city?_s = PM:ASIA (accessed 25 February 2012).

Ashworth, G.J. and Graham, B. (2005) 'Senses of Place, Senses of Time and Heritage', in G.J. Ashworth and B. Graham (eds) *Senses of Place: Senses of Time*, Hants: Ashgate Publishing Ltd, pp. 3–12.

Buruma, I. (2002) 'The Nanking Massacre as a Historical Symbol', in F.F. Li, R. Sabella and D. Liu (eds) *Nanking 1937, Memory and Healing*, London and New York: M.E. Sharp, Inc., pp. 3–32.

Callahan, W. (2007) 'Trauma and Community: The Visual Politics of Chinese Nationalism and Sino-Japanese Relations', *Theory & Event*, *10*(4): 1–14.

Crang, M. (1994) 'On the Heritage Trail: Maps of Journeys to Olde Englande', *Environment and Planning D: Society and Space*, *12*: 341–355.

Dann, G.M.S. (1998) 'The Dark Side of Tourism', *Etudes et Rapports/Studies and Reports, Serie L*. Aix-en-Provence: Centre International de Recherches et d'Etudes Touristiques.

Dann, G.M.S. and Seaton, A.V. (2001) 'Introduction', in G.M.S. Dann and A.V. Seaton (eds) *Slavery Contested Heritage and Thanatourism*, New York: Haworth Hospitality Press, pp. 1–30.

Du, W. (2012) 'Tourism Motivation to Dark Tourism Sites: A Case Study of the Memorial to the Victims of Nanjing Massacre', unpublished thesis, Glasgow Caledonian University, Glasgow, UK.

Falk, R. (2002) 'Redressing Grievances: Assessing the Nanjing Massacre', in F.F. Li, R. Sabella and D. Liu (eds) *Nanking 1937 Memory and Healing*, New York and London: East Gate Books, pp. 10–32.

Foley, M. and Lennon, J. (1996) 'JFK and a Fascination with Assassination', *International Journal of Heritage Studies*, *2*(4): 195–197.

Halbwachs, M. ([1950] 1968) *La Mémoire Collective [Collective memory]*, Paris: Presses Universitaires de France.

Hu, H.C. (1944) 'The Chinese Concepts of Face', *American Anthropologist*, *46*(1): 45–64.

Huigen, P.P.P. and Meijering, L. (2005) 'Making Places: A Story of De Venen', in G.J. Ashworth and B. Graham (eds) *Senses of Place: Senses of Time*, Hants: Ashgate Publishing Ltd, pp. 19–30.

Lennon, J. and Foley, M. (2000) *Dark Tourism: The Attraction of Death and Disaster*, London: Cassell.

Lennon, J. and Smith, H. (2004) 'A Tale of Two Camps: Contrasting Approaches to Interpretation and Commemoration in the Sites at Terezin and Lety, Czech Republic', *Journal of Tourism Recreation Research*, *29*(1): 15–25.

Lowenthal, D. (1985) *The Past is a Foreign Country*, Cambridge: Cambridge University Press.

Nanjing City Government (n.d.) *Sightsee Bus Tour*. Available at http://english.nanjing.gov.cn/ly/200812/t20081216_256814.htm (accessed 25 May 2012).

National Bureau of Statistics of China (n.d.) *China Statistical Database*. Available at http://219.235.129.58/reportYearBrowse.do (accessed 25 May 2012).

Nisbett, R.E. (2003) *The Geography of Thought*, London: Nicholas Brealey Publishing.

Paez, D., Basabe, N. and Gonzalez, J.L. (1997) 'Social Processes and Collective Memory: A Cross-Cultural Approach to Remembering Political Events', in J.W. Pennebaker,

D. Paez and B. Rime (eds) *Collective Memory of Political Events, Social Psychological Perspectives*, Mahwah, NJ: Lawrence Erlbaum Associates, Inc., pp. 147–189.

Proshansky, H.M. (1978) 'The City and Self-Identity', *Environment and Behavior*, 10(2): pp. 147–169.

Rojek, C. (1993) *Ways of Escape: Modern Transformations in Leisure and Travel*, London: Macmillan.

Schouten, F.F.J. (1995) 'Heritage as Historical Reality', in D.T. Herbert (ed.) *Heritage Tourism and Society*, London: Mansell.

Seaton, A.V. (1996) 'Guided by the Dark: From Thanatopsis to Thanatourism', *International Journal of Heritage Studies*, 2(4): 234–244.

Seaton, A.V. (2001) 'Sources of Slavery – Destinations of Slavery: The Silences and Disclosures of Slavery Heritage in the UK and US', in G.M.S. Dann and A.V. Seaton (eds) *Slavery, Contested Heritage and Thanatourism*, New York, London and Oxford: The Haworth Hospitality Press, pp. 107–129.

Seaton, A.V. and Lennon, J. (2004) 'Thanatourism in the Early 21st Century: Moral Panics, Ulterior Motives and Alterior Desires', in T.V. Singh (ed.) *New Horizons in Tourism: Strange Experiences and Stranger Practices*, Wallingford and Cambridge: CABI Publishing, pp. 63–82.

Seaton, A. V. (2009) 'Thanatourism and Its Discontents: An Appraisal of a Decade's Work with some Future Issues and Direction', in *The Sage Handbook of Tourism Studies*, T. Jamal and M. Robinson (eds), London: Sage Publications, pp. 522–542

Sharpley, R. and Stone, P. (eds) (2009) *The Darker Side of Travel, The Theory and Practice of Dark Tourism*, Bristol, Buffalo and Toronto: Channel View Publications.

Slade, P. (2003) 'Gallipoli Thanatourism, the Meaning of ANZAC', *Annals of Tourism Research*, 30(4): 779–794.

Stone, P. (2006) 'A Dark Tourism Sepctrum: Towards a Typology of Death and Marcabre Related Toursit Sites, Attractions and Exhibitions', *Tourism: An Interdisciplinary International Journal*, 54(2): 145–160.

Stone, P. and Sharpley, R. (2008) 'Consuming Dark Tourism: A Thanatological Perspective', *Annals of Tourism Research*, 35(2): 574–595.

Tang, W.F. and Iyengar, S. (2011) 'The Emerging Media System in China: Implications for Regime Change', *Political Communication*, 28(3): 263–267.

Tarlow, P. (2005) 'Dark Tourism: The Appealing Dark Side of Tourism and More', in M. Novelli (ed.) *Niche Tourism: Contemporary Issues, Trends and Cases*, Oxford: Elsevier, pp. 47–57.

Tokushi, K. (2002) 'Remembering the Nanking Massacre', in F.F. Li, R. Sabella and D. Liu (eds) *Nanking 1937, Memory and Healing*, London and New York: M.E. Sharp, Inc., pp. 75–94.

Tunbridge, J.E. and Ashworth, G.J. (1996) *Dissonant Heritage: The Management of the Past as a Resource in Conflict*, Chichester: John Wiley.

Wight, A.C. and Lennon, J. (2007) 'Selective Interpretation and Eclectic Human Heritage in Lithuania', *Tourism Management*, 28: 519–529.

Yoshida, T. (2002) 'Refighting The Nanking Massacre: The Continuing Struggle over Memory', in F.F. Li, R. Sabella and D. Liu (eds) *Nanking 1937, Memory and Healing*, London and New York: M.E. Sharp, Inc., pp. 154–180.

Zhu, C. (2012) *A Public Protest Letter to Takashi Kawamura, the Mayor of Nagoya*. Available at http://www.nj1937.org/rss_show_news.asp?id = 3662 (accessed 23 March 2012).

5 The contribution of dark tourism to place identity in Northern Ireland

Maria Teresa Simone-Charteris, Stephen W. Boyd and Amy Burns

Introduction

According to Henderson (2007), tangible and intangible heritage reflects peoples' identities and representations of this can, in turn, influence how people see themselves and their country. Nation-states are very selective with regard to what cultural heritage resources to develop and promote as not only are they pivotal to the formation and maintenance of a national identity for the domestic visitors, but they also influence how destinations are seen by 'Others' (Lanfant 1995; Wood 1984). However, while states may encourage the development of certain types of cultural heritage resources and forms of tourism that enable them to present themselves to the wider world on their terms, they cannot exercise complete control over this activity. As a consequence, a state may be represented in a way that it would not choose. This, in turn, may generate forms of tourism demand that a state would not seek to encourage. Such a situation may be considered as unwelcome or even unacceptable by the host community and may compromise the political and cultural identity that it wishes to present to the wider world (Burns 2005; Morgan and Pritchard 1998). Sometimes, in fact, the physical remains of the past offer up an identity that many of those in the present wish to distance themselves from, even while, at the same time, recognizing it as part of their history. This is the dilemma of 'undesirable' heritage (Macdonald 2006), also referred to as 'atrocity heritage' (Ashworth 2002), 'dissonant heritage' (Tunbridge and Ashworth 1996), 'conflict heritage' (McDowell 2008) and 'negative heritage' (Meskell 2002). In some cases dark tourism can be considered as an example of this type of heritage.

Northern Ireland is representative of the dilemma of 'identity versus economy' (Light 2000; Tunbridge 1994) as it is faced by a demand versus supply conundrum with regard to the development and promotion of dark heritage tourism. The National Tourist Organization (NTO), the Northern Ireland Tourist Board (NITB) and other public sector tourist bodies are reluctant to officially market dark tourism as a distinct niche product, leaving few mainly private sector companies to offer visitors with an experience of sites and events linked to the region's turbulent past (Simone-Charteris and Boyd 2011). The reason for this is that in Northern Ireland, dark heritage tourism divides public opinion, and while some see it as an opportunity to transform the legacy of what came to be known as the 'Troubles' (Devine and Connor 2005), others believe it exacerbates differences and sectarianism (Crooke 2001). On the other hand, notwithstanding the controversy it generates, dark heritage tourism is attracting increasing numbers of visitors to Northern Ireland especially in the cities of Belfast and Londonderry/Derry (LD).

Based on a mixed method approach incorporating a survey of 300 visitors to three dark tourism attractions in Northern Ireland and structured interviews of public and private sector organizations, this chapter aims to explore the contribution of dark tourism to place identity in Northern Ireland through a demand perspective by investigating the motivations that inspire visitors to visit dark tourism attractions, and through a supply perspective by investigating the views of tourism organizations and bodies within the Province on the management, interpretation and promotion of sites associated with death and atrocity.

National and place identity in tourism

Identity can be described as one's understanding of the question 'Who am I?' As one's self identity indicates how 'self' is different from 'other', national identity also encompasses unique characteristics that differentiate one nationality from another (Renshon 2005). A communal culture, its beliefs and mode of life are part of the shared identity of a certain people living in a certain place at a certain time. This communal state of being might be understood as the ethos of a place, which characterizes and creates its distinctiveness (Kotler and Gertner 2002). The ethos or ontology of a place is based mainly on the meanings of people's social interactions, constructions and understanding of the past and of their relevance to the present. The ways in which these interactions are established shape the place identity and a collective sense of being and belonging, that is, national identity (Dixon and Durrheim 2000).

National identity is related to tourism because of the shared need for uniqueness and difference, an important element in tourism marketing. A central role of tourism marketing is to create a unique image that sets a given destination apart from other places. Thus, national identity can be incorporated into tourism branding as a way of showcasing how each country is exceptional and worthy of a visit (Huang and Santos 2011). Promotional materials are imbued with messages about 'who we are' and 'how we want you to see us' (Light 2001: 1055). As such, official promotional materials can be read as expressions of political and cultural identity aimed at both domestic and international audiences. Cultural heritage is often used by destinations to this end. According to McLean (1998), heritage offers representations of a nation's past with which the individuals of that nation may identify, while Lanfant (1995) notes that national heritage is perceived by international visitors as a marker of the nation.

According to Pitchford (2008: 3), identity tourism is a comprehensive term where collective identities are "represented, interpreted and potentially constructed". The term "encompasses the notion that tourism and finding out more about one's cultural identity is something that has broad appeal" (White and Frew 2011). Identity tourism can be contrasted with the "gaze" (Urry 1990) and "frequently involves the generation of significant personal meaning for the visitor" (White and Frew 2011). This is linked to the recent emergence of a branch of heritage tourism that emphasizes visiting "spaces considered by the visitors as relevant to their own heritage" (Poria, Biran and Reichel 2009: 92). This form of heritage tourism is pursued by those who are either searching to understand their own sense of identity (Prentice and Andersen 2007), or looking to create their own interpretation of the past. In the latter case, tourists might use their personal knowledge and combine it with the site experience to gain insights about their individual heritage (Poria *et al.* 2009). Genealogy provides a sense of belonging to a larger family or ethnic group and the distinctiveness of this belonging allows people to reconstruct and reaffirm their identities. Genealogical tourism attracts visitors who find personal meaning in the sites they visit and who "recognize personal legacy motives" (McCain and Ray 2003: 716).

Chronis (2005), however, goes one step further by affirming that sense of belonging and affirmation of self identity are provided not only through family ties and state identification but also through emotional connection. By using Gettysburg, USA as an example, he highlights how visitors at dark heritage attractions become linked to known and unknown individuals and their stories of human suffering through empathy. This way, isolated accounts of death and destruction are transformed into a community story: a story that belongs to a group rather than to a person, a sort of imagined community. Chronis (2005), Craik (1997) and Richter (1983) argue that tourists embark on their journeys with already formed images, mainly the product of popular cultural representations and of touristic discourse, their own historical background, preconceptions, ideological values and interpretational aptitude. During the course of the touristic experience, they constantly fill narrative gaps, recontextualize the narrative events in terms of their own experiences and actively engage their imagination. Hence, the experience of cultural heritage attractions is co-constructed in the present through the interaction of producers and consumers. In other words, it is the contemporary view of the past; of what people look for in the past, that shapes the past.

It follows that destinations cannot entirely control how they are seen by the outside world, so forms of tourism demand may emerge that are discordant with the way that they imagine themselves and wish to be imagined by others (Light 2007). One example is a form of political tourism that has developed in Central/Eastern Europe since the fall of state socialism. After 1989, the curiosity of foreign visitors about life behind the 'iron curtain' has forced a representation of socialist heritage. The states concerned have done little to encourage this. On the contrary, they were trying to move on from their past of political oppression, to assert their 'Europeanness' by joining the EU, and to present themselves as modern and cosmopolitan (Hall 2004). Other examples include 'Dracula Tourism' in Romania (Light 2007) and the case of this chapter, dark tourism in Northern Ireland (Simone-Charteris and Boyd 2011). This situation is problematic for the countries involved since it directs attention to a past that is rejected or that they have not come to terms with yet. This dilemma has been described as 'identity versus economy': such a past can attract foreign visitors and generate revenue, but at the same time it collides with identity-building (Light 2000; Tunbridge 1994).

Interpretation of historical sites of any type often causes debate, and those sites whose cultural or historical significance rests on the highly emotive issue of human suffering excite particularly deep and intensely fought divisions among scholars and stakeholders. Dark heritage tourism sites often embody multiple layers of contested historical and cultural meanings attached to them by different groups, and the motivations of the visitors tend to be at least as complex (Crooke 2001; Strange and Kempa 2003). The tourism generated by dissonant heritage rarely enjoys support from the governing bodies and official tourism associations. Many dark heritage sites pass through phases of contested meaning or significance, being reviled as shameful in one era due to the recentness of events, only later, as historical sensibilities shift, to be celebrated (Causevic and Lynch 2007; Lennon 2005; Wilson 2011). However, international examples suggest that social memory is often affirmed, and national identity thus served, by those sites that embody the darkest narratives (Wilson 2011).

Dark tourism

Dark tourism has been in evidence for centuries (Lennon 2005; Seaton 1996; Sharpley and Sundaram 2005; Stone 2006). What is different today is the extent of dark tourism and the academic interest it has aroused (Cochrane 2002; Lennon and Foley 2000; Stone 2006; Stone and Sharpley 2008). Tourism scholars have endeavoured to define or label death-related tourist activity as 'thanatourism' (Dann 1994; Seaton 1996), 'black-spot tourism' (Rojek 1993), 'morbid tourism' (Blom 2000), 'grief tourism' (Trotta 2006) and 'atrocity tourism' (Ashworth 2002), and produce a typology comprising battlefield, cemetery, disaster, ghost, plantation, holocaust, prison, suicide and doomsday tourism (involving visits to places which are under threat) (Trotta 2006). Attention has also been focused on exploring the reasons underpinning tourists' desires to seek out dark sites or experiences. Notwithstanding these attempts, the literature remains eclectic and theoretically fragile (Stone 2006; Stone and Sharpley 2008).

A number of definitions exist of dark tourism. According to Foley and Lennon (1996: 198), 'dark tourism' relates primarily to "the presentation and consumption (by visitors) of real and commodified death and disaster sites". Tarlow (2005: 48) adds a temporal dimension to Foley and Lennon's definition and identifies dark tourism as "visitations to places where tragedies or historically noteworthy death has occurred and that continue to impact our lives". Both definitions are quite broad and lack attention to motivation. In contrast, Seaton (1999) argues that dark tourism emerges from 'thanatoptic tradition' (the contemplation of death) that originated in the Middle Ages. He proposes that thanatourism is the "travel dimension of thanatopsis" defined as "travel to a location wholly, or partially, motivated by the desire for actual or symbolic encounters with death, particularly, but not exclusively, violent death" (Seaton 1996: 240).

Given the diverse range of sites, attractions and exhibitions that are associated with death and the morbid, attempts have been made to identify different intensities of dark tourism (Stone 2006; Stone and Sharpley 2008). Miles (2002), for example, proposes that a distinction can be made between 'dark' and 'darker' tourism where sites *of* death are darker than sites associated *with* death. The concept of different shades of dark tourism is also explored by Stone (2006), who proposes a spectrum of dark tourism suppliers based on the 'macabreness' within a dark tourism product comprising dark fun factories, exhibitions, dungeons, resting places, shrines, conflict sites and camps of genocide.

From a demand perspective, equally diverse are the motives of tourists who visit and consume these products: for instance, curiosity; nostalgic/nationalistic/patriotic reasons (to be part of a collective sense of identity or survival, such as visits by Australians and New Zealanders to Gallipoli); remembrance and commemorative purposes; educational interests (such as visits to the Port Arthur Historic Site, Tasmania); empathy with the victims (Gettysburg, USA); search of novelty and authenticity; overcoming childlike fears; celebration of crime or deviance (bloodlust); or risk-taking (dicing with death) (Ashworth 2002; Causevic and Lynch 2007; Dann 1998 as cited in Stone 2006; Light 2007; Seaton 1999; Shackley 2001; Slade 2003; Stone 2006; Stone and Sharpley 2008; Wilson 2011). The chapter now sets the background for the study by addressing the context of tourism in Northern Ireland.

Setting the background: tourism in Northern Ireland

In discussing the case of tourism in Northern Ireland it is helpful to subdivide time into distinct periods. For the purposes of this chapter the following time periods and characteristics are outlined: prior to 1969 as a period of pre-violence where a normal tourism environment operated, 1969–94 as a period of overt violence dominated by terrorist activity, and post 1994 to the present as a period of post-violence with the cessation of terrorist activities and the ongoing development and maturing of tourism (Boyd 2012).

In the pre-violence phase, Northern Ireland had a strong domestic tourism focus where attention was focused on seaside resorts and 'bucket and spade' type holidays at resort destinations along its northern coastline. Baum (1995) noted that by the late 1960s, tourism in Northern Ireland was at a pace commensurate to that of similar destinations in the British Isles; all this was to change over the next time period (1969–94) as the Irish Republican Army (IRA) began their long campaign of violence against the British government and its presence within Northern Ireland. Boyd (2000) stated that the period 1969–94 were years lost to tourism investment, development and growth; it would not be until 1991 that visitor numbers returned to pre-violence levels with over one million staying visitors. The 1970s were perhaps the darkest years for tourism in Northern Ireland; 1973 recorded the lowest ever number of tourists trips at 435,000, and the 'Troubles' came to symbolize the conflict situation in Northern Ireland and how the media presented the country to British and international audiences. It was over this

Table 5.1 Total visitor figures and revenue: select years between 1974 and 1989

	Staying visitors (tourists)			Day visitors (excursionists)		All visitors
Year	Trips	Nights	Spend (£m)	Trips	Spend (£m)	Spend (£m)
1974	486,800	3,424,200	13.1	3,494,000	8.8	21.9
1978	628,100	4,321,400	30.6	3,529,000	13.2	43.8
1981	588,000	4,206,100	42.2	3,200,000	17.8	60.0
1983	865,300	5,641,400	72.1	5,500,000	120.0	192.1
1987	942,800	6,638,700	91.4	N/A	N/A	N/A
1989	1,090,600	6,636,400	136.3	N/A	N/A	N/A

Source: NITB (1980; 1990).

decade that the symbols of a dark past were being forged in the communities; their viewpoints and defence portrayed in murals and graffiti. The 1980s was a decade of slow change with staying visitors from the United Kingdom (UK) and Republic of Ireland (ROI) rising alongside robust growth in tourist revenue (see Table 5.1) (NITB 1980; 1990).

By the end of the 1980s the perception of Northern Ireland in the marketplace was still one of fear, with visitor numbers showing a strong correlation to terrorist incidents and bombings (Moorhead 1991; Buckley and Klemm 1993) and where there lacked strong investment in tourism and development of infrastructure (Leslie 1999); understandable in the political and economic climate of the time. The start of the 1990s witnessed a sea change in politics where engagement with the IRA continued through its political wing Sinn Fein culminating in a ceasefire in August 1994. This first ceasefire resulted in a 20 per cent rise in visitor numbers over 1995, with over 1.5 million visitors recorded for the first time (Boyd 2000). The signing of the Good Friday Agreement in 1998 saw devolved power given back to Northern Ireland; it also provided the platform to build a lasting peace, develop a new political base and establish an external environment against which tourism could build for the future by helping to establish a safer climate for potential visitors: a key ingredient in the diet of any successful destination (Boyd 2012). At the same time, the built landscape of the communities at the heart of the violence had been changed, with peace walls erected and communities separated, creating the spaces for opportunities for dark tourism to emerge. Table 5.2 illustrates that between 1995 and 2009, the predominant pattern was one of growth both in terms of out-of-state visits and revenue, creating the base of a developing and more mature visitor destination (NITB 2009a).

Growth targets set for 2020 are ambitious: a £1 billion industry with 25 per cent more pure holiday visitors. The strategy of the NITB is set around a clear brand of "confidently moving on" and inviting visitors to "experience our awakening" and "uncover our stories". Unfortunately, none of this awakening or storytelling is developing around a clear dark tourism infrastructure and product base. Dark places of interest have developed as part of private sector initiatives in tourism, but the number of attractions and products remains small. This is disappointing, as

Table 5.2 Visitors to Northern Ireland and revenue generated (1995–2009)

Year	Out-of-state visits	Revenue (£m)	Domestic visits	Revenue (£m)
1995	1,557,000	214	613,000	57
1996	1,436,000	206	607,000	60
1997	1,415,000	208	570,000	60
1998	1,477,000	217	543,000	63
1999	1,655,000	265	510,000	57
2000	1,480,000	251	952,000	123
2001	1,511,000	271	892,000	123
2002	1,615,000	262	910,000	121
2003	1,896,000	284	847,000	99
2004	1,985,000	313	749,000	81
2005	1,972,000	357	1,390,000	146
2006	1,979,000	371	1,350,000	139
2007	2,107,000	376	1,154,000	159
2008	2,076,000	396	1,024,000	144
2009	1,918,000	337	1,375,000	192

Note: Change in the methodology from 2005 means data prior to 2005 is not comparable.
Domestic visits and revenue prior to 2005 relate to holiday visits only. Data since 2005 relates to total domestic trips (including VFR, business and other) and is therefore not directly comparable with data prior to 2005.
Source: NITB (2009a)

a number of researchers have identified how parts of heritage tourism can be linked to community peace building (see Anson 1999; Simone-Charteris and Boyd 2010) and where murals, once a symbol of struggle, have found transformation in tourism initiatives and are part of wider bus/black cab/walking city sightseeing tours offered by private sector organizations including ex-prisoners' organizations (McDowell 2008). Murals in Belfast and LD have become popular with the media, which use them to convey a sense of distinctiveness, place and authenticity (see Figure 5.1). However, they have become even more popular with tourists, who see them as a *matériel* remnant of the conflict, a legacy of the last 30 years, a reminder of a past that should not be forgotten or concealed (McCormick and Jarman 2005; Tripwolf 2012).

The Museum of Free Derry in LD, which focuses on the civil rights era of the 1960s and the Free Derry/early Troubles era of the 1970s, attracted 17,000 visitors in 2011 including American civil rights leader Jesse Jackson (Derry Journal 2011). The Museum's location, Glenfada Park, might not be glamorous with the Museum's entrance resembling a run-down back alley, but it is strategic as it is central to most of the events covered by the displays. The main battleground for the Battle of the Bogside was only yards away at the front of Rossville Flats, as was one of the main killing grounds on Bloody Sunday with two killed and five injured directly in front of the Museum's building, which still holds two bullet strikes on its face. Glenfada Park also places the Museum of Free Derry only yards away from the Bloody Sunday Monument, Free Derry Corner and the Bogside artists' murals, all of which are attracting large numbers of tourists (The Museum of

Figure 5.1 Mural of Bobby Sands on Belfast's Republican Falls Road

Free Derry 2005). It follows that the Museum of Free Derry is instrumental in reaffirming its domestic visitors' national identity but also the identity of international visitors who are able to identify themselves as part of an imagined community through empathy with the victims of the conflict. To this end, the Museum of Free Derry is engaged in collaborative projects with Robben Island Museum in South Africa and several concentration camps in Poland and the Czech Republic, and regularly receives visitors from the Basque Country, Catalonia and Palestine due to parallels being drawn by the international communities (Simone-Charteris and Boyd 2010), which explains the mural at the right side of the Museum's entrance in support of Palestine (see Figure 5.2).

Among other dark tourism attractions popular with visitors to the Province are the Apprentice Boys of Derry Memorial Hall, which commemorates the Siege of LD 1688–89; the Hands Across the Divide Monument in LD, which symbolizes the spirit of reconciliation (between the Loyalist and Republican communities) and hope for the future; the Belfast Peace Walls, which separate Catholic and Protestant neighbourhoods; the Orange Order Parades, which take place in July across the Province and celebrate the victory of William III, Prince of Orange over King James II at the Battle of the Boyne in 1690; and several small memorials and gardens cemeteries, found in and around Belfast and LD, that are tied to certain events and people, for example Milltown Cemetery where Bobby Sands and other hunger strikers are buried who died in the early 1980s seeking to be recognized as political prisoners. Even churches in the Province echo political views and, as a consequence, have become popular with dark tourists as in the case of St Columb's

Figure 5.2 Museum of Free Derry

Cathedral in LD, which contains artefacts from the Great Siege of Derry and was used by the Protestant army to observe the Catholic enemies during that time.

Furthermore, the Province's dark tourism product offering is about to expand. Plans are underway to redevelop the Maze Prison/Long Kesh site on the outskirts of Belfast, which contains the infamous H-block jails and was the theatre of the hunger strikers' protests in 1981, into a Peace Building and Conflict Resolution Facility that will promote the success of the peace process (Belfast Telegraph 2010). In addition, a major £2.5 million scheme to restore the Gatehouse and Governor's corridor at the Crumlin Road Gaol in North Belfast will be completed by late 2012. The restoration project will provide new facilities and improved accessibility for both locals and visitors with an aim to increase visits to the Gaol, which received 27,000 visitors during its 2009 tour programme (Northern Ireland Executive 2010). Both projects are funded by public sector money (together with EU funding in the case of the Maze Prison). The remainder of the chapter focuses on a case study highlighting the contribution of dark tourism to place identity in Northern Ireland.

The contribution of dark tourism to place identity in Northern Ireland

Dark tourists and place identity: a demand perspective

A total of 300 visitors were surveyed at three attractions related to dark tourism in Northern Ireland, namely, the Museum of Free Derry, St Columb's Cathedral also in LD and the Belfast City Open Bus Tour (that takes in the murals on the Protestant and Falls Roads) between June and October 2008. Of the survey participants, 41 per cent were male and 59 per cent were female. A wide number of age groups were represented with the largest group being that between the ages of 26 and 35 (28 per cent) followed by the 18–25 age group, which comprised 24 per cent and those 46–55, 18 per cent. A further 12 per cent of respondents comprised those aged 56–65, with 11 per cent between the ages of 36 and 45, 5 per cent representing the 66+ group, and 2 per cent under the age of 18. These results indicate that visitors to dark tourism attractions tend to be quite young when compared with other reported heritage tourism studies (Herbert 2001).

With respect to country of origin, the majority of visitors came from the UK (40 per cent). This is unsurprising given the domestic market, the UK, generates most visits to Northern Ireland together with ROI. Seventeen per cent of respondents were resident in North America. This could be explained in terms of genealogy as many Irish migrated to the USA and Canada following the Irish Famine in the mid-nineteenth century. This is a relevant finding as genealogy provides a sense of belonging to an ethnic group and the distinctiveness of this belonging allows people to reconstruct and reaffirm their identities (McCain and Ray 2003; McLean 1998; Prentice and Andersen 2007). The third biggest group, comprising 11 per cent of visitors, came from Germany, not surprising as according to statistics published by the NITB (2009a), Germany was the biggest European tourism market for Northern Ireland based on number of trips, nights and spend. The rest of the survey comprised of visitors from Australia (7 per cent), ROI (6 per cent), France and Denmark (5 per cent), Austria and Italy (4 per cent), Spain and Catalonia (3 per cent) and a further 7 per cent from other countries, which the authors combined in one group because of the very low numbers of respondents per country.

As stated earlier in the chapter, Chronis (2005) affirms that a sense of belonging and affirmation of self identity are provided not only through family ties and state identification but also through emotional connection and empathy. In the case of German visitors, sense of belonging and affirmation of self identity could be provided through the emotional connection deriving from parallels being drawn between their fascist past that culminated in the division of Germany into East and West following World War II, with the sectarian history of the Republican and Loyalist communities in the Province. In this respect, the Province's past could be interpreted as the story of an imagined community that transcends physical borders. Similar interpretations can be applied in the cases of Austrian and Italian visitors owing to the association of their respective countries with Fascist Germany during World War II; and Spanish and Catalan visitors due to various attempts on behalf of Catalonia to gain autonomy status.

When asked to indicate the main reason why they visited Northern Ireland, the vast majority of tourists replied 'Holiday/Leisure/Recreation' (69 per cent), followed by 'Visiting Friends and Relatives' (VFR) (18 per cent), 'To Study/School trip/University' (7 per cent), 'Business/Conference' (4 per cent) and 'Other' (2 per cent). These results do not reflect NITB's statistics on purpose of visit (NITB 2009b), especially concerning the third main reason provided. However, they support the view in the dark tourism literature that educational interest is one of the reasons why tourists visit dark tourism attractions (Ashworth 2002; Causevic and Lynch 2007; Light 2007; Seaton 1999; Shackley 2001; Slade 2003; Stone 2006; Stone and Sharpley 2008; Wilson 2011). Regarding the relevance of dark tourism attractions to the overall visit, only 15 respondents (5 per cent) stated that 'Visiting historical attractions' was 'Not Relevant' to them and only 41 visitors (14 per cent) stated that 'Visiting places associated with the Troubles' was 'Not Relevant'. Moreover, the large majority of those surveyed described visiting dark tourism attractions as 'A part of my trip' (72 per cent) as opposed to 'Not Relevant' (20 per cent) and 'The main purpose of my trip' (8 per cent). This highlights that despite not being the sole reason for visiting the Province, dark heritage attractions are popular with visitors and, therefore, are an important component of the tourism product offering in Northern Ireland.

Visitors were also asked to indicate the main motivation for visiting dark tourism attractions. Out of the 300 surveyed, more than half (54 per cent), replied 'I want to learn more about the conflict that involved Loyalists and Republicans', with a further 28 per cent replying 'Curiosity', 16 per cent 'I empathize with the cause of Republicans' and 2 per cent 'I empathize with the cause of Loyalists'. Again, the results are in line with the existing dark tourism literature that highlights educational interest, curiosity and empathy with the victims among the motives of tourists who visit and consume places associated with death and suffering. These findings are in line with Craik's (1997: 118) view that tourists take with them the 'prior knowledge, expectations, fantasies and mythologies' generated in and by their culture of origin and this cultural baggage will circumscribe their encounter with the destination. In this respect, the perspective of visitors also contributes towards the formation and maintenance of Northern Ireland's identity as seen by 'Others'.

Respondents were presented with a scale from 1 to 10 where 1 was 'a tourist not interested in dark heritage' and 10 was 'a tourist very interested in dark heritage', and were asked to rate themselves. Sixty-nine visitors (23 per cent) rated themselves an 8 and 44 visitors (15 per cent) rated themselves a 7; both toward the upper end of scale. This finding may be linked to Richter's (1983) opinion that specific itineraries might be viewed as representing ideological values of the tourists and their beliefs and convictions. In this light, tourists to the Province might be looking to reaffirm their own identities during the course of their experience of dark tourism attractions, while at the same time, reinforcing their preconceived image of Northern Ireland by attaching meanings to it, which in turn affect the national identity of the destination as seen by the international community.

When asked about their ability to obtain information on dark tourism attractions in the Province, 58 per cent of visitors indicated that it was either 'easy or very easy'. This is a surprising finding given the lack of public sector promotion, but rather confirms that too often destinations cannot control how they are seen by the outside world and the forms of tourism demand that it might generate (Light 2007). When asked about post-visit perceptions of Northern Ireland, less than half of those surveyed (44 per cent) indicated that their views had changed, and reasons included: 'I know more about the conflict' (44 per cent), which highlights the educational value of dark tourism; 'Better/more beautiful than expected' (20 per cent); and 'More peaceful/safer than expected/was before' (17 per cent). In relation to their experience of the dark tourism attractions, the vast majority of respondents (74 per cent) replied that it was positive, with 45 per cent indicating that it was 'Good/Interesting', 22 per cent 'Very good/Very interesting', 4 per cent 'Excellent' and 4 per cent 'Educational'. Finally, visitors were asked if they intended to return to Northern Ireland in the future. The vast majority of respondents replied 'Yes' (81 per cent), the main reasons provided for this being 'To do more sightseeing' (41 per cent), 'I had an enjoyable experience' (22 per cent) and 'To VFR' (22 per cent). The main reasons provided by those who replied 'No' (10 per cent) were 'I want to visit other countries' (63 per cent) and 'It is costly' (13 per cent).

Overall, the results indicate that visitors are satisfied with the dark tourism product Northern Ireland is offering, which is promising given that dark places of interest have mostly developed as part of private sector initiative in tourism. In addition to descriptive statistics, the authors attempted to perform cross tabulation to compare data, for instance, visitors' country of origin against motivations for visiting dark tourism attractions and other variables. Unfortunately, due to the small sample size, the Chi square test assumption of an expected cell count of a minimum of five was violated, hence cross tabulations could not be undertaken.

Dark tourism and place identity: a supply perspective

Twenty-one structured interviews of public sector bodies and private sector organizations including two visitor and convention bureaux, city councils, the NITB, the Orange Order, organizations involved with walking, bus and taxi tours, community organizations, two museums and political parties took place over a two-month period in 2008. All interviews were recorded, transcribed verbatim and deconstructed in order to identify key themes. The emergent findings follow. The primary explanation provided by the NITB for the exclusion of dark tourism from the organization's product development portfolio and promotional material is that the Troubles are very recent, people are still hurting and, therefore, there is a need to be sensitive. NITB Culture, Heritage and Activity Tourism Manager stated that:

> A lot of people are still hurting in Northern Ireland and it is a very sensitive situation where a lot of people have moved on but we still have the Victims' Commission... We know people are interested [in dark tourism], we are happy working with the different bodies and hopefully when this [government] policy comes out we will be able to put [the dark tourism attractions] on our website... We'll let the consumers make their choice... But anything that we do on the last 30 years has to be balanced and fair.
> (R. Lightbody, Belfast, 2008, pers. comm.)

The NITB's explanation supports Causevic and Lynch's (2007), Lennon's (2005) and Wilson's (2011) view that dissonant heritage rarely enjoys support from the governing bodies and official tourism associations, unless a certain chronological distance exists between what is being consumed and the tourists consuming it, which makes the experience acceptable. Regarding the Province's political parties, they have very different stances concerning dark tourism and cannot reach an agreement with regard to its development and promotion (Northern Ireland Assembly Official Report 2008). For example, according to Sinn Féin member Paul Maskey:

> Dark tourism has massive potential to grow the tourism industry and will assist in the regeneration of many areas of social need throughout the North... People are interested and curious about the North's history. They want to be told that history by the people who have lived through it. Dark tourism showcases the North to the rest of the world in a positive manner.
> (Northern Ireland Assembly Official Report 2008)

Conversely, Ulster Unionist Party (UUP) member David McClarty, argued that:

> Northern Ireland is still a divided society, within which, unfortunately, sectarianism is still rife... Tours often glorify division and our violent past... That is a sure way to remain in the past... Many of the tours pay attention to the suffering that victims of terrorist atrocities still undergo... Political tourism can be seen as a cynical attempt to make money out of other people's suffering.
> (Northern Ireland Assembly Official Report 2008)

The views above highlight the 'identity versus economy' dilemma, whereby a dissonant past attracts foreign visitors and generates revenue, but at the same time, according to some, it collides with identity-building (Light 2000; Tunbridge 1994). On the one hand, dark tourism allows the past to re-emerge and potentially disrupt efforts at post conflict identity construction (Young and Light 2006). On the other hand though, dark heritage attractions in Northern Ireland serve as reminders of the past and educate future generations. Even if it is of a dissonant nature, dark tourism in Northern Ireland allows for the saving and establishing of a cultural identity and nation-building (Smith and Puczkó 2011).

However, dark tourism is not considered to be as controversial and divisive by the communities as it is by the statutory authorities as evidenced by the fact that Republican and Loyalist ex-prisoners organizations in Belfast and LD cooperate on a regular basis. For instance, Coiste na nIarchimí Political Tours Co-ordinator explained that:

> Coiste [Republican ex-prisoners organization] would encourage unionists, loyalists to participate in their own tours and we are happy to give them any training that we can give them... We have a very sound dark tourism,

wherever people go, whatever side of the political divide, they want to explore further afield. I think it's beneficial to the communities... William Smith is an ex-UVF [Ulster Volunteer Force] prisoner. We have a fairly good relationship. We are serious about reaching across the divide. The guns are gone, the war is gone... and now we are confident that we can move that political situation on.

(S. Kelly, Belfast, 2008, pers. comm.)

In addition, a number of organizations that are currently not engaged in collaborative projects with the other community stated that they would like to do so in the future. For instance, the Co-ordinator of Free Derry Tours, a community organization in the Bogside in LD, which takes visitors around the Republican murals, stated that:

You will probably find official dark tourism projects in the next couple of years, all government funded, all nice and straightforward, not too controversial explaining the Troubles. That sort of misses the point. I would be more in favour of supporting projects in Unionist areas if it's going to create employment rather than co-operate with whatever body just for the sake of supporting dark tourism... All the areas that are most affected [by the Troubles] are working class areas. If we tell the story it should benefit the areas that are affected the most.

(M. Cooper, LD, 2008, pers. comm.)

From the examples above, it follows that dark tourism is allowing the two main communities to overcome around 30 years of mistrust, suspicion, prejudice and hatred, thus letting them come to terms with and accept their shared identity. The findings confirm that those sites whose cultural or historical significance rests on the highly emotive issue of human suffering excite particularly deep and intensely fought divisions (Crooke 2001; Strange and Kempa 2003). However, more importantly, they confirm Wilson's (2011) view that social memory is often affirmed, and national identity thus served, by those sites that embody the darkest narratives.

Conclusion

This chapter outlines the contribution of dark tourism to place identity in Northern Ireland from a demand and supply perspective. The findings have highlighted that the NITB is reluctant to promote dark tourism mainly due to the recentness of the conflict and the fact that the consequent healing process is still ongoing in Northern Ireland; a position that is also shared by some political parties. Because of this, it would seem that the Province is faced by the dilemma of 'identity versus economy' (Light 2000; Tunbridge 1994): should dark tourism attractions be developed and promoted because they attract visitors and, as consequence, contribute to the regional economy or should the Province try to protect its cultural and political identity? A closer examination of the findings however, reveals that this is not a real conundrum for Northern Ireland as dark tourism does not disrupt attempts to build and maintain its national identity following the cessation of the Troubles. On the contrary, it enhances this process in a number of ways.

First, by understanding dark tourism sites and events linked to the Province's turbulent past, visitors develop a deeper appreciation of the destination's national identity. Second, despite the statutory authorities' wish and attempts to distance themselves from the past, that past has shaped Northern Ireland as it is today and continues to shape the identity of the local peoples and the wider domestic market. Third, dark tourism is allowing the Republican and Loyalist communities to overcome many years of mistrust, suspicion, prejudice and hatred by means of cooperative projects such as tours that provide visitors with a comprehensive picture of the conflict, which in turn, enhance their acceptance of their shared identity. Fourth, dark heritage attractions allow some tourists to explore their own identities through genealogy tourism as in the case of North American visitors to the Province, but also through emotional connection and empathy with known and unknown victims of the conflict as members of an 'imagined community' (Chronis 2005) as, possibly, in the case of German, Catalonian and Palestinian visitors (Simone-Charteris and Boyd 2010).

According to Frew and White (2011), with the advance of globalization and its homogenizing effect on culture as well as ever increasing competition in the tourism industry at world, national and regional levels destinations need to concentrate their efforts on the provision of a distinctive product to be successful. Dark heritage attractions communicate Northern Ireland's unique story of conflict and subsequent peace building. As such, they represent the Province's most distinctive resource. This is reflected by the growing demand for dark tourism in Northern Ireland. As indicated by the findings, current visitors to the Province are generally satisfied with the dark tourism product offered even though dark places of interest have mostly developed as part of private sector initiatives in tourism so far. The intervention of statutory authorities in terms of provision of infrastructure, interpretation and marketing would unlock the full potential of dark tourism in Northern Ireland and assist in the provision of an even better product for dark tourists.

References

Anson, C. (1999) 'Planning for Peace: The Role of Tourism in the Aftermath of Violence', *Journal of Travel Research*, *38*: 57–61.
Ashworth, G.J. (2002) 'Holocaust Tourism: The Experience of Kraków-Kazimierz', *International Research in Geographical and Environmental Education*, *11*(4): 363–67.
Baum, T. (1995) 'Ireland – The Peace Dividend', *Insights*, July, A9–A14.
Belfast Telegraph (2010) 'Maze to Become Troubles Museum'. Available at http://www.belfasttelegraph.co.uk/news/local-national/northern-ireland/maze-to-become-troubles-museum-14893526.html (accessed 3 March 2012).
Blom, T. (2000) 'Morbid Tourism: A Postmodern Market Niche with an Example from Althorpe', *Norwegian Journal of Geography*, *54*(1): 29–36.

Boyd, S.W. (2000) '"Heritage" Tourism in Northern Ireland: Opportunities Under Peace', *Current Issues in Tourism*, *3*(2): 150–74.

Boyd, S.W. (2012) 'Tourism in Northern Ireland: Before Violence, During and Post Violence', in R.W. Butler and S. Wantaee (eds) *Tourism and War*, London: Routledge.

Buckley, P.J. and Klemm, M. (1993) 'The Decline of Tourism in Northern Ireland', *Tourism Management*, *14*(3): 184–94.

Burns, P. (2005) 'Social Identities, Globalization and the Cultural Politics of Tourism', in W. Theobald (ed.) *Global Tourism*, 3rd edn. Amsterdam: Elsevier, pp. 391–405.

Causevic, S., and Lynch, P. (2007) 'The Significance of Dark Tourism in the Process of Tourism Development after a Long-term Political Conflict: An Issue of Northern Ireland', paper presented at conference 'ASA 2007: Thinking Through Tourism', London Metropolitan University, London, 11 April.

Chronis, A. (2005) 'Coconstructing Heritage at the Gettysburg Storyscape', *Annals of Tourism Research*, *32*(2): 386–406.

Cochrane, P. (2002) 'Dark Tourism – Exploring the Dark Side'. Available at http://www.hyperhistory.org/index.php?option = displaypage&Itemid = 767&op = page (accessed 5 September 2008).

Craik, J. (1997) 'The Culture of Tourism', in J. Urry and C. Rojek (eds) *Touring Cultures*, London: Routledge, pp. 113–36.

Crooke, E. (2001) 'Confronting a Troubled History: Which Past in Northern Ireland's Museums?' *International Journal of Heritage Studies*, *7*(2): 119–36.

Dann, G. (1994) 'Tourism: The Nostalgia Industry of the Future', in W. Theobald (ed.) *Global Tourism: The Next Decade*, Oxford: Butterworth Heinemann, pp. 55–67.

Derry Journal (2011) 'FREE Admission to Museum of Free Derry'. Available at http://www.derryjournal.com/community/free-admission-to-museum-of-free-derry-1-3346672 (accessed 16 May 2012).

Devine, A. and Connor, R. (2005) 'Cultural Tourism – Promoting Diversity in the Aftermath of Conflict', paper presented at conference 'Tourism and Hospitality Research in Ireland: Exploring the Issues', University of Ulster, Portrush, 14–15 June.

Dixon, J. and Durrheim, K. (2000) 'Displacing Place Identity: A Discursive Approach to Locating Self and Other', *British Journal of Social Psychology*, *39*: 27–44.

Foley, M. and Lennon, J. (1996) 'JFK and Dark Tourism: A Fascination with Assassination', *International Journal of Heritage Studies*, *2*(4): 198–211.

Frew, E. and White, L. (2011) 'Research Directions for Tourism and National Identities', in E. Frew and L. White (eds) *Tourism and National Identities: An International Perspective*, Oxon: Routledge, pp. 215–18.

Hall, D. (2004) 'Branding and National Identity: The Case of Central and Eastern Europe', in N. Morgan, A. Pritchard and R. Pride (eds) *Destination Branding: Creating the Unique Destination Proposition*, Amsterdam: Elsevier, pp. 111–27.

Henderson, J.C. (2007) 'Communism, Heritage and Tourism in East Asia', *International Journal of Heritage Studies*, *13*(3): 240–54.

Herbert, D. (2001) 'Literary Places, Tourism and the Heritage Experience', *Annals of Tourism Research*, *28*(2): 312–33.

Huang, W. and Santos, C.A. (2011) 'Tourism and National Identity in the United States: The Case of Washington, DC', in E. Frew and L. White (eds) *Tourism and National Identities: An International Perspective*, Oxon: Routledge, pp. 14–25.

Kotler, P. and Gertner, D. (2002) 'Country as Brand, Product, and Beyond: A Place Marketing and Brand Management Perspective', *Journal of Brand Management*, *9*: 62–82.

Lanfant, M. (1995) 'International Tourism, Internationalization and the Challenge to Identity', in M. Lanfant, J. Allcock and E. Bruner (eds) *International Tourism: Identity and Change*, London: Sage, pp. 24–33.

Lennon, J. (2005) 'Journeys into Understanding'. Available at http://www.guardian.co.uk/travel/2005/oct/23/darktourism.observerescapesection (accessed 1 September 2008).

Lennon, J., and Foley, M. (2000) *Dark Tourism: The Attractions of Death and Disaster*, London: Continuum.

Leslie, D. (1999) 'Terrorism and Tourism: The Northern Ireland Situation – A Look Behind the Veil of Certainty', *Journal of Travel Research*, 38: 37–40.

Light, D. (2000) 'Gazing on Communism: Heritage Tourism and Post-Communist Identities in Germany, Hungary and Romania', *Tourism Geographies*, 2: 157–76.

Light, D. (2001) '"Facing the Future": Tourism and Identity-Building in Post-socialist Romania', *Political Geography*, 20: 1053–74.

Light, D. (2007) 'Dracula Tourism in Romania: Cultural Identity and the State', *Annals of Tourism Research*, 34(3): 746–65.

Macdonald, S. (2006) 'Undesirable Heritage: Fascist Material Culture and Historical Consciousness in Nuremberg', *International Journal of Heritage Studies*, 12(1): 9–28.

McCain, G. and Ray, N. (2003) 'Legacy Tourism: The Search for Personal Meaning in Heritage Travel', *Tourism Management*, 24: 713–17.

McCormick, J. and Jarman, N. (2005) 'Death of a Mural', *Journal of Material Culture*, 10(1): 49–71.

McDowell, S. (2008) 'Selling Conflict Heritage through Tourism in Peacetime Northern Ireland: Transforming Conflict or Exacerbating Difference?' *International Journal of Heritage Studies*, 14(5): 405–21.

McLean, F. (1998) 'Museums and the Construction of National Identity: A Review', *International Journal of Heritage Studies*, 3: 244–52.

Meskell, L. (2002) 'Negative Heritage and Past Mastering in Archaeology', *Anthropological Quarterly*, 75(3): 557–74.

Miles, W.F.S. (2002) 'Auschwitz: Museum Interpretation and Darker Tourism', *Annals of Tourism Research*, 29(4): 1175–78.

Moorhead, P. (1991) 'An Examination of the Relationship between Terrorism, the Media and Tourism with Reference to the Northern Ireland Tourism Product', unpublished MSc thesis, University of Surrey.

Morgan, N., and Pritchard, A. (1998) *Tourism Promotion and Power: Creating Images, Creating Identities*, Chichester: Wiley.

Northern Ireland Assembly Official Report (Hansard) (2008) 'Northern Ireland Assembly', *Hansard*, 27, 19 February.

Northern Ireland Executive (2010) 'Ministers Announce Restoration Project at Crumlin Road Gaol'. Available at http://www.northernireland.gov.uk/news/news-ofmdfm/news-ofmdfm-news-releases-june/news-ofmdfm-130610-ministers-announce-restoration.htm (accessed 21 March 2012).

Northern Ireland Tourist Board (NITB) (1980) 'Tourism Facts 1979'. Available at http://www.nitb.com/ResearchIntelligence/HistoricDataandReports.aspx barometer (accessed 30 November 2012).

Northern Ireland Tourist Board (NITB) (1990) 'Tourism Facts 1989'. Available at http://www.nitb.com/ResearchIntelligence/HistoricDataandReports.aspx barometer (accessed 30 November 2012).

Northern Ireland Tourist Board (NITB) (2009a) 'Tourism Facts 2009'. Available at http://www.nitb.com/ResearchIntelligence/HistoricDataandReports.aspx barometer (accessed 30 November 2012).

Northern Ireland Tourist Board (NITB) (2009b) 'Knowing the Visitor: Tourism Facts 2009'. Available at http://www.nitb.com/ResearchIntelligence/HistoricDataandReports.aspx barometer (accessed 30 November 2012).

Pitchford, S. (2008) *Identity Tourism: Imaging and Imagining the Nation*, Bingley: Emerald.

Poria, Y., Biran. A. and Reichel, A. (2009) 'Visitors' Preferences for Interpretation at Heritage Sites', *Journal of Travel Research*, *1*: 92–105.

Prentice, R. and Andersen, V. (2007) 'Interpreting Heritage Essentialisms: Familiarity and Felt History', *Tourism Management*, *3*: 661–76.

Renshon, S.A. (2005) *The 50% American: Immigration and National Identity in an Age of Terror*, Washington DC: Georgetown University Press.

Richter, L.K. (1983) 'Tourism Politics and Political Science: A Case of not so Benign Neglect', *Annals of Tourism Research*, *10*(3): 313–15.

Rojek, C. (1993) *Ways of Escape*, Basingstoke: Macmillan.

Seaton, A.V. (1996) 'From thanatopsis to thanatourism: Guided by the dark', *Journal of International Heritage Studies*, *2*(2): 234–44.

Seaton, A.V. (1999) 'War and Thanatourism: Waterloo 1815–1914', *Annals of Tourism Research*, *26*(1): 130–58.

Shackley, M. (2001) 'Potential Futures for Robben Island: Shrine, Museum or Theme Park?', *International Journal of Heritage Studies*, *7*(4): 355–63.

Sharpley, R. and Sundaram, P. (2005) 'Tourism: A Sacred Journey? The Case of Ashram Tourism, India', *International Journal of Tourism Research*, *7*(1): 161–71.

Simone-Charteris, M.T. and Boyd, S.W. (2010) 'Northern Ireland Re-emerges from the Ashes: The Contribution of Political Tourism Towards a More Visited and Peaceful Environment', in O. Moufakkir and I. Kelly (eds) *Tourism, Progress and Peace*, Wallingford: CABI, pp. 179–98.

Simone-Charteris, M.T. and Boyd, S.W. (2011) 'The Potential for Northern Ireland to Promote Politico-religious Tourism: An Industry Perspective', *Journal of Hospitality Marketing & Management*, *20*: 457–83.

Slade, P. (2003) 'Gallipoli Thanatourism: The Meaning of ANZAC', *Annals of Tourism Research*, *30*(4): 779–94.

Smith, M. and Puczkó, L. (2011) 'National Identity Construction and Tourism in Hungary: A Multi-Level Approach', in E. Frew and L. White (eds) *Tourism and National Identities: An International Perspective*, Oxon: Routledge, pp. 38–51.

Stone, P.R. (2006) 'A Dark Tourism Spectrum: Towards a Typology of Death and Macabre Related Tourist Sites, Attractions and Exhibitions', *Tourism: An Interdisciplinary International Journal*, *54*(2): 145–60.

Stone, P.R. and Sharpley, R. (2008) 'Consuming Dark Tourism: A Thanatological Perspective', *Annals of Tourism Research*, *35*(2): 574–95.

Strange, C. and Kempa, M. (2003) 'Shades of Dark Tourism: Alcatraz and Robben Island', *Annals of Tourism Research*, *30*(2): 386–405.

Tarlow, P. (2005) 'Dark Tourism: The Appealing "Dark" Side of Tourism and More', in M. Novelli (ed.) *Niche Tourism: Contemporary Issues, Trends and Case*, Oxford: Elsevier, pp. 47–57.

The Museum of Free Derry (2005) 'Glenfada Park'. Available at http://www.museumof freederry.org/location.html (accessed 16 May 2012).
Tripwolf (2012) 'Peace Lines'. Available at http://www.tripwolf.com/en/guide/show/17634/ Northern Ireland/Belfast/Peace-Lines (accessed 2 April 2012).
Trotta, J. (2006) 'Grief Tourism'. Available at http://www.grief-tourism.com (accessed 1 September 2008).
Tunbridge, J. (1994) 'Whose Heritage? Global Problem, European Nightmare', in G. Ashworth and P. Larkham (eds) *Building a New Heritage: Tourism, Culture and Identity in the New Europe*, London: Routledge, pp. 123–34.
Tunbridge, J.E. and Ashworth, G.J. (1996) *Dissonant Heritage: Managing the Past as a Resource in Conflict*, Chichester: Wiley.
Urry, J. (1990) *The Tourist Gaze: Leisure and Travel in Contemporary Societies*, London: Sage.
White, L. and Frew, E. (2011) 'Tourism and National Identities: Connections and Conceptualizations', in E. Frew and L. White (eds) *Tourism and National Identities: An International Perspective*, Oxon: Routledge, pp. 1–10.
Wilson, J.Z. (2011) 'Dark Tourism and National Identity in the Australian History Curriculum: Unexamined Questions Regarding Educational Visits to Sites of Human Suffering', in E. Frew and L. White (eds) *Tourism and National Identities: An International Perspective*, Oxon: Routledge, pp. 202–14.
Wood, R. (1984) 'Ethnic Tourism, the State, and Cultural Change in Southeast Asia', *Annals of Tourism Research*, *11*: 353–74.
Young, C. and Light, D. (2006) 'Communist Heritage Tourism: Between Economic Development and European Integration', in D. Hassenpflug, B. Kolbmüller and S. Schröder-Esch (eds) *Heritage and Media in Europe: Contributing towards Integration and Regional Development*, Weimar: Bauhaus Universität, pp. 249–63.

6 Dark tourism, heterotopias and post-apocalyptic places
The case of Chernobyl

Philip R. Stone

Introduction

On 26 April 1986, during a procedural shut down of reactor number four at the Chernobyl nuclear power plant in the Ukrainian Soviet Socialist Republic (now Ukraine), a catastrophic surge of energy led to a vessel rupture and, subsequently, resulted in the world's worst nuclear accident. The reported numbers of deaths from the disaster vary enormously, including from the radioactive fallout that encroached great swathes of northern Europe, to the apparent generational health maladies that now affect local populations. Nevertheless, despite obvious health and safety concerns, illegal tourism to Chernobyl has flourished over the past decade or so. In 2011 – the 25th anniversary of the disaster – the Ukrainian government sanctioned official tours to the site, as well as to the nearby abandoned 'ghost-town' of Pripyat.

Arguably, therefore, Chernobyl has become a destination associated with dark tourism and the 'darker side of travel' (Sharpley and Stone 2009; Stone 2011). The purpose of this chapter is to critically explore the touristification of Chernobyl and, in particular, examine how a place of industrial disaster can convey broader political narratives and identity. Indeed, Chernobyl is a monument to the secrecy and failings of the Cold War, a warning from history of a nuclear-energy utopia and a place located within the 'badlands of modernity' that can provide a surreal counter-hegemonic representation of space (Hetherington 1997). Chernobyl and the exclusion zone around it is where the technologies and disciplines of social orders are out of sequence and suspended with globalization and a new world order; a place misaligned with respect to normal or everyday space. It is also a place now consumed as a tourist experience which, in turn, allows for a potential resequencing and reconstruction of the past, creating a new space where microcosms of society are perceived. Thus, Chernobyl as a space of technical, political and cultural importance allows, through its touristic production and consumption, for a valorization of an alternate social ordering. In so doing, Chernobyl is viewed as a heterotopia – a ritual space that exists outside of time – in which time is not only arrested but also notions of Otherness are consumed in a post-apocalyptic place.

However, questions remain as to how Chernobyl can be framed as a psychogeographical space. Particularly, how is Chernobyl perceived as Other? What are the potential roles of dark tourism and the rituals of the tourist experience in co-constructing the place? Moreover, does Chernobyl provide a blueprint of how other 'dark tourism' sites might be constructed as marginal spaces? Through the application of Foucault's diverse, if not contested, concept of heterotopia, this chapter critically examines Chernobyl and its commodification within a conceptual heterotopian framework. In short, the research outlines Foucault's principles of heterotopias and, subsequently, offers an exploratory synthesis with tourism at Chernobyl. Ultimately, by examining Chernobyl as a heterotopia, the study suggests the popularizing of Chernobyl through dark tourism means the politics of the past are interfaced with the present, and that utopian ideals of the former Soviet Union are exposed within the petrified ruins of a heterotopian place. The first task, however, is to briefly locate the concept of heterotopia within broader social theory before reviewing Chernobyl and its subsequent touristification into an-Other place.

Chernobyl as heterotopia: 'the Other place'

In 1966, during a French radio interview on 'Les Hétérotopies', the renowned philosopher and social theorist Michel Foucault adopted the tone of an old traveller telling children amusing tales about the marvellous places he had visited. Subsequently, during an architectural lecture the following year, Foucault introduced the perplexing term 'heterotopia' to describe an assortment of places and institutions that interrupt the apparent continuity and normality of ordinary everyday space (Foucault 1967 [1984]). Foucault suggested 'heterotopias' – as opposed to 'utopias' as invented places – are real spaces where the boundaries of normalcy within society are transgressed. Literally meaning 'of Other Places', Foucault argued that heterotopias inject a sense of alterity into the sameness, and where change enters the familiar and difference is inserted into the commonplace. Indeed, heterotopias are spaces of contradiction and duality, as well as places of physical representation and imagined meaning. Foucault used a broad array of everyday examples and places to illustrate his heterotopian idea, including the school, military service, the honeymoon, old people's homes, psychiatric institutions, prisons, cemeteries, theatres and cinemas, libraries and museums, fairs and carnivals, holiday camps, saunas, brothels, motels, the Jesuit colonies and the ship. In short, however, heterotopias may be broadly defined as real places, but are perceived to stand outside of known space and, thus, create a sense of the alternative. Since Foucault's original conception, scholars have used the term heterotopia somewhat loosely as they pursue a direct connection with the topic of their study of public–private spaces within a 'post-civil society' (Dehaene and De Cauter 2008). Given such an array of examples, it is easy to understand, perhaps, the vastness of the concept, as well as its contention. Nonetheless, and stripped of its philosophical verbiage, the notion of heterotopias as alternative social spaces existing within and connected to conventional places, offers a thought-provoking idea that can stimulate further investigation into fundamental interrelationships between space, experience and culture.

Ultimately, heterotopias can be physical or mental spaces that act as 'other places' alongside existing spaces. As revealed shortly within the context of Chernobyl and dark tourism, heterotopias conform to a number of principles. These include places where norms of conduct are suspended either through a sense of crisis or through deviation of behaviour. Heterotopias also have a precise and determined function and are reflective of the society in which they exist. They also have the power to juxtapose several real spaces simultaneously as well as being linked to the accumulative or transitory nature of time. Heterotopias are also places that are not freely accessible as well as being spaces of illusion and compensation. In short, Foucault argued that we are now in an era of simultaneity, juxtaposition, of proximity and distance, of side-by-side and of the dispersed.

With its all-encompassing and vaguely defined parameters, Foucault's idea of heterotopia has been a source of both inspiration and confusion in the application of conceptual frameworks that shape public space. While a full critique of 'heterotopology' is beyond the scope of this study, the paradox of heterotopias is that they are spaces both separate from yet connected to all other places. In essence, heterotopias are spaces within places and places within spaces. Therefore, in our contemporary world heterotopias are everywhere and, consequently, highlight the public–private binary opposition (Dehaene and De Cauter 2008). Indeed, heterotopian places are collective or shared in nature, and are often perceived as marginal, interstitial and subliminal spaces. It is in this conceptual framework that heterotopias open up different, if not complex, layers of relationships between space and its consumption. Heynen (2008) argues that heterotopia, while being a 'slippery' term to employ, offers potentially rich and productive readings of different spatial and cultural constellations and, accordingly, justifies the continuing use of the concept. On that premise, therefore, the space of Chernobyl as a contemporary tourism place can be viewed under a heterotopian lens. Firstly, however, an overview of the accident at Chernobyl provides a context for tourism to the site.

Chernobyl and the 'dead zone'

Chernobyl, a site approximately 130km north of Kiev in the Ukraine and about 20km south of the Belarusian border, is no longer merely a nuclear power plant, but a term used to describe the calamitous events of 26 April 1986 when one of the nuclear reactors caught fire then exploded. Subsequently, the word 'Chernobyl' has entered a contemporary lexicon not only to mean devastation and contamination of the physical environment, but also as a term used to denote cultural destruction or a collapse in social relations (see, for example, McKernan and Mulcahy 2008). Chernobyl has also come to represent the 'standard' by which other nuclear accidents can be compared, including the 2011 tsunami-triggered disaster at Fukushima Daiichi nuclear power plant in Japan. In particular, Chernobyl is used to determine the severity of nuclear accidents on the International Nuclear and Radiological Event Scale, of which it currently holds the most severe of classifications (IAEA 2012). The four Soviet-designed graphite reactors at Chernobyl were constructed between 1970 and 1983, and when the accident occurred, it caused the largest uncontrolled radioactive release into the environment ever recorded for any civilian operation, including plutonium, iodine, strontium and caesium (IAEA 2012). Ultimately, the disaster was the result of a flawed reactor design that was operated with inadequately trained personnel and, arguably, a direct consequence of Cold War isolation and the resulting lack of a health and safety culture.

The explosion destroyed reactor number four at Chernobyl, killing two plant workers on the night of the accident, and a further 28 operators and fire fighters died within a few weeks as a result of Acute Radiation Sickness (WNA 2012). During the aftermath, up to 600,000 people, including soldiers, miners, plant workers and fire fighters from across the former Soviet Union – referred to as 'liquidators' – were drafted in to decontaminate the site. The decontamination process included a hastily constructed concrete 'sarcophagus' which entombed the entire fourth reactor and the estimated 200 tonnes of highly radioactive material that remains deep inside. The sarcophagus allowed the continuing operation of the other reactors at the plant, of which the final reactor was producing energy up until 2000. As the sarcophagus is now leaking radiation from the destroyed reactor, the International Shelter Implementation Plan in the 1990s began raising the expected cost of US$1.2 billion for a new durable confinement structure. Construction on a New Safe Confinement Shelter commenced in April 2012 and is due to be completed by 2016 (WNA 2012).

While debate over the number of deaths attributed to the disaster is still ongoing, partly due to lack of accurate records and politically contested criteria to determine Chernobyl-related mortality, a Greenpeace report suggests approximately 270,000 cancers within the affected region have been caused by the accident (Greenpeace 2006). Greenpeace also conclude that since the disaster, 60,000 people in Russia and 140,000 people in Belarus and the Ukraine have died as a direct result of the incident. The report also examines ongoing health impacts of Chernobyl and argues that radiation from the disaster has had a devastating effect on survivors, including the liquidators; damaging immune and endocrine systems, leading to accelerated ageing, cardiovascular and blood illnesses, psychological disorders, chromosomal aberrations and an increase in foetal deformations (Greenpeace 2006).

Initially, the Soviet authorities denied an accident had even occurred, and only admitted the disaster when a radioactive monitoring device at the Forsmark Nuclear Power Plant in Sweden alerted the world. Whereas the former Soviet Union wanted to downplay the incident, Medvedev (2011) argues its Cold War enemies wanted to extract a political advantage. This was no more apparent than in the forced, yet delayed, evacuation of the nearby town of Pripyat and its population of approximately 47,500 inhabitants. A town built in the 1970s to serve the Chernobyl nuclear power complex, the iconography of Pripyat – or 'atomgrad' – represented Soviet youth, modernity and progress (Phillips 2004), yet was systematically looted and vandalized in the immediate aftermath of the evacuation. The evacuation of Pripyat two days after the explosion and of a further 116,000 people a day later from villages within an arbitrary 30km radius around Chernobyl created what is now commonly referred to as the 'dead zone'. Hence, the Chernobyl disaster turned Pripyat, an example of blocky architectural Brezhnev baroque, from an icon of modern Soviet planning and technology into an icon of Soviet political ineptness, bureaucratic incompetence and technological calamity.

While there are no precise temporal or spatial boundaries, Chernobyl has had an enduring traumatic effect. The self-imposed exclusion zone that still surrounds the disaster site and the continuing hazards that remain within (as well as outside) are highly disputed. Indeed, the scientific community appears divided on how dangerous the dead zone actually is, which 'hot-spot' areas are the most contaminated, what diseases have been or are being caused and who can contract them (WNA 2012). For the layperson, including increasing numbers of tourists visiting the 'zone', the issue is even more acute. Arguably, however, experiencing radioactive danger may inject a sense of both thrill and anxiety for the contemporary tourist; yet the danger is invisible to the human senses and can only be mediated through specialized technology, such as Geiger counters and dosimeters. Of course, the chronology of radioactive pollution is far beyond human life spans or sociocultural memory. In spite of that, or perhaps even because of that, Goatcher and Brunsden (2011) suggest there is a sense of the sublime in visiting Chernobyl – a sensation of seeking something there. Certainly, the birth defects, the still births, the tiredness, the headaches, the cancers, the deformed wildlife, the suffering and the physical dislocations are real, lived, experienced – and to the people affected they are clearly not natural (Fairlie, Sumer and Nyagu, 2006; Petryna 2002). These hazards elude the senses and our descriptive language; they remain un-grasped and misunderstood, yet can now be experienced in a 'dark tourism moment'. Thus, the touristification of Chernobyl and its dead zone is well underway and it is to this that the chapter now turns.

Chernobyl: towards touristification

In 1979, Andrei Tarkovsky released his critically acclaimed film *Stalker*, in which a professional tour guide – the Stalker – takes two travellers on a spiritual journey into a forbidden Zone in search of a mysterious room that can grant one's deepest wish. Shot in and around an abandoned power station in Estonia, and inspired by the saga of 'alien zones' from the 1972 novel *Roadside Picnic*, Tarkovksy's *Stalker* uses cinematic imagination to transform ghostly beautiful rural landscapes and industrial topography into a science fiction terrain of a restricted and hazardous Zone. In the story, the Zone's origins were a 'breakdown at the fourth bunker' – Chernobyl's fourth reactor 'broke down' – and with an enigmatic narrative and photography of ruinous and empty quality, the film has come to be seen as prophetic of the Chernobyl disaster (Coulthart 2006; Dyer 2009). Moreover, with many of the cast and crew, including Tarkovsky, dying prematurely of cancer – attributed somewhat to the polluted Estonian power station film set – the film provides a surreal popular culture narrative in which the real zone at Chernobyl can be consumed.

Consequently, tales of Chernobyl and its dead zone are becoming entrenched in popular culture. Examples include video games such as *S.T.A.L.K.E.R: Shadow of Chernobyl* and *S.T.A.L.K.E.R: Call of Pripyat*; the horror mutant movie *Chernobyl Diaries* depicting 'extreme tourism' to the exclusion zone (Parker 2012) and fiction novels such as the thriller *Chernobyl Murders* (Beres 2008). These combine to provide meta-narratives in which the contemporary tourist to Chernobyl then consumes industrial ruins, environmental contamination and political decay. With an increasing number of Internet blogs and online photographic galleries dedicated to Chernobyl and Pripyat, creating a demand, perhaps, for 'toxic holidays', the Ukrainian government has now officially sanctioned tourism to the dead zone (Russia Today 2012). Of course, tourism to Chernobyl may have more to do with the continuing economic impacts of the disaster, as well as showcasing Chernobyl's 'dark heritage' to the influx of foreign visitors to the Euro 2012 football tournament, which was co-hosted by the Ukraine (with Poland). Indeed, as 6 per cent of the national budget of the Ukraine is currently devoted to Chernobyl-related benefits and programmes, there is a political desire to return some of the polluted land to productive use (Choi 2011).

Thousands of people have undertaken illegal so-called 'Cherno-tours' over the past decade or so (Bennetts 2011). However, the recent licensing of tours by the Ukrainian authorities allows tourists approved access to the dead zone, complete with a 'Stalker' guide and dinner in the Chernobyl canteen. Additionally, the highly regulated tours offer tourists an opportunity to wander through the nuclear ghost town of Pripyat or to feed the unusually large and sometimes deformed catfish that reside in the nuclear power plant cooling pond (Lehren 2012). Moreover, tourists armed with individual Geiger counters can visit a number of deserted villages within the zone. Many of these former settlements are in much better condition than Pripyat and offer a unique glimpse into Soviet rural life. For instance, St Michael's Church in the village of Krasnoe is still used for worship by the small number of elderly people who illegally returned to their homes after the disaster (Bennetts 2011), but have since been granted residency on an individual basis (Choi 2011). For a fee, tourists embarking on a 'riveting toxic adventure' can now meet with these dead zone residents, and explore how they live in the world's most radioactive ecosystem (Blackwell 2012).

While measures employed to guard tourists against radiation include protective clothing and radiation badges, visitors still have to sign official waiver forms to relinquish any claim against ill health. The disclaimer that the Ukrainian government will not be liable for possible deterioration of visitors' health because of their trip, suggests that "it's safe, but don't blame us if you get cancer" (Lyons 2011: 1). It is this, perhaps, that is the most obvious of indicators that tourists are about to enter the *zone*; a petrified ruin on an unprecedented scale that invites an altogether different mediation on not only spoiled landscapes, but also on man's technological folly and even, perhaps, of civilization itself (Dobraszczyk 2010). Crucially, however, it is the tourist gaze of the formerly forbidden zone where the normative, rather than being erased, is modified – or rather more precisely – where the norms of ordinary life are under suspension. Thus, it is here that the 'other place' of Chernobyl is both witnessed and consumed, and dark tourism and heterotopology collide. Indeed, the principles of Foucault's heterotopias, which have been uniquely entitled for this study and contextualized within the tourist experience at Chernobyl, remain the focus of this chapter.

Dark tourism and the 'dead zone': a heterotopian framework

While the interpretation, application and theoretical (de)construction of Foucault's heterotopias is contested, as is the nature and scope of dark tourism, a number of heterotopian principles can shine light on Chernobyl as a tourism place and its relationship with the cultural condition of contemporary society. In particular, Foucault offered six principles that loosely outlined his notion of heterotopia. Undoubtedly, these principles will always possess inherent author bias in any interpretation. Notwithstanding this predisposition, the six principles of 'heterotopology' can be applied to the touristification of Chernobyl and the dead zone.

Principle #1: heterotopias of crisis and deviation

The first principle of heterotopias is that they are universal. In other words, every culture has them, although the forms they take are heterogeneous (Topinka 2010). Foucault defined two types of heterotopias; namely, heterotopias of crisis and, subsequently, heterotopias of deviation. In his heterotopias of crisis, Foucault suggested these were forbidden places reserved for individuals in times of social, cultural or political crises. Certainly, Chernobyl and its dead zone is a place of socio-cultural and political crisis, a remnant 'forbidden' place that highlights the upheavals and divisions of the Cold War and its sustained state of political and military tension. Yet, the post-Cold War world in which Chernobyl is now located offers new pressures, including religious fundamentalism, economic uncertainty, the unipolarity of the United States, the potential collapse of the Euro-zone, the geopolitical implications of the Arab Spring and a rebalancing of international hegemony with the rise of China. Consequently, Chernobyl might be perceived as a place in which the old world order offered a sense of (in)security, both in terms of socio-cultural identity as well as military-industrial complexes. Thus, touristification of Chernobyl and its dead zone permits crises of the old world order and its technological failings and political divisions to be consumed, yet contemporary tourists are simultaneously connected to the new world order of turbulent transformations in society, culture, politics and economics. Therefore, Chernobyl as a heterotopia of crisis is where tourists can not only separate crises of the past, but also can (re)connect to present predicaments and contemplate future quandaries.

Importantly, however, the very fact that tourists are present at Chernobyl – a site of crisis – might suggest that tourist behaviour is deviant in relation to the required norm, thus revealing Foucault's emergent heterotopia of deviation from heterotopias of crisis. Foucault originally argued that leisure in a society of consumption was a form of idleness and, in turn, a sort of deviation (or even crisis). Consequently, the term 'deviant leisure' has entered academic parlance to suggest behaviour in a place that goes against the prevailing moral grain of society (Stebbins 1996; Rojek 1999). Indeed, deviant leisure is commonly viewed as sensation-seeking behaviour that is immoral, unhealthy or even dangerous (Williams 2009). Of course, so-called deviant leisure activity in any dark tourism environment is relative and socially constructed within a framework of cultural norms (Biran and Poria 2012). Even so, Chernobyl as a site of catastrophe is arguably a heterotopia of deviation in the sense that tourists are perpetrating deviant leisure. Yet, in this context, the very idea of deviance possesses qualities of a serious, even therapeutic leisure activity (Stebbins 2007). In other words, deviant leisure is serious in that it offers tourists time and space to reflect upon otherwise taboo topics – in this case death, decay and the causes of disaster (Stone and Sharpley forthcoming). Consequently, Chernobyl as a heterotopia of deviation can provide a participatory tourist experience that is potentially fulfilling, rich in personal, political, technological and environmental meaning and, as a result, has the capability of building social or 'mortality' capital (Stone 2012a; 2012b).

Principle #2: heterotopias of functionality

The second principle suggests that each heterotopia has a precise and determined function within a society. Moreover, the same heterotopia can have duality of function, depending on the synchrony of the culture in which the heterotopia is located. In other words, heterotopias of functionality permit the connection of another place with ordinary cultural spaces. Foucault illustrated this functionality by arguing that cemeteries, as sacred spaces of the dead, have been relocated from the spiritual centre of the city to the outskirts of living places. As he points out, "the cemetery no longer constitutes the sacred and immortal belly of the city, but the 'other city', where each family possesses its dark dwelling" (Foucault [1967] cited in Dehaene and De Cauter 2008: 19). Ultimately, Foucault argues that the cardinal displacement of the cemetery and its heterotopian function allow the dead to be distant yet, importantly, also allow the living to connect with their dead.

This duality of both providing distance and allowing connection is inherent in Chernobyl as a heterotopia of functionality. Indeed, Chernobyl can function as a place where tourists may learn about a new world in the face of the collapse of old hegemonic securities. As Alexievich (1999: 174) points out after her visit to Chernobyl:

> [t]here are two states, separated by barbed wire: one is the zone, the other, everything else. People come to the zone as they do to a cemetery. It's not just their house that is buried here, but an entire era. An era of faith. Of science. In a just social ideal.

Consequently, Chernobyl and the dead zone now function as icons of a failed political dogma as well as being symbolic of distant utopian ideals and Soviet power. Yet, the site is also consumed by tourists as a pyramid of our technical age, a tomb of technological tragedy and a symbol of our ruin to generations to come and, so, connects us to the fragility of our progress outside the zone.

Principle #3: heterotopias of juxtaposition

The third principle suggests that heterotopias have the power to juxtapose in a single real place several spaces that are in themselves incompatible. It is here where the dead zone of Chernobyl offers the strange mixing up of conventional notions of ruins and monuments, yet is juxtaposed with the return of normality, of residents, of wildlife and of tourism and commerce. Of course, wandering through, gazing upon and celebrating ruins has a long history. Edensor (2005), for example, argues that since the Renaissance onwards, the pleasure of ruins arrives from the juxtaposition of experiencing the impact of the past in the present; an opportunity to gaze on technological creations; as well as revelling in the gothic qualities of death and decay. Chernobyl as a heterotopia of juxtaposition offers such combinations to tourists and, as such, the dead zone is slowly being brought back to life. In Pripyat, for example, Dobraszczyk (2010) juxtaposes both his trepidation and delight in the arbitrary arrangements of once-ordered things – broken strip lights in a supermarket; the reappearance of utopian objects from the past – socialist icons left in a room; and the excess of meaning generated by inexplicable objects and juxtapositions – rusted hat stands alone in a decaying hall. Consequently, Pripyat is an empty place of both the familiar and the uncanny.

These juxtapositions present Pripyat as an alternative space – indeed, as a post-apocalyptic space – within the proverbial order of modern places. Yet, the town of Pripyat is a space of tragedy and the strange decomposition of the place serves to remind tourists of decay and incommensurable loss. However, as noted earlier, Pripyat's ruin is largely the result of systematic looting, rather than natural decay or the accident, and its meaning "is irrevocably bound up with violent human agency rather than technological failure or the return of nature" (Dobraszczyk 2010: 381). Even so, Pripyat has been dubbed a "modern Pompeii" (Todkill 2001), and its juxtapositions of the real and the familiar with the surreal and the alien allow tourists to consume not only a sense of ruinous beauty and bewilderment, but also a sense of anxiety and incomprehension in a petrified place that mirrors our own world.

Principle #4: heterotopias of chronology

Heterotopian places begin to function fully when individuals find themselves in a sort of absolute break with their traditional time (Foucault 1967). While tourists to Chernobyl are clearly breaking from the routine of ordinary life by the act of visitation, what is more important perhaps is how a Chernobyl tourist experience can offer a sense of both the accumulation and transition of time. Indeed, the fourth principle suggests heterotopias are linked to slices of time, termed by Foucault as 'heterochronism'. In other words, Chernobyl as a heterotopia of chronology is similar to a museum. As such it accumulates time and collects evidence of an age in a perpetual and indefinite manner. Hence, tourists consume not only the disaster of Chernobyl and inherent socio-cultural, political and environmental meanings, but also the era in which the disaster occurred. Metaphorically speaking, time at Chernobyl is stored and accumulated for generations to come, allegorically stopped by the concrete sarcophagus around reactor number four and monumentalized. However, the improvised and precarious nature of the current sarcophagus – symbolically associated with the Kremlin-based sarcophagus of

Vladimir Lenin and Marxism–Leninism ideals – has come to represent a socialist era that failed. Hitherto, Chernobyl is not dead; it is just set in stone.

When the accident occurred in 1986, time was arrested and the mandated zone around the site essentially ceased to function at that moment. Apocalyptic visions of ruined cities within cinematic and literary imaginations over the past century or so have preconditioned us to ruination, fear and decay; yet, blurred distinctions between the real and the surreal within the dead zone are now part of the (dark) tourist experience. Although these distinctions are being conserved and accumulated by the museumification of Chernobyl, Foucault argues for another type of heterochronism. Particularly, while heterotopias of chronology can be linked to accumulation and conservation of time, there are heterotopias that are linked to time in its most futile, most transitory and most precarious state (Foucault 1967). Foucault suggested these heterotopias existed in festive mode and were not eternitary, but chronic. Hence, the ever-recurring and habitual nature of tourism to Chernobyl can reveal it as a heterochronism that is fleeting and transient. Tourists visiting Chernobyl are regulated to spend short periods in the dead zone and consume the landscape in a moment. It is here that heterotopias of chronology come together, both by witnessing the accumulation of time at Chernobyl and by the temporary touristic consumption of the dead zone.

Principle #5: heterotopias of (de)valorization

The fifth principle suggests that heterotopias presuppose a system of opening and closing that both isolates them and makes them penetrable. Termed here as heterotopias of (de)valorization, heterotopian places must have a system of rituals or what Foucault called 'purifications' in order to both valorize (open up) and de-valorize (close down) the space. As Foucault (1967 cited in Dehaene and De Cauter 2008: 21) notes, "one can only enter with a certain permission and after having performed a certain number of gestures". In the case of Chernobyl, the rituals of valorization and gaining (temporary) access to the site are evidenced in the regulatory framework and the payment of fees that now surrounds tourist applications to enter the zone. Moreover, the gestures of medical disclaimers as well as the issuing of health and safety equipment to tourists prior to their Chernobyl experience provide a basis for Foucault's purification rites – a way of valorizing the dead zone as an-Other place. On leaving the zone, tourists are subject to physical checkpoints and further health and safety testing before being allowed to exit. Again, these apparent purification rituals de-valorize the extraordinary place of the dead zone and allow the tourist back into ordinary space.

However, on the contrary, Foucault argued that heterotopias of (de)valorization that look like pure and simple openings and closings generally conceal certain exclusions. He suggested that one "can enter into heterotopian places, but in fact it is only an illusion: one believes to have entered and, by the very fact of entering, one is excluded" (Foucault 1967 cited in Dehaene and De Cauter 2008: 21). It is here that a staged authenticity of Chernobyl is perceived as tourists ritually enter a decaying landscape that is contrived somewhat by human intervention. Indeed, the ghost town of Pripyat has seen thousands of visitors, many of them urban photographers who have (re)arranged ordinary everyday items to create juxtapositions for emblematic effect. For example, in a ruined school in Pripyat, toy dolls left by evacuated children have been posed with baleful looking gasmasks – a graphic image of the threat to youth – an image subsequently consumed by tourists as real yet is staged (Russia Today 2012). Arguably, therefore, despite being allowed valorized access to the place, manufacturing the presentation of artefacts potentially excludes tourists from the authentic reality of the evacuation itself.

Principle #6: heterotopias of illusion and compensation

The final trait of heterotopias is that they create illusions that expose all real spaces and, as result, create a place that is Other. In turn, this can compensate us for the angst of the contemporary world in which we live. In short, heterotopias of illusion and compensation bring binaries between the real and surreal into focus. Indeed, at Chernobyl, the reality of the place is consumed as a surreal tourist attraction. Yet, the question remains, what is the 'attraction'? Ruined landscapes are presented as visions of technical and political folly, and consumed as society's superciliousness for the natural environment as well as a warning of apocalypse to civilization itself. The illusion of course is the authorities' endeavour to try to persuade tourists that the manufactured calamity of Chernobyl has been regulated, limited and thus controlled. Tourists consume this ostensible illusion as they wander through the dead zone, arbitrarily protected by Geiger counters that sing warnings of impending ailments. However, while tourists attempt to capture the horror of Chernobyl, the Otherness of the place begins to elude the senses and a feeling of the sublime can give way to feelings of a pervasive anxiety inherent in contemporary society (Goatcher and Brunsden 2011). Hence, not only does Chernobyl represent a microcosm of an apocalyptic world, the ordinary world outside the dead zone is brought to the fore and exposed for all its political disorder and fragile societal frameworks in which we are all located.

Consequently, the tourist experience in the Other place of Chernobyl can produce a heterotopia of compensation. Indeed, the place of Chernobyl offers a counterbalance space that links us to present-day concerns of the possible ruin of our own environments. Therefore, the Chernobyl tourist experience takes place in a (relatively) safe and socially sanctioned environment in which feelings of helplessness in preventing the accident stimulate an enhanced awareness of the fragility of our modern world. In that context, any notion of helplessness caused by a Chernobyl tourist experience is compensated as a positive and life-enhancing response to the inevitable (Dobraszczyk 2010), and even, according to Sennett (1994), a quality of being that stimulates an enhanced awareness of others. As Dobraszczyk (2010: 387) states, "if the voices of Chernobyl and Pripyat are to speak to us clearly, they must do so through the ruin that bears witness to them... in this sense, ruins become the foundation on which to build the future".

90 *Philip R. Stone*

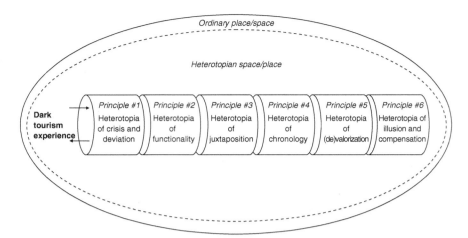

Figure 6.1 A dark tourism cylinder: a conceptual model showing the dark tourism experience within a heterotopian framework

Conclusion

This chapter arises from a simple yet fundamental interest in the psychogeographical attributes of dark tourism. Adopting a Foucaultian perspective of heterotopias, the research offers a contextualized conceptual framework in which to locate dark tourism experiences and their interrelationship with a place of death and disaster. Of course, Foucault's notion of heterotopias, derived from a lecture in 1967, is frustratingly incomplete, inconsistent and even incoherent (Soja 1996). Yet, despite these acknowledged characteristics and limitations, this study has interpreted key principles of Foucault's heterotopias and applied them within the context of dark tourism to Chernobyl, Pripyat and the surrounding dead zone. In so doing, six heterotopian principles have been correlated with the touristification of Chernobyl and, consequently, illustrate how a site of catastrophe can be consumed within the contemporary visitor economy.

Of course, this research has offered only a preliminary and exploratory synthesis between the philosophical notion of heterotopia and dark tourism. Undoubtedly, further theoretical research and empirical interrogation at a variety of dark tourism sites will be required to reveal the extent and support for dark tourism as heterotopias. Even so, as the summative model illustrates (see Figure 6.1), dark tourism places may exist in a conceptual cylinder of heterotopian space, whereby each principle of heterotopia in no particular order, rather than giving a linear experience, combines to provide an encompassing tourist encounter of Other places.

In summary, Chernobyl is now an-Other place. It exists alongside ordinary spaces of the everyday, yet it is a place where disaster has been captured and suspended. It is a place of crisis, of deviation, of serious reflection. It has a functionality that is determined by its touristic consumption and, in turn, is reflective of the society in which we exist. A surreal place to juxtapose our apocalyptic nightmares, Chernobyl is both real and imagined. It is a space for time and of the time, a place that accumulates the failures of a political era and consumed by transient tourists in dark tourism moments. Finally, Chernobyl possesses rituals to valorize its penetrability, to allow temporary access to a so-called dead zone that is both illusionary and compensatory. Chernobyl is a heterotopia that allows us to gaze on a post-apocalyptic world, in which the familiar and uncanny collide. Indeed, tourists now ritually consume the place as a site of environmental disaster, failed technology and political collapse. Yet, Chernobyl and its dead zone is a surreal space that reflects the reality of our contemporary world – a world exposed by dark tourism.

References

Alexievich, S. (1999) *Voices from Chernobyl: Chronicle of the Future*, trans. A. Bouis, London: Aurum Press.
Bennetts, M. (2011) 'A Day Trip to Chernobyl'. Available at http://www.lonelyplanet.com/ukraine/travel-tips-and-articles/76503 (accessed 28 May 2012).
Beres, M. (2008) *Chernobyl Murders*, USA: Medallion Press.
Biran, A. and Poria, Y. (2012) 'Reconceptualising Dark Tourism', in R. Sharpley and P.R. Stone (eds) *Contemporary Tourist Experience: Concepts and Consequences*, Abingdon, Oxon: Routledge, pp. 59–70.
Blackwell, A. (2012) *Visit Sunny Chernobyl: And Other Adventures in the World's Most Polluted Places*, New York: Rodale Books.
Choi, C.Q. (2011) 'The Worst Nuclear Plant Accident in History: Live from Chernobyl'. Available at http://blogs.scientificamerican.com/guest-blog/2011/03/15/the-worst-nuclear-plant-accident-in-history-live-from-chernobyl/ (accessed 29 May 2012).
Coulthart, J. (2006) 'The Stalker Neme'. Available at http://www.johncoulthart.com/feuilleton/2006/12/07/the-stalker-meme/ (accessed 28 May 2012).
Dehaene, M. and De Cauter, L. (2008) 'Heterotopia in a Postcivil Society', in M. Dehaene and L. De Cauter (eds) *Heterotopia and the City: Public Space in a Postcivil Society*, Abingdon, Oxon: Routledge, pp. 3–9.
Dobraszczyk, P. (2010) 'Petrified Ruin: Chernobyl, Pripyat and the Death of the City', *City*, *14*(4): 371–389.
Dyer, G. (2009) 'Danger! High-radiation Arthouse!' Available at http://www.guardian.co.uk/film/2009/feb/06/andrei-tarkovsky-stalker-russia-gulags-chernobyl (accessed 28 May 2012).
Edensor, T. (2005) *Industrial Ruins: Space, Aesthetics and Materiality*, Oxford and New York: Berg.
Fairlie, I., Sumner, D. and Nyagu, A. (2006) *The Other Report on Chernobyl (TORCH)*, Berlin/Brussels/Kiev: The Altner Combecher Foundation & The Hatzeldt-Foundation.
Foucault, M. ([1967] 1984) 'Des espaces autres. Une conférence inédite de Michel Foucault', *Architecture, Mouvement, Continuité*, 5 (October): 46–49.
Foucault, M. ([1967] 2008) 'Of Other Spaces', trans. L. De Cauter and M. Dehaene, in M. Dehaene and L. De Cauter (eds) *Heterotopia and the City: Public Space in a Postcivil Society*, Abingdon, Oxon: Routledge, pp. 13–29.

Goatcher, J. and Brunsden, V. (2011) 'Chernobyl and the Sublime Tourist', *Tourist Studies*, *11*(2): 115–137.

Greenpeace (2006) 'The Chernobyl Catastrophe: Consequences on Human Health'. Available at http://www.greenpeace.org/international/en/publications/reports/chernobylhealthreport/ (accessed 19 May 2012).

Hetherington, K. (1997) *Badlands of Modernity: Heterotopia and Social Ordering*, London: Routledge.

Heynen, H. (2008) 'Heterotopia Unfolded?' in M. Dehaene and L. De Cauter (eds) *Heterotopia and the City: Public Space in a Postcivil Society*, Abingdon, Oxon: Routledge, pp. 311–323.

IAEA (2012) 'In Focus: Chernobyl'. Available at http://www.iaea.org/newscenter/focus/chernobyl/ (accessed 19 May 2012).

Lehren, A.A. (2012) 'Walking the Streets of a Nuclear Ghost Town'. Available at http://travel.nytimes.com/2012/05/27/travel/near-chernobyl-touring-a-disaster.html (accessed 28 May 2012).

Lyons, R. (2011) 'Chernobyl: When Truth Went into Meltdown'. Available at http://www.theaustralian.com.au/news/features/chernobyl-when-truth-went-into-meltdown/story-e6frg6z6-1226027914874 (accessed 29 May 2012).

McKernan, J. and Mulcahy, K.V. (2008) 'Hurricane Katrina: A Cultural Chernobyl', *The Journal of Arts Management, Law and Society*, *38*(3): 217–232.

Medvedev, Z. (2011) *The Legacy of Chernobyl*, 2nd edn, Nottingham: Spokemans Books.

Parker, B. (2012) *Chernobyl Diaries*, USA: Warner Bros.

Petryna, A. (2002) *Life Exposed: Biological Citizens after Chernobyl*, Princeton, NJ: Princeton University Press.

Phillips, S.D. (2004) 'Chernobyl's Sixth Sense: The Symbolism of an Ever-present Awareness', *Anthropology and Humanism*, *29*(2): 159–185.

Rojek, C. (1999) 'Deviant Leisure: The Dark Side of Free-time Activity', in E.L. Jackson and T.L. Burton (eds) *Leisure Studies: Prospects for the Twenty-first Century*, State College, PA: Venture, pp. 81–96.

Russia Today (2012) 'Chernobyl Exclusion Zone Reopens for Extreme Tourism'. Available at http://www.rt.com/news/prime-time/chernobyl-exclusion-zone-tourism-219/ (accessed 29 May 2012).

Sennett, R. (1994) *Flesh and Stone: The Body and the City in Western Civilization*, London and Boston: Faber.

Sharpley, R. and Stone, P.R. (eds) (2009) *The Darker Side of Travel: The Theory and Practice of Dark Tourism*, Bristol: Channel View Publications.

Soja, E. (1996) *Thirdspace: Journeys to Los Angeles and Other Real-and-Imagined Places*, Oxford: Blackwell.

Stebbins, R.A. (1996) *Tolerable Differences: Living with Deviance*, 2nd edn, Toronto: McGraw-Hill Ryerson.

Stebbins, R.A. (2007) *Serious Leisure: A Perspective for Our Time*, New Brunswick, NJ: Transaction.

Stone, P.R. (2011) 'Dark Tourism: Towards a New Post-disciplinary Research Agenda', *International Journal of Tourism Anthropology*, *1*(3/4), 318–332.

Stone, P.R. (2012a) 'Dark and Significant Other Death: Towards a Model of Mortality Mediation', *Annals of Tourism Research*, *39*(3): 1565–1587.

Stone, P.R. (2012b) 'Dark Tourism as "Mortality Capital": The Case of Ground Zero and the Significant Other Dead', in R. Sharpley and P.R. Stone (eds) *The Contemporary Tourist Experience: Concepts and Consequences*, Abingdon, Oxon: Routledge, pp. 30–45.

Stone, P.R. and Sharpley, R. (forthcoming) 'Consuming "Dark Leisure": Sex, Death and Ontological Meanings of the Taboo', in S. Elkington and S. Gammon (eds) *Contemporary Perspectives in Leisure: Meanings, Motives and Lifelong Learning*, Abingdon, Oxon: Routledge.

Todkill, A. (2001) 'Overexposure: The Chernobyl Photographs of David McMillian', *Canadian Medical Association Journal*, *164*(11): 1604–1605.

Topinka, R.J. (2010) 'Foucault, Borges, Heterotopia: Producing Knowledge in other Spaces', *Foucault Studies*, *9*: 54–70.

Williams, D.J. (2009) 'Deviant Leisure: Rethinking "the Good, the Bad, and the Ugly"', *Leisure Sciences: An Interdisciplinary Journal*, *31*(2): 207–213.

World Nuclear Association (2012) 'Chernobyl Accident 1986'. Available at http://www.world-nuclear.org/info/chernobyl/inf07.html (accessed 19 May 2012).

Part II
Destination management

7 Pagan tourism and the management of ancient sites in Cornwall

Chantal Laws

Introduction

This chapter seeks to locate pagan engagement with sacred sites and ancient places within the context of dark tourism, with a particular regard for the process of meaning-making and place identity formation that is generated, and to consider the implications for site management in light of the increasingly inclusive policy strategies that characterize a modern heritage industry.

This engagement, which might be broadly termed pagan tourism, has received relatively little attention to date, and much of the research is located within the religious/spiritual tourism literature. While spiritually motivated travel has become an increasingly popular focus for study it is the nature of religious tourism in its more traditional forms (such as visits to cathedrals or temples as a form of modern 'pilgrimage') which are most clearly modelled, for example, through the work of Shackley (2001) and Timothy and Olsen (2006), with the requirements of more liminal groups such as pagan visitors, or as they might prefer to be identified, users (given the serious and intent nature of their visitor behaviour), remaining largely untreated to date.

Pagan interactions with heritage sites often receive sensationalist coverage from the British media, for example during the midwinter and midsummer solstice celebrations at Stonehenge, where images of Druids, New Age travellers, archaeologists and police battling over access have become iconic images of the continued clash between mainstream and alternative lifestyle choices in contemporary Britain. Prominent ancient sites such as Stonehenge (as discussed by Hetherington 2000), Avebury (see Harvey 2008 for a critique of the heritage identity of this site) and Glastonbury (Digance and Cusack 2002) function as identity lodestones for a very diverse range of groups that may be loosely defined as pagan or New Age, yet represent a fluid set of subcultural identities with equally divergent attitudes to heritage. There is no overarching definition to encompass the full diversity of pagan beliefs and practice but the Pagan Federation (2011) propose that paganism is the ancestral religion of the whole of humanity. Blain and Wallis (2001) in an extensive study of contemporary alternative spirituality and heritage engagement have defined these groups as 'the tribes of Paganism' and suggest that *paganisms* may be a more appropriate term to encompass the array of tribal identities that are identifiable amongst pagan users of heritage sites in the United Kingdom.

Contemporary visits to sites of sacred interest have recently been defined as being on the dark tourism (Sharpley 2009) or thanatourism (Seaton 2010) spectrum, and with the generation of an increasing volume of critical appraisal of the dark tourism phenomenon, an opportunity is afforded to consider pagan notions of place identity within this alternative analytical framework. However, the association of paganisms with an understanding of dark tourism is by no means yet established. Seaton (2010) has outlined that academic research into motivations for thanatourism as a consumer experience remains an area where data is sparse; certainly this is the case for pagan tourism, although previous studies (for example, Attix 2002; Bowman 1994, 2002; Hale 2006; Laws 2007) have identified that these tourists are affluent, allocentric, well-educated and highly individualized travellers, who may 'fly under the radar' of the service machinery of mass tourism and therefore operate at the fringes of official tourism and heritage management interactions.

For the author it is this notion of otherness associated with New Age and pagan ideologies and behaviours that is evocative of dark tourism's preoccupation with the seemingly macabre, as there is an inherent implication of a gaze upon the other in any such identification. Spiritual tourism exhibits 'darkness', in that it draws on occult or esoteric practices in the truest meaning of the word, such practices being perceived as hidden or obscured when considered from a mainstream perspective (Hunt 2003). Dark tourism also shares a degree of syncretism and *bricolage* with alternative belief systems, and both may indeed be expressions of postmodern attitudes to identity construction in their (re)imagining of past and place (Hale and Payton 2000; Hunt 2003). That occultism has become synonymous in current parlance with the macabre or grotesque is in itself noteworthy, indicating perhaps that the coterminous relationship of gazing on otherness inherent in touristic consumption expresses something about the disjunct in contemporary society between the secular and the sacred.

This chapter focuses on the ancient pre-Christian heritage of the West Penwith area of Cornwall, which is designated as an Area of Outstanding Natural Beauty (Cornwall AONB Partnership 2011a; 2011b) and recognized by ICOMOS for an exceptionally rich historic landscape, having, at several thousand registered sites, the highest density of ancient monuments in western Europe. Yet West Penwith is a working industrial and agricultural landscape, which also supports a thriving domestic tourism market and pressures on the traditional preservation ethos in the management of local heritage sites are therefore inevitable and increasing. To illustrate the form that more inclusive site management approaches can take this chapter concludes by considering interventions by the Cornish Ancient Sites Protection Network (CASPN), which was established in 1997 in response to the potential impact of a hallmark dark tourism event, namely the northern hemisphere's solar eclipse of August 1999, with Cornwall being the only area of British landfall to experience totality.

Dark tourism perspectives on place identity

Dark tourism is a relatively recent introduction to the tourism lexicon, having been first outlined and defined by Lennon and Foley in 1996. These authors emphasize that chronological nearness to recent death is a defining factor, and that mediated consumption of such death or disaster placed the phenomenon firmly in the latter portion of the twentieth century. Dark tourism is thus an intimation exclusively of late and postmodernity, which omits the large proportion of 'dark' heritage sites that pre-date the twentieth century.

While Lennon and Foley (2000: 12) acknowledge that such places are host sites for tourism consumption and have been subject to mediation through films, novels and television, they state that events associated with them "did not take place within the memories of those still alive to validate them" and that "the events of ancient and medieval battles, etc., do not posit questions, or introduce anxiety and doubt about, modernity and its consequences". It is this particular aspect of the commodification of anxiety and doubt through the processes of design and interpretation of sites and associated products or experiences that for these authors exemplifies dark tourism. The historic antecedents of early tourist journeys, such as pilgrimage, as a form of proto-dark tourism are acknowledged but the chronological distance from the past, and lack of direct personal recall at ancient sites forms a disjunct that is, in their opinion, insurmountable. This conception of the distant past as a closed resource is in direct contrast to the work of Seaton (1996), which, in focusing more on the expression of *thanatopsis* in touristic activity, allows for immediate connections in recognition of the universality inherent in the human experience, including death.

Authors such as Stone (2006; 2011) and Wight (2006) provide detailed accounts of both the development of dark tourism studies since Lennon and Foley's work, and the key debates and issues that continue to surround the terminology. At one level, the development of the increasingly nuanced typologies of tourism can be argued as part of a self-serving trend within academic circles. Sharpley and Stone (2009: 6) acknowledge that the "increasingly diluted and fuzzy" meaning of the term may be symptomatic of such research-led preoccupations. However, as outlined by Novelli (2005) the increasing specialization of tourism industry services reflects the growing agency of the consumer in shaping their own travel experience and Sharpley and Stone recognize, along with Seaton (2010), that the notable lack of research into demand-side perspectives has hampered the growth of the field.

In a more recent piece, Stone (2011) calls for a post-disciplinary approach to the further development of dark tourism studies. Here, in adopting the framework proposed by Coles *et al.* (2006: 6) he recognizes that the study of dark tourism necessitates engagement with insights from other academic fields in order to fully comprehend and map the fundamental interrelationships that dark tourism has to the "broader cultural condition of society" (p. 6), principally in the areas of secularization, spirituality and memorialization, and it is in these aspects that we find the potential nexus with pagan perspectives.

Connecting spiritual and dark tourism

Spiritual or religious tourism is further established as a discrete field of study and has a more substantial body of literature. In defining the term, Timothy and Olsen (2006) offer a broad explanation, acknowledging that even that most established form of religious tourism, the pilgrimage, is the product of a multiplicity of motivations, attitudes and behavioural mindsets. Modern pilgrimage is further conceived as a journey undertaken in quest of a place or state believed to embody a valued ideal, whereas religious tourism requires visitation to physical sites that are sacrosanct and ritually separated from the profane space of everyday life. Shackley (2001) further defines visits to sacred sites as the seeking of authentic experience through sense of place and/or a sacred atmosphere.

Spiritually motivated visits to heritage sites are perceived as fluid and often allocentric activity, contingent on a range of factors in the personal and professional realms that make concrete identification of such practices hard to quantify, a characteristic also shared by the dark tourist.

New Age and pagan tourism

According to Digance (2006: 38), "New Age followers emphasize transformation of the self... with an emphasis on the experiential": such self-reflexivity is often partnered by more externalized attributes which, as identified by Timothy and Conover (2006), are the belief in the sanctity of nature, harmony of the cosmos and the resurrection of ancient spiritual traditions. New Age tourism is also extremely place-specific and such tourists have been identified as avid and affluent travellers (Attix 2002), tying in with Bowman's (1994) identification that the prosperity wing of New Ageism is as significant for the development of a pagan tourism industry as the more prevalent tribe of counter-culture travellers that are foregrounded in popular culture representations (Hetherington 1992, 1998, 2000).

Neo-paganism is often considered as a sub-set of the New Age movement, although as Pearson (2002) acknowledges the connection remains contested: while contemporary pagan practice does indeed share common ground (particularly in the United States), the traditions of those following a European/Celtic path are more locally oriented and circumscribed by particular identity characteristics (York 2002). Timothy and Conover (2006) state that neo-paganism can generally be understood as a set of modern beliefs informed and inspired by ancient (pre-Christian) religious practices whose core tenets are respect for nature and homage to ancient traditions, informed by principles of animism and the existence of an ancestral heritage.

Most notable for understanding pagan attitudes to heritage sites is this relationship with an ancestral past, where prehistoric monuments are conceived as "living places imbued with sacred energy and not as relics from a completed past" (English 2002: 9). This is at odds with the established conventions of heritage management, where the past is deterministically viewed as a closed product that necessitates professional intervention to be made meaningful in the present.

This dichotomy also informs neo-pagan tourist consumption, and influences both forms of travel to, and behaviour at, the destination. Here, the notion of the tourist gaze (Urry 1990) is challenged by MacCannell's identification of a second gaze, which is "structured by the understanding, conscious or not, that visibility presupposes invisibility, that in every seeing there is an unseen" (2001: 23). For the pagan tourist there is an acknowledgement that the site, or sight, of their gaze is only one layer in a complex palimpsest of the material and intangible. Spiritual tourism therefore combines elements of "identity, intangibility, memory and remembering, performance, place and dissonance" (Smith 2006: 300) in the consumption of sacred heritage spaces, and it is the influence of the tourist gaze upon heritage conservation and interpretation strategies that forms the next focus for discussion.

Heritage site management, paganisms and dark place identity

The concept of heritage is described by Tunbridge and Ashworth as "a contemporary product shaped from history" (1996: 20), which is a selective retelling of the past. This product-led approach necessitates the use of segmentation techniques to package sites to suit particular audiences, and the success of heritage planners in this regard largely depends on their empathy for the needs of particular consumer groups. However, the range of paganisms with which users may be engaged makes any such segmentation exercise increasingly complex, particularly where anxiety over the seemingly macabre nature of site use is present.

Wallis and Blain (2001) have documented the many challenges that unfamiliarity, anxiety and hostility present (see, for example, 2001, 2006, 2008; and with Letcher 2009) and their research could certainly be argued to demonstrate a classic case of dissonance, where one form of discourse is marginalized in favour of a more acceptable politico-cultural narrative of the past. However, Tunbridge and Ashworth (1996) identify that the very process of creating partisan and polarized identities of inclusion/exclusion demonstrates naivety and point instead to the fluid nature of heritage discourse and its contingent relationship to prevailing societal trends. Harvey (2008: 32) further observes that heritage today "appears to be far less strident" and "led by the losers in society" indicating a contingent kind of place identity.

Dark tourist places

Dark tourism and New Age spirituality act as signifiers of the breakdown of mass society and the rise of highly individualized discourses of identity (Maffesoli 1996). Seaton (2010) acknowledges that control of such discourses is a critical issue given that "travel undertaken to maintain or construct individual identity, however temporarily through remembrance of people and things past, real or imagined, at locations associated with or dedicated to them" (2010: 535) is a defining characteristic of the thanatouristic experience. Wight (2006) expands on this point by critiquing the power of tourism production to create constructed narratives of past events, which can manipulate visitors into particular configurations of politics and power.

Clearly, place in the sense of being "a socially constructed site or location in space marked by identification or emotional investment" (Barker 2003: 40) is important in the construction of such narratives, yet dark tourism shows us that these are not necessarily fixed and that locations and the meanings attached to them are mutable and polysemic. Furthermore, sites can be placed along a spectrum of attractions (Sharpley and Stone 2009) and interestingly for this discussion the notion of authenticity is key in identifying 'shades' of dark tourism at sites and attractions, a preoccupation shared with heritage management and cultural tourism, where authenticity has particular resonance for interpretation strategies at locations that are numinous (Paine 2000), auratic (Seaton 2009) or dissonant (Tunbridge and Ashworth 1996) in character.

Lennon and Foley (2000) conceive of dark tourism sites as venues for staging anxieties and doubts, while Tarlow (2005) and Sharpley and Stone (2009) recognize sites as places of nostalgia that play host to the search for novelty that may typify the experience of postmodernity. There is some debate about the purposefulness of such staging, with Lennon and Foley stating that visitors who approach sites as 'specialists' lack the serendipitous nature of the mass tourist chancing upon a site as part of an organized itinerary or happenstance proximity. This position does not sit easily with the stance adopted by later authors, for example Wight (2006), who emphasize instead the highly individualized and fragmented nature of postmodern touristic experience when engaging with sites. Rojek (1993) expands further on this by identifying dark tourism as a place-bound spectacle: to continue with this analogy, spectacles require actors and theories of performativity in tourism, and (Crouch 2009) tell us that the agency of participants in shaping their own experiences are full of intent, whether consciously expressed through deliberate intercession or not.

In this manner, 'specialists' can become bona fide dark tourism consumers, as much as the chance visitor, particularly as they may engage with a range of otherwise discrete identity discourses (Pearson 2002). Those users who adopt a specialist role provide a bridge between the standard production/consumption dichotomy that informs much site management practice as well as the wider tourism industry; privileging certain forms of authority and expertise while disenfranchizing others. This further supports Tunbridge and Ashworth's (1996) argument that dissonance is subjective rather than fixed, and also resonates with Lowenthal's (1985) classic appraisal of whether the past is indeed ever a closed resource.

Lennon and Foley's (2000) position on the character of visitors appears at odds with their equally emphatic statement on the nature of dark tourism itself, namely the individual mediated nature of consumption. Their thesis appears grounded in the conventional structures of a 'Fordist' tourism industry, which Novelli (2005) argues is a veneer placed upon a highly complex and diverse agglomeration of services that is itself experiencing the fragmentation of increased specialization.

Novelli configures this fragmentation into a series of niches: religious tourism forms a sub-set of the cultural tourism micro-niche, situated more in the mainstream and established industry of mass tourism, whereas dark tourism is 'other' (2005: 9). Any discussion of the contemporary nature of emerging and niche forms of tourism is by necessity an arbitrary snap-shot at a given point, yet Novelli's approach does appear to echo some of the challenges of understanding the relationship between a modern dark tourism phenomenon and the management approaches of heritage site professionals at places of ancient significance, in that cultural tourism and heritage studies have already acceded to the status of an established discipline whereas dark tourism awaits further definition.

'Dark' spirituality?

Such imbalance masks the shared history of both niches in the counter-culture movements of the 1960s, which in turn drew on cultural references from earlier times. Bowman (1994: 143) perceives a continuum of interest in making an ancient past present in modern society through place-making and identity construction, recognizing "recurring periods of fascination... simply marked by peaks and troughs" that encompass the work of seventeenth- and eighteenth-century antiquarians and nineteenth-century romantics, which in turn supported what Seaton (2010) terms a 'thanatoptic tourism tradition'. Hunt (2003) further identifies the importance of pre-modern memes such as 'the noble savage' in the development of contemporary alternative religions, with Bowman (1995; 2002) recognizing that for many adherents of Celtic spirituality, identity is constructed in reference to a European aboriginal tribe existing in some form of Golden Age, which contrasts starkly with the perceived inadequacies of contemporary social order.

Here again, otherness is emphasized by association with peripheral places and the distant past: in considering the relationship between New Age advocates and a contemporary service industry constructed around their elective affinity, Bowman (1994: 147) recognizes that such religion "may in many respects be described as the commodification of the arcane and the obscure". The process of seeking to make the past present correlates with Tarlow's (2005) identification of dark tourism as a form of reflexive or restorative nostalgia, and Sharpley and Stone's (2009) suggestion that shared consumption such as mourning at iconic dark tourism sites forges a sense of *communitas* in the present: in this way the act of dark tourism also embodies a life-affirming quality for those engaged in the process of meaning-making.

Ancient sites may be particularly suited as canvases for meaning-making and (re)interpretation for contemporary audiences: as Jacquetta Hawkes famously stated, "Every age has the Stonehenge it deserves – or desires" (1967: 174). Letcher *et al.* (2009) in discussing the mediated images of pre-history in contemporary society identify the inherently unknowable qualities of the very distant past as ideal for polysemic interpretations, yet also acknowledge that many prehistoric sites have perhaps become trapped in their own clichéd status as iconic objects of national identity. Much of the preservation ethos surrounding sites of national significance, particularly those which have been given further specialized status through inscription on the World Heritage Site list, is concerned with maintaining sites as closed texts and past relics. As Letcher *et al.* identify, this approach constitutes change as degradation and as such "contemporary activities must necessarily be regarded as potentially threatening" (2009: 171). In this way, the ritual activity demanded by current pagan user groups as part of their site engagement cannot be considered 'real' as it falls outside of a boundary of closure that is decided upon by heritage professionals as the ultimate arbiters of meaning.

However, away from these iconic sites where meanings have become concrete and dissonance is evident, there appear to be opportunities for alternative approaches to site management based on the concept of *ritual landscape*: a term that gained popularity among archaeologists in the 1980s as part of the post-processual movement and has since been adopted by other interest groups, notably those counter-culture 'tribes' for whom the phrase resonates with their own vision of a living sacred site.

This approach has been highly influential for alternative place narratives constructed around the ancient Celtic sites of Cornwall, and we will now turn to consider how pagan identities have informed approaches to site management there, and wider influences on the tourism industry that is vital to the Cornish economy.

Case study: Cornwall as a dark tourist destination

Research conducted by the Cornwall Tourist Board (CTB) in 2000 and 2005 identified that the county's tourism industry is predominantly comprised of small and micro enterprises that together generate approximately 30 per cent of the region's gross domestic product, employing 25 per cent of the workforce, and attracting over 4 million visitors yearly with an expenditure of over €1.7 billion in 2003.

Tourism is a key income generator following the decline of the traditional industrial base, ranging from traditional family-based 'bucket and spade' holidaying to high-profile visitor attractions such as the Tate St Ives or the Eden Project, which exemplify the instrumental approach of tourism-led regeneration. Diversification of tourism product has shifted seasonality from the established high/no season model of summer family vacations to a year-round cultural tourism, which may provide a more sustainable model for future development (CTB 2005). In 2006 large sections of the county were inscribed onto the World Heritage Site list as the Cornwall and West Devon Mining Landscape (UNESCO 2011).

Research by South West Tourism (SWT) gathered in 2005 identifies that Cornwall is a unique and distinct destination brand clearly understood by its customers, and offers a range of touristic experiences or 'brand clusters' within a small geographical area. SWT locate the mythical aspects as part of Cornwall's 'unique historical legacy' (2005: 8).

Locating Cornwall's spiritual tourism

Cornwall's resources for spiritual tourism are diverse and cover a long time-span, from the prehistoric monuments of West Penwith to the sites of early Celtic Christianity and later Methodist heritage. Furthermore, there is an increasingly visible and active New Age community in Cornwall, focused principally on West Penwith and the area surrounding Tintagel/Boscastle, but increasingly spread throughout the county comprising a range of individuals and groups acting "as guardians of sites, educators of site-users and volunteers to restore sites" (Blain and Wallis 2006: 213). They actively contribute to the local tourist economy as "a whole New Age spiritual service industry" (Bowman 1994: 143), as artists and craftspeople, authors, tour guides, accommodation providers, shop owners as well as heritage and tourism advisors. What attracts many to the county if not born there is something that Phillips (2006: 3 citing Dimbleby 2005) identifies as the unique characteristic of this most western point of the UK:

> What you find as you go west is a different kind of Britishness; you find the Celtic view of the world, driven west by successive invasions but which has survived and in some ways is reviving: the idea of life not as something that is absolutely rational and ordered but something where you have to listen carefully to inner voices and spirits and the strangeness of things.

Hale notes that there are a whole range of services that array themselves as part of the county's distinct Celtic identity. Despite "Celticity being asserted more vigorously than at any time in the past" (2006: 274), the multiplicity of meanings surrounding a Celtic heritage remains ambiguous and Hale perceives the association of Celtic identity with primitive or superstitious behaviours as problematic for the county's tourism. Spiritual 'Celtic pilgrims' may still be viewed with disfavour through association with subcultural groups that have a reputation for damage and destruction, again reflecting anxiety over otherness despite the benefits they may in fact bring to the tourism economy.

The solar eclipse of August 1999 raised both opportunities and challenges for spiritual tourism in Cornwall and is identified by Hale (2006: 279) as "the single biggest disaster in the marketing of Cornwall" of recent years. Hale apportions blame squarely with the county council who treated the hallmark event as a potential crisis and reacted negatively to the predicted influx of tourists, anxious about the "proliferation of hippies and weirdos" it would attract. Again, anxiety over marginal groups looms large in the official strategy, but concerns for the impact of the solar eclipse on sites associated with indigenous spirituality were, in this case, shared by local pagan groups, and their response is also significant as it led in part to the formation of CASPN, the focus of the case study here.

Cornwall's spiritual heritage landscape

As outlined previously, Cornwall has a rich heritage resource for ancient pre-Christian and 'Celtic' consumption. Robb (1998) explores the area of West Penwith, Cornwall as a ritual landscape construct within the context of heritage tourism, identifying that in contrast to archaeological attractions which are marketed principally in isolation and large enough to contain the monument which is conserved within a contemporary context, the Penwith landscape is densely populated with upstanding monuments from the Neolithic and Bronze Age. This, coupled with the continuation of ancient stone boundaries and relatively low density of human habitation, creates a strong sense of separation from the modern world, making Penwith's heritage sites uniquely placed to offer connection with an imagined past that re-enchants the viewer (Letcher *et al.* 2009).

Robb (1998) identifies that West Penwith was largely ignored by archaeologists until the late twentieth century, and thus much of the available interpretation of sites such as Mên an Tol (see Figure 7.1) originates from the local community, often with an emphasis on pagan and earth mysteries perspectives on landscape interpretation. Earth mysteries is a tradition which, as described by Hetherington (1998: 336), "challenges the modes of understanding offered by modern science and seeks to find in the landscape forgotten practices of knowing and understanding both natural and social", again demonstrating the broad interests that can be associated with paganisms.

The mystical landscape quality at Mên an Tol as described by Robb (1998) is illustrated below. The name simply means 'holed stone', and this type of monument is very rare in the county. Constructed in the Bronze Age, the site's original purpose remains unknown: the stones may have been rearranged, which has done much to confuse the archaeological stratigraphy; yet, if the current arrangement is correct, then the holed stone at the centre of the monument may have been used as a lens to observe important astrological events or ritual landmarks (CHES 2007).

Figure 7.1 Mên an Tol monument, West Penwith

The stones have a strong tradition as a place to cure various ailments and avert ill-fate, and have an established local heritage narrative, which more recently has included contemporary ritual use. That this has led to contention is demonstrated by the damage done to the stones by an alternative protest group in 1999 using an accelerant identified as napalm (Wallis 2003). This incident also contributed to the groundswell of frustration with misrepresentation by extreme users that led ultimately to the formation of CASPN; a silhouette of the stones is now clearly identifiable as their logo and features prominently on site signage installed at ancient sites across the county.

West Penwith has since acceded to more official status as an AONB and become integrated into a wider environmental, tourism and heritage planning framework, yet, as an area in recent transition, the potential for alternative place interpretation within the conceptual framework of dark tourism remains.

Contrast between mainstream and alternative users at sacred sites in Penwith is further illustrated by the holy well at Madron, near Penzance (see Figure 7.2), which comprises a natural spring and twelfth-century bapistry known also as Boswarthen chapel. Many visitors revere the site as having spiritual significance, and both pagan and Christian groups are regular users (CASPN n.d.) in addition to those

Figure 7.2 A 'Cloutie' tree at Madron Holy Well, marking the way to the original well head and showing the difficult access

who visit on an annual pilgrimage, or happen on the site through local signage as the more conventional casual dark tourist. Many leave an offering by tying clouties or cloths (a practice with a long history of tradition in British folklore) to trees near the source of the spring. This practice has in the past been criticized as heathen, untidy and offensive; branches with clouties attached were reported to have been removed in 1996 (Petherick 1999), again sparking frustration from alternative users regarding the lack of empathy to their needs. The practice of marking a visit at the trees around the spring as the 'true' site rather than at the chapel, which is the more tangible landmark, demonstrates how narratives of place can be subverted by alternate interactions. The Cornwall Heritage Environment Service (CHES) reported on a recent conservation project (Preston-Jones and Mossop 2007), which demonstrates increased sensitivity to the activity around the spring, although the improvements were still criticized by some as intrusive to the site's character. CASPN also provides low-key interpretive guidance at Madron, both on site and virtually through their website (CASPN n.d.), which supports a respectful, minimal trace approach.

The Cornish Ancient Sites Protection Network

CASPN describes itself as "a local partnership organization that protects and conserves the ancient sites and monuments of Cornwall, so that people of all ages and abilities can enjoy and appreciate them forever" (CASPN n.d.). The network includes representatives from a wide range of organizations and community groups that share an interest in Cornwall's ancient sites, including the National Trust, CHES, Cornwall Archaeological Society, English Heritage, English Nature, Cornwall Wildlife Trust, Cornwall Heritage Trust, Penwith District Council (Sustainable Tourism and Community Regeneration), Penwith Access and Rights of Way, Penlee Gallery and Museum, Madron Community Forum, Zennor Parish Council, Cornish Earth Mysteries Group, Pagan Federation, Pagan Moot, Meyn Mamvro and the Order of Bards, Ovates and Druids.

The partnership seeks to "bring people together to care for the sites with a shared sense of place and identity" and has three specific aims: to facilitate and promote research and educational activities; promote a feeling of involvement and ownership within the wider community; and improve public access, both intellectual and physical. In part this is achieved through practical approaches that involve site management and preservation such as vegetation clearance, path maintenance and rubbish removal, as well as interpretive strategies and signage (see Figure 7.3) in addition to higher-level stakeholder management such as community engagement, building relationships with landowners and official bodies as well as the development of a sustainable heritage-tourism led strategy for year-round visitor and site management. The partnership has received funding from the National Lottery Awards for All scheme, from the local community development trust and the AONB, but is currently run primarily on a voluntary basis. The organization achieved registered Trust status in 2000 and is currently applying to become a charity (Straffon 2012 [pers. comm.]).

Figure 7.3 CASPN signage at Madron Holy Well

Established in 1997 as a response to a number of issues, which included the impending solar eclipse and vandalism at sites such as Mên an Tol, the primary concern was to protect the fragile heritage of key sites and to coordinate the somewhat disparate activities of heritage custodians. CASPN's approach differed greatly from the oft-criticized strategy of official heritage preservation by bringing together a diverse committee of representatives across the range of mainstream and alternative user groups: while this strategy is now commonplace as part of community-oriented heritage and archaeology planning in the UK, at the time it was somewhat revolutionary given the prevailing lack of common ground at ancient sites that Blain and Wallis have identified.

The chair of CASPN, Cheryl Straffon, has reflected on the development of Cornish spiritual tourism (Laws 2007), recognizing a range of site engagements from casual visitors to regular pagan users with the supply of organized spiritual tourism the biggest potential threat. Tour operators are beginning to demand better infrastructure and improved facilities at sites that were not designed for high volume visitors and calling on local pagans to act as guides for niche groups mainly from the US and Germany (interestingly, places where New Age and neo-pagan identities are particularly strong). Clearly, this requires a balance of conflicting priorities but direct involvement was framed as an effective and proactive method to ensure that appropriate management and considerate use was actively promoted.

Most significant was the awareness of changing opinions among the officio-academic community:

> today archaeologists are beginning to look not just at the content of the site, but the possible uses of the sites, that relationship to the landscape as a 'spiritual being' and that has been a huge shift... I do dread the day though that we might get specific spiritual themes set up because one of the joys of all this is that currently it is open and organic.
>
> (Straffon 2007 [pers. comm.])

CASPN is a bridging organization, incorporating voices from the mainstream of the heritage industry as well as the fringe, acknowledging that none has precedence and that discourse with regard to heritage is about finding consensus on the small scale as well as in the grand place narrative.

Conclusion

The intention here was to frame the interaction of pagan users at ancient historic sites within the conceptual framework of dark tourism, to explore whether the identification of spiritually motivated travel on the spectrum of dark tourism could offer a fresh perspective on a complex area where notions of identity and place were still subject to debate despite the availability of relevant research from disciplines and areas within disciplines such as archaeology, heritage management, heritage tourism, Celtic studies, cultural studies and consumer behaviour.

The fragmented nature of the literature belies a number of shared themes, and it emerges that while each niche strives for distinction as a valid academic field (Robb's identification in 1998 of heritage tourism as a non-academic subject being a case in point!), there is significant commonality to be found. Principally the foci are the inter-connectedness of place and self; the competing trends for group versus individual identity; and the search for ontological security in the face of an increasingly fragmented, hyper-real and mediated world, with the notion of authenticity and its strong linkage to place permeating much of the discussion.

It can be argued that dark and spiritual tourism are linked by their preoccupation with evoking 'otherness' in the present context, be this explicitly linked to a reflection on death or to activities that, operating outside of the mainstream, play with seemingly macabre memes. Mediation, interpretation and (re)imagining are key, and the discursive play between opposing or discrete ideologies necessary for the fluidity of place meaning-making that dark tourism engenders. Much like the landscape of heritage sites themselves, which accrete multiple meanings over time, conceptual tourism frameworks exist as palimpsests: as areas such as West Penwith proceed from the fringes of academic scrutiny towards mainstream status as privileged landscapes within the heritage tourism industry, so perhaps their openness to multivalent shades of darkness declines.

Ultimately, state of being emerges as the key concern: Hetherington (1992) notes that concerns over the rise of counter-cultures within the mainstream of late modernity reflect ontological insecurity, while Blain and Wallis (with Letcher 2009) in their framing of prehistoric sites as locations for re-enchantment, suggest that pagan engagement with heritage sites involves proactive questioning of the ontological status quo, and Stone (2011) also puts forward a strong argument that dark tourism challenges the status of being in making absent death present in the everyday. Spiritual and dark tourist consumption can thus be conceived as transgressive, and in breaking with the boundaries of conventions of time, space and place, also transformative.

As Smith (2006: 308) summarizes the challenge: "It is... understanding the use that places and processes of heritage are put to in the present, the way the present constructs it, the role that heritage plays and the consequences it has", that is vital. It is the composite understanding that can be achieved through a post-disciplinary approach that is the real strength for research into sites of dark tourism in this regard. Organizations such as CASPN also display these post-disciplinary characteristics, and while their aims are by no means fully achieved, the journey from fear of otherness and the seemingly macabre to effective dialogue and action bodes well for collaborative heritage site management approaches despite the growth of dark tourism from niche to populist status.

References

Attix, S.A. (2002) 'New Age-oriented Special Interest Travel: An Exploratory Study', *Tourism Recreation Research*, 27(2): 51–58.

Barker, C. (2003) *Cultural Studies: Theory and Practice*, 3rd edn, London: Sage.

Blain, J. and Wallis, R.J. (2006) 'Pasts and Pagan Practices: Moving Beyond Stonehenge', *Public Archaeology*, 5. Available at Sheffield Hallam University Research Archive (SHURA): http://shura.shu.ac.uk/61/ (accessed 7 November 2011).

Blain, J. and Wallis, R.J. (2008) 'Sacred, Secular, or Sacrilegious? Prehistoric Sites, Pagans and the Sacred Sites Project in Britain', in J. Schachter and S. Brockman (eds) *(Im)permanence: Cultures In/Out of Time*, Pittsburg: Penn State University Press, pp. 212–223.

Bowman, M. (1994) 'The Commodification of the Celt: New Age/Neo-pagan Consumerism', in T.Brewer (ed.) *The Marketing of Tradition: Perspectives on Folklore, Tourism and the Heritage Industry, Folklore in Use: Applications in the Real World (2)*, Enfield Lock, Middlesex: Hislarik Press.

Bowman, M. (1995) 'The Noble Savage and the Global Village: Cultural Evolution in New Age and Neo-pagan Thought', *Journal of Contemporary Religion*, 10(2): 139–149.

Bowman, M. (2002) 'Contemporary Celtic Spirituality', in A. Hale and P. Payton (eds) *New Directions in Celtic Studies*, Exeter: University of Exeter Press, pp. 69–94.

Coles, T., Hall, C.M. and Duval, D.T. (2006) 'Tourism and Post-disciplinary Enquiry', *Current Issues in Tourism*, 9(4&5): 293–319.

Cornish Ancient Sites Protection Network (n.d.) *Madron Well and Baptistry*. Available at http://www.cornishancientsites.com/Madron%20Well%20&%20Baptistry.pdf (accessed 16 May 2012).

Cornwall AONB Partnership (2011a) *07: West Penwith in the Cornwall Area of Outstanding Natural Beauty Management Plan 2011–2016*. Available at http://www.cornwall-aonb.gov.uk/management-plan/west-penwith.html (accessed 13 October 2011).

Cornwall AONB Partnership (2011b) *Cornwall Area of Outstanding Natural Beauty Management Plan 2011–2016*. Available at http://www.cornwall-aonb.gov.uk/management-plan/index.html (accessed 13 October 2011).

Cornwall Historic Environment Service (2007) 'Access to Monuments: Men-an-Tol, Madron'. Available at http://www.historic-cornwall.org.uk/a2m/bronze_age/stone_circle/men_an_tol/men_an_tol.htm (accessed 16 May 2012).

Cornwall Tourist Board (2000) *Tourism Strategy for Cornwall: Delivery Distinctive Difference*. Available at http://www.cornwalltouristboard.co.uk/files/doc/ctb.strategy.web.doc (accessed 27 June 2007).

Cornwall Trust Board (2005) *Promoting Cornwall to the World: Cornwall Marketing Strategy 2006–2010*. Available at http://www.cornwalltouristboard.co.uk/documents/TourismMarketingStrategyDec2005.doc (accessed 27 June 2007).

Crouch, D. (2009) 'The Diverse Dynamics of Cultural Studies and Tourism', in M. Robinson and T. Jamal (eds) *The Sage Handbook of Tourism Studies*, London: Sage, pp. 82–97.

Digance, J. (2006) 'Religious and Secular Pilgrimage: Journeys Redolent with Meaning', in D.J. Timothy and D.H. Olsen (eds) *Tourism, Religion and Spiritual Journeys*, London: Routledge.

Digance, J. and Cusack, C. (2002) 'Glastonbury: A Tourist Town for All Seasons', in G. Dann (ed.) *The Tourist as a Metaphor for the Social World*, Oxford: CABI.

English, P. (2002) 'Disputing Stonehenge: Law and Access to a National Symbol', *Entertainment Law*, 1(2): 1–22.

Hale, A. (2006) 'Selling Celtic Cornwall: Changing Markets and Meanings', in K. Meethan, A. Anderson and S. Miles (eds) *Tourism Consumption and Representation: Narratives of Place and Self*, Wallingford: CABI.

Hale, A. and Payton, P. (2000) (eds) *New Directions in Celtic Studies*, Exeter: University of Exeter Press.

Harvey, D.C. (2008) 'The History of Heritage', in B. Graham and P. Howard (eds) *The Ashgate Research Companion to Heritage and Identity*, Aldershot: Ashgate.

Hawkes, J. (1967) 'God in the Machine', *Antiquity*, 41(163): 174–180.

Hetherington, K. (1992) 'Stonehenge and its Festival: Spaces of Consumption', in R. Shields (ed.) *Lifestyle Shopping: The Subject of Consumption*, London: Routledge.

Hetherington, K. (1998) 'Vanloads of Uproarious Humanity: New Age Travellers and the Utopics of the Countryside', in T. Skelton and G. Valentine (eds) *Cool Places: Geographies of Youth Cultures*, London: Routledge.

Hetherington, K. (2000) *New Age Travellers: Vanloads of Uproarious Humanity*, London: Cassell.

Hunt, S.J. (2003) *Alternative Religions: A Sociological Introduction*, Aldershot: Ashgate Publishing.

Laws, C. (2007) 'Myth, Magic and the Marketplace: The Preservation and Interpretation of Cornwall's Arthurian Heritage within a Spiritual Tourism Context', in *Proceedings of the Things that Move: The Material Worlds of Tourism and Travel Conference held at the Centre for Tourism and Cultural Change*, Leeds, July 2007.

Lennon, J. and Foley, M. (2000) *Dark Tourism: The Attraction of Death and Disaster*, London: Continuum.

Letcher, A., Blain, J. and Wallis, R.J. (2009) 'Re-viewing the Past: Discourse and Power in Images of Prehistory', in M. Robinson and D. Picard (eds) *The Framed World: Tourism, Tourists and Photography*, Farnham, Surrey: Ashgate Publishing.

Lowenthal, D. (1985) *The Past is a Foreign Country*, Cambridge: Cambridge University Press.

MacCannell, D. (2001) 'Tourist Agency', *Tourist Studies*, *1*: 23–37.
Maffesoli, M. (1996) *The Time of the Tribes: The Decline of Individualism in Mass Society*, trans. Don Smith, London: Sage.
Novelli, M. (2005) (ed.) *Niche Tourism: Contemporary Trends, Issues and Cases*, Oxford: Butterworth-Heinemann.
Pagan Federation (2011) *Introduction to Paganism*. Available at http://www.paganfed.org/paganism.shtml (accessed 17 May 2012).
Paine, C. (2000) (ed.) *Godly Things: Museums, Objects and Religion*, London: Leicester University Press.
Pearson, J. (2002) (ed.) *Belief Beyond Boundaries: Wicca, Celtic Spirituality and the New Age*, Aldershot: Ashgate Publishing.
Petherick, R. (1999) *Madron Well, Cornwall*. Available at http://people.bath.ac.uk/prsrlp/kernunos/england/madron.htm (accessed 4 December 2011).
Phillips, C. (2006) 'Mystical Geographies of Cornwall', unpublished thesis, University of Nottingham. Available at http://etheses.nottingham.ac.uk/744/1/Mystical_Geographies_of_Cornwall.pdf (accessed 28 October 2011).
Preston-Jones, A. and Mossop, M. (2007) *Madron Well, Cornwall: Conservation and Access Works, June 2007, Report No: 2007R035*, Historic Environment Service, Cornwall County Council. Available at http://www.cornwall.gov.uk (accessed 4 December 2011).
Robb, J.G. (1998) 'The Ritual Landscape Concept in Archaeology: A Heritage Construction', *Landscape Research*, *23*(2): 159–174.
Rojek, C. (1993) *Ways of Escape: Modern Transformations in Leisure and Travel*, Basingstoke, UK: Macmillan Press.
Seaton, A. (2009) 'Purposeful Otherness: Approaches to the Management of Thanatourism', in R. Sharpley and P.R. Stone (eds) *The Darker Side of Travel: The Theory and Practice of Dark Tourism*, Bristol: Channel View Publications.
Seaton, A. (2010) 'Thanatourism and its Discontents: An Appraisal of a Decade's Work with Some Future Issues and Directions', in T. Jamal and M. Robinson (eds) *The Sage Handbook of Tourism Studies*, London: Sage.
Shackley, M. (2001) *Managing Sacred Sites: Service Provision and Visitor Management*, London: Continuum.
Sharpley, R. (2009) 'Tourism, Religion and Spirituality', in T. Jamal and M. Robinson (eds) *The Sage Handbook of Tourism Studies*, London: Sage.
Sharpley, R. and Stone, P.R. (2009) *The darker side of travel: The theory and practice of dark tourism*, Bristol: Channel View Publications.
Smith, L. (2006) *Uses of heritage*, London: Routledge.
South West Tourism (2005) *Towards 2015: Shaping Tomorrow's Tourism*. Available at http://www.towards2015.co.uk/downloads/vision_0105.pdf (accessed 27 June 2007).
Stone, P.R. (2006). 'A Dark Tourism Spectrum: Towards a Typology of Death and Macabre Related Tourist Sites, Attractions and Exhibitions', *Tourism: An Interdisciplinary International Journal*, *54*(22): 145–160.
Stone, P.R. (2011) 'Dark Tourism: Towards a New Post-disciplinary Research Agenda', *International Journal of Tourism Anthropology*, *1*(3/4): 318–332.
Straffon, C. (2007) Chair of the Cornish Ancient Sites Protection Network. Interview with C. Laws and S. Stuart, 5 July 2007.
Straffon, C. (2012) Chair of the Cornish Ancient Sites Protection Network. Email correspondence, 23 March 2012.

Tarlow, P. (2005) 'Dark Tourism: The Appealing "Dark" Side of Tourism and More', in M. Novelli (ed.) *Niche Tourism: Contemporary Trends, Issues and Cases*, Oxford: Butterworth-Heinemann.

Timothy, D.J. and Conover, P.J. (2006) 'Nature Religion, Self-spirituality and New Age Tourism', in D.J. Timothy and D.H. Olsen (eds) *Tourism, Religion and Spiritual Journeys*, London: Routledge.

Timothy, D.J. and Olsen, D.H. (2006) (eds) *Tourism, Religion and Spiritual Journeys*, London: Routledge.

Tunbridge, J.E. and Ashworth, G.J. (1996) *Dissonant Heritage: The Management of the Past as a Resource in Conflict*, Chichester: John Wiley and Sons.

United Nations Scientific and Cultural Organization (2011) World Heritage List: Cornwall and West Devon Mining Landscape. Available at http://whc.unesco.org/en/list/1215 (accessed 4 December 2011).

Urry, J. (1990) *The Tourist Gaze*, London: Sage.

Wallis, R.J. (2003) *Shamans/Neo-shamans: Ecstasy, alternative archaeologies and contemporary Pagans*, London: Routledge.

Wallis, R.J. and Blain, J. (2001) 'Sacred Sites, Contested Rites/Rights: Contemporary Pagan Engagements with the Past', Sheffield: Sheffield Hallam Centre for Human Rights.

Wight, A.C. (2006) 'Philosophical and Methodological Praxes in Dark Tourism: Controversy, Contention and the Evolving Paradigm', *Journal of Vacation Marketing*, *12*(2): 119–129.

York, M. (2002) 'Contemporary Pagan Pilgrimages' in W.H. Swatos, Jr. and L. Tomasi (eds) *From Medieval Pilgrimage to Religious Tourism: The Social and Cultural Economics of Piety*, Westport, CT: Praeger.

8 Soviet tourism in the Baltic states

Remembrance versus nostalgia – just different shades of dark?

Brent McKenzie

Introduction

Is there a difference between remembrance tourism and nostalgia tourism? As argued by Orbasli and Woodward (2009), remembrance tourism aims to focus on emblematic historic sites, particularly those of major conflicts, with a goal of presenting a tourist experience that provides a testimony of a people's history. Although 'remembering' may force one to recall those moments that many would like to forget, its value lies in its ability to retain lessons from the past (Richter 2002). Similarly, but in a different context, nostalgia tourism also deals with the past, but while remembrance arguably focuses more on an educational aspect, nostalgia tourism as suggested by Caton and Santos (2007) looks at historical events, with an aim to promote kitschy and longing representations of the past. Drawing on these two concepts as they relate to dark tourism research, this chapter examines their status within the context of 'Soviet' tourism in the Baltic States of Estonia, Latvia and Lithuania.

With their return to independence in 1991, the Baltic States of Estonia, Latvia and Lithuania ended a 50-year period of forced incorporation into the Soviet Union. One of the earliest post-Soviet economic successes was their collected ability to reignite their long dormant tourist industries. A key component of the tourist agenda was to provide opportunities for visitors to learn about the struggles that had occurred during the Soviet period. Thus, one aim of this chapter is to better understand the underlying motivations and perceptions of those that offer, support/do not support, or frequent such attractions in Estonia, Latvia and Lithuania.

This chapter aims to advance the extant literature in dark tourism research in general, and in the Baltic States specifically. One of the premises of this study was that all three countries, as former Republics in the Soviet Union from 1944 to 1991, would have a similar focus in terms of the Soviet period and how it is portrayed today. As will be shown, this was not always the case. There was a need to better understand the potential for differences in how Soviet tourism sites or attractions relating to the Soviet period were developed, managed and promoted. This was accomplished through a three-stage process. The first was to review the existing literature on tourism in the Baltic States during the Soviet period in order to better understand the role that tourism played in each country's economic, social and political make up. The second was to provide a review of the various dark tourism sites, memorials, tours and exhibitions that relate to the Soviet period. The third step was to collect various narratives of stakeholders that were involved in this realm of Soviet tourism, by way of personal interviews and correspondence by the author with actual visitors to these destinations; representatives of the official travel boards of the various countries/regions; and providers of such tours. As will be discussed, these findings help contribute to a greater comprehension of the impact such a form of tourism has upon country branding, and by extension the larger field of destination marketing in Estonia, Latvia and Lithuania.

In order to establish the background to this study, the chapter provides both a historic and present day perspective on the concept of dark tourism as it pertains to 'Soviet' tourism in Estonia, Latvia and Lithuania. This will be accomplished through a grounding of the concept of dark tourism in the Baltic States, and highlights how these types of attractions, sights and experiences have been documented in the academic and popular press. The next section provides a historical reflection on tourism in Estonia, Latvia and Lithuania, during the Soviet period, followed by a brief discussion of some of the major dark tourism sites that exist in each country today. The subsequent section presents the findings of the aforementioned interviews with stakeholders involved in dark tourism in each of the three countries. The chapter concludes with both concerns and opportunities for the future of dark tourism as it pertains to the Baltic Soviet past.

Dark tourism in the Baltic States: an overview

One way in which to judge the evolution of how a tourism niche such as dark tourism has changed and evolved over time is to examine tourism texts and tourist guides. With respect to Estonia, Latvia and Lithuania, one such source is the *Lonely Planet* series of travel books devoted to this region. Beginning in 1994 with the publishing of *Baltic States and Kaliningrad* (Noble 1994) through to the subsequent five editions of *Estonia, Latvia and Lithuania* (Williams, Gaudie and Noble 1997; Williams, Hermann and Kemp 2000; Kemp 2003; Williams and Blond 2006; Bain 2009); the sites, attractions and commentary about Soviet tourism in this region have continued to grow and change.

In the *Baltic States and Kaliningrad* volume (Noble 1994), there was a section entitled 'Soviet Nostalgia' (p. 137), which discusses where Lenin's statue used to be in Tallinn, and a short reference to a 1924 statue near the Tallinn train station of the armed uprising of the Tallinn proletariat. Interestingly there were no similar sections about Latvia or Lithuania, and in fact the specific term 'Soviet Nostalgia' could not be found in any subsequent editions.

Each volume included a number of Soviet dark tourism sites, predominantly the occupation museums, and World War II cemeteries and memorials (see Figures 8.1, 8.2 and 8.3). In the third edition in 2003, a discussion of the Latvian People's Front Museum, which housed an exhibit that depicted an office where the main participants met who worked on the campaign to lead to Latvia's re-independence from the Soviet Union, was presented. The exhibit included Soviet

Figure 8.1 Soviet World War II Memorial, Antakalnis Cemetery, Vilnius, Lithuania

period furniture and an early computer, and provided visitors (predominantly international tourists) an opportunity to view first hand the trappings of the 'Soviet' period.

The fifth edition (Bain 2009) represented the first time that the term 'Soviet' in the guise of both heritage and nostalgia sites was mentioned in the book's index. Interestingly, there were no sites in the index listings for Estonia. There continued to be a number of references to Soviet-related tourist sites and this edition saw the first inclusion of a company that offered Soviet tours.

More recently, in the 2011 book *1000 Ultimate Sights* (Bain *et al.* 2011), also published by the *Lonely Planet* group, there were four attractions listed in the Baltic States that would fall into the category of dark tourism: the Karosta Military Prison, the Pension Līgatne Nuclear Bomb shelter in Latvia, the Museum of Genocide and Grutas Park (colloquially known as 'Stalin World') in Lithuania. There were no listings of sites in Estonia. These attractions fall into the category of 'remembrance' tourism (Nuclear Bomb Shelter, and Genocide Museum) and 'nostalgia' (Karosta Prison, and Stalin World).

Estonia, Latvia and Lithuania were the three most western Republics of the Soviet Union, and were the 'richest' republics in terms of per capita income during the communist period (O'Connor 2006). Unlike many of the other republics of the Union of Soviet Socialist Republics (USSR), the Baltic States had

Figure 8.2 Soviet World War II Memorial, Estonian Defence Forces Cemetery, Tallinn, Estonia

previously experienced a period of independence between the world wars, and thus with independence re-established in 1991, there was an overt emphasis on the 're-branding' of each country as a distinct, individualist, stand-alone nation (Kaneva 2011).

In reality, most of the outside world continued to refer to the three countries collectively as the Baltic States (or even the pejorative terms 'Ex-Soviet', 'Ex-Communist', or even 'Russian'); this fact was not necessarily surprising, as the early 1990s saw each country's central government promote the creation of a museum, and special exhibits, to bring to light their shared experiences under the Communist system. Each country focused on the establishment of a major museum dedicated to the remembrances, and atrocities of the Soviet period. The capital cities of Tallinn, Estonia; Riga, Latvia; and Vilnius, Lithuania opened, respectively, the Museum of Occupation of Estonia; the Museum of Occupation of

Figure 8.3 Soviet World War II Memorial, Pokrov Cemetery, Riga, Latvia

Latvia; and the Museum of Genocide Victims in Lithuania. A constant theme of the exhibits in these museums was to communicate to the outside world the harsh and often brutal oppression placed upon many of the citizens of these countries. Although the museums included exhibits related to the atrocities inflicted on these countries by Nazi Germany, the dominant message was aimed at the Communist period.

As noted, these museums fall within the realm of dark tourism and the sub-category of 'remembrance' tourism (Sharpley and Stone 2009). In this case, the remembrance allows for the saving and establishing of an identity, particularly a cultural identity; and by extension the values of citizenship (Metro-Roland 2008). In other words, these museums highlight to the outside world that each country was distinct and had a distinct people and culture that did not disappear, despite the excessive repression inflicted upon them during the Soviet period.

A more recent phenomenon was the growth of so called 'Soviet' tourism, under the guise of 'nostalgia' tourism (Caton and Santos 2007). Examples include Soviet 'Nostalgia' tours in Estonia (Tourism Estonia 2011), the opportunity to stay at former USSR leader Brezhnev's Dacha in Jurmala, Latvia (Baltic Features 2009), and 'Stalin World' near Druskininkai, Lithuania (Grūto Parkas 2011). Unlike the remembrance attractions, which generally caused little controversy inside each country, there were regular articles and postings about these nostalgia attractions and sites.

Tourism in the Soviet period

Prior to their joint return to independence in 1991, the Baltic States greatly mirrored the rest of the Soviet Union with regard to tourism. As Estonia, Latvia and Lithuania were Republics within the USSR, their tourist industry differed to a degree from the other countries such as Poland and Hungary that fell within the Soviet Bloc (see Hall 1991). During 'Soviet times', 1941–91, tourism was primarily seen as a means of educating Soviet citizens into promoting 'Homo Sovieticus' ('Soviet Man') and not economic ends, while leisure tourism was viewed as "non-productive" (Gorsuch 2003).

There was a focus on two forms of tourism – domestic and foreign. Since travel and free movement was often heavily restricted in the Soviet Union, Soviet citizens were encouraged to remain within the borders of the Soviet Union in order to avoid the dangers of travel (Gorsuch 2003). There was an overt attempt to develop an official ignorance in Soviet citizens' minds about foreign (non-Socialist) countries in order to adhere to Soviet doctrine, resulting in the vast majority of leisure travel occurring within the Soviet Union.

As noted by Koenker (2009), the main function of the Soviet citizen's vacation was therapeutic. The aim of a vacation was to help ensure a physically and mentally sound Soviet citizen. This type of tourism related to rest and relaxation, in contrast to what was known as 'turizm', which related to travel in order to experience the new (Gorsuch and Koenker 2006). There was also a genuine lack of need for domestic travel as most companies/industries had their own vacation properties that were available to workers and their families at no charge (Joost 2009). Therapeutic travel consisted of health spas or resorts, with a collection of medical facilities, sanatoria, scenery and services (Koenker 2009). Travel to see and do was recommended for healthy adults who were interested in increasing their travels while strengthening their physique in rather demanding conditions. These travels included "hiking through the nature reserves of the Caucasus or Crimea before concluding with several days' stay at a seaside tourist base" (Koenker 2009: 408).

In terms of international tourists, for almost a decade after the death of Stalin in 1953, general tourism to the USSR was basically closed to foreigners (Chabe 1969). Even if visas to enter were issued, the tourist faced many challenges and extreme regulations (Kostiainen 2002). In addition to the difficulty in obtaining the visa itself, just crossing a border from the West into the USSR was an extremely stressful process, as visitors were met by "strict aggressive soldiers and customs officials pointing rifles" (Kostiainen 2002: 2).

All foreign tourism fell within the realm of the Soviet tourist agency, *Intourist*. The tourism agency was established in 1929 with the goal of providing tourism for foreigners to meet people from their occupational group. *Intourist* was responsible for the staffing of tourist guides, employing hotel floor coordinators and recruiting citizen informers. All *Intourist* employees were aligned with the Soviet Secret Police, the KGB (Komitet Gosudarstvennoy Bezopasnosti), (Chabe 1969). Tourists were only permitted to stay in approved accommodation for international guests and had to purchase packaged tours (Hall, Smith and Marciszewska 2006).

Travel regulations prohibited tourists from deviating from approved tours and those that violated these regulations were subject to removal from the Soviet Union (Siverson, Groth and Blumberg 1980). Not surprisingly, the majority of foreign tourism took place in capital cities of the Soviet Union (Shaw 1991). The main form of tourism was classified as cultural tourism, where tourists were shown the cultural, historic and economic achievements of the Soviet Union. The time spent at each attraction was strictly enforced, as there was fear of prolonged exchanges between foreign tourists and Soviet citizens (Kostiainen 2002).

Soviet tourism was not dissimilar to other tourism of the time as one of the aims was to increase service related revenues, and more importantly, the earning of hard currency. Soviet tourism also had a goal of promoting the ideals of the Socialist system to outsiders (Shaw 1991). By forcing foreign tourists to follow a stringent itinerary and monitoring their movements and interactions within the citizens of the Soviet Union, the aim was for the portrayal of a favourable image, while minimizing the potential for the confirmation of negative perceptions (Burns 1998).

Soviet tourism in the Baltic States

It was not until the late 1980s, under the leadership of Mikhail Gorbachev and the period of Perestroika ('Restructuring'), and Glasnost (Openness), that foreign tourist restrictions began to ease (Hall *et al.* 2006). As noted by Vallen and Levinson (1989), there was an overt change in the demeanour of the tourist personnel, who began to understand the financial rewards of better service. This was particularly true in the Baltic States. As early as 1968, regular passenger ferry service on the SS *Tallinn* began between Helsinki, Finland and Tallinn, Estonia, resulting in the development of tourism-related services in Tallinn. The most overt example of this tourism orientation was the building of the Viru Hotel, which was the first hotel built within the Soviet Union by a non-Soviet nation (it was built by Finland in exchange for Soviet oil and gas and opened in 1973). Regular ferry service between Helsinki and Tallinn also lead to the establishment of a tourism niche that continues to exist today – namely, tourists that come to Estonia to purchase lower-priced alcohol. In 1971 an article in *The New York Times* appears to be the first mention of vodka tourism as it pertained to Finnish tourists travelling to Estonia for this purpose (Juckett 1971).

There were also a number of Soviet books and guides published for Western tourists, such as *Noukogude Eesti* (Soviet Estonia, 1978), which included pictures of Soviet statues and memorials, and focused editions of the publication *Soviet Life* on Estonia in 1979 (*Estonia Today*), and the Baltic States in 1980 (*The Baltic Republics: Forty Years of Soviet Power*). These publications often represented the sole opportunity for the promotion of these regions to potential Western tourists, particularly to those expatriates from the region. Other English language publications during the Soviet period that featured the Baltic States included *National Geographic*, which published articles such as *Estonia: At Russia's Baltic Gate* (December 1939); *Return to Estonia* (April 1980); and *The Baltic Nations: Estonia, Latvia, and Lithuania Struggle Toward Independence* (November 1990).

Tourism and country branding in the Baltic States

Thus, by 1991 the Baltic States tourism sector was ready to flourish (Jarvis and Kallas 2008). Although day visitors (mainly cruise ship tourists) continued to represent the largest sector of foreign tourists, there was a concentrated effort to increase the number of overnight visitors (Hall *et al.* 2006). The success of this endeavour was heavily dependent upon improved infrastructure (for example, Western-quality hotels and restaurants) and transportation capabilities (mainly taxis and buses). The Baltic States began to extend the breadth of their targeted tourist market beyond their nearby Scandinavian and Northern European markets (as well as a marked downturn in Russian tourists) to the rest of Europe. Furthermore, with all three countries' entrance into the European Union in 2004, the previously noted border issues were essentially eliminated. There continued to be a focus on tourists with cultural ties to the region from North America (Nichols 2001).

Each of the three countries was determined to develop a brand identity. As noted, labels such as Baltic States, Former-Soviet Union, even Russian were terms that each country had to struggle with in their own way. In the case of Estonia and Latvia, country brand slogans and logos helped to lead this brand identity. 'Welcome to Estonia' (with the 'EST' highlighted as it is the European short-form for the country), and Latvia's slogan 'The Land that Sings' to highlight its musical heritage (Szondi 2007). Lithuania tended to focus mainly on building its hotels and support services, as by 1996 demand for accommodation had exceeded supply. Lithuania saw less of a need to re-brand itself, as it felt it was much better known than Estonia and Latvia to the outside world. Lithuanian tourism identified the country's historic sites and places of cultural value as defining its brand. Additionally, in the late 1990s Latvia's development of ecotourism represented a bid to encourage tourism outside of the capital city, Riga (Hall *et al.* 2006).

As noted, the growth in Estonian tourism was judged to be quite successful (Worthington 2001). In addition to Estonia's geographic proximity to Finland, tourism in Estonia even during the Soviet period was not a new occurrence. Tallinn was a popular site for New Year celebrations by many of those from other parts of the Soviet Union, particularly from Russia. Similar to Latvia, the new tourist sites that developed in Estonia were often described in terms of Estonian community, heritage and tradition (Saarinen and Kask 2008). The Estonia tourist industry viewed tourism as a way to help to promote the country's process of transitioning, or its 'return to Europe', originally with the slogan 'Positively Transforming' (Worthington 2001), and later with the aforementioned 'Welcome to Estonia'.

Soviet dark tourism in the Baltic States

With respect to the dark tourism sector, each of the Baltic States has a number of offerings in this field. As shown in Table 8.1, each country has what would be classified as remembrance and nostalgia sites. In sheer numbers, of the three

Table 8.1 Selected examples of dark sites in Estonia, Latvia and Lithuania

	Estonia	Latvia	Lithuania
Museums	Museum of Occupations; Estonian War Museum – General Laidoner Museum; KGB Cells Museum – Tartu; KGB Museum – Viru Hotel; Soviet Life Exhibit	Museum of the Occupation of Latvia; Latvian Museum of Prison History – Jurmala	Grutas Park (Stalin World); Museum of Genocide Victims
Tours/ attractions	Soviet Tours – Blue Drum Group; Bronze Soldier – Defence Forces Cemetery; Prison of Patarei	Liepaja Naval Port; Soviet Bunker in Ligatne; Pokrov Cemetary; Victory Memorial to Soviet Army	1984 Survival Drama in Soviet Bunker; Vilnius Antakalnis Military Cemetery

countries, Latvia has the greatest number of sites, while Estonia the least. This fact is reflected in a search of tourist brochures, websites and travel publications. But in order to go beyond the published materials on this subject, and in order to advance the understanding of the role of Soviet tourism in Estonia, Latvia and Lithuania, a series of interviews and data collection was conducted with various tourism stakeholders in each of the three countries. This data gathering, which was qualitative in nature, consisted of one-to-one interviews, as well as guided questionnaires. The author had previously experienced the often-sensitive nature of talking about the Soviet period in each of these countries, particularly as it pertains to a sympathetic portrayal of those times. Thus, the interviews and questionnaires were broader in nature than the Soviet period to encompass the tourist sector and branding issues in general (Netemeyer, Bearden and Sharma 2003).

During 2009 and 2010, the author visited Estonia, Latvia and Lithuania to conduct face-to-face interviews, while email correspondence was also used to supplement the initial contacts. As the aim of the data collection was to provide input from a variety of stakeholder sources, tourism providers, governmental agencies and tourists were targeted to provide insights about dark tourism, under the guise of Soviet tourism in the Baltic States. The subjects were contacted by the author through relationships previously developed from numerous trips to each country, and each participant was briefed as to the nature of the study. The participants were also provided with a definition of dark tourism and once the term was defined, specific questions were asked. As was to be the case, the term dark tourism was found not to be commonly used, and often was not recognized by the subjects. One interesting finding was that the dark tourism attraction providers did not feel that the service that they provided should be classified as dark tourism (McKenzie 2009–2010).

In Estonia, in the case of the Soviet Experience tours, there was a belief that this firm was providing history-tainment, and that although the essence of the experience was based upon the Soviet period, there were no political aims. They said:

> It is to experience local flavour, and we are doing Soviet programmes a lot. We have the Soviet bus. Sometimes we meet a crowd in the airport. We ask them all for passports. We show them Soviet propaganda... we are yelling in Russian... we talk in English so that they understand... of course Europeans and Americans realize immediately that it's a joke so they play along... we take them to interrogation, photo sessions, and finger printing sessions... we don't talk about the Soviet period, we don't show them about the Soviet period, we immerse them in the activities... then they learn more about the culture and history through experience... that's our concept.
>
> (Tourism owner/operator, Tallinn)

When pressed about any controversy that comes from Soviet tourism, the response was, "For us it's ridiculous, because we are not making any political demonstration, we are talking about the history... Vikings weren't exactly the nicest people, and no one seems to have any issue with Viking themed attractions" (Tourism owner/operator, Tallinn).

This finding contrasts with comments from the Tallinn tourism bureau. Although the bureau representative had no difficulty in talking about Soviet tourism, there was a marked departure in terms of the impact that such tourism brings to the Estonian marketplace:

> people still think that this is a Soviet country... it took us many, many, many, years to make them understand... It [Soviet tourism] is not our main topic, of course. Our typical old town, which definitely attracts more people than a couple of Soviet buildings... from our surveys of Tallinn, we can't see any unique interest in that [Soviet] kind of tourism or attractions. Of course there are people who want to see these types of attractions. It is interesting for people to listen to their tour guides talk about what happened here during the Soviet period, so there are sightseeing tours by bus that provide this information. It is not hidden, not in any way, but it is not promoted.
>
> (Tourism bureau representative, Tallinn)

In contrast to the findings from the interview in Estonia, the interview with a representative of the Latvian tourist development agency provided insight about the type of tourist that would be attracted to Soviet tourism:

> yes it's [Soviet-related tourism] popular in Riga... we pass some places where you can see Soviet life or Soviet places like military bases and it's quite popular... foreign tourists mostly are interested in these sites, less so from people from Eastern Europe... if we can make our history interesting for tourists, why not?
>
> (Tourism bureau representative, Riga)

The insights from correspondence with the representative from Lithuania were similar to that of the Latvian interview. Particularly similar was the discussion about the role of Soviet tourism and Lithuanian history. What proved interesting was the suggestion as to how Soviet tourism is interpreted by those of different generations:

> Soviet sites are popular among the older people who lived in Lithuania during Soviet times, even if they had some bad experience when living during it... for younger people, it is a good way of learning Lithuanian history in unusual places, but it is often less interesting to this generation of Lithuanians, as this historical period had little direct connection to them. For foreigners these sites are part of the Soviet times so it is very interesting... they are intrigued by this period and purchase many 'Soviet' souvenirs... but they have difficulty in understanding the real meaning of what it was like during the Soviet period.
> (Tourism bureau representative, Vilnius)

Also surprisingly, there was a stated expectation that Soviet-related tourism was beneficial in terms of both remembrances for Lithuanians, but also as an agent of change:

> This [Soviet] kind of tourism is interesting for older people who lived their childhood during Soviet times because of their remembrance of innocence and beauty during their younger years... because older people are better able to compare the level of development in Lithuania after the influence of the Soviet times they can see parallels and differences in how it was then, and how it is today.
> (Tourism bureau representative, Vilnius)

When taken together, there was a clear indication that tourism providers and tourism industry representatives acknowledged that Soviet tourism does play a role in the overall tourism industry, even if it is a small role. However, in face-to-face discussions by the author with foreign tourists, there was a noticeably higher indication that Soviet-related tourist attractions and sites were one of the key highlights of visiting this region of the world (McKenzie 2009–2010). This finding may have been a result of a general ignorance by foreign tourists, particularly cruise ship tourists who may only spend a day, or even a few hours, in the country, as they would also refer to the Baltic States as 'former Russian'. Furthermore, Soviet remembrance in general, and nostalgia tourism specifically, were considered attractions that many tourists would only visit once, and that there would be a limited interest in learning more about the true facts of the period.

Through the data gathering stage of this research, it was apparent to the author that each Baltic country's approach to Soviet tourism was different. While Estonia, Latvia and Lithuania have a number of Soviet tourism sites and attractions to offer, the official government position varies. In Latvia and Lithuania the government tourism representatives demonstrated a more relaxed attitude about the Soviet period and offering Soviet tourism. For both Latvia and Lithuania there was an overt hesitation to being defined by Soviet tourism, but there was an acceptance that it was natural to share parts of their history with the world (McKenzie 2009–2010). In contrast, the interviews in Estonia suggested a more negative position about the Soviet period and Soviet tourism. Those interview findings are mirrored in the Estonia popular press, which supports the fact that the majority of Estonians do not feel comfortable talking about the Soviet period in a positive, or even neutral, way. Furthermore, any Soviet era-related tourism that did take place in Estonia was to be independently run and not at all recognized or supported by official governmental agencies and departments.

Conclusion

A persistent problem that Estonia, Latvia and Lithuania must confront or accept is that some tourists will continue to see the Baltic Region as being ex-Soviet. This becomes an economic issue if tourists are visiting expecting to see evidence of a Soviet region and instead are confronted with fully transitioned European countries. It is suggested that this issue could be addressed through a continued focus on the branding and marketing of Baltic sites and attractions that ignore the Soviet period, while also allowing for, or at minimum not suppressing, different types of sites and attractions that relate to the Soviet period of history. While each of the three nations has been working towards marketing a more professional branding of their country, there continues to be a lack of evidence that this goal has been fully achieved. As it has been just over 20 years since the return of their re-independence, this may not be surprising, as countries, like other brands, take years of development and refinement to clarify and solidify their image to the rest of the world (Chlivickas and Smaliukienė 2009). The reality is that there is no way of getting around the fact that rightly or wrongly, the Soviet period is a defining characteristic of the history of each of these countries. Be it under the guise of remembrance or nostalgia there continues to be an opportunity to develop and support the various aspects of dark tourism in this realm. The empirical findings tend to suggest that Estonia has done the best job in distancing itself from the Soviet period, and increasingly is viewed as a European country (which has further benefited from its adoption of the Euro in 2011). This contrasts with Latvia and Lithuania, who arguably have done the best job of integrating their local Soviet history into their larger history.

Thus, it remains to be seen if the growth of remembrance versus nostalgia in dark tourism as it relates to Soviet tourism in the Baltic States will, as found in Sharpley and Stone (2009), 'lighten' (dark tourism that is more kitsch and entertainment related) or 'darken' (dark tourism that is more directly related to death, authenticity and education). The fact that the breadth of offerings in this tourism niche continues to grow in all three countries suggest that future research in this field will benefit from longitudinal studies of how all involved stakeholders, both tourist providers and tourists themselves, react to this dark tourism niche.

References

Bain, C. (2009) *Estonia Latvia & Lithuania*, 5th edn, Footscray, Victoria, Australia: Lonely Planet Publications.

Bain, C., Harkin, P., James, K., Koehner, H., Sellers, S. and J. Wall (eds) (2011) *Lonely Planet: 1,000 Ultimate Sights*, Footscray, Victoria, Australia: Lonely Planet Publications.

Baltic Features (2009) *Latvia's Soviet Holiday Heaven Finds A New Place In The Sun*. Available at http://balticfeatures.wordpress.com/2009/08/17/latvias-soviet-holiday-heaven-finds-a-new-place-in-the-sun/ (accessed 18 June 2011).

Burns, P. (1998) 'Tourism in Russia: Background and Structure', *Tourism Management*, 19(6): 555–565.

Caton, K. and Santos, C. (2007) 'Heritage Tourism on Route 66: Deconstructing Nostalgia', *Journal of Travel Research*, 45(4): 371–386.

Chabe, A.M. (1969) 'Soviet Tourism: An Open Door to a Closed Society', *Social Studies*, 60(2): 57–65.

Chlivickas, E. and Smaliukienė, R. (2009) 'International Region as a Brand Origin: Conceptualization and Review', *Journal of Business Economics and Management*, 10(2): 141–148.

Gorsuch, A.E. (2003) 'There's No Place Like Home, Soviet Tourism in Late Stalinism', *Slavic Review*, 62(4): 760–785.

Gorsuch, A.E. and Koenker, D.P. (eds) (2006) *Turizm: The Russian and East European Tourist Under Capitalism and Socialism*, New York: Cornell University Press.

Grūto Parkas (2011) *Founding History*. Available at http://www.grutoparkas.lt/istorija-en.htm (accessed 3 July 2011).

Hall, D. (ed.) (1991) *Tourism and Economic Development in Eastern Europe and the Soviet Union*, London: Belhaven.

Hall, D., Smith, M. and Marciszewska, B. (eds) (2006) *Tourism in the New Europe: The Challenges and Opportunities of EU Enlargement*, Oxfordshire: CABI.

Jarvis, J. and Kallas, P. (2008) 'Estonian Tourism and the Accession Effect: The Impact of European Union Membership on the Contemporary Development Patterns of the Estonian Tourism Industry', *Tourism Geographies*, 10(4), 474–494.

Joost, J. (2009) Telephone interview with the author [Recording in possession of author], 16 September 2009, Tallinn, Estonia.

Juckett, E. (1971) 'The Vodka Special to Estonia', *New York Times*, 29: 32.

Kahu, M. and Kahu, M. (1978) *Soviet Estonia (Nõukogude Eesti)*, Tallinn: Eesti Raamat.

Kaneva, N. (ed.) (2011) *Branding Post-Communist Nations: Marketizing National Identities in the 'New' Europe*, New York: Routledge.

Kemp, C. (2003) *Estonia Latvia & Lithuania*, 3rd edn, Footscray, Victoria, Australia: Lonely Planet Publications.

Koenker, D.P. (2009) 'Whose Right to Rest? Contesting the Family Vacation in the Postwar Soviet Union', *Comparative Studies in Society and History*, 51(2): 401–25.

Kostiainen, A. (2002) *The Soviet Tourist Industry as Seen by the Western Tourists of the Late Soviet Period*, XIII International Congress of Economic Historians. Available at http://users.utu.fi/aukosti/Soviet%20Tourism.html (accessed 18 June 2011).

McKenzie, B. (2009–2010) Personal interviews [Notes in possession of author].

Metro-Roland, M.M. (2008) 'A Nostalgia for Terror', in D.C. Knudsen, C.E. Greer, M.M. Metro-Roland and A.K. Soper (eds) *Landscape, Tourism, and Meaning*, Aldershot, Hampshire: Ashgate Publishing.

Netemeyer, R.G., Bearden, W.O. and Sharma, S. (2003) *Scaling Procedures: Issues and Applications*, Thousand Oaks, CA: Sage Publications.

Nichols, K. (2001) 'Tourism as a Nation Building Tool in the Baltic Republics', *Middle States Geographer*, *34*: 1–9.

Noble, J. (1994) *Baltic States and Kaliningrad*, Footscray, Victoria, Australia: Lonely Planet Publications.

O'Connor, K. (2006) *Culture and Customs of the Baltic States*, Westport, CT: Greenwood Publishing Group.

Orbasli, A. and Woodward, S. (2009) 'Tourism and Heritage Conversation', in T. Jamal and M. Robinson (eds) *The Sage Handbook of Tourism Studies*, London: Sage Publications.

Richter, L.K. (2002) 'The Politics of Heritage Tourism Development: Emerging Issues for the New Millennium', in D. Pearce (ed.) *Contemporary Issues in Tourism Development*, London: Routledge.

Saarinen, J. and Kask, T. (2008) 'Transforming Tourism Spaces in Changing Socio-political Contexts: The Case of Parnu, Estonia, as a Tourist Destination', *Tourism Geographies*, *10*(4): 452–473.

Sharpley, R. and Stone, P.R. (eds) (2009) *The Darker Side of Travel: The Theory and Practice of Dark Tourism*, Bristol: Channel View Publications.

Shaw, D. (1991) *Tourism & Economic Development*, London: Belhaven Press.

Siverson, R.M., Groth, A.J. and Blumberg, M. (1980) 'Soviet Tourism and Detente: 1958–1977', *Studies in Comparative Communism*, *13*(4): 356–368.

Soviet Life (1979) 'Special Issue: Estonia Today', O.P. Benyukh (Editor in Chief), *7*(274), Washington: Embassy of the Union of Soviet Socialist Republics.

Soviet Life (1980) 'The Baltic Republics: Forty Years of Soviet Power', O.P. Benyukh (Editor in Chief), *8*(287), Washington: Embassy of the Union of Soviet Socialist Republics.

Szondi, G. (2007) 'The Role and Challenges of Country Branding in Transition Countries: The Central and Eastern European Experience', *Place Branding and Public Diplomacy*, *3*(1): 8–20.

Tourism Estonia (2011) *Soviet and Estonian Military Tours*. Available at http://www.visitestonia.com/en/soviet-military-estonia-tours (accessed 22 September 2011).

Vallen, J.J. and Levinson, C. (1989) 'The New Soviet Tourism', *The Cornell H.R.A Quarterly*, February: 73–79.

Williams, N. and Blond, B. (2006) *Estonia Latvia & Lithuania*, 4th edn, Footscray, Victoria, Australia: Lonely Planet Publications.

Williams, N., Gaudie, R. and Noble, J. (1997) *Estonia Latvia & Lithuania*, Footscray, Victoria, Australia: Lonely Planet Publications.

Williams, N., Hermann, D. and Kemp, C. (2000) *Estonia Latvia & Lithuania*, 2nd edn, Footscray, Victoria, Australia: Lonely Planet Publications.

Worthington, B. (2001) 'Riding the "J" Curve: Tourism and Successful Transition in Estonia', *Post-Communist Economies*, *13*(3): 389–400.

9 Turning the negative around
The case of Taupo, New Zealand

Alex Morales

Introduction

Dark tourism is a subject that has caught the interest of scholars for the past two decades. Lennon and Foley (2000) explored this area in their book, providing a stepping stone for other academics interested in this topic. In New Zealand, the subject has not been studied in detail yet, even though there are many tourist sites that could be considered as places for engaging in dark tourism. Equally, they are places that have shaped the community and New Zealand's identity. Taupo is an example of this, since the community's identity has been re-shaped by the events that took place in January 2008, when Scottish backpacker Karen Aim was murdered near a local school in this vibrant tourist destination. This not only changed the small town, it also had an impact in New Zealand as a country, as it attracted the attention of the international media who promptly reported every update of this tragic case.

This case study will look at the media representations of this violent crime in New Zealand, and will illustrate how a small community has interpreted and managed a violent event. In this particular case, the community came together and showed respect regarding the loss of a precious life, and worked together to help prevent crimes of this nature from occurring in the future. This chapter outlines the circumstances of how Karen Aim died while visiting New Zealand, from the moment it happened until the time her killer was caught. The chapter also explores how the small community of Taupo reacted to this atrocity and how they vowed to never forget, as the incident left a permanent imprint on the identity of the small town and indeed, the nation.

The role of the media in forming perceptions of a tourist destination

As this case study looks at the media portrayal of a dark event, it is important to look at the impact of the media in forming or re-shaping tourists' perceptions of a destination. According to Nielsen (2001), a negative media event occurs when the mass media is communicating bad news, threats, irritations or other matters that can be seen as unfavourable for the audience. (Mass media refers to all media technologies that are intended to reach a large audience via mass communication.

This chapter is informed using Internet media primarily, and secondarily using printed media.) A significant issue concerning the way media outlets communicate is their reliability; it is always questionable as their reports may or may not be true, and even if 'true', the reporting can be biased (Hall and O'Sullivan 1996). Hall, Timothy and Duval (2003) expressed that tourism is irrevocably bound up with the concept of security; consequently, tourists' behaviour and destinations are deeply affected by perceptions of safety, security and risk (Hall *et al.* 2003). Incidents portrayed in the media regarding crime around the world create a sense that criminal activity cannot be controlled, which causes a generalized fear of crime; this idea was named collective security (Hall *et al.* 2003). As broadcast and printed media compete for higher ratings, reporting incidents of crime with a 'shock factor' seems to be the norm nowadays. People are de-sensitized and are not afraid to look at grim images in news reports. As the use of portable technology increases (i.e., cell phones, tablets, notebooks) and the dissemination of information becomes instant, it has a significant impact on how we perceive the world; it is evident that the power of the media is clearly critical in influencing both tourist and political reactions to security issues (Hall and O'Sullivan 1996; Carter 1998). Similarly, Nielsen (2001) points out that it does not make any difference if the report is based on actual facts. The end result is that people feel shocked or afraid and their degree of scepticism increases and is reflected in their decision making.

In 1990, Lombardi suggested that through communication in the media, and through real experience, an image of a destination is (re)created in the minds of visitors after an event has occurred. Echtner and Ritchie (1991) suggested that a human act or a natural catastrophe can transform the reputation, image and marketability of the most popular tourism destinations overnight. The murder of Karen Aim in Taupo, New Zealand resulted in a tsunami of overseas attention. Her attack was so vicious that when the police arrived they found her barely conscious, but she was able to tell them her name. The details of her attack were reported in the British media and in Scotland in particular.

Silverstone (1999) suggested that by understanding the media's role, a link can be drawn to the issues concerned with tourists' motivation and how expectations are related to the tourists' decisions. On the same line of thought, Beirman (2003) proposed that the role of effective media communication is critical for tourist authorities in democratic countries where the media's role is to inform the general public. The concept of freedom of the press in these countries means that public relations management is an important communications tool for tourism operators because they have an obligation to report on recovery and restoration efforts (Beirman 2003). These efforts promote a sense of trust, as the community recognizes that after something bad has happened everyone knows what to do and how to react, in order to reassure potential visitors that even though something negative has occured, they are capable of dealing with and recovering from it. As it happened in Taupo, the community's response was to provide strong support for Karen's family as well as helping the police to find the perpetrator. This will be explored in more detail later on in this chapter.

In world standards, New Zealand has a small proportion of tourists that fall victim to crime. In 2008, former CEO of Tourism New Zealand, George Hickton expressed:

> crime occurs, and regrettably sometimes that crime will affect tourists who visit New Zealand, but it should be kept in the context that millions of tourists visit New Zealand each year and go home safely and experience a trip without incident.
>
> (*Waikato Times* 2008)

While some high-profile crimes against tourists have been undeniably shocking, the risk to visitors is put into perspective by the sheer number of tourists coming to New Zealand, with almost 2.6 million international arrivals as of May 2012 (Ministry of Economic Development 2012). But, if such a small proportion of tourists actually fall victim to crime, why is it such a big story when they do?

Four days after Karen Aim's murder in January 2008, Chattrice Maihi-Carrolls, a 43-year-old New Zealander and a mother of five, died of stab wounds at her home in Napier (*Waikato Times* 2008). The crime received little attention and police said they were surprised at how little public response there was. Media commentator Jim Tully (2008) said there is "no doubt" that a crime of violence, and even minor theft, against tourists attracts stronger media coverage than non-tourists. Tully said, "I suspect attacks on tourists contradict our view of ourselves as friendly, welcoming, easy-going people... [and], often, there is a strong human interest dimension because of their circumstances and the impact on their families" (*Waikato Times* 2008).

In 2003, a New Zealand Department of Courts survey (Morris *et al.* 2003) showed that the public believed that violent crime made up about two-thirds of all reported crime – when it actually represented about 9 per cent. All of those surveyed thought crime was on the increase, when the opposite was the case. This shows that disproportionate media coverage impacts upon the perception of crime and opens a wide gap between reality and perception, as well as raising questions about how we bridge the gap.

The role of the media is pivotal in shaping perceptions about crime – and it is useful to compare how printed media in different countries treat notorious crimes, for example, tourists killed while on holiday. By understanding how events like this are portrayed in other countries, it is possible to anticipate the possible impacts and to try to understand if potential visitors to New Zealand might be influenced by these types of reports. Lexow and Edelheim (2004) defined the media as a third party that tourists are likely to trust, and they are therefore influenced by the media in their decision-making process. They concluded that tourists have different perceptions of motivational factors, and this conclusion supports the idea that the media plays a paramount role in travel behaviour because it influences tourists' decisions. They also recognize that further research is needed to establish the extent to which the tourism experience is shaped by the media.

Tourism and crime

Safety, tranquillity and peace are necessary conditions for prosperous tourism (Pizam and Mansfield 1996). Pizam and Mansfield stated that as leisure is a discretionary activity, most tourists will not spend their money to go to a destination where their safety may be in jeopardy. The occurrence of crime against tourists has been recognized slowly in the tourism literature (Jud 1975; Newman 2000; Pizam 1982; Pizam and Mansfield 1996). There is increasing evidence to suggest that where crime, safety and security concerns are evident, travellers postpone or cancel their travel plans (Edgell 1990; WTO 1996; Goodrich 2002). Where travel continues, tourists often modify their behaviour within the destination in response to risk, to the point where their travel experience can be significantly impaired (Edgell 1990). Increased crime can generate national and international interest. In particular, with crimes against international tourists, coverage of these acts in their home countries can be continuous, and in some cases extreme. According to Dimanche and Lepetic (1999), adverse media coverage and the public's perception of personal safety will have a significant and lasting effect on the decision to travel to a particular destination.

Given the significant contribution that tourism makes to New Zealand's economy (Ministry of Economic Development 2012), it is important that the information disseminated to tourists, in relation to their safety, is updated and accurately portrays the level of risk they may face without sensationalizing or scaring potential visitors. The rising evidence of the impacts of crime related to tourism on destinations has become acknowledged as an inevitable dilemma, and efforts towards prevention have been and are being addressed. In 1990, the Hague Declaration on Tourism stated that in order for tourism to flourish and develop, it required safety for all visitors and their personal property; as well as safety and protection of tourist sites and facilities (Edgell 1990: 190). For some tourist destinations, it is hard to fulfil the promise of a safe visit, but this provides the guidelines to start managing risks and decrease cases where tourists are victimized. In the case of New Zealand, which is seen as a relatively 'safe' destination, these principles can help ensure that this 'safe' image is maintained and not jeopardized by incidents of crime against international tourists.

Crime in New Zealand

New Zealand spends millions of dollars cultivating an international image as clean, green and safe. Such is the portrayal of New Zealand as a paradise in the long running marketing campaign '100% Pure New Zealand', which now has added the twist of '100% Pure You', but as the *Waikato Times* expressed, "having visitors beaten, raped and murdered is not exactly '100% Pure'" (*Waikato Times* 2008).

The publicity generated due to these attacks had the potential to damage New Zealand's reputation internationally. Paradoxically, New Zealand is one of the safest places in the world, according to the Global Peace Index (2010/2011). This is perhaps one of the reasons why it is big news when a tourist is victimized in

New Zealand, which may feed the perception that it is a potentially unsafe place. In March 2010 the New Zealand Institute, who describe themselves as "a non-partisan think-tank committed to generating innovative ideas to improve social, economic, and environmental outcomes for New Zealand" (NZI 2010), published the report *NZahead*, a type of report card that "seeks to arm New Zealanders with a big picture view of our overall, long-term performance" (NZI 2010: 1). The NZI used 16 measures from the social, environmental and economic dimensions to provide a balanced and comparative view of all strengths and weaknesses, opportunities and threats. According to the report, a country with high incidences of violence is more likely to have a high assault rate.

Tourism New Zealand (TNZ) annual Visitor Experience Monitor Research looks at international visitors' satisfaction levels. It surveys the seven key markets (Australia, the UK, US, Japan, South Korea, China and Germany), and it is broken down into seven areas: accommodation; food and beverage; internal transport; activities; i-SITE centres, which provide information to visitors face to face; environment; and safety. In November 2010 TNZ reported that the overall satisfaction with safety in New Zealand was again high in 2009/10, with international visitors scoring it 8.8 out of a possible 10. Safety was among the most satisfying aspects of a New Zealand holiday.

In 2009, a New Zealand Department of Conservation (NZDOC) survey sent to international visitors revealed that although international visitors were not concerned about their safety when visiting New Zealand, they suffered graver consequences than the domestic visitors, as they tended to lose everything. This could be another reason why these events make international headlines, as international visitors tend to be more vulnerable and in need of more support in order to recover. The survey identified vehicle crime in car parks at outdoor recreation and tourist destinations as a problem for New Zealand's visitors and destination managers. It was reported that currently no public agencies are fully addressing the problem, and that the impact of this type of crime is poorly understood. The NZDOC study illustrates the vision and strategies the New Zealand tourism industry could focus on. When information is disseminated and shared in a sensible way, aiming to inform rather than scare, it provides a wealth of material for future tourists to prepare and be up to date while being in New Zealand.

One more approach worth looking at is the Māori over-representation within the New Zealand Justice System. Owing to the fact that the perpetrator of this case study is identified as Māori, it is imperative to look at the Māori population and its social issues. A report by the New Zealand Corrections Department (2007) proposed that there is no reason to believe being Māori causes criminal behaviour; unquestionably, criminal behaviour is associated with risk factors other than ethnicity, such as lack of educational achievement, unemployment, poor health, low socio-economic status, a dysfunctional family and a negative peer environment. This report also points out that Māori are over-represented in the risk factors that contribute to criminal behaviour, hence are over-represented in crime statistics. Roughly half of all the justice offenders and victims identify as Māori (Statistics New Zealand 2009), a proportion far greater than would be expected for the size of the population. About 14 per cent of New Zealand's population identify themselves as Māori. Later in this chapter the details of the perpetrator's circumstances will be discussed.

Dark tourism: the accidental place of remembrance

Part of human nature appears to involve being fascinated by the concept of death, through a combination of reverence or morbid curiosity and superstition. Stone's (2006) ideas about the complexities of defining dark tourism include two propositions that are relevant to this chapter: a) the distinction between purposefully constructed sites, attractions or exhibitions, that interpret or recreate events or acts associated with death, and the macabre and so-called 'accidental' or non-purposeful sites. That is, those sites, such as cemeteries, memorials or disaster sites that have become tourist attractions 'by accident' because of their relationship with turbulent and tragic events; and b) the fundamental reasons why and how dark sites/experiences are produced or supplied – for example, political reasons, for remembrance purposes, for education, for entertainment or for economic gain. The core of Stone's ideas are relevant to the circumstances of a tragic incident that occurred in Taupo and generated a sequence of events that created a new phase for the town and for its people. This event created an 'accidental' site of remembrance where the town was brought together. Lennon (2010) suggested that sites linked with death tend to exert a dark fascination for visitors and are often linked to crime locations and the perpetration of lawful and unlawful acts. He suggests that "dark tourism sites can create policy dilemmas for civic and local authorities as these locations have an ability to generate headlines, media coverage and visitation" (Lennon 2010: 220).

This case study is about the tragic murder of Karen Aim; it is based on information found in national newspapers in their online format, as well as some international online newspapers and web logs, in order to understand how an atrocity like Karen's murder can affect and re-shape a small town, and indeed a nation.

Taupo and Karen Aim

Taupo is a popular resort town located at the outlet of Lake Taupo, New Zealand's largest lake; it has a population of 32,418 (Statistics New Zealand 2006); 8,643 people of the total population identify themselves as Māori (Statistics New Zealand 2006). Taupo is situated in the central North Island, midway between Auckland and Wellington. It is four hours by road from Auckland and five hours from Wellington. As a tourist destination, Taupo offers activities such as fishing, boating, walking, white-water rafting and jet boating.

Karen Aim arrived in Taupo to work in a local art business for a couple of months; she made friends and quickly became an active member of the small community. She was a 26-year-old Scottish backpacker travelling around New Zealand on a holiday working visa. On 17 January 2008, after a night out with friends, she decided to walk back to her apartment alone, in the early hours of the morning. The last sighting of her was from a dairy's camera footage, when she waved goodbye to her friends. On her way back, she walked past a local college, where a disturbance was taking place. When police officers arrived at the scene and discovered her on the road nearby, she was still conscious and managed to give her name. Karen died later in hospital. A few months later a 15-year-old was apprehended and charged with her murder. He was sentenced to life in prison.

The media in New Zealand followed the case closely, reporting the developments of the case in detail and encouraging people to help the police find the perpetrator(s). The British media followed the case closely, with reports titled 'Last Steps of Briton Murdered in New Zealand' (*Telegraph* 2008), 'New Pictures Show Final Moments of British Woman Bludgeoned to Death in New Zealand' (Mail Online 2008) and 'Karen Aim Murder: Funeral for Backpacker Killed in New Zealand' (Sky News 2008). The national media was focused on reporting the progress of the investigation, of finding the perpetrator, encouraging possible witnesses to come forward; as well as reporting on how the town was coping with the incident. National reports were published, with titles such as 'Judge Dismisses Broughton's Story as He Gives Life Sentence for Karen Aim Murder' and 'Karen Aim's Father Will Fight Any Parole Bid by Jahche Broughton' (3news.co.nz reports 2009). Not much was published about the young man's background, apart from mentioning that he was raised by his religious grandparents in Taupo, and that he considered himself to be a ladies' man; he also fancied the gangster look, smoked marijuana and drank alcohol (Eriksen and Rowan 2009). A cousin Broughton had talked to about killing Karen told the police that he had a "mean temper" and that he was quite big; the cousin also spoke about Broughton's plan of disposing of Karen's body by throwing her into the Waikato River, but as there was too much traffic around he decided to leave her where the attack took place (Eriksen and Rowan 2009). On 5 February 2009, Broughton confessed to murdering Miss Aim; he had been due to go on trial in the High Court at Rotorua on 9 February 2009. He also pleaded guilty to one count of wounding with intent to cause grievous bodily harm to another woman, aged 17, in Taupo on 5 January 2008 (*New Zealand Herald* 2009a). Thanks to his confession his family was spared having to sit through the expected four to five week trial. The family arrived that same week, to attend the trial; they decided to stay for Broughton's sentencing on 6 March 2009. Before confessing, Broughton maintained he was innocent, claiming that a gang member was the real perpetrator.

Karen's case appeared in the media throughout 2008, 2009 and 2010. The focus during 2008 was the reporting of what happened, from the day of the attack to the day the perpetrator was caught; 2009 focused on the court case and the community's involvement and developments of the case. In early 2010 the case was still making headlines when Karen's father was interviewed about New Zealand. He stated that he "didn't hate the place, he hated the killer" (*New Zealand Herald* 2010). Brian Aim also expressed gratitude to the New Zealand people and government for all the support his family had received. In 2011 the *Dominion Post* featured an article titled 'Motive still mystery for murdered tourist's dad' (Watson 2011). It recounted the case and quoted Karen's father on how he was resigned to never knowing why his only daughter was killed, as well as how he agreed with the coroner Wallace Bain on his conclusion on the inquest into Karen's killing; the coroner's judgment was that a lack of supervision by Broughton's parents had contributed to her murder. That same year the *Scotsman* online paper reported about the inquest too; interestingly, no more was mentioned about the inquest in the New Zealand media. In 2012, the *Daily Record* paper in Britain reported that "Family of New Zealand Murder Victim Karen Aim Will Demand Killer Stays in Prison" (Barry 2012); it reported that Brian Aim would send a letter to the parole board to request that his daughter's killer remain in prison for the rest of his life.

The national media played a pivotal role in the development of this case, how it was handled by the police and how the community reacted to it. It showed that a small community can and should aim to work together to recover from the attention a negative event can bring to it. Events like Karen's murder can re-shape the image of a small community such as Taupo, a town that prides itself on being one of New Zealand's top tourist destinations. The town relies on visitors, but being a dangerous place where a tourist could be killed is not the image it wants to portray to the world. After Karen was murdered, a memorial service took place on 29 January 2008, followed by the establishment of the Karen Aim Memorial Working Group. The first initiative of this group was to collect enough money to send a close friend to Scotland to take her body back to her family, as well as presenting a book of condolences that was made available in town for a few days so the community could express their feelings of sympathy for Karen's parents. In addition, Taupo mayor Rick Cooper encouraged members of the community to sign the book and make a donation to the fund. He asked all of the caring people of the Taupo community to come along to this memorial service or sign the book of condolence to pay respect to Karen and show support for her family. The rest of the money was used for a permanent memorial for Karen, within the Taupo township. The memorial was unveiled on 1 March 2009, as a wooden seat placed at the location where she liked to visit and admire the view of Lake Taupo. The seat features an engraved plaque with her name and nickname 'Our Peedie Buddo'. Her parents and brother came to New Zealand for the memorial unveiling, and after the ceremony they were presented with a painting of Karen. The memorial is a constant reminder of a life taken, and it aimed to ensure that the people of Taupo will not forget what happened to Karen Aim. The media reported that the Aim family stayed in New Zealand for a month. They expressed that they wanted to visit where Karen died and thus have some closure on the horrendous event. The Aim family also said that they were overwhelmed by the kindness New Zealanders had shown them following the tragic death of their daughter.

One more way in which the Working Group used the money donated was by initiating two youth art scholarships (Taupo District Council 2008). In 2008 the spokesperson of the Working Group, Reverend John Howell said:

> We hope Karen's memory will live on through art and in the development of young people who may make a creative contribution to our humanity. We also

hope the Taupo community will honour Karen's memory by committing to living without violence and to work to make our town a safer place.

(Taupo District Council 2008)

The scholarships were granted to two art students pursuing education at a tertiary institution. The students were asked to produce a piece of art suitable for display in a public space – either in Taupo or in the Orkneys, Scotland, where Karen came from – before graduating from their tertiary study. By the end of 2008 the Working Group had secured funding for another three years, and was planning on securing more funds for the future. The main donations came from the public, Creative Arts Taupo, Craters of the Moon Trust, Rotary Club of Taupo and Mayor Rick Cooper.

An online tribute was set up for Karen Aim on the Respectance.com page. This online tribute and memorial website provided a tool for all the people who knew Karen to leave a message, especially for people that were not able to travel to New Zealand to say farewell to her. This website still exists and people can and do still leave messages. One message reads:

Although we did not know Karen personally, we are fellow Orcadians having a holiday in New Zealand and felt compelled to visit the seat by the Lake dedicated to her memory, drive by the school where she so tragically was murdered and visit Lava Glass where she worked. The owners of the campsite where we are staying kindly pointed us in the right direction and told us that Karen was admired by the whole community here in Lake Taupo and is very much missed. She was just trying to be a good citizen on that fateful night.

(Talpa 2008)

Messages like this show that the memorial site provides a virtual place for people to mourn.

Conclusion

Gibson (2006) noted that criminal activity, and particularly murder, in any place is a serious concern and in general it will cause business to reduce due to fears of personal safety. Lennon (2010) argued that crimes that demonstrate the darker side of human nature can similarly stimulate increased visitation. He also stated that such sites represent the record, the context and, in some cases, the evidence of crime. "Their conservation, educational potential and dark appeal deserves comprehension and a voice" (Lennon 2010: 226).

Karen Aim's family and the local community in Taupo were left with unanswered questions when Karen Aim was murdered: Why did the perpetrator commit the crime? Did Karen suffer? This murder left the community mourning a tragedy that marked the town deeply, and the sense of sympathy and regret brought the small town together to try to make sense of the horrific situation. The Taupo community managed to work together to prove to the world that their small town was not a dangerous place. They wanted to portray an image that friendly and caring people lived there, and show that they were deeply sorry about the dark event that had taken place. The community wanted to repair their positive tourist image because they truly felt the blow of losing a young visitor in such a devastating way. Consequently, they created a place to remember, a place to be able to look at and think 'never again', a place to show support and respect for the loss of a beloved daughter and sister.

This case also raised the issue of visitors' taking risks while visiting New Zealand. It added another case to the statistics of Māori committing crime, as well as underlining the social issues that are deeply engraved in today's society in New Zealand: the unspoken truth about broken families, family violence and youth problems, which are all roots of the country's issues. At the end of the day, in order to provide a safe environment for visitors, whether domestic or international, families have to feel safe and secure within their own environment.

Gathering the lessons learnt from Karen's murder, this chapter acknowledges that from that day, the city of Taupo was forever linked to Scotland, in debt for having taken one of its daughters. Although Karen's family and fellow countrymen lost someone in the most tragic way, they still believe New Zealand to be a beautiful place worth visiting; not only for what the community and the country did for the family and for finding her killer, but mainly because Karen herself loved New Zealand so much.

References

3news.co.nz (2009a) 'Judge Dismisses Broughton's Story as He Gives Life Sentence for Karen Aim Murder', 3News. Available at http://www.3news.co.nz/Judge-dismisses-Broughtons-story-as-he-gives-life-sentence-for-Karen-Aim-murder/tabid/423/articleID/97253/Default.aspx#ixzz1qej3KCi7 (accessed 15 January 2012).

3news.co.nz (2009b) 'Karen Aim's Father Will Fight Any Parole Bid by Jahche Broughton', 3News. Available at http://www.3news.co.nz/Karen-Aims-father-will-fight-any-parole-bid-by-Jahche-Broughton/tabid/423/articleID/97825/Default.aspx#ixzz1qeiruqoB (accessed 16 December 2012).

3news.co.nz (2009c) 'Memorial Unveiled for Murdered Backpacker Karen Aim', 3News. Available at http://www.3news.co.nz/Memorial-unveiled-for-murdered-backpacker-Karen-Aim/tabid/423/articleID/93377/Default.aspx (accessed 5 June 2012).

Barry, M. (2012) 'Family of New Zealand Murder Victim Karen Aim Will Demand Killer Stays in Prison', *Daily Record* UK. Available at http://www.dailyrecord.co.uk/news/uk-world-news/2012/01/22/family-of-new-zealand-murder-victim-karen-aim-will-demand-killer-stays-in-prison-86908-23712588/ (accessed 18 May 2012).

Beirman, D. (2003) *Restoring Tourism Destinations in Crisis: A Strategic Marketing Approach*, Wallingford: CABI.

Carter, S. (1998) 'Tourists' and Travellers' Social Construction of Africa and Asia as Risky Locations', *Tourism Management, 19*(4):349–458.

Dimanche, F. and Lepetic, A. (1999) 'New Orleans Tourism and Crime: A Case Study', *Journal of Travel Research, 38*(1):19–23.

Echtner, C.M. and Ritchie, J.R.B. (1991) 'The Measurement of Destination Image: An Empirical Assessment', *Journal of Travel Research, 31*:3–13.

Edgell Sr., D.L. (1990) *International Tourism Policy*, New York: Van Nostrand Reinhold.

Eisler, R. (2007) 'Dark Underbelly of the World's Most "Peaceful" Countries', *Christian Science Monitor*. Available at http://www.csmonitor.com/2007/0726/p09s01-coop.htm. (accessed 6 January 2011).

Eriksen, A. and Rowan, J. (2009) 'Karen Aim's Killer Fancied Gold Chains and Bling Earrings', *New Zealand Herald*. Available at http://www.nzherald.co.nz/nz/news/article.cfm?c_id=1&objectid=10555446 (accessed 5 May 2011).

Gibson, D.C. (2006) 'The Relationship Between Serial Murder and the American Tourism Industry', *Journal of Travel and Tourism Marketing*, 20(1):45–60.

Global Peace Index (2010) 'Methodology, Results and Findings for Institute from Economics and Peace', Australia: Vision for Humanity. Available at http://www.visionforhumanity.org (accessed May 2011).

Goodrich, J.N. (2002) 'September 11, 2001 Attack on America: A Record of the Immediate Impacts and Reactions in the USA Travel and Tourism Industry', *Tourism Management*, 23: 573–580.

Hall, C.M. and O'Sullivan, V. (1996) 'Tourism, Political Stability and Violence', in A. Pizam and Y. Mansfeld (eds) *Tourism, Crime and International Security Issues*, New York, Wiley, pp. 105–121.

Hall, C.M., Timothy, D.J. and Duval, D.T. (eds) (2003) *Safety and Security in Tourism: Relationships, Management, and Marketing*, Binghamton, NY: Haworth Hospitality Press.

Jud, G.D. (1975) 'Tourism and Crime in Mexico', *Social Science Quarterly*, 56: 342–330.

Lennon, J. (2010) 'Dark Tourism and Sites of Crime', in D. Botterill and T. Jones (eds) *Tourism and Crime*, Oxford: Goodfellow Publishers.

Lennon, J. and Foley, M. (2000) *Dark Tourism: The Attraction of Death and Disaster*, London: Continuum.

Lexow, M. and Edelheim, J.R. (2004) 'Effects of Negative Media Events on Tourists' Decisions', in W. Frost, G. Croy and S. Beeton (eds) *Proceedings of International Tourism and Media Conference, Tourism Research Unit*, Melbourne: Monash University, pp. 51–60.

Lombardi, R. (1990) 'Communicating with the Public about Major Accidents Hazards', in H. Gow and H. Otway (eds) *Report: Commission of the E.C.*, London: Elsevier Science.

Mail Online (2008) 'New Pictures Show Final Moments of British Woman Bludgeoned to Death in New Zealand'. Available at http://www.dailymail.co.uk/news/article-509040/New-pictures-final-moments-British-woman-bludgeoned-death-New-Zealand.html (accessed 6 February 2012).

Mansfeld, Y. (1999) 'Cycles of War, Terror, and Peace: Determinants and Management of Crisis and Recovery of the Israeli Tourism Industry', *Journal of Travel Research, Past Ethnic Conflict*, 38: 30–36.

Ministry of Economic Development (2012) *Key Tourism Statistics*. Available at http://www.med.govt.nz/sectors-industries/tourism/pdf-docs-library/key-tourism-statistics/key-tourism-statistics.pdf (accessed 2 May 2012).

Morris, A., Reilly, J., Berry, S. and Ransom, R. (2003) *The New Zealand National Survey of Crime Victims 2001*, Wellington: Ministry of Justice.

New Zealand Department of Conservation (2009) *Vehicle Crime at Outdoor Recreation and Tourist Destinations: Prevalence, Impact and Solutions*. Available at http://www.doc.govt.nz/documents/science-and-technical/sfc298.pdf (accessed 9 October 2010).

New Zealand Department of Corrections (2007) *Over-representation of Maori in the Criminal Justice System: An Exploratory Report*. Available at http://www.corrections.govt.nz/_data/assets/pdf_file/0004/285286/Over-representation-of-Maori-in-the-criminal-justice-system.pdf (accessed 10 May 2012).

New Zealand Herald (2008) 'Big Turnouts Expected at Memorial Services', New Zealand Herald Online. Available at http://www.nzherald.co.nz/nz/news/article.cfm?c_id=1&objectid=10489251 (accessed 18 May 2012).

New Zealand Herald (2009a) 'Karen Aim's Parents Relieved Boy, 15, Admits Murder', New Zealand Herald Online. Available at http://www.nzherald.co.nz/nz/news/article.cfm?c_id=1&objectid=10555298 (accessed 15 January 2012).

New Zealand Herald (2009b) 'Karen Aim's Killer Fancied Gold Chains and Bling Earrings', New Zealand Herald Online. Available at http://www.nzherald.co.nz/nz/news/article.cfm?c_id=1&objectid=10555446 (accessed 4 February 2012).

New Zealand Herald (2009c) 'Karen Aim Memorial Unveiled in Taupo', New Zealand Herald Online. Available at http://www.nzherald.co.nz/nz/news/article.cfm?c_id=1&objectid=10559468 (accessed 7 May 2012).

New Zealand Herald (2009d) 'Parents of Slain Tourist and Accused Teen to Meet', New Zealand Herald Online. Available at http://www.nzherald.co.nz (accessed 10 January 2012).

New Zealand Herald (2009e) 'Teen's Guilty Plea to Killing Scottish Tourist to Stand', New Zealand Herald Online. Available at http://www.nzherald.co.nz/nz/news/article.cfm?c_id=1&objectid=10560032 (accessed 6 January 2012).

New Zealand Herald (2009f) 'Tourist Karen Aim's Killer Sentenced Today', New Zealand Herald Online. Available at http://www.nzherald.co.nz/nz/news/article.cfm?c_id=1&objectid=10563622 (accessed 6 January 2012).

New Zealand Herald (2010) 'I Hate the Killer, not the Country, says Karen's Dad', March 28. Available at http://www.nzherald.co.nz/nz/news/article.cfm?c_id=1&objectid=10634801 (accessed 11 May 2012).

New Zealand Institute (2010) *NZahead Report Card*. Available at http://www.nzinstitute.org/index.php/nzahead/ (accessed 2 February 2011).

Newman, H. (2000) 'Hospitality and Violence: Contradictions in a Southern City', *Urban Affairs Review*, 35(4): 541–558.

Nielsen, C. (2001) *Tourism and the Media*, Sidney: Hospitality Press Pty Ltd.

Pizam, A. (1982) 'Tourism and Crime: Is There a Relationship?' *Journal of Travel Research*, 20: 7–10.

Pizam, A. (1999) 'A Comprehensive Approach to Classifying Acts of Crime and Violence at Tourism Destinations', *Journal of Travel Research*, 38: 5–12.

Pizam, A. and Mansfeld, Y. (eds) (1996) *Tourism, Crime and International Security Issues*, Chichester and New York: Wiley.

Pizam, A., Tarlow, P. and Bloom, J. (1997) 'Making Tourists Feel Safe: Whose Responsibility Is It?' *Journal of Travel Research*, 36 (1): 23–28.

Richter, L.K. and Waugh W.L., Jr. (1986) 'Terrorism and Tourism as Logical Companions', *Tourism Management*, 7(4): 230–238.

Silverstone, R. (1999) *Why study The Media?* London: Sage Publication.

Sky News (2008) 'Karen Aim Murder: Funeral for Backpacker Killed in New Zealand'. Available at http://news.sky.com/story/569062/karen-aim-murder-funeral-for-backpacker-killed-in-new-zealand (accessed 6 February 2012).

Statistics New Zealand (2006) 'Quickstats about Taupo'. Available at http://www.stats.govt.nz/Census/2006CensusHomePage/QuickStats/AboutAPlace/SnapShot.aspx?id=2000021&type=ta&ParentID=1000008&p=y&printall=true (accessed 17 May 2012).

Statistics New Zealand (2009) 'Review of Crime and Criminal Justice Statistics Report 2009'. Available at http://www.stats.govt.nz/~/media/Statistics/browse-categories/

people-and-communities/crime-justice/review-crime-criminal-justice-statistics/rccjs-report-2009.pdf (accessed 17 May 2012).

Stone, P.R. (2006) 'A Dark Tourism Spectrum: Towards a Typology of Death and Macabre Related Tourist Sites, Attractions and Exhibitions', *Tourism: An Interdisciplinary International Journal*, 52(2): 145–160.

Talpa, M. (2008) 'Karen Aim Tribute'. Available at http://www.respectance.com/KarenAim/ (accessed 15 December 2011).

Taupo District Council (2008) 'Book of Condolence for Karen Aim'. Available at http://www.infonews.co.nz/news.cfm?l=1&t=0&id=13032 (accessed 18 May 2012).

Telegraph (2008) 'Last Steps of Briton Murdered in New Zealand'. Available at http://www.telegraph.co.uk/news/worldnews/1575949/Last-steps-of-Briton-murdered-in-New-Zealand.html (accessed 5 May 2011).

Tourism New Zealand (2010) 'Visitor Experience Monitor Research – Safety'. Available at http://www.tourismnewzealand.com/markets-and-stats/other-research/visitor-experience-monitor/ (accessed 18 January 2012).

Tully, J. (2008) 'A History of Broadcasting in New Zealand', in J. Tully (ed.) *Intro: A Beginner's Guide to Professional News Journalism*, Wellington: New Zealand Journalists Training Organisation, pp. 371–382.

Waikato Times (2008) 'Trouble in Paradise'. Available at http://www.stuff.co.nz/waikato-times/life-style/247811/Trouble-in-paradise (accessed 6 February 2012).

Watson, M. (2011) 'Motive Still Mystery for Murdered Tourist's Dad', Stuff.co.nz. Available at http://www.stuff.co.nz/dominion-post/news/6058320/Motive-still-mystery-for-murdered-tourists-dad (accessed 18 May 2012).

World Tourism Organization (1996) *Tourist Safety and Security: Practical Measures for Destinations*, Madrid: World Tourism Organization.

10 Commemorating and commodifying the Rwandan genocide

Memorial sites in a politically difficult context

Peter Hohenhaus

Introduction

Contemporary Rwanda's identity is largely determined by two aspects: mountain gorillas and the 1994 genocide. This is particularly true from a tourism perspective. Most foreign visitors to the country go there almost solely to see the gorillas, which is thus the country's main source of tourism revenue. Arguably there is even a dark element in mountain gorilla tracking, inasmuch as these close relatives to humans are among the most endangered species on Earth. Furthermore, the grave of Dian Fossey (of *Gorillas in the Mist* fame) at her former research station in the mountains, where she was murdered, has become an associated pilgrimage destination.

However, many tourists also take in at least one of the genocide memorials while in Rwanda, in particular the Gisozi Centre in the capital Kigali, whereas the more demanding rural sites are less frequently visited. Going to these constitutes the very darkest kind of dark tourism. All these memorials showcase how place identity shapes site management – at least at the premier 'national' memorials. Here, recent developments have resulted in a more standardized, streamlined commodification. This remains surrounded by controversy, however, both with regard to the nature of the memorials and from a political perspective. Place identity, it will be argued here, is crucial in this context both for local 'sited-ness' and the greater 'national identity' as well as for the experiences foreign tourists have at these places.

Historical background: the 1994 Rwandan genocide

There are numerous comprehensive accounts of the Rwandan genocide, such as Gourevitch (1998), Prunier (1995/1997), Melvern (2000) and Dallaire (2004) to name a few. Those wishing to try to better understand the whole context of the Rwandan genocide are referred to works such as these. Here, only the briefest of summaries of the background can be provided.

The ethnic/political roots of the conflict have a long history. The Tutsi group, as cattle herders, traditionally enjoyed a greater socio-economic status over the farming Hutu majority. This was reflected in a political system exploited and reinforced by the arriving colonial powers. The actual ethnic distinctions had already become rather blurred after centuries of intermarriage. However, in the eugenics-inspired 'race craze' of the first few decades of the twentieth century the Tutsi–Hutu divide became institutionalized when the Belgian 'masters' introduced the system of identity cards that had to specify ethnicity for each Rwandan citizen. This would later prove a crucial element in the genocide, since without these cards the selection of Tutsi could not have worked the way it did.

Towards the end of their colonial rule, the Belgians, in an ill-devised attempt at providing for 'majority rule', turned the old system on its head and installed Hutu leaders in positions of power instead of Tutsi, which in turn alienated the latter. When Rwanda was finally released into independence in 1962 it found itself in an extremely volatile socio-political situation. From 1959, there had already been violent clashes, and large numbers of Tutsi fled into exile in the northern neighbour Uganda. It was there that the rebel army of the Rwandan Patriotic Front (RPF) formed. At the beginning of the 1990s, insurgent activities of the RPF in the north of Rwanda increased while at the same time similar ethnic clashes between Hutu and Tutsi repeatedly erupted in the southern neighbour Burundi. In Rwanda the regime of President Habyarimana was coerced into the Arusha Accords – a peacekeeping effort that also provided for the stationing of a United Nations (UN) contingent in the country. Fearing political losses, extremist Hutu organizations stepped up their openly racist anti-Tutsi propaganda – while in the background full-scale genocide was already being meticulously prepared.

The incident that triggered the eventual outbreak of the genocide came about on 6 April 1994 when Habyarimana's plane was shot down near Kigali airport (to this day it remains unclear who was responsible for this attack). Within hours a well-planned choreography of carnage unfolded: key Tutsi figures as well as moderate Hutu politicians were executed; soldiers and militia began going from house to house rounding up the Tutsi population by means of prepared name-lists, using identity cards as a main selection criterion – and the slaughter commenced. Crucially, ten Belgian UN soldiers were also murdered, a move specifically aimed at triggering a hasty UN withdrawal. Indeed, rather than reinforcing its peacekeeping troops, the UN did mostly withdraw, leaving only a minimal, under-equipped rump force on the ground, too powerless to intervene in the systematic massacres that were now spreading across the country.

In addition to Hutu government soldiers and the mostly radio-disseminated propaganda, it was the Interahamwe militia that was instrumental in the execution of the genocide, staffing roadblocks, spreading orders and taking the lead in blood-lust rampages. While the soldiers had guns and grenades, most of the killers used simple clubs and farming tools such as hoes and machetes to literally hack their victims to pieces. Most disturbingly, ordinary Hutu peasants were also coerced into participating. As Diamond (2011: 311–328) points out, another major factor fuelling the violence were disputes over land ownership that had, rather independently from ethnicity, come about through critical overpopulation – and worryingly this is still a massive problem. See also Mironko (2006) for further non-ethnic motives involved in the genocide.

It was the RPF that decided to intervene rather than stand by. A highly trained rebel army, the RPF managed to push out the Hutu forces – alongside a wave of refugees of civilian Hutu, who, fearing reprisals, streamed westwards towards neighbouring Zaire/Congo (where the Hutu extremists are still part of the ongoing conflicts in that battered part of Africa). However, after 100 days of massacres that cost an estimated 800,000 lives the genocide in Rwanda finally ceased.

Aftermath, commemoration, politics and place identity

At the end of the genocide Rwanda was in tatters, its infrastructure largely destroyed and plagued by an ongoing refugee crisis. Yet the economic 'miracle' that the country has since performed is nothing short of astounding: from possibly the poorest country in Africa (or the entire world) in 1994 to an economic powerhouse with the capital city Kigali aspiring to become a kind of African Singapore, a financial and economic hub for the whole East/Central African region.

With regard to commemoration, Rwanda has quickly shown a remarkable willingness to confront its violent past, that is, to engage in the process frequently referred to by the German term *Vergangenheitsbewältigung* or 'coming to terms with the past' (as is the standard, though insufficient, English translation). Of the several organizations that have formed to this end, the Commission Nationale de Lutte contre le Génocide (CNLG), or National Commission for the Fight against Genocide, is taking a lead in the actual management of many of the relevant sites. Furthermore, the UK-based non-governmental organization (NGO) Aegis Trust was invited to participate in the task.

It is beyond this chapter's scope to go into the difficult socio-political or legal issues of rebuilding and ongoing judicial processes. Suffice it to say that the Rwandan state policy of reconciliation involves rather drastic regulations regarding (former) ethnic identities to be replaced by a uniform national identity. Effectively it is "outlawing ethnicity" (Williams 2007: 111). The former identity card system was abolished and 'divisionism' has been made a criminal offence. In short, these days all Rwandans are supposed to identify with being Rwandans only, not Tutsi or Hutu. It may be "little more than façade" (Beech 2009: 220), but apparently one that is deemed necessary by the (Tutsi-led) government.

This principle of reconciliation also puts a strain on commemoration. For one thing, the old ethnic division can hardly be left unmentioned in the context of the genocide. The necessary differentiation between victims and perpetrators has to be 'divisionist' per se: it was Hutu who slaughtered Tutsi. While this point cannot be avoided, some of the Rwandan genocide memorials try to at least counterbalance it by pointing out that some Hutu were also killed, and in particular by highlighting individual cases of 'good Hutu' who risked their own lives to save individual Tutsi from being slaughtered. In reality, however, such stories are rarely as noble as one would wish. Such saviours may have rescued their own brother-in-law, say, or a neighbour, but still participated in killing sprees on other occasions during the genocide (cf. Mironko 2006). Such ambivalence sits rather uncomfortably in between documentation vs. reconciliation efforts, and it is thus no great surprise to find that the genocide memorials generally omit reference to this complicated aspect.

What the genocide memorials typically do add to their documentation and presentation of evidence is an overt 'lest we forget' warning that history must not be allowed to repeat itself. This 'never again' credo takes an extreme form in Rwanda: it is national policy. The force with which this is employed can also be seen as echoing the memory of the international community's failure to stop the genocide. This certainly forms a crucial part of contemporary Rwanda's sense of self-reliance in its national identity – and thus is also an element of the place identity of the genocide memorial sites. Conversely, it makes the foreign, especially Western visitor even more of an outsider than usual in Africa. This forms part of the dark tourist experience in Rwanda too, especially in that memorial visitors who come from the relevant First World countries may feel a certain share of the international community's collective guilt with regard to the Rwandan genocide.

Dark tourism in Rwanda: genocide memorial sites

As 'genocide tourism', visiting the Rwandan genocide memorials clearly ranks among the very darkest categories of dark tourism – see, for instance, the scales suggested in Stone (2006) and Sharpley (2009). However, it seems reasonable to presume that there are very few people who travel to Rwanda solely for genocide tourism. Naturally, there are no statistical figures to back this presumption up, so it remains speculative. But the experience gained first-hand on a field trip in December 2010/January 2011 corroborates this speculation.

The only place where any other visitors were encountered was at the Gisozi memorial in the capital Kigali. These were small groups of British and American tourists who were on larger organized trips focused on ecotourism (especially mountain gorilla tracking) – that is, the visit to the Gisozi memorial was made part of their itinerary, whether on demand or not, because it is considered the 'Number One site in the city' even from a mainstream tourism perspective (see Briggs and Booth 2007: 102; or the 'things to do in Kigali' entry on TripAdvisor n.d.). That is to say, such visitors are most likely not dedicated dark tourists but rather what can be called 'casual' dark tourists – see Walter (2009: 54), who theorizes that most dark tourism consumption takes the form of mere 'side trips'.

While this may apply to the easily accessible Gisozi site, most other genocide memorials in the country require much more dedicated effort just to get there. This effort can be part of the specific dark tourism experience where it resembles a 'pilgrimage'. In that sense most genocide tourism in Rwanda is indeed 'pitch black' dark tourism (cf. the categories hinted at in Lonely Planet's *Bluelist* 2007: 124).

The massacres of the genocide were perpetrated in hundreds of places and accordingly there are numerous, typically smaller and less developed memorial sites all over Rwanda, many of which have come into being as private initiatives on the part of survivors – see Meierhenrich (2002–2010), who provides a comprehensive survey of genocide-related sites in Rwanda. However, a few particular sites have gained the status of 'national' memorials. These are mostly run under

146 Peter Hohenhaus

the auspices of the CNLG, while Gisozi in Kigali is primarily in the hands of the British NGO Aegis Trust. Given that these national memorials are the prime institutions that present the topic of the genocide to tourists, it is of particular importance how their subject matter is 'commodified' (in the sense of Lennon and Foley 2000: 5f). The following sections therefore aim to look into the respective commodification approaches at these sites and provide a general overview.

The main memorial sites

As indicated above, on a field trip in December 2010/January 2011, I was able to personally experience the six major memorial sites in Rwanda. Brief accounts for each of these are given below, roughly ordered according to accessibility for foreign tourists.

Gisozi, Kigali Genocide Memorial

The site in the Gisozi district of the Rwandan capital is on the one hand a cemetery, with mass graves for 250,000 genocide victims from Kigali. These are set in a 'memorial garden', which also contains a wall of victims' names and various sculptures. More importantly from a dark tourism perspective, Gisozi features a memorial museum too. Admission is nominally free, though there are fees for photography permits, audio-guide hire or tours with a 'live' guide. Adjoining the centre is a museum shop that sells books, DVDs, T-shirts and general souvenirs.

The main exhibition, designed by the Aegis Trust and opened in 2004, takes the form of a modern memorial museum and includes text-and-photo panels, documents, artefacts and multi-media installations, which soberly outline the events, its prehistory and aftermath. Part of the exhibition is a room containing several glass display cabinets in which victims' skulls and bones are neatly arranged and subtly illuminated (see Figure 10.1). Finally, there is a theatre-like large room lined at the back with thousands of victims' photographs, while at the front video recordings of survivor/witness testimonies are projected onto a large screen.

Nyamata

The genocide memorial site at the church in Nyamata is an altogether different incarnation of commemoration of atrocity. Here victims' blood-stained clothes form the shocking core of what visitors get to see. They are strewn all over the church pews in a tangled mass that makes it difficult to discern individual garments. This 'frozen-in-time' approach to memorialization (Cook 2006: 295) does indeed provide a rather graphic illustration of the mass of victims that had gathered here for safety but were instead brutally slaughtered.

At this memorial, visitors are given a compulsory guided tour and the guide explains details such as the blood stains on walls or on the altar, where a couple of representative artefacts have been placed, including a machete. In the centre of the building, steps lead down to a morgue-like space with white-tiled walls and a centrally placed coffin. This, the guide calmly explains, contains the body of a

Commemorating the Rwandan genocide 147

Figure 10.1 Display of victims' skulls at Gisozi Genocide Memorial, Kigali

woman who had been raped and mutilated. On top of the coffin, a few skulls and bones are placed together with one of those infamous identity cards. Behind the church there is another section: mass graves under a protective roof. One of the mass graves is accessible through a hatch, and steps leading down allow visitors to literally walk among the dead, whose skeletal remains are piled high on either side.

Ntarama

Less shocking and less developed than Nyamata, but of a similar style is the Ntarama Memorial. Here too it was a church compound where the victims had gathered under the false illusion of safety and where the slaughter was conducted with similar brutality. The memorial site of today consists of the comparatively small, simple brick chapel and various ancillary buildings. In one of the buildings, skulls and bones are piled, in another, blood-stained clothes hang from the walls. Victims' personal belongings can also be viewed on shelves in another building. Protective roofs have been erected over the buildings and a memorial garden has been added adjacent to the site. As at Nyamata, visitors are greeted and given a tour by an official guide.

Murambi

This is the most controversial site. Here, at this former school complex, not only skulls and bones are on display, but whole semi-mummified bodies of victims dug up from a mass grave, semi-preserved by lime (which, ironically, has coloured their skin white). This display of hundreds of contorted bodies, often with visible mutilations, has attracted much comment and criticism. Recently, an accompanying exhibition has been added, which was designed in co-operation with the Aegis Trust. Unfortunately I cannot personally comment on this exhibition because at the time of my visit it still had not opened yet – its official opening took place in May 2011. However, a recent description by Vernon (2011) suggests that it is quite similar in style to that at Gisozi. Visits to this new exhibition are probably on a self-guided basis as well, whereas the outbuildings of the former school campus, especially those containing the bodies, will presumably remain accessible by guided tour only.

Bisesero

This site is somewhat exceptional as it also celebrates resistance: the Tutsi who fled to this steep hilltop location managed to fight back and hold out longer against their attackers than anywhere else. It was thus surprising to find that of all the memorial sites visited, this looked the least developed and most in need of refurbishing – the concrete structures were visibly crumbling. The inside of the string of small buildings in the landscaped compound was even inaccessible at the time of my visit, since the local caretaker was nowhere to be found. However, my driver-guide reported from previous visits that here, too, the heart of the display is piles of bones and skulls. These were still stored in an adjacent shed being prepared for transferral to proper display cabinets within the actual memorial site's buildings.

Nyarubuye

At this church-and-convent complex in the south-east of Rwanda, the slaughtered victims were mostly Tutsi refugees already on their way to neighbouring Tanzania. It is now one of the most developed memorial sites outside Kigali. It includes a large memorial garden where there is a rostrum for ceremonies attended by foreign dignitaries. The museum part contains yet more neatly arranged skulls and bones, alongside an array of artefacts such as various tools of the brutal slaughter. The local guide readily explained many a grisly detail regarding the use of such tools. The exhibition also contains a damaged Jesus statue from the church – and the guide explained that it was deliberately targeted by the Hutu attackers because its facial features were associated with Tutsi (long nose, small lips, etc.). In other words, the racist elements of the genocide are clearly spelled out here. In contrast to other such sites, the church at Nyarubuye remains in operation and is freely accessible, while the museum in the former convent can be visited by guided tour only.

Evaluation: common threads and contrasts

Comparing all six of these memorials in early 2011, a number of differences as well as several aspects of resemblance emerge. The main points are summarized in Table 10.1.

Table 10.1 Overview of the six national genocide memorial sites in Rwanda

	Gisozi	Nyamata	Ntarama	Murambi	Bisesero	Nyarubuye
Tourist accessibility	High	Mid-high	Mid-high	Mid-low	Low	Low
Degree of place authenticity	Mid-low	High	High	High	High	High
Prescribed mode of visitation	Self-guided or guided	Guided	Guided	Guided	Guided	Guided
Degree of interpretive commodification	Very high	Mid-low	Low	Mid-high	Low	Mid-low
Degree of commercialization	Low	None	None	None	None	None
Photography permitted	Yes (for a fee)	No	No	No	No	No
Graphic nature of displays (especially of human remains)	Mid-low	High	Mid-high	Very high	Mid-low	Mid-high

One common thread is that all the memorials rely heavily on place authenticity, least so Gisozi, but very poignantly so at all the other sites. Likewise, they all employ the display of perpetrators' weapons, victims' personal effects and, most crucially, their human remains. Gisozi is the least graphic in this respect, whereas at some of the other memorials it is very 'raw' and undeniably the decisive element.

Notable is also the absence of commercialization. Only Gisozi has a museum shop and fees levied for extra services, such as guides – though not for profit as such, since all proceeds are said to support the centre's maintenance. At least nominally, admission to all six sites is free of charge. However, at all six sites visitors are 'encouraged' to leave a donation – and at all places other than Gisozi there is a degree of pressure that visitors are exposed to in this respect (see also Cook 2006: 289). The guides urge visitors to sign and leave a comment in the guest book where you are also expected to note down the amount left as a donation.

Similarly, only Gisozi allows self-guided visits of the entire site, while still offering audio-guides and/or guided tours led by a staff member as an alternative. At all other sites visitors are greeted by a local guide, and led on a compulsory guided tour – with the possible exception of Bisesero, which could not be assessed in this respect. In addition, it is the guide's duty to police a no-photography rule.

There is a certain degree of correlation between accessibility for tourists and the degree of commodification. Some of the memorials are in very isolated rural locations and rather 'raw', with little more than damaged buildings and remains of victims to be seen (except for Murambi, which now has its newly added exhibition too). Conversely, at Gisozi, the most easily independently accessed site, the memorial museum is the least graphic and the most 'Westernized' in style and approach.

One generalization that emerges is that the Gisozi Centre stands out among the six sites assessed, clearly being the one most geared towards tourism in general. Not too surprisingly, then, on Internet travel platforms it is often taken to be '*the* genocide memorial' in Rwanda – many tourists are clearly not even aware of the existence of the other sites.

Developments in site management

Apart from physical preservation/development efforts, such as the corrugated metal roofs at Ntarama, and extensions such as the new exhibition at Murambi, relatively recent streamlining/standardizing developments in general site management strategies have come into effect. Formerly most of the rural memorial sites were first developed as places of remembrance set up and/or looked after by survivors acting as caretakers (see, for instance, Sharp 2007). However, officially appointed employees now receive visitors and give guided tours, which these days are also available in English. In part this reflects a general current policy of promoting English to complement the native national language, Kinyarwanda, and to join, or even replace, the previous colonial language, French, as an international *lingua franca* for Rwanda (cf. *Rwanda Dispatch*, 2010: 14–29). It can be assumed that the provision of English guiding at these memorial sites is also a gesture towards better accommodating international visitors in a global tourist market. In Kigali, this had already been in place from the beginning. The exhibitions at Gisozi and later Murambi were designed for self-guided visits and are trilingual: all text panels and labels are in Kinyarwanda as the main language with translations into French and English in smaller script.

Another recent development concerns control of tourist behaviour. A new no-photography rule has been introduced at all genocide memorial sites except for Gisozi, where visitors can purchase a photo permit on site as they arrive at the reception desk. At all other places visitors would have to apply at the CNLG headquarters in Kigali for a photo permit to be exceptionally granted in advance. This strict policy of restricting visitor behaviour is evidently a recent development. Accounts of visits can be found on the Internet that are accompanied with graphic images taken at the site, and from these it is apparent that no such restrictions were in place only a few years ago. Apparently, at Murambi guides used to almost encourage visitors, telling them "it is ok to take photographs" – see the testimony quoted in Beech (2009: 220); cf. also Sharpley (2012). When I visited, the new rules were strictly enforced: no cameras or recording devices of any sort could be taken inside. I have since (repeatedly) enquired with the CNLG when and why this policy was implemented. Unfortunately, however, my questions have been left unanswered. I can thus only presume that this new policy must have been primarily motivated by anxieties over ethics.

Controversy and dilemma

Mentioning the ethnic division that was a main factor underlying the genocide has become taboo in contemporary Rwanda. The Hutu–Tutsi distinction is supposed to be avoided. The dilemma in the context of genocide memorials is clear. One simply cannot portray the genocide appropriately without recourse to the ethnic element.

Indeed, the genocide memorials seem to be exempt from the 'national identity' legislation that otherwise holds in the country. While the country's 'divisionism' laws passed under the ruling RPF's 'One Rwanda' policies are even invoked to justify widespread suppression of political opposition, the foreign NGO status of the Aegis Trust at the Gisozi Centre puts it in a special position "freed from direct government prohibition" (Williams 2007: 111). This is evidently not limited to this site alone. Clearly spelled-out references to the ethnic/racist substratum of the massacres were also encountered at other memorial sites, especially at Nyarubuye.

A particular ethical concern with regard to most of Rwanda's genocide memorials is the display of human remains, most starkly the bodies at Murambi. This ultimately shocking display of horror triggers repulsion reflexes including very strong concerns about the legitimacy of such displays and whether it violates the victims' dignity. Yet, the reluctance of visitors from the Western First World to accept the public display of corpses may also have much to do with the established 'sequestration of death' from Western postmodern societies (see, for example, Stone 2009 or Walter 2009). The theory of 'sequestered' death refers to the observation that the topic of death is publicly present. For example, in fiction and the media, real death is hidden away and has become 'medicalized'. In that sense death has been made more *abstract* in contemporary Western society. Openly public confrontation with death is typically avoided – unlike earlier in history, or in some non-Western societies.

The issue of 'dignity' in conjunction with display of the dead does indeed appear to be seen in quite a different way by some Rwandans. For instance, Freddy Mutanguha, country director for the Aegis Trust in Rwanda, states:

> There are those who feel that only reburial can offer dignity for the dead, but some survivors ask what dignity there is in being forgotten. They fear that unless the ultimate evidence of genocide is there to see, it could be denied and perhaps one day happen again.
>
> (Aegis Trust 2011)

In a similar vein, Williams (2007: 46) points out that in the Rwandan case the graphic display of bodies/remains may actually be 'required' – as there was so little media coverage of the genocide within Rwanda and signs of genocide-denial have already emerged. The hope is that by displaying the 'unmistakable' actual bodies such denial is made impossible (see Cook 2006: 281). Still, for the dark tourist experience, the encounter with these bodies clearly remains a most powerful one, one that is easily overwhelming, as many a visitor testimony illustrates, for example the personal endnote in Sharp (2007). I can confirm this from my own experience. Out of the hundreds of dark tourism sites I have visited I found Murambi possibly the very darkest and emotionally most taxing of them all (more on my evaluation of Murambi and the other Rwandan genocide memorials can be found in Hohenhaus 2012).

Different dimensions of place identity

Place authenticity and local group identity

The significance of 'authenticity' of any place of commemoration has been amply discussed (see, for example, Sharpley and Stone 2009: 115; Williams 2007: 25, 77) – both for historical fact, in the sense of 'it happened *here*', and also for remembrance. Genocide survivors' group identity is crucially shaped by the places of the atrocities in question. For them it is primarily a place where they come to remember. So there is a potential clash of motivations: that of mourners vs. that of tourist outsiders. If the two meet, the encounter might become 'uncomfortable', as Williams (2007: 145) reports about such a case at Ntarama. Indeed, tourists are advised to at least ensure their visit to Rwandan genocide memorials does not coincide with the commemorative services held at these places every April (cf. Briggs and Booth 2007) when the relevant place identity is, in a sensitive way, restricted to those directly affected by it.

National identity

The state policy of reconciliation is itself steeped in dilemma. The still recent history of the genocide is clearly a defining element of the Rwandan psyche, yet mentioning its ethnic root cause has become taboo as 'divisionism' under current policies that stipulate a unified and reconciled national identity. While this is, as any assumed 'national identity', rather artificial and abstract, it is nevertheless a crucial element in the evaluation of Rwandan genocide memorials. Not least because of the theoretical clash between the official policy of reconciliation that aims to level out ethnic differences and the educational/representational need to preserve the memory of what brought this policy about in the first place. Thus the memorial sites have to constitute places exempt from the otherwise nationwide policy, also allowing local group identities related to past tragedy to coexist alongside the stipulated unified 'national identity'.

Destination place identity from the foreign tourist point of view

Perhaps most interesting with regard to dark tourism is the notion of place identity not from the usual point of view of the actual 'proprietors' of the places concerned (local or national), but from the point of view of the outside visitor who only briefly comes to occupy that same space. It has been emphasized what an important role 'sited-ness' of a place plays for the dark tourist experience (Williams 2007: 77, 182). Conversely, the important interplay of 'a tourist's own identity' with that of the place has been underscored too (Sharpley and Stone 2009: 117). We might call this 'temporary place identity'. In the case of the Rwandan genocide memorials outside the capital this is largely determined by two factors: the 'pilgrimage effort' it takes to get there and a latent feeling of being a voyeuristic 'intruder' (Beech 2009: 223). It is in any case an undeniably intense experience – with much of it taking the nature of what Williams (2007: 100) described as 'from head to stomach'. The latter is particularly true for Murambi, where visitors frequently report 'stomach-churning' emotional effects on encountering the display of preserved corpses.

There is some counterbalance of this in the form of visitation being by guided tour – which sets a certain frame for the physical and temporal setting of the experience. In fact, Cook (2006: 288) reports a telling discrepancy between her visitor group's behaviour, who repeatedly felt compelled to 'pause' for respectful silent contemplation, and the guide's rushing them on to see all the rooms full of displayed bodies, as if to emphasize the enormity and incomprehensibility of the scale of the tragedy. These days, further counterbalance is provided at Murambi through the new exhibition, which redirects visitors' attention to the 'head' rather than 'stomach' through interpretive commodification.

At the Kigali Memorial Centre, the setting is almost the total reverse of that at the rural sites. Here the commodification is decidedly 'Westernized' in style, and clearly geared towards foreign tourist visitation. It is also the least graphic – the few displays of human remains are subdued, almost sanitized, and the emphasis is on information through text and audio-visual means. At the same time, it is by far the most accessible site both physically and emotionally and is accordingly the one most 'popular' with foreign tourists. It is regarded as one of the 'things you do when in Kigali'. Its 'consumption' is the least demanding with regard to 'temporal place identity', being so similar to numerous memorial museums the world over.

Conclusion

Overall, the efforts made in Rwanda with a view to an adequate approach to commemoration of one of human history's most horrific episodes can be regarded as highly commendable. Still, the commodification of the genocide at the relevant memorial sites faces dilemmas as well as controversy.

One notable element of this is the friction between documentation needs and national reconciliation policies. This correlates with discrepancies between the 'prescribed' national identity and the place identity of the genocide memorials. The former is supposed to eschew ethnic identity in favour of an assumed universal national identity of 'we're all Rwandans, not Tutsi or Hutu'. In contrast, reference to the ethnic element of the genocide is unavoidable for the memorials, where it cannot be left unmentioned that overall it was Tutsi who were the victims and Hutu the perpetrators.

For the 'temporary place identity' that foreign dark tourists find themselves in at these memorials, the experience is furthermore influenced by a certain awkwardness that derives from an uneasy feeling of a part of the collective guilt that the 'international community' has to bear for not having prevented the genocide when it could have done so at the time. That is, here the foreign tourist's own national identity collides with the locals' identity. Moreover, this can lead to uncomfortable feelings of being a voyeuristic intruder, as the place identity of the memorial sites appears to belong more to the Rwandans themselves than to tourists. However, foreign tourist visitation is increasingly encouraged and catered for at these sites – if to varying degrees. In terms of site management this is reflected in several recent changes in policies, such as English-language provision, newly imposed restrictions on tourist behaviour, and a more standardized overarching concept in general. Yet, there are also marked differences in commodification between the Gisozi memorial and the rural sites outside the capital. The former is primarily a more conventional memorial museum with a Western-style interpretive commodification through text panels, photos, documents and multi-media installations and thus somewhat less dark in consumption. It is also the most accessible of the sites and therefore the one most visited by foreign tourists. The rural memorials, on the other hand, are genuinely of the very darkest kind of dark tourism. They require a pilgrimage effort of getting there and expose tourists to a much more 'difficult' experience.

The display of human remains is a particularly controversial element in this. Even though all Rwandan genocide memorials include a degree of this, the very 'raw' and 'frozen-in-time' approaches at sites such as Nyamata and Murambi are of the very darkest nature possible. The display of the bodies at Murambi is accordingly seen as especially problematic – in particular by Westerners, who are used to the 'sequestration' of death in their own societies and thus tend to be quite disturbed by such encounters with the dead. However, this shocking display of bodily remains is defended in Rwanda as a necessary measure in order to prevent genocide denial within the country. So the site management decision in this regard is made rather with the local population and local/national policies in mind, much less so for foreign tourists.

The various strata of interplay of place identity and dark tourism, both in terms of commodification of genocide commemoration and tourists' consumption experience, are thus particularly distinctive in Rwanda. Arguably, the Rwandan case is even unique. And it certainly is about the darkest form of tourism available anywhere on Earth.

References

Aegis Trust (2011) 'New Memorial Opens at Murambi, Rwanda', 25 May. Available at http://www.aegistrust.org/Aegis-Rwanda/genocide-memorial-opens-at-murambi-rwanda.html (accessed 18 April 2012).

Beech, J. (2009) 'Genocide Tourism', in R. Sharpley and P. Stone (eds) *The Darker Side of Travel: The Theory and Practice of Dark Tourism*, Bristol: Channel View, pp. 207–223.

Briggs, P. and Booth, J. (2007) *Rwanda: The Bradt Travel Guide*, 3rd edn, Chalfont St Peter: Bradt.

Cook, S.E. (2006) 'The Politics of Preservation in Rwanda', in S.E. Cook (ed.) *Genocide in Cambodia and Rwanda: New Perspectives*, New Brunswick and London: Transaction Publishers, pp. 281–299.

Dallaire, R. (2004) *Shake Hands with the Devil: The Failure of Humanity in Rwanda*, London: Arrow.

Diamond, J. (2011) *Collapse*, 2nd edn, London and New York: Penguin.

Gourevitch, P. (1998) *We Wish to Inform You that Tomorrow We Will Be Killed with Our Families*, New York: Picador.

Hohenhaus, P. (2012) *dark-tourism.com – The Online Travel Guide to Dark, Unusual and Weird Places Around the World*.
Lennon, J. and Foley, M. (2000) *Dark Tourism*, London: Thomson.
Lonely Planet (2007) *Bluelist: The Best in Travel 2007*, Melbourne, Oakland and London: Lonely Planet Publications.
Meierhenrich, J. (2002–2010) *Through a Glass Darkly: Genocide Memorials in Rwanda 1994–present*. Available at http://genocidememorials.cga.harvard.edu/home.html (accessed 18 April 2012).
Melvern, L. (2000) *A People Betrayed: The Role of the West in Rwanda's Genocide*, London: Zed.
Mironko, C. (2006) 'Ibitero: Means and Motive in the Rwandan Genocide', in S. E. Cook (ed.), *Genocide in Cambodia and Rwanda: New Perspectives*, New Brunswick and London: Transaction Publishers, pp. 163–189.
Prunier, G. (1995/1997) *The Rwanda Crisis: History of a Genocide*, London: Hurst & Company.
Rwanda Dispatch (2010) Issue 24, December 2010, Kigali.
Sharp, J. (2007) 'Rwanda Genocide Memorial', 13 February 2007, report for *The World* radio programme. Transcript available at http://www.pri.org/theworld/?q = node/7997 (accessed 18 April 2012).
Sharpley, R. (2009) 'Shedding Light on Dark Tourism', in R. Sharpley and P. Stone (eds) *The Darker Side of Travel: The Theory and Practice of Dark Tourism*, Bristol: Channel View, pp. 3–22.
Sharpley, R. (2012) 'Towards an Understanding of "Genocide Tourism": An Analysis of Visitors' Accounts of their Experience of Recent Genocide Sites', in R. Sharpley and P. Stone (eds) *Contemporary Tourist Experience: Concepts and Consequences*, Abingdon: Routledge, pp. 95–109.
Sharpley, R. and Stone, P. (2009) '(Re)presenting the Macabre: Interpretation, Kitschification and Authenticity', in R. Sharpley and P. Stone (eds) *The Darker Side of Travel: The Theory and Practice of Dark Tourism*, Bristol: Channel View, pp. 109–128.
Stone, P. (2006) 'A Dark Tourism Spectrum: Towards a Typology of Death and Macabre Related Tourist Sites, Attractions and Exhibitions', *Tourism*, 54(2): 145–160.
Stone, P. (2009) 'Making Absent Death Present: Consuming Dark Tourism in Contemporary Society', in R. Sharpley and P. Stone (eds) *The Darker Side of Travel: The Theory and Practice of Dark Tourism*, Bristol: Channel View, pp. 23–38.
TripAdvisor (n.d.) 'Things to Do in Kigali', entry on *TripAdvisor* website. Available at http://www.tripadvisor.com/Attractions-g293829-Activities-Kigali.html (accessed 18 April 2012).
Vernon, P. (2011) 'Murambi Genocide Memorial', posted on *Rwanda Travel News by Bradt's Rwanda Guide* in December 2011. Available at http://bradtrwandaupdate.wordpress.com/2011/12/11/murambi-genocide-memorial/ (accessed 18 April 2012).
Walter, T. (2009) 'Dark Tourism: Mediating Between the Dead and the Living', in R. Sharpley and P. Stone (eds) *The Darker Side of Travel: The Theory and Practice of Dark Tourism*, Bristol: Channel View, pp. 39–55.
Williams, P. (2007) *Memorial Museums*, Oxford and New York: Berg.

11 Dark tourism and place identity in French Guiana

Olivier Dehoorne and Lee Jolliffe

Introduction

Dark tourism is defined as visitation to places such as murder sites, battlefields and cemeteries (Lennon and Foley 2006). Types of dark tourism sites vary and Stone (2006) identifies a spectrum of such sites, from dark to light depending on the nature of death associated with the site, the distance in time from the death and the nature of the site (existing or purpose built). The author also classifies seven types of the dark tourism product as: dark fun factories; dark exhibitions; dark dungeons; dark resting places; dark shrines; dark conflict sites; and dark camps of genocide. Stone (2006) indicates that defunct prisons such as Alcatraz and Robben Island, once converted into museums or heritage sites, have subsequently become popular tourist sites.

This chapter focuses on the case of French Guiana (Guyanne) – an overseas region of France on the coast of South America – in terms of Stone's (2006) dark dungeon type of product: "sites and attractions which present bygone penal and justice codes to the present day consumer, and revolve around (former) prisons and courthouses". This type of site is thought to occupy the middle ground of the dark tourism spectrum proposed by Stone (2006). Such sites were not initially designed for tourism but due to their historical association with aspects of dark history, they offer potential for the development of dark tourism.

As Sharpley and Stone (2009) note, the management of dark tourism sites such as those found in French Guiana raises complex moral and ethical issues related to interpretation and the visitor experience. However, from the perspective of tourism management, sites with a dark history also have the capacity to contribute to the identities of the places where they are located. In colonized territories such sites may also reflect the sense of place of the colonizing country while in the case of those territories transitioning to independence they may, as sites of reflection, contribute to an emerging sense of national identity (Carrigan 2010).

National identity is increasingly being connected to tourism, as it is the identity of a place that differentiates it from other destinations (Hayes and MacLeod 2007). Historic site management can play a key role in the development of identity for a nation (Howard 2003) as well as in the development of tourism attractions and products that will appeal to visitors, thus attracting them to visit one location over another. Experiences of place can also be packaged as tourism products, such as routes that have the potential to contribute to local and regional economic development (Briedenhann and Wickens 2004). Tied into the growing international interest in the heritage associated with pain and shame (Logan and Reeves 2009), dark history resources thus have a potential for tourism development.

Based on secondary sources, we review the historical context to the dark history and related national identity of French Guiana, from both historical and literary sources. As Howard (2003) indicated, literature can be a powerful source for understanding post-colonial tourism. Second, based on available documentation we identified the dark history sites and components of the tourism product of the territory, within Stone's (2006) theory of dark tourism product types. In examining the main sites open to the public, we used a case study approach advocated by Yin (2009). In particular, we drew from official documentation from the French Guiana Tourism Committee and other related reports on tourism development. Third, we examined the tourism context in terms of the policy setting of French Guiana that might have influenced the development of dark tourism. Fourth, our analysis and conclusion draws upon the literature on dark tourism, for example as a context to examine both the current and future directions of French Guiana's dark tourism sites in both its tourism product and sense of national identity. In essence, consideration is given as to how the dark tourism sites contribute to the current place identity, in a territory that many observers have noted not to have a national identity (Collomb 1999; Jolivet 1990; Mam-Lam-Fouck 1992).

Dark history in French Guiana

The image of French Guiana is inseparable from the history of the territory as a penal colony, for example as immortalized as in the book *Papillon* by Henri Charrière, later made into a film (Toth 2006). To understand the current tourism situation, an account needs to be made of the dark history associated with the destination. The historical legacy of this young country consists of 86 years (1852–1939) as a penal colony with many prisons and, over time, about 90,000 prisoners deported by the French justice system from France. It is the story of prisons arranged on the perimeter of the coastline with the resident convicts condemned to disappear in this part of the world, this 'piece of hell on earth' (Montabo 2004; Pierre 2000). Worn down by epidemics of yellow fever (which affected the convicts just as much as the guards) and hunger, this was a double condemnation, to die in exile in oblivion but also in slow suffering more than 7,000 kilometers from the powerful French mother country.

This piece of land on the South American continent (86,504 km^2) has the configuration of an island, which no one can escape: the country set between the 20 kilometers of coastline contained by strong shore currents and fearsome sharks, the immense rivers of Maroni to the west and Oyapock to the east, which are both natural borders with Suriname and the Brazilian state of Amapa. In addition, the endless extent of the impenetrable, frightening forest, with wild beasts and feared insects, chief among them the mosquitoes that infest the marshes that extend over the sedimentary rocks of the Quaternary.

The memory of the convicts in Guiana and the architectural heritage of the prisons represent for both locals and visitors a grim episode in the history of France. Worn down by disease and hunger, sinking into oblivion, the convict was sentenced to long suffering resulting in a slow death. This past still clings to French Guiana today and its history is one of a land of exile and punishment (Spieler 2012). This is not a touristic destination driven by positive, attractive and rewarding values. 'The Green Hell' image (Pierre 2000) is still maintained in media announcements through sensational reporting, with the tantalizing and recurring themes: drugs, violence, training camps of the French foreign legions in the middle of the jungle (Paqueteau 1986; Pétot 1986; Spieler 2012).

The 230,000 inhabitants of Guiana (INSEE 2010) seem to bear the burden of this history (Mam-Lam-Fouck 1992; 1996). The population is divided between the descendants of indigenous Amerindians established in the forest near rivers and sometimes in the vicinity of Bushenengués (the 'Negroes of the forest') whose ancestors, during the time of the slave trade, fled slavery and relocated along the rivers (Piantoni 2002). The rest of the population includes misplaced Europeans, descendants of convicts and Hmong refugees who arrived during the last Indochinese wars. The population also consists of Brazilian gold miners, often clandestine, that plague the confines of the territory (Piantoni 2011), not to mention the Brazilian prostitutes who converge towards the capital and the Haitian economic and environmental refugees. There has therefore been a constant passage of migrants through the country, including officials and European engineers working on the aerospace base at Kourou. Today, as a result of positive demographic growth, half of the population is under the age of 20 and almost 30 per cent do not have French citizenship. Immigrants to Guiana come from 139 countries, mainly Brazil, Suriname, China, Haiti and other European countries (European Parliament 2010).

The repulsive connotations rooted in the legacy of the prison maintained through the many clichés that characterize the legacy of a 'colony' (Memmi 1957) are actively opposed by the contemporary Guyanese. This old territory, yet young country (administratively a French overseas region but will benefit from a more direct governance with the 2014 elections), under construction with emerging infrastructure tends to highlight these resources and diversity. In a land of crossbreeding, various minorities mix and mingle in this country where more than half of its current residents were born outside of French Guiana. Today, aspects of a multicultural society are set against a backdrop of a rich natural area burdened by the stigma of the past.

The first who were condemned of common rights in France arrived in French Guiana in 1852, in this isolated land that hitherto had only received political prisoners. The abolition of slavery had reduced labour in the colonies while European industries faced social troubles. The French government's decision to deport convicts was based on both economic and political motives (similar to those of the British Crown, at the same time as Botany Bay in Australia) (Bernard 2000). The government estimated that 6,000 prisoners from France were too expensive to maintain in their home country and should be deported into forced labour, which was a cheaper and more efficient way to facilitate French colonization. France established a penal settlement on the prison with the deportation of their undesirable population. The 'social leprosy' (Memmi 1957) that proliferated in the slums and outside of the French cities thus led to developing remote French Guiana, which at the time had a population of less than 25,000 souls (Londres 1932). Those convicted of theft, forgery, fraud and desertions in France were sent to prison in French Guiana (as well as in the colony of New Caledonia); criminals who escaped the death penalty joined those just sentenced to forced labour.

After more than three weeks of travel from France in cages, without proper hygiene, prisoners were sorted first in the coastal islands of the territory and later at a processing station on the coast: the political prisoners were directed to Devil's Island (like Captain Dreyfus in 1898), the most dangerous common law criminals on Royal Island and the others scattered across the territory. To consolidate the settlement, there was the principle of 'doubling': "When a man is sentenced five to seven years of forced labour, once the sentence is completed, he must remain here the same number of years in. If sentenced to more than seven years, the term used was 'perpetual residence'" (Londres 1932). Then, the 'law of relegation' (1885) sent to the prison colony the repeated offenders convicted of petty offences, with no possibility of return to France. Special camps were reserved for citizens of colonies such as Annamite, Indochinese, Malagasy and women at a prison in Mana (1858).

It is through the writings of reporter Albert Londres, who worked for three weeks investigating French Guiana in 1923, that the public discovered the injustices of the prison system:

> Prison is not a well-defined, unchangeable punishment machine. It is a factory of misfortune that functions without a plan or matrix. One will search in vain for the template used to shape the convicts. She crushes them, that's all, and the pieces go where they may. The law allows us to cut the head of the assassins, not to pay us their heads.
>
> (Londres 1932)

In addition to this philosophical view, Albert Londres also provided descriptive evidence of the extreme conditions under which the convicts existed:

> I had never seen 50 men in a cage before... They were preparing for their night. They were swarming in the room. From five o'clock in the evening to five o'clock in the morning they are free – in their cage. The convict begins to release. As long as they are under sentence, they are fed (badly), we lay them down (badly) and they are dressed (badly). While looking at the results, it is the brilliant minimum. When their five or seven years are completed, we kick them out of the camp.
>
> (Londres 1932)

The system continued like this until the last convoy of November 1938. At that point about 9,000 people remained. This was a population made up of about 3,300 convicts, just as many freed convicts that were obliged to remain due to doubling of their sentences and about 2,000 relegated convicts.

But is this dark history as a prison colony, reflected in the historical literature on French Guiana, echoed today in the country's heritage attractions (historical sites and museums)? Is this dark history interpreted as part of the tourism product of contemporary French Guiana? The next section of the chapter identifies those sites related to the dark history that are currently open to the public.

Dark tourism sites in French Guiana

A number of sites in the country are associated with the dark history as a penal colony (see Table 11.1). Most are found along the coast of the country. A small archipelago grouping of three islands – Royal Island (Île Royale), Saint Joseph Island (Île Saint-Joseph) and Devil's Island (Île du Diable) (the latter known for the imprisonment of Captain Dreyfus) – was established in 1852 and utilized until 1951 as a penal colony. Another dark tourism site in French Guiana, Transportation Camp (Camp de la Transportation), established in 1854 at Saint-Laurent-du-Maroni, was used until the end of World War II as a reception site for convicts before they were transported elsewhere.

The French Guiana Tourism Committee does not currently seem to promote these sites as part of dark tourism but does list them as historical sites. The Salvation Islands are only accessible by boat as part of an excursion, and guided tours are only offered at Royal Island. Another limitation is that the tours are usually provided in French. However, a recent tourism report indicates the intention to develop some of these areas for tourism with investment planned for improvements of tourism infrastructure at both the Salvation Islands and the Transportation Camp (Atout France Delegation Guyane 2010).

Tourism context in French Guiana

The country is an administrative department of France. However, after local requests for a more participative form of governance in 2010 the French government has approved a new, more autonomous system for both Guiana and Martinique that could have implications for tourism development:

> Guiana will create a new unique self-governing entity (*collectivités uniques*) merging the competences of the department and region. It will be established as a unique council (with 51 members) and executive power represented by the President of the Council and standing committees (*Commission permanente*). The first election will take place in 2014, at the same time as regional and local elections in metropolitan France. The members of the Council will be elected in the general elections in a complex two-round proportional system.
>
> (European Parliament 2010)

Table 11.1 Dark tourism sites listed in French Guiana

Site	Location	Significance
Transportation camp (Camp de la Transportation)	Saint-Laurent-du-Maroni	Camp used for arrival and processing of prisoners. Open to the public for guided tours
The 'Official District'	Saint-Laurent-du-Maroni	The central part of town represents the space the state built as needed for administration of the prison
Salvation Islands (Îles du Salut) Royal Island (Île Royale) St Joseph Island (Île Saint-Joseph) Devil's Island (Île du Diable)	Located 15 km north of Kourou	Used for the creation of a penal colony in 1852. Île Royale was the headquarters, Île Saint-Joseph was a prison with cells, and Île du Diable was for political prisoners. Only Île Royale is open to the public. Two-hour guided tours begin at the Director's House, which displays exhibits on the history of the islands as a penal colony
Saint-Louis Island	Located in the middle of the Maroni River, near St Laurent	This island housed the lepers who were evacuated from the Salvation Islands
St Jean du Maroni	Located 17 km from St Laurent	A large camp of 16 huts housing the relegated 'crowbars' (convicts) who completed their sentence condemned to end their lives in isolation
Annamites Prison of Eel Creek (La Crique des Anguilles)	This site is 45 km east of Cayenne in the territory of the municipality of Montsinery-Tonnegrande	Housed convicts from Indochina's colonies where life expectancy was very low
Departmental Museum (Musée Départemental)	Cayenne	Exhibits of the penal colony are displayed. Open limited hours. Small admission fee

Source: French Guiana Tourism Committee (2012)

Tourism has recently become an important sector of the economy. For example, in 2010 there were more than 100,000 visitors, who generated 333,000 hotel nights (Euromonitor 2012). However, few of those who visit are motivated by an interest in heritage, as it is reported that three quarters of this visitation is for professional reasons connected with the Guiana Space Centre. The tourists come primarily from metropolitan France (more than half of them) along with others involved in the European Space Program (European Parliament 2010). There is a modern international airport in Rochambeau near the capital of Cayenne with air connections to metropolitan France, the USA, South America and the French Antilles.

It reportedly served more than 400,000 passengers in 2009 (European Parliament 2010). While a large proportion of these visitors are business tourists connected with the Space Centre, considerable numbers are also VFRs (visiting friends and relatives). With modest arrivals, tourism represents a turnover of €70 million, representing 10 per cent of gross domestic product (INSEE 2010). The territory lists barely 1,200 hotel rooms. Thus, this emerging destination is not always able to meet the demand of tour operators for group space, due to a lack of sufficient accommodation capacity. The cities contain some traditional hotel facilities but outside the cities, the accommodation is more rustic: visitors can sleep under large cabanas, in hammocks or spend the night in canoes to watch the alligators. The destination is currently promoted as a land of adventure, a huge playground for adults, between the descent of turbulent rivers, adventure trails, large forest walks and exploring the coastal islands.

An overall strategy for the development of Guiana includes developing infrastructure; promoting local employment and indigenous economic development; guaranteeing the cohesion of Guiana's society and developing its diversity (European Parliament 2010). Tourism is included within the second objective of developing the economy of the region along with the agriculture, fishing, wood industry, mining, construction and space sectors.

The government of French Guiana is also reportedly working on a National Tourism Strategy for the period of 2011–12. It is not known if 'heritage tourism' or 'dark tourism' features within the strategy. In 2011 the government called for public input into the strategy. Local tourism promotion is the responsibility of the French Guiana Tourism Committee, a government office. There is potential for regional partnerships towards developing new products and thus increasing tourism, for example as mentioned in the Suriname Tourism development plan:

> While to date the number of French visitors to Suriname are few, the potential of the French market is also limited for Suriname in the future, however, a combination programme together with French Guyana *(Guiana)* could be striven for and promoted.
>
> (Suriname n.d.)

Tourism partnerships and co-operation in addition to being with Suriname could also include Brazil. For example, this could fit within the European Union funded 'Amazonia' programme of technical assistance that includes the goal of increasing cross border business that could include tourism (European Parliament 2010).

With limited air access (main flights are from Paris and other French territories in the Americas, for example Guadeloupe to Martinique to Cayenne, with a few flights arriving directly from Brazil and the USA), modest tourism arrivals and a lack of suitable infrastructure, tourism in Guiana is considered to be still at an early stage of development. The primary resource for tourism, the natural environment, has been promoted (for nature and ecotourism) over the historic environment (buildings and sites) as the latter will require investment (conservation, restoration, interpretation) to be brought up to a standard that will attract visitors and ensure their satisfaction. The country review of tourism Euromonitor (2012) does not even mention the historic sites related to the dark history:

> French Guiana is more than just a spaceport. It is rich in green tourism attractions, such as its Amazonian rainforest, which is abundant in flora and fauna, and its rivers. French Guiana also has beautiful beaches, while sport fishing can be practiced in the Caribbean Sea. For those seeking culture, Cayenne offers museums, local Indian communities can be found in Guiana Amazonian Park, while coastal towns celebrate Carnival.

The architectural legacy of the penal colony is therefore for the most part unrecognized as a resource for tourism. As previously identified, the coastal remains of the numerous prison facilities, with many jails built between 1851 and 1940, are scattered over the Salvation Islands, 15 km from Kourou with Royal Island, St Joseph Island, and Devil's Island, containing some renovated buildings while other ruins are covered by vigorous vegetation. On the coastline, the major cities such as Cayenne house the buildings of the former colonial administration, and just below Fort Cépérou in Saint-Laurent-du-Maroni is the Transportation Camp. No effort seems to have been made to link these sites. With sites being nationally administered, local authorities (the regions, municipalities and related organizations) seem to be disinterested in tourism development.

In addition, the country does not yet have the necessary infrastructure in the form of hotels and related services to bring an increased number of visitors for the purpose of heritage or dark tourism. At present the only dark tourism experiences visitors may encounter are often 'accidental', if they visit the museum in Cayenne or any of the sites associated with the former penal system. Only the most adventurous of visitors will visit the most famous site associated with the dark history of the colony, Devil's Island, as it is only accessible by private boat.

The dark dungeon types of sites of French Guiana, identified earlier in the chapter, are not promoted for 'dark tourism'. They are as of yet relatively undeveloped for tourism, available to those adventurous tourists who seek them out but not actively featured by the local tourism commission, other than being acknowledged as historical sites and listed as such for tourist activity.

The black history of the country has been identified in this chapter as being a positive attribute for potentially developing dark tourism, as well as a component of the identity of the country. These sites are also part of the history of France, serving as a reminder of the former harsh penal code of that country. Consequently, they could be of interest to visitors from France, who currently comprise the majority of the visitors.

With a number of sites historically associated with processing and housing of prisoners there should be potential for them, once developed and interpreted for tourism, to be packaged in the form of tours, or even tourism routes. The creation of tourism routes commemorating the formal penal colony sites could be important not only for tourism but also as sites of reflection for the current residents of the country, and as sites that have the potential to create a sense of a shared past in the form of national identity.

However, to be ready for tourism consumption the sites representing the dark heritage of the country, of which only a few are now available for visitors, need to be accessible to visitors and developed with adequate interpretation. Recent funding to improve interpretation of some of the dark tourism sites is a good sign. The museums in Cayenne, while containing exhibits on the penal colony, could also benefit from additional resources for upgrading facilities and improving public access.

Conclusion: a dark history unrecognized

The patrimonial inheritance of the penal colony has not yet been recognized. As identified in this chapter related tourism developments are thus random. Some locations are open to tourism, but they are not integrated into the overall process of tourism development in the country, since no specific tourism circuit or route is marketed. Yet tourism demand is constant and it is inconceivable for a visitor to travel to French Guiana without visiting or at least becoming aware of some remains of the former prison system during their stay.

This painful past that is still so close, whose connotations still tarnish the country's image, is not yet integrated into a real process of cultural heritage. Fundamentally, the prevailing sentiment of public opinion is rather in the direction of retraction of the story of this legacy as it is viewed as being heavy and painful, which hinders the development of the country as a nation (Mam-Lam-Fouck 1992).

In current tourism promotions French Guiana prefers to sell its image of a welcoming land through events like the Carnival, a festival season occurring immediately before Lent, consisting of street parades with costumes and music and local cuisine reflecting the local cultures, as well as its technological jewel, the Kourou Space Center and its biodiversity. However, touristic communications and campaigns work to reduce the potentially manly and sometimes brutal image of the destination, marketing French Guiana as a land of adventurers. This is a form of collective amnesia, or deliberate forgetting of some aspects of the past (Timothy and Boyd 2003). To the observer, it seems that French Guiana wishes to shape its new tourism image by erasing the rough edges of the history of yesteryear, replacing it with a more user-friendly one, built around offering a practice of soft ecotourism, of serene adventure far from the past and the image of the prison. This is reflected by the current website of the Tourism Committee under the slogan of 'Incredible Guiana'. This marketing promotion featuring aspects of history, geography, nature, adventure, space and tradition is coordinated locally by the local office in Cayenne and implemented for Europe out of an office in Paris.

The current position, carried unanimously by politicians, must be understood in the context of a young country, whose identity is under construction, which turns to a bright future under the value of land resources (aerospace, biodiversity, the promising start of off-shore oil production). The current heritage approaches emphasize the country's first people, with the ancestral Amerindian populations, but the history of the penal colony is still unexploited for the moment. However, there are some signs that the potential for utilizing the dark history of this place for tourism may be recognized, with improvements budgeted for the sites associated with this history and with a call for public input into a national tourism strategy.

References

Atout France Delegation Guyane (2010) *La Tourisme en Guyane: La Synthesese du Diagonastic et des Recommendations Strategiques*, Cayenne: L'Agence de développement touristique de la France.

Bernard, M. (2000) *La Colonisation Pénitentiaire en Australie, 1788–1868*, Paris: L'Harmattan.

Briedenhann, J. and Wickens, E. (2004) 'Tourism Routes as a Tool for the Economic Development of Rural Areas – Vibrant Hope or Impossible Dream?' *Tourism Management*, 25(1): 71–79.

Carrigan, A. (2010) *Postcolonial Tourism: Literature, Culture and Environment*, New York: Routledge.

Collomb, G. (1999) 'Entre Ethnicité et National: A Propos de la Guyane Socio-anthropologie', *Socio-anthropologie*, 6.

Euromonitor (2012) *Country Report, Travel and Tourism in French Guiana*, London: Euromonitor International.

European Parliament (2010) *Economic, Social and Territorial Situation of French Guiana*, Brussels: European Parliament Directorate-General for Internal Policies.

French Guiana Tourism Committee, French Guiana (2012) Available at http://www.tourisme-guyane.com/en.html (accessed 6 July 2012).

Hayes, D. and MacLeod, N. (2007) 'Packaging Places: Designing Heritage Trails Using an Experience Economy Perspective to Maximize Visitor Engagement', *Journal of Vacation Marketing*, 13(1): 45–58.

Howard, P. (2003) *Heritage: Management, Interpretation, Identity*, London: Continuum International Publishing Group.

INSEE (2010) National Institute of Statistics and Economic Studies, Paris.

Jolivet, M.J. (1990) 'Entre Autochtones et Immigrants: Diversité et Logique de Positions Créoles Guyanaises', *Etudes créoles*, 8(2): 1–32.

Lennon, J. and Foley, M. (2006) *Dark Tourism*, London: Thomson Learning.

Logan, W. and Reeves, K. (2009) *Places of Pain and Shame Dealing with Difficult Heritage*, London: Routledge.

Londres, A. (1932) *Au Bagne*, Paris: Albin Michel.

Mam-Lam-Fouck, S. (1992) *Histoire de la Guyane Contemporaine (1940–1982). Les Mutations Économiques, Sociales et Politiques*, Paris: Editions Caribéennes.

Mam-Lam-Fouck, S. (1996) *Histoire de la Guyane Française. Les Grands Problèmes Guaynais: Permanence et Évolution*, Cayenne: Ibis Rouge.

Memmi, A. (1957) *Portrait du Colonisé, Précédé du Portait du Colonisateur*, Paris: Buchet/Chastel.

Montabo, B. (2004) *L'Histoire de la Guyane: Tome 2, de 1848 à Nos Jours*, Paris: Orphie.

Paqueteau, B. (1986) *Grande Muette, Petit Écran: Présence et Représentations du Militaire dans les Magazines de Reportage: 1962–1981*, Paris: Fondation Pour Les Études de Défense Nationale.

Pétot, J. (1986) *L'Or de Guyane: Son Histoire, ses Hommes*, Paris: Editions Caribéennes.

Piantoni, F. (2002) 'Les Recompositions Territoriales dans le Maroni: Relation Mobilité-environnement', *Revue Européenne des Migrations Internationales [En ligne]*, *18*(2): 1–31.

Piantoni, F. (2011) *Migrants en Guyane*, Paris: Actes Sud Beaux-Arts.

Pierre, M. (2000) *Bagnards: La Terre de la Grande Punition, Cayenne 1852–1953*, Paris: Autrement.

Sharpley, R. and Stone, P.R. (2009) *The Darker Side of Travel: The Theory and Practice of Dark Tourism*, Bristol, UK: Channel View Publications.

Spieler, M.F. (2012) *Empire and Underworld: Captivity in French Guiana*, Cambridge, MA: Harvard University Press.

Stone, P.R. (2006) 'A Dark Tourism Spectrum: Towards a Typology of Death and Macabre Related Tourist Sites, Attractions and Exhibitions', *Tourism*, *54*(2): 145–160.

Suriname (n.d.) *Suriname Tourism Development Plan*. Available at http://www.hitchcock.itc.virginia.edu/Suriname/texts/plan.pdf (accessed 25 June 2012).

Timothy, D.J. and Boyd, S.W. (2003) *Heritage Tourism*, Harlow: Pearson Education Limited.

Toth, S.A. (2006) *Beyond Papillon. The French Overseas Penal Colonies 1852–1952*, Lincoln, NE: University of Nebraska Press.

Yin, R.K. (2009) *Case Study Research: Design and Methods*, Thousand Oaks, CA: Sage Publications.

12 Place identities in the Normandy landscape of war

Touring the Canadian sites of memory

Geoffrey R. Bird

Introduction

The aim of this chapter is to examine the relationship between remembrance and tourism in a landscape of war, specifically the area in Normandy where Canadians fought in World War II. On D-Day, 6 June 1944, American, British and Canadian troops landed in Normandy in the largest amphibious assault in history, and then fought for 80 days before liberating Paris. With a total population of 11 million, one million Canadians volunteered for military service. Forty-four thousand Canadians were killed in the war, of which roughly 6,000 Canadians died in the Battle of Normandy. For many Canadians, D-Day is emblematic of Canada's cultural memory of World War II (see Goddard 2004; Granatstein and Morton 1989). As Keegan (2004: xiii) notes, the feat of taking of Juno Beach in particular was 'an extraordinary achievement for a country of Canada's modest population... a source of enormous Canadian national pride'. Canadians therefore tour the Normandy beaches, towns, and surrounding fields as they collectively represent a national heritage landscape.

The purpose of this research is to provide a better understanding of the significance of tourism, war memory, landscape and meaning in the twenty-first century and to examine how these phenomena interrelate and influence the post-veteran generation. This study also involves understanding the emotional and symbolic meaning associated with the landscape of war. In his examination of the phenomenology of landscape, Tilley (1994: 35) acknowledges, "the affective, emotional and symbolic significance of the landscape... the relationship between people and the land, and the manner in which it is culturally constructed, invested with powers and significances". Tilley's perspective on the affective, emotional and symbolic significance of landscapes helps us to understand how the presentation of various sites of memory, individually and collectively, functions to construct emotionally resonant meanings for Canadian tourists.

The chapter draws upon doctoral fieldwork, involving observation of guided bus tours and the annual D-Day commemorations over several years. The research also includes key informant interviews representing museum and cemetery management, visitors, tour guides and veterans along with visitor online feedback and reflexive journal writing. In this context, the research draws upon ethnography to understand the social and cultural phenomenon of war remembrance as evoked through experiencing a landscape of war.

Winter and Sivan (1999: 6) describe war remembrance as the "act of gathering bits and pieces of the past, and joining them together in public". In this way, whereas commemorations such as Remembrance Day in Commonwealth countries or Memorial Day in the United States represent the ritual and traditions created by society to remember (see Marshall 2004), the meaning of remembrance differs from person to person and evolves from generation to generation (see Winter 2006). Despite the concerns of authors such as Cole (1999), Scates (2008) and Winter (2009), tourism is indeed a resonant and meaningful act of remembrance, whereby the post-veteran generation can gather where a battle occurred, and connect with bits and pieces of the past to make meaning. In this sense, Edensor's (1998) concept, the tourist performance of remembering, is useful here, reflecting that the tourist brings their own positionality to a site, making meaning of national culture memory and other local narratives by way of imagining the past, taking photographs, collecting souvenirs or as is often the case, leaving mementoes (see Sather-Wagstaff 2008). The next section provides a review of literature to help us consider place identity from the perspective of landscapes, markers and sense of place.

The Normandy landscape of war: markers and sense of place

It is helpful at this point to conceptually redefine battlefields as a landscape of war. According to Filippucci (2004: 41) a landscape of war stands as:

> a separate 'landscape' not only because they are generally set apart from inhabited areas and dedicated to the dead rather than the living, but also because they largely materialize a national rather than local narrative of the war, centred on the lives and death of soldiers and troops and investing part of the... land with national and even international significance. In practice, these sites symbolically co-opt the local landscape through monuments that celebrate the land as the site of suffering and object of the sacrifice.

This definition is relevant to this research because the memorialization of Normandy has international significance for several nations, including Canada. Normandy is also significant in that it is a heritage landscape that is geographically distant from the respective homelands: people must travel overseas in order to experience and physically connect with a significant chapter in their national history.

Filippucci's definition aligns with the description of battlefield markers provided by MacCannell (1976: 129), when he describes a standard set of markers, including The Cemetery, The Museum (with its display of rusted arms), The Monument to a General or Regiment, The Polish Cannon with its welded balls, The Battle Map and the (optional) Reconstructed Fortification. These markers may be viewed as commonplace in military heritage sites, but MacCannell's observation also implies dismissing the complexity of symbolic meaning. Contrary to MacCannell's comment, memorials and monuments take many forms, as noted by authors such as Borg (1991) and Michalski (1998). Ryan (2007: 3) also acknowledges the complexity of markers when he argues that there are multiple truths to a battlefield, owing to one's own cultural memory of the war, and therefore, markers are more readily identified than they are understood. Notable markers in Normandy include memorials, museums, plaques, relics of war and war cemeteries. At last count, Holt and Holt (2004) recorded 400 memorials, monuments, plaques, street names, cemeteries, museums and relics of war specifically dedicated to D-Day and the ensuing 80-day Battle of Normandy. In addition, commemorations for D-Day and the Battle of Normandy number about 600 events annually (Normandie Mémoire), which mark both time and space.

Whereas authors such as MacCannell (1976), Lennon and Foley (2000), Diller and Scofidio (1994) and Edwards (2009) have written about the Normandy battlefields, the various national cultural memories – American, British, Canadian, French, German and Polish (to name the main nationalities involved) – have not been taken into account. One may argue that the legend of D-Day has been Americanized, described as 'Ambrosification' by one British battlefield tour guide the author met, in recognition of the popularity and influence of the American historian Stephen Ambrose (1992; 1994). The hegemony is also reflected in the popular Hollywood movies such as *Saving Private Ryan* (Spielberg 1998) and the television series *Band of Brothers* (Spielberg and Hanks 1998), which fuel the tourist performance of remembering with imagery. That the Americans played a pivotal role in World War II cannot be questioned. The American Sector, with sites such as Omaha Beach and Pointe-du Hoc, is the most visited sector, with the Normandy American Cemetery receiving 1.5 million visitors a year. Despite this, the Canadian sector, like the British Sector, is distinct in terms of how it is memorialized, forming a distinct national storyscape (see Chronis 2005). There are scores of markers in the Canadian sector, each one sponsored by a regiment, family or community wishing to commemorate a specific event or individual. In addition, themed tour routes, designated by maple leaf-emblazoned signs placed along country roads, pass through villages where Canadian flags stand in town squares and in the windows of local houses and schools. As independent in focus and as varied in story these markers are, they collate to form Canada's place identity in Normandy.

Added here to the list of war markers is sense of place, representing an intangible reference to the subjective and emotional attachment people have to a place (Agnew 1987). For Seaton (2009a: 96), "the defining feature of thanatourism" is the "auratic quality" of the site, attributed to its association with death. Similar to sense of place, the auratic quality of a site involves certain attributes: it is shared by a community, socially constructed in a space, it evolves over time, and the significance of the site is subjectively attributed by the individual, "often without much reflection" (Seaton, 2009a: 96). Employing the new term helps to describe such sites of memory and the specific management challenges involved in avoiding heritage dissonance (Tunbridge and Ashworth 1996). Auratic quality can gain greater theoretical weight by drawing from the more familiar term of sense of place.

In the context of landscapes of war, the natural environment plays a significant element in imagining the past. Several authors note the power of the natural environment in creating a sensory experience. For example, Mels (2004) links sense of place to what he refers to as the geography of rhythms, a resonance fostered from the significance of a place, the interconnecting of sensory feelings from the experience – seeing, smelling, touching, tasting and hearing – to meanings associated with the human condition. To illustrate further, in describing the Gallipoli battlefield, Scates (2006: 40) notes that "much of the wonder of Gallipoli has to do with... its natural setting". Gough (2004: 252) argues that the power of the Somme is created by its very emptiness, noting the resonance of "cherished open spaces... [that] should not become littered with ill-considered 'monumentalia'". Piekarz (2007: 29) also values the lack of materiality at the site of the 1685 Battle of Sedgemoor, as it allows "for the field to act as a canvas on which one's imagination can play". Each of these examples reflects what Tuan (2004: 45–46) defines as a sense of place established by three criteria: a perception of permanence, a sense of history that has an emotional quality and finally, an "intimate tie between place and self". This point is relevant to this research because it acknowledges sense of place as part of place identity and tourist meaning-making.

Whereas individual sites have their own unique sense of place, a tour would involve experiencing a number of sites, each offering a different story and insight of the battle. For example, a visit to Normandy in June might involve visiting a few museums, a landing beach, a cemetery and possibly a battlefield close to the coast, as well as perhaps attending one of the literally hundreds of commemorations that take place from June to August. In this sense, the visitor may engage in what Benediktsson and Lund (2010) metaphorically describe as conversations with landscape, multiple interactions with place identity that evoke meaning with regard to themes such as national identity, social identity and nostalgia as well as how the visitor identifies with death and war. Despite the Canadian sense of identity associated with the sites discussed here, place identity is more complex, yet richly demonstrated, when we consider these various other conversations that occur in the tourist performance.

A multiple-voice approach is employed here to reflect what Hertz (1997: xii) describes as a "visible narrator and co-participant". Tourist meditations evoked by war and death can be a highly personal and emotionally charged matter, as Dunkley (2007) argues, with the deeper conversation taking place with oneself. Collins and Gallinat (2010: 29) argue that researchers can broaden and enrich their research by trusting "their own personal and cultural biographies as significant sources of knowledge". Writing in the third person is the primary format, with parts written in the reflexive first person and italics. Providing the first person perspective allows the researcher to capture the tourist moment (Cary 2004) in its unabridged and subjective form. Incorporating a reflexive element in the research is therefore important to co-participate in the thoughts and feelings associated with a battlefield tourism experience.

What follows are five vignettes, each based on a different site of memory. Each vignette also demonstrates how a range of interactions and sensory experiences

Place identities in Normandy 171

with the landscape of war affect the tourist performance of remembering. In addition, various dimensions of the tourism–remembrance relationship are illustrated, such as the role of cultural memories (see Sturken 1997), heritage dissonance (Tunbridge and Ashworth 1996) and the politics of remembrance (Seaton 2009a). The first vignette explores Juno Beach, presented separately from the Juno Beach Centre, the fifth vignette. In this way, the visitor experience of the beach as a site of memory is distinguished from the management challenges involved in representing and interpreting Canada's war heritage.

Exploring the sense at Juno Beach

The landing beaches themselves are among the most iconic sites of memory for D-Day. As Bastable (2004: 12) writes:

> Even now, [the D-Day beaches] have a stillness about them, a solemn air that makes you inclined to tread softly and keep your voice to a whisper. You go mindfully when you explore the landing grounds, as if you were in a church. And it is not hard to tell where this sense comes from: it is the sanctity of spilt blood. You can still sense it, though the tides have washed over the beaches forty thousand times since the day of battle.

Bastable's quote exemplifies what Baldacchino (2010: 767) notes as the power of sand to evoke "time, impermanence...[and] a place of solace". Baldacchino (2010: 763) also notes how the sand can be a "powerful, visual, emotive and experiential component" that is culturally determined, a point emphasized for Canadians at Juno as it is in particular for American visitors to Omaha Beach. The sand is therefore significant as nature's relic of war, conveying both the memory of D-Day and the aura of battle.

For Cartier and Lew (2005: 3) a beach is often viewed as a touristed landscape, one that is associated with joyful family summer holidays. In contrast, in their interpretation of the D-Day beaches, Diller and Scofidio (1994) see the holiday beach as being in conflict with a memorialized landing beach: the sun bathers, a macabre parallel of bodies lying in the sand, in dissonance with the war memory. Such an interpretation leads to the question of what is appropriate in maintaining the auratic quality of the landing beaches that, at the height of the summer, are populated with families enjoying the seaside. While Lefebvre (1991: 310) notes that beaches are often viewed as a landscape for the purpose of pleasure, they are also evocative places (Bærenholdt 2004) and warrant further examination of their meaning beyond what is provided by Diller and Scofidio.

Comments from Canadian tourists visiting Juno Beach reflect their attempts to imagine the soldier's experience. One Canadian, Ian, muses on his connection with the memory of soldiers landing on 6 June: "Feel the sand under foot. Just feel the contact. Look up and see the German placements. Try to time it that the tide is out [when visiting], you see the distance to sprint." Ian's comment demonstrates an emotional connection with the landscape at an intimate level of

172 *Geoffrey R. Bird*

meaning, gaining a common tactile and imagined perspective of a soldier advancing on the beach. Furthermore, as Julia explains, "I think there is something that's visceral about actually getting to touch the earth and walk on the beach and the soil where all of that actually happened... it is a different level of understanding." Julia is illustrative of White (2000) when he describes the significance of emotion in the process of identifying with a war memory, and the resonant dimension gained by being physically proximate to where the event occurred. The examples here therefore highlight the range of cognitive and emotional thoughts that are part of the tourist performance and the unique power, or resonance, experienced in a landscape of war.

Moving inland from Juno, Canadian troops liberated many villages and towns by 6 June, including the village of Basly. The intention of the next vignette is to explore what the author experienced at the annual commemoration in this village. In addition to identifying as a Canadian, what is emphasized is the interaction between Canadian and French cultural memories of war and how they are reflected and overlap in place identity.

Patriotism at Basly Village

The service at Basly (see Figure 12.1), a small village a few miles from Juno Beach, is to commemorate its liberation by Canadian troops. The stone monument cut in the shape of a maple leaf stands festooned with flowers and wreaths, surrounded by about 100 locals and a few Canadians. Speaking in French, a booming voice sets the tone: "Thousands of Canadians were killed in order that we could be free." Silence. The words echo across the square. The presenter continues, speaking about the young soldiers, as volunteers, who came to fight in a war far away from those they loved. I think about some of the veterans I know, and the places they came from: the prairies, small towns on the west coast of Canada, so far removed from this place. I imagine them cautiously entering this square, fearful of what might be around the next corner. I sense an earnest reverence for the Canadians who came here to fight, a shared affinity amongst the French and the few Canadians present.

As if emotionally primed by the steady flow of speeches and poetry about the war dead, about freedom won, about foreigners coming from the other side of the world to fight, the crowd unleashes *La Marseillaise*. Their voices raised and singing with emotion, the anthem fills the town square. Aux armes, citoyens! To arms, citizens! Voices quivering, those around me do not hold back. The historical concepts of occupation, of oppression, fear and then liberation, take on a living, emotional charge here. Many of those around me either lived through, or grew up hearing about, Nazi occupation and the day the Canadians came. The Canadian national anthem follows, and the small number of Canadians present do our best to have our voices heard. Afterward, a Frenchman smiles and shakes my hand. I am invited to the local hall for a vin d'honneur. The sun sets on French and Canadian flags caressed to dance

Figure 12.1 Flags and anthems: local commemoration on 6 June 2008 at Basly

by the summer breeze. It is a powerful moment, one tinged with patriotism as well as a sense of personal attachment toward this community.

(Bird, Field Notes 2008)

A range of themes can be discussed with regard to these observations. First, there is the researcher/tourist, as sympathetic insider (Goldenberg 1992), who feels a connection to the place through the ritual narratives of commemoration and the interaction with French and Canadian people. What is affirmed in the commemoration is that World War II represents the 'good war' (see Granatstein 2005; Pauwels 2002; Terkel 1984), a just cause that overcame Nazi tyranny. As Torgovnick (2005: 22) explains, Normandy represents "a synecdoche for the Allied victory, for the triumph of democracy over totalitarianism, and, once the Nazi camps had been breached and opened, for a system of evil that shocked the world". Thus, the significance of D-Day, as embodied in the commemoration in Basly, is that the event embodies both historical and mythic themes that represent World War II as a just and heroic war.

The narrative of the Basly commemoration, like many town commemorations in the Canadian Sector, reflects a shared cultural memory between France and Canada: a Norman town's liberation by Canadian soldiers. There is a sense of pride for Canadian visitors who, upon viewing the Canadian flags and experiencing the locals' recognition of Canada, assimilate the Canadian victory as a reflection of their own Canadian identity. Yet the multiple layers of war heritage at a given site can evoke a range of memories, as Winter and Sivan (1999) and Seaton (2009a) argue. In the case of Basly, the narrative also reflects what Farmer (1999: 208) describes as the "organization of silences" in French commemoration, which do not speak of collaboration and Vichy. In addition, Footitt (2004) also argues that closer inspection of the French experience during the Battle of Normandy reveals conflicting views about the Allies that influence the war memory of liberation. An example of these experiences are the Allied bombing of cities and towns (see Beevor 2009), soldiers looting farmhouses and fraternization (see Footitt 2004), which has led to problematizing what is remembered, forgotten and silenced.

As Mosse (1990) argues, the problem of remembering can be assuaged by the use of myth. Myths, Boym (2001: 54) asserts, "are not lies but rather shared assumptions that help to naturalize history and make it liveable". As Hedges (2002: 23) writes, myth in the context of war "allows us to make sense of mayhem and violent death". A national war memory, as elicited in the Basly commemoration, is free of complexities and conveys a purified history, what Mosse (1990) describes as the "Myth of the War Experience". However, it is important to note that war memories are not solely fabricated by the state. For example, in the aftermath of World War I, Vance (1997: 267) notes that myth of that war was borne out of grief, hope and a search for meaning. In the case of Basly and other towns, what is remembered, in fact celebrated, is liberation and victory. There is an earnest sense of gratitude felt in the community toward Canadians who fought here. The confirmation of Canadian nationhood, of the values and lives invested in Canada's war effort, are embodied in the place identity of a town and manifested in its commemoration.

Taken from another perspective, this experience represents a tourist moment, whereby the sense of being a tourist is erased, and that the narrative and experience in this site of memory creates a sense of belonging (Cary 2004: 73). Rather than standing as passive consumer, as Bagnall (2003: 95) describes, the Canadian researcher gains a different insight and connection about the meaning of war remembrance. Research on battlefield tourism in France such as the Somme does not typically involve taking into account the local voice, as the non-French-speaking tourist/researcher misses the chance to interact with the French, muting the French war memory. Gaining insight into the French war memory means gaining insight in the struggle with the past, vacillating between the French memories of resistance, collaboration, deportation and indifference (see Hewitt 2008; Rousso 1991).

The next vignette focuses on the place identity associated the Canadian War Grave at Beny-sur-Mer. Two themes are explored here. First, the place identity of the cemetery is considered in terms of dominant and instrumental symbols (Turner 1967). Second, the vignette focuses on the experience of a Canadian veteran returning with his family, and the topic of familial kinship that is a significant theme in perpetuating war remembrance and war pilgrimage (see Lloyd 1998; Scates 2006; Winter 2006, 2009).

Lines of graves at Beny-sur-Mer

Approximately 2,000 Canadians are buried at the Beny-sur-Mer Canadian War Cemetery. As with all Commonwealth war graves, the site was designed and maintained by the Commonwealth War Graves Commission. The meaning of a military cemetery, what Seaton (2000: 68) describes as a "hub of signifiers", cannot be underestimated, nor can it be readily dismissed as a form of state propaganda to mythologize the dead and the cause of war (see Mosse 1990). Nevertheless, war cemeteries do indeed possess powerful symbolism. Turner (1967: 31) defines a dominant symbol as a shrine, "consisting of several objects in configuration". Instrumental symbols are the means by which the goals of the dominant symbol are attained (Turner 1967: 32). For a war cemetery, the row of gravestones can be viewed as a dominant symbol of sacrifice for the nation, and the humanism of an individual gravestone may be viewed as an instrumental symbol. This form of symbolism is now explored.

McGeer (2008) provides insight into the timeless significance of a military cemetery by focusing on the personal inscriptions engraved on many gravestones. He notes:

> the abundance and diversity [of] individual expressions of sorrow and consolation, touching, heartfelt, and permanent, spoke more poignantly than any memorial for the burden of loss borne by thousands of parents, wives, and children for the rest of their lives.
>
> (McGeer 2008: v)

A personal inscription cited by McGeer (p. 16) is for Trooper Robert Lawrence Morton, 24 years old (see Figure 12.2), and exemplifies the personal mourning and a sense of solace of perhaps a fiancée or a wife:

> A beautiful future planned, only to end in a dream.
> Dear, my thoughts are ever of you and what might have been.

Such moving inscriptions are unique to Commonwealth gravestones, signifying a personal and often private message. Figure 12.2 also presents the typical format of a Commonwealth gravestone. To refashion a phrase by Turner, the gravestone represents a forest of identities, with the individual identified by his family and familial names, rank, regiment, age, religion and nationality, all of which represent forms of kinship to which the visitor may associate her or himself (see Palmer 2005). In addition, there is the narrative of love and loss with which McGeer (2008) identifies. Collectively, these identities cosmologically frame one man, providing a number of triggers that may engage the onlooker, a phenomenon that is made even more powerful when multiplied across row upon row of gravestones.

Whereas the main intent of this research is to focus on remembrance by the post-veteran generation, the experience of families visiting with their veteran fathers represents the passing on of the family history, what Winter (2006)

Figure 12.2 Gravestone of Trooper Morton, Beny-sur-Mer, Canadian Military Cemetery

describes as the familial kinship of war remembrance. The sense of familial obligation to remember forms a central part of the continuance of war memory beyond the veteran generation and exemplifies the notion of next of kin as social agents of remembrance (Winter 2006). In this sense, touring the landscape of war facilitates the succession of family war memories to the next generation. For example, Cullis, a Canadian veteran, took a trip with his daughter and grandchildren. With his photographs taken from the landing craft he piloted in 1944, Cullis is able to locate the spot where he landed. The triangulation of veteran/father narrative, a specific location and the old photographs establish a strong family ownership to both story and place. The result is what Cullis' son Mark describes as a "passing on of family history". Similar in significance is the experience at Beny-sur-Mer cemetery. The cemetery draws both Cullis and his family in what Bachelor (2004: 97) explains is part of the mourning process and cemeteries, "an inexplicable innate compulsion to visit". The forest of symbols of the gravestones, in particular the date of death, affect Cullis, something that becomes a feeling shared by his family. As Cullis explains, "we were at the Canadian cemetery and I got quite tearful. I realized I was so lucky. I was there with my grandchildren and showing them around, and for all of these other guys their date of death was June 1944." In this way, Cullis engages in what Bachelor (2004) describes as maintaining an emotional bond with the dead that involves seeking solace from emotions of grief. This meaning is transmitted to the family as witnesses to Cullis' emotional experience in the cemetery, a powerfully symbolic site that can provoke conversations about one's own mortality.

In summary, this vignette illustrates the social agency of memory and how familial kinship plays an important role in preserving the individual memories of war (Winter 2006). Part of this legacy involves visiting the landscape of war and recounting wartime events, in this case evoked by the instrumental symbolism of a gravestone, thereby anchoring family memory in a place. The next vignette provides another example of what Park (2010) aptly entitles "emotional journeys into nationhood" but one that is more conflicted than the experience at Basly. Whereas the ritual elements are similar to other commemorations attended throughout Normandy, each commemoration has its own tone of remembrance, framed by the war experiences of that landscape. From a thanatourism perspective, the tourist readily experiences the auratic quality of the Other of Death at the Abbaye d'Ardenne, the site where Canadian prisoners of war were executed.

Unthinkable endings at Abbaye d'Ardenne

> A crowd of Canadians and French gather in a small clearing adjacent to the Abbey. It is a solemn commemoration, with the events of June 8th recalled, and the 16 names of those executed recited. The moment of silence is filled with the rustle of leaves overhead, as a stand of trees sways to a gentle wind. The juxtaposition of the beauty of nature adds to the emotion for me, as I think it might have been the last sound these men heard before being shot. It might be a familiar sound to them, as it is for me: trees we would find in Nova Scotia or British Columbia. The photographs provide a sense of presence, reminding me of their youth and innocence, with eyes expressing the hope of youth. The commemoration is challenged in that it cannot offer a rationale or sense of closure to what happened here. Instead, I am haunted by the inhumanity of this place. The Piper's Lament breaks the silence.
>
> (Bird, Field Notes 2009)

This place is what Bell (1997: 813) describes as a "landscape of ghosts", with a haunted sense of place that narrative, ritual memorials and landscape have enshrined in the site (see Figure 12.3). Winter (2009: 62, 70) asserts that the search for meaning in World War II commemoration is "infinitely more complex", a comment that holds veracity when considering the memory of what occurred at the Abbaye d'Ardenne and other sites such as Authie, Audrieu and Le Mesnil-Patry (see English 2011). Of those Canadians killed between 6 and 11 June 1944, one out of every seven was executed by members of the 12th SS Panzer Division (Margolian 1998: 123–124).

Abbaye d'Ardenne provokes thoughts of the Other of Death (Seaton 2009a). I find the site quite troubling; there is no conclusion, no heroism to deflect the story of murder, no way to rationalize the loss without stepping away from the details and thinking about the larger victory. The fruitless search for meaning reflects in what Geertz (1975: 30) describes as "in search of all-too-deep-lying turtles",

Figure 12.3 Abbaye d'Ardenne: site of Canadian executions

resulting in losing "touch with the hard surfaces of life". Abbaye d'Ardenne represents a senseless atrocity, amplifying the complexity and irreconcilability of certain war memories.

The Canadian tourist performance of remembering at Abbaye d'Ardenne involves leaving objects and mementoes behind, as also occurs at Beny-sur-Mer cemetery (see Figure 12.4). Bachelor (2004) describes such rituals as establishing a relationship between those remembering and the remembered. The act also reflects what Park (2010: 117) describes as the "socio-psychological dimensions of heritage" and how "personal perceptions... subjective sentiments and collective social memories contribute to the long-term tourism appeal" of heritage sites. In this light, it is the power of being there that instills a shared sense of collective remembrance. The sense of place is enabled by the sensory element such as the familiar and peaceful sound of wind rustling the trees. Like the physicality of a place as a site of memory, sound acts as an intersection in time and space, a bond shared between those who awaited execution in June 1944 and those who come to bear witness and to remember in a contemporary setting.

The final section explores the challenges of the Juno Beach Centre with establishing its place identity. The vignette represents the politics of remembrance involved in representing and interpreting war (see Cole 1999; Linenthal and Engelhardt 1996).

Place identities in Normandy 179

Figure 12.4 Flags, poppies and crosses left behind at the Abbaye d'Ardenne

Politics of remembrance at the Juno Beach Centre

The Juno Beach Centre (JBC) is what Linenthal (1991) would describe as a "ceremonial center", the site where the main official Canadian commemorations take place, with several war memorials, an interpretive exhibit on Canada's war effort as well as one about Canada itself comprising the site. With no government funding at the start, the initiative to establish an interpretive centre on Juno Beach was led by veterans who turned to the general public to help fund the project. The surge of popular support ultimately embarrassed the government into participating (see Granatstein 2004: A20). Although receiving some government funding, the JBC, as the only Canadian World War II interpretive site outside of Canada, is still run by a non-profit entity.

As this site is often considered hallowed ground for Canadians (Goddard 2004; Granatstein and Morton 1989; Granatstein and Neary1995), there has always been much attention and expectation brought to bear on the JBC. Controversies regarding the representation of the Canadian war effort reflect the politics of remembrance (Seaton 2009b). The concept of the heritage force field (Seaton 2001; Sharpley 2009) is useful here, as it acknowledges the range of memory activists (Winter 2006) such as next of kin, local communities, veterans, site management, visitors, the media as well as the state, who stake claim to the war memory and how it is best represented.

Briefly, there are several challenges faced by the JBC. First, the mandate given to the Centre is to tell the story of Canada's involvement in World War II, not only of D-Day. As Garth Webb, D-Day veteran and Chair of the Centre, clarifies, the mandate of the site "is not a D-Day memorial. This is dedicated to Canadians of World War II to tell their story". Despite the good intentions of representing the stories of all Canadian veterans, this broader mandate raises interrelated challenges of implementation and generating visitor revenue. For example, in 2008, the JBC presented an exhibit on Canada's involvement in the Italian Campaign. Much to the discomfort of D-Day veterans, they are placed on a pedestal of heroes, while other campaigns were forgotten, such as the Canadians fighting in Italy, referred to as the D-Day dodgers (see Dancocks 1991). The difficulty placed upon JBC management is attracting visitors to Juno Beach to view an exhibit that memorializes the battles in Italy.

This example reflects what Joly (2000: 50) would describe as typical when veterans take the lead role in the development of a museum. Joly points to the success of the *conseil scientifique,* or expert steering committee, that was created for the design of the First World War Museum in Péronne, an initiative that "revolutionized thinking" (Joly 2000: 50) by providing academic input from the three main warring parties. Such an approach is difficult in the context of World War II given that controversy can readily occur with regard to how World War II is interpreted (see Linenthal and Engelhardt 1996; Nobile 1995). Joly describes the prevalence of micro memories that dominate museum portrayals of world war museums, resulting in localized narratives that are unable to connect with a larger audience. In the case of the JBC, the micro memory is not a localized narrative, but a shallow and broad memory, one lacking deep narrative linked to the immediate landscape of war, yet presenting the entire breadth of the Canadian war effort. The result is described by a Canadian historian and guide: "One of my problems with the Juno Beach Centre is that [visitors] read kind of basic stuff about the war." In essence, the JBC does not offer a deep description and interpretation of the nearby battles owing to its mandate to acknowledge the entire Canadian war effort.

This controversy spills over into another challenge, criticism owing to the lack of artefacts and a reliance on interpretive boards and video clips. As John, a Canadian guide reflects, "Something is missing. Is it to have more 'hands-on' stuff, or to have some different kinds of artefacts in there? It doesn't capture what I am feeling." This concern is reflected in a Canadian newspaper editorial that criticized the Centre as being "artifact-light and text-heavy", "bleak", "uninspired" and at times inaccurate in its narrative of Canada before the war (Granatstein 2004: 20). A larger issue is the limited link that the JBC, although located on the Canadian landing beach, has with the beachscape. Guided tours by young Canadians employed by JBC provide sufficient interpretation of adjacent war memorials and a nearby German bunker, but the tour is limited in that staff cannot extend the tour to the entire stretch of Juno Beach, a distance of about eight kilometers, nor inland to where the battle raged for three months. The result is a limited narrative of the Canadian war effort in Normandy that in turn may hasten the forgetting of Canadian war heritage.

The contested nature of the Canadian war memory as illustrated at the Juno Beach Centre involves a complex and delicate balance between the interests of the veteran voice and those wishing to ensure remembrance of the immediate landscape of war. The transition from the veteran to the post veteran era will inevitably alter the representation of Canadian war heritage. In this context, an underlying theme in the Canadian cultural memory of war is the passionate debate as to how the national war story should be represented and interpreted in Normandy.

Conclusion

Five sites in the Canadian sector of the Normandy landscape of war were selected on the basis of what may be typically experienced on a tour during the June commemorations. Each site evokes a different dimension of Canada's cultural memory of war. The landing beach itself represents a uniquely powerful site, as it draws the visitor's imagination to make meaning of the sense of place. The war grave cemetery at Beny-sur-Mer involves a forest of symbols (Turner 1967) that trigger connection with the visitor. Whereas the commemoration at Basly evokes a sense of Canadian identity, the experience is a powerful example of shared remembrance with the French war memory of liberation, exemplifying how cultural memories converge in certain place identities. The place identity of Abbaye d'Ardenne, one of several sites where Canadian prisoners of war were executed, conveys the atrocity of war, and stands as a memory unresolved with the more mythic generalist interpretation of D-Day. Finally, the Juno Beach Centre, the ceremonial hub in the Canadian Sector, embodies the politics of remembrance associated with representing and interpreting war and the challenges of management in working with various stakeholders to memorialize the site's auratic quality.

Collectively, these places represent a mix of meanings that draw upon feelings of national identity, but also social identity, as evident in the conveying of family history at the cemetery, as well as thoughts of death and war, such as at the Abbaye d'Ardenne. Throughout these vignettes, place identity has been constructed through the sensory experience coupled with the visitor's imagination. Not discussed here, but an integral part of meaning-making, is the role of tour guides, guide books and other mediating agencies. Authors such as Chronis (2005) and Iles (2006) provide excellent examples of the important role interpretation plays in battlefield tourism.

Certain notable historical battles are not discussed in this chapter. For instance, at St Lambert sur Dives, a small interpretive site marks where Major David Currie of the South Alberta Regiment was awarded the Victoria Cross for his leadership and bravery. Verrières Ridge, Carpiquet and Caen are also notable sites in Canada's military history in Normandy (see Copp and Bechthold 2008). Future research could examine place identity of these sites and the efforts of the Canadian Battle Monuments Foundation to establish memorials and interpretive information.

The research findings demonstrate the complexity of the context, conflicts and contributions of the tourism–remembrance relationship. First, they reveal the central role of tourism and the tourist in the co-construction of meaning and engagement in remembrance. This also involves consideration of narratives and voices that are remembered, forgotten as well as silenced in place identity. Second, the research underlines the power of a memorialized landscape of war in evoking a connectedness with national cultural memories of World War II. Finally, the research identifies the politics of remembrance in Canadian war heritage at a time when living memory, represented by veterans, is fading, and tourism grows in prominence as a guardian of that important memory.

References

Agnew, J.A. (1987) *The United States in the World Economy: A Regional Geography*, Cambridge: Cambridge University Press.
Ambrose, S.E. (1992) *Band of Brothers: E Company, 506th Regiment, 101st Airborne: From Normandy to Hitler's Eagle's Nest*, New York: Simon & Schuster.
Ambrose, S.E. (1994) *D-Day, June 6, 1944: The Climactic Battle of World War II*, New York: Simon & Schuster.
Bachelor, P. (2004) *Sorrow & Solace: The Social World of the Cemetery*, Amityville, NY: Baywood.
Bærenholdt, J.O. (2004) *Performing Tourist Places*, Aldershot: Ashgate.
Bagnall, G. (2003) 'Performance and Performativity at Heritage Sites', *Museum and Society*, 1(2): 87–103.
Baldacchino, G. (2010) 'Re-placing Materiality: A Western Anthropology of Sand', *Annals of Tourism Research*, 37(3): 763–778.
Bastable, J. (2004) *Voices from D-Day*, Newton Abbot: David & Charles.
Beevor, A. (2009) *D-Day: The Battle for Normandy*, London: Viking.
Bell, M.M. (1997) 'The Ghosts of Place', *Theory and Society*, 26(6): 813–836.
Benediktsson, K. and Lund, K.A. (2010) *Conversations with Landscape*, Burlington, VT: Ashgate.
Borg, A. (1991) *War Memorials: From Antiquity to the Present*, London: Leo Cooper.
Boym, S. (2001) *The Future of Nostalgia*, New York: Basic Books.
Cartier, C. and Lew, A. (eds) (2005) *Seductions of Place: Geographical Perspectives on Globalization and Touristed Landscapes*, New York: Routledge.
Cary, S.H. (2004) 'The Tourist Moment', *Annals of Tourism Research*, 31(1): 61–77.
Chronis, A. (2005) 'Co-constructing Heritage at the Gettysburg Storyscape', *Annals of Tourism Research*, 32(2): 386–406.
Cole, T. (1999) *Selling the Holocaust: From Auschwitz to Schindler: How History is Bought, Packaged and Sold*, New York: Routledge.
Collins, P., and Gallinat, A. (2010) *The Ethnographic Self as Resource: Writing Memory and Experience into Ethnography*, New York: Berghahn Books.
Copp, T., Bechthold, M., Laurier Centre for Military Strategic and Disarmament Studies, and Canadian Battlefields Foundation (2008) *The Canadian Battlefields in Normandy: A Visitor's Guide*, 3rd edn, Waterloo, ON: Laurier Centre for Military, Strategic and Disarmament Studies.
Dancocks, D. (1991) *The D-Day Dodgers: The Canadians in Italy, 1943–1945*, Toronto: McClelland & Stewart.
Diller, E. and Scofidio, R. (1994) *Visite aux Armes: Tourismes de Guerre [Back to the front: Tourisms of War]*, Caen: F.R.A.C. Basse-Normandie.

Dunkley, R.A. (2007) 'Re-peopling Tourism: A "Hot Approach" to Studying Thanatourist Experiences', in I. Ateljevic, A. Pritchard and N. Morgan (eds) *The Critical Turn in Tourism Studies: Innovative Research Methods*, Oxford: Elsevier.

Edensor, T. (1998) *Tourists at the Taj: Performance and Meaning at a Symbolic Site*, London and New York: Routledge.

Edwards, S. (2009) 'Commemoration and Consumption in Normandy, 1945–1994', in M. Keren and H.H. Herwig (eds) *War Memory and Popular Culture: Essays on Modes of Remembrance and Commemoration*, London: McFarland.

English, J.A. (2011) *Surrender Invites Death: Fighting the Waffen SS in Normandy*, Mechanicsburg, PA: Stackpole.

Farmer, S.B. (1999) *Martyred Village: Commemorating the 1944 Massacre at Oradour-sur-Glane*, Berkeley, CA: University of California Press.

Filippucci, P. (2004) 'Memory and Marginality: Remembrance of War in Argonne, France', in F. Pine, D. Kaneff and H. Haukanes (eds) *Memory, Politics and Religion: The Past Meets the Present in Europe*, London: Lit.

Footitt, H. (2004) 'Liberating France without the French: Grammars of Representation', in W. Kidd and B. Murdoch (eds) *Memory and Memorials: The Commemorative Century*, Aldershot: Ashgate, pp. 167–177.

Geertz, C. (1975) *The Interpretation of Cultures: Selected Essays*, London: Hutchinson.

Goddard, L. (2004) *D-Day Juno Beach: Canada's 24 Hours of Destiny*, Toronto: Dundurn.

Gold, J.R. and Gold, M.M. (2003) 'Representing Culloden. Social Memory, Battlefield Heritage and Landscapes of Regret', in S.P. Hanna and V.J. Del Casino (eds) *Mapping Tourism*, Minneapolis, MN: University of Minnesota Press.

Goldenberg, S. (1992) *Thinking Methodologically*, New York: HarperCollins.

Gough, P. (2004) 'Sites in the Imagination: The Beaumont Hamel Newfoundland Memorial on the Somme', *Cultural Geographies*, 11(3): 235–258.

Granatstein, J.L. (2004) 'War Stories, Told Badly', *National Post*, Toronto, 17 June.

Granatstein, J.L. (2005) *The Last Good War: An Illustrated History of Canada in the Second World War, 1939–1945*, Vancouver: Douglas & McIntyre.

Granatstein, J.L. and Morton, D. (1989) *A Nation Forged in Fire: Canadians and the Second World War 1939–1945*, Toronto: Lester & Orphen Dennys.

Granatstein, J.L., and Neary, P. (1995) *The Good Fight: Canadians and World War II*, Toronto: Copp Clarke.

Hedges, C. (2002) *War Is a Force that Gives Us Meaning*, New York: PublicAffairs.

Hertz, R. (ed.) (1997) *Reflexivity & Voice*, Thousand Oaks, CA: Sage Publications.

Hewitt, L.D. (2008) *Remembering the Occupation in French Film: National Identity in Postwar Europe*, Basingstoke: Palgrave Macmillan.

Holt, T. and Holt, V. (2004) *Major & Mrs Holt's Guide to the Normandy Landing Beaches*, 4th edn, Barnsley, UK: Leo Cooper.

Iles, J. (2006) 'Recalling the Ghosts of War: Performing Tourism on the Battlefields of the Western Front', *Text & Performance Quarterly*, 26(2): 162–180.

Joly, M. (2010) 'War Museums in France', in S. Blowen, M. Demossier and J. Picard (eds) *Recollections of France: Memories, Identities and Heritage in Contemporary France*, New York: Berghahn Books, pp. 33–51.

Keegan, J. (2004) 'Forward', in T. Barris (ed.) *Juno: Canadians at D-Day, June 6, 1944*, Toronto: T. Allen.

Lefebvre, H. (1991) *The Production of Space*, Malden, MA: Blackwell.

Lennon, J. and Foley, M. (2000) *Dark Tourism*, London: Continuum.

Linenthal, E.T. (1991) *Sacred Ground: Americans and their Battlefields*, Urbana: University of Illinois Press.

Linenthal, E.T. and Engelhardt, T. (1996) *History Wars: The Enola Gay and other Battles for the American Past*, New York: Metropolitan Books.

Lloyd, D.W. (1998) *Battlefield Tourism: Pilgrimage and the Commemoration of the Great War in Britain, Australia and Canada, 1919–1939*, New York: Berg.

MacCannell, D. (1976) *The Tourist: A New Theory of the Leisure Class*, London: Macmillan.

McGeer, E. (2008) *Words of Valediction and Remembrance: Canadian Epitaphs of the Second World War*, St Catharines, ON: Vanwell.

Margolian, H. (1998) *Conduct Unbecoming: The Story of the Murder of Canadian Prisoners of War in Normandy*, Toronto and London: University of Toronto Press.

Marshall, D. (2004) 'Making Sense of Remembrance', *Social & Cultural Geography*, 5(1): 37–54.

Mels, T. (2004) *Reanimating Places: A Geography of Rhythms*, Burlington, VT: Ashgate.

Michalski, S. (1998) *Public Monuments: Art in Political Bondage 1870–1997*, London: Reaktion.

Mosse, G.L. (1990) *Fallen Soldiers: Reshaping the Memory of the World War*, Oxford: Oxford University Press.

Nobile, P. (1995) *Judgment at the Smithsonian*, New York: Marlow.

Palmer, C. (2005) 'An Ethnography of Englishness: Experiencing Identity through Tourism', *Annals of Tourism Research*, 32(1): 7–27.

Park, H.Y. (2010) 'Heritage Tourism: Emotional Journeys into Nationhood', *Annals of Tourism Research*, 37(1): 116–135.

Pauwels, J.R. (2002) *The Myth of the Good War: America in the Second World War*, Toronto: J. Lorimer.

Piekarz, M. (2007) 'It's Just a Bloody Field! Approaches, Opportunities and Dilemmas of Interpreting English Battlefields', in C. Ryan (ed.) *Battlefield Tourism*, Oxford: Elsevier.

Rousso, H. (1991) *The Vichy Syndrome: History and Memory in France since 1944*, Cambridge, MA: Harvard University Press.

Ryan, C. (2007) *Battlefield Tourism: History, Place and Interpretation*, London: Elsevier.

Sather-Wagstaff, J. (2008) 'Picturing Experience: A Tourist-Centred Perspective on Commemorative Historical Studies', *Tourist Studies*, 8: 77–103.

Scates, B. (2006) *Return to Gallipoli: Walking the Battlefields of the Great War*, Cambridge: Cambridge University Press.

Scates, B. (2008) 'Memorializing Gallipoli: Manufacturing Memory at Anzac', *Public History Review*, 15: 47–59.

Seaton, A.V. (2000) '"Another Weekend Away Looking for Dead Bodies...": Battlefield Tourism on the Somme and in Flanders', *Tourism Recreation Research*, 25(3): 63–77.

Seaton, A.V. (2001) 'Sources of Slavery – Destinations of Slavery: The Silences and Disclosures of Slavery Heritage in the UK and US', in G. Dann and A.V. Seaton (eds) *Slavery, Contested Heritage and Thanatourism*, Binghampton, NY: Haworth.

Seaton, A.V. (2009a) 'Purposeful Otherness: Approaches to the Management of Thanatourism', in R. Sharpley and P. Stone (eds) *The Darker Side of Travel: The Theory and Practice of Dark Tourism*, Bristol: Channel View.

Seaton, A.V. (2009b) 'Thanatourism and its Discontents: An Appraisal of a Decade's Work with some Future Issues and Directions', in T. Jamal and M. Robinson (eds) *The Sage Handbook of Tourism Studies*, London: Sage.

Sharpley, R. (2009) 'Dark Tourism and Political Ideology: Towards a Governance Model', in R. Sharpley and P. Stone (eds) *The Darker Side of Travel: The Theory and Practice of Dark Tourism*, Bristol: Channel View Publications, pp. 145–166.
Spielberg, S. (1998) *Saving Private Ryan*, Dream Works Pictures.
Spielberg, S. and Hanks, T. (2001) *Band of Brothers*, HBO Miniseries.
Sturken, M. (1997) *Tangled Memories: The Vietnam War, the AIDS Epidemic, and the Politics of Remembering*, Berkeley, CA: University of California Press.
Terkel, S. (1984) *The Good War: An Oral History of World War Two*, New York: Pantheon Books.
Tilley, C.Y. (1994) *A Phenomenology of Landscape: Places, Paths, and Monuments*, Providence, RI: Berg.
Torgovnick, M. (2005) *The War Complex: World War II in our Time*, Chicago: University of Chicago Press.
Tuan, Y.-F. (2004) 'Sense of Place: Its Relationship to Self and Time', in T. Mels (ed.) *Reanimating Places: A Geography of Rhythms*, Aldershot: Ashgate.
Tunbridge, J.E. and Ashworth, G.J. (1996) *Dissonant Heritage: The Management of the Past as a Resource in Conflict*, Chichester: Wiley.
Turner, V.W. (1967) *The Forest of Symbols: Aspects of Ndembu Ritual*, Ithaca, NY: Cornell University Press.
Vance, J.F.W. (1997) *Death So Noble: Memory, Meaning, and the First World War*, Vancouver: UBC Press.
White, G. (2000) 'Emotional Remembering: The Pragmatics of National Memory', *American Anthropological Association*, 27(4): 505–529.
Winter, J.M. (2006) *Remembering War: The Great War between Memory and History in the Twentieth Century*, New Haven, CT: Yale University Press.
Winter, J.M. (2009) *The Legacy of the Great War: Ninety Years on*, Kansas City, MO: University of Missouri Press; National World War I Museum.
Winter, J.M. and Sivan, E. (1999) *War and Remembrance in the Twentieth Century*, New York: Cambridge University Press.

Part III
Place interpretation

13 Holocaust tourism in a post-Holocaust Europe
Anne Frank and Auschwitz

Kimberley Partee Allar

Introduction

This chapter looks at two places that represent different extremes in Holocaust tourist destinations in post-war Europe. One place is compact and focuses on an individual's story. The other is expansive and memorializes the suffering of over a million victims. These two places are not only the most visited Holocaust sites in Europe, but their names have become symbols, universally recognizable and representative of the Holocaust. On the one hand, there is the Anne Frank House, a place where no blood was shed but the suffering of a young girl is recorded and remembered. This site approaches the Holocaust from an individual level, through an examination of the life of one person. On the other hand, there is Auschwitz–Birkenau, a place where 1.1 million persons were murdered and thousands more suffered immeasurable brutality (Piper 1994).

In their different ways, both sites represent the Holocaust, and both have been visited for different reasons by millions of people. Unlike many memorials and museums around the world, specifically those in Israel and the United States, these sites are where the actual events happened; thus, they are primary sources of the Holocaust. Beginning with an inquiry into the reasons why these sites were initially preserved, this chapter examines how these places have evolved over the past 60 years into iconic sites and universal images that represent the Holocaust, while also briefly commenting on the debates and controversies surrounding their development.

Anne Frank

Anne Frank's diary is used as an educational tool for learning and studying the Holocaust by millions of school children throughout the world (Moger 1998). Annelies Marie Frank, born on 12 June 1929 in Frankfurt-am-Main, was the second daughter of Otto and Edith Frank. In response to the increasing persecution of Jews in Germany, Otto moved his family to Amsterdam in 1933. The family prospered there until the Nazi occupation of the Netherlands in 1940 instituted measures excluding Jewish persons from all spheres of social life. By 1942 Otto Frank, with the cooperation and help of his business colleagues, organized a hiding place in the upstairs annex of his former workplace, the Opekta Works office building located at 263 Prinsengracht in the centre of Amsterdam. On 6 July 1942, the Frank family, later followed by the van Pel family and Fritz Pfeffer, moved into the Secret Annex. For the next two years, these eight Jewish occupants lived in fear and absolute silence, before being betrayed by an unknown informant. During this time Anne kept a meticulous diary recording her activities in hiding as well as her thoughts, feelings and dreams. On 4 August 1944, the Gestapo broke into the Secret Annex and arrested everyone, including their Dutch protectors. The Jews who had been hiding were sent to Westerbrook, a transit camp for Jews to places further east and then on to Auschwitz in September. Anne and Margot eventually ended up in the concentration camp of Bergen-Belsen, where both sisters died of typhus in March 1945, one month before the camp's liberation.

Otto was the only member of the group to survive. He received Anne's diary from Miep Gies, one of the rescuers who had discovered it after the family's arrest. After reading the diary, Otto decided to publish the work, in accordance, he believed, with Anne's wishes (Prose 2009).

The diary, the fame, the museum

Like any iconic figure, Anne Frank and her resulting image as the innocent Holocaust victim, was an evolutionary process. The Anne Frank House has been visited by millions of people throughout the world, and her diary has been read by millions more (AFH 2011). How did Anne Frank, a young Jewish-German girl living in the Netherlands and recording an adolescent's diary, become a universally recognized figure? And how did her hiding place and virtual prison for two years become a site of pilgrimage, as well as a popular tourist site?

Publicity surrounding Anne and her diary began almost immediately after the war; however, it would be another ten years before it achieved any significant international attention. In April 1946, a Dutch journalist reflected on the power of this seemingly inconsequential diary of a child ("schijnbaar onbetekenende dagboek van een kind"), proclaiming that Anne's spirit ("geest") and childish voice embodies the real hideousness of fascism, more so than all the evidence presented at Nuremburg ("in dit door een kinderstem gestamelde 'de profundis' alle afzichtelijkheid van het fascisme belichaamd, méér dan in alle processtukken van Neurenberg bij elkaar") (Romein 1946). This article, written only 13 months after Anne's death, was the first to recognize the diary's future importance and role in delivering and shaping post-war memory. After the diary's publication in the Netherlands in 1947 under the title *Het Achterhuis* (*The Secret Annex*), subsequent publications followed in Germany and France (both in 1950), and then in English as *Anne Frank: The Diary of a Young Girl* in 1952. The diary was scripted into a Pulitzer Prize-winning Broadway play and was adapted into a film in 1959, which won three Academy Awards. Finally, in 1995 an unexpurgated edition was published in English, revealing the diary in full for the first time as entries pertaining to Anne's sexuality and difficult relationship with her mother had been previously removed. Today, the diary, having been read and translated into 50 different languages, is one of the most popular books in the world (Enzer and Enzer 2000).

The diary's notoriety led to a movement to memorialize the hiding place and create a permanent site of remembrance for Anne. In December 1954 the Dutch newspaper *De Nieuwe Dag* reported that Anne Frank's 'Secret Annex' was marked for demolition in order to make way for a new office block along the canal. Otto's former office building:

> the spot where the 'Secret Annex' is located, right up to the Westermarket will be taken up by ateliers and offices of the clothing factory N.V. Berghaus. It is not known when the demolition work will begin.
>
> (DND 1954)

Fortunately, this destruction never took place. Otto Frank, in collaboration with Amsterdam's Mayor Gijs van Hall, moved to save the site by appealing for popular support to turn the building into a museum. The place had already become a sight of pilgrimage for "countless foreign visitors" who wished to see the place where Anne had hidden and to pay homage to her memory (DND 1954). Fundraising and support, both domestic and international, was widely successful and allowed plans for a permanent museum at the House to become a reality (Young 1994).

The Anne Frank Museum at 263 Prinsengracht opened on 3 May 1960. *The New York Times* briefly reported its opening, noting that Otto Frank wished the site would be not only a memorial to Anne and her suffering, but also "a building in which the ideals of Anne will find their realization" (NYT 1960). Two years later, the Museum was mentioned in several travel articles and advertisements in the United States highlighting tourist destinations within Amsterdam (NYT 1962). Four years after the museum's opening one travel writer concluded that while in Amsterdam, "An American reader finds this book [the diary]... tragic and tender. When one puts it down and visits the narrow house at 263 Prinsengracht where Anne lived, the impact is overpowering" (NYT 1964). The site retains this emotional reaction today. Nearly ten years after reading the diary in the seventh grade, I finally visited the museum in March 2009. Despite the many years that had passed, Anne's words remained a vivid guide that clearly illustrated the angst, hope, love and frustration she recorded during her two years in hiding.

During the second half of the twentieth century, the Annex emerged as an established tourist site, a must-see destination in the Netherlands. In the first year alone 9,000 people visited the Secret Annex. These numbers grew exponentially throughout the following decades from 180,000 in 1970, to 600,000 in 1990, to over one million in 2007 (AFH 2011). Throughout the years the museum has grown and adjusted its presentation in order to accommodate the increasing number and variety of visitors. This process entailed the reinforcing of structures, establishing of educational programmes and exhibits, and the presentation of a more universal message that would speak to diverse audiences about current issues. The museum is a self-directed tour that is designed to encourage free exploration and individual learning. According to the official museum webpage, "The House is a museum where visitors are given the opportunity to personally envision what happened on this very spot" (AFH 2012). While the rooms of the Secret Annex retain their authentic state, they are empty as the furniture was removed immediately following the August arrest. However, detailed information, documents and objects belonging to the former occupants are displayed along the walls. Furthermore, the building adjacent to the former office has been incorporated into the museum and houses both temporary and permanent exhibitions, including an interactive programme that highlights current human rights violations around the world. The popularity and success of the museum has ensured that the Secret Annex is fully incorporated into the tourist attractions of Amsterdam and represents an important tourist facility for the city.

While there are many reasons for the rise in popularity of the Annex as a tourist destination, one of the most self-evident explanations was the rise in public awareness of and interest in the Holocaust on a global scale. Increased interest in the Holocaust by the wider public can be further observed by examining the 60-year history of the Memorial Museum of the Concentration Camp at Auschwitz–Birkenau. While the two sites are located in separate countries and present different histories, both witnessed dramatic international attention and recognition as the most prominent sites displaying the horror of the Holocaust. An examination of the timeline for post-war Auschwitz – with particular attention to events after the fall of the Soviet Union in 1989 when foreign travel to Poland was relaxed – will reveal some of the key movements and public attitudes that have led to the exponential growth of the Holocaust tourism industry over the past two decades.

Auschwitz

Konzentrationslager Auschwitz was the largest and deadliest concentration and extermination centre during the history of the Third Reich (Dwork and van Pelt 1996). The camp was built outside of the Polish town of Oswiecim in southeastern Poland, 30 miles outside of Krakow. It was initially constructed for Polish political prisoners in 1940, yet its purpose changed dramatically in 1942 when Heinrich Himmler, head of the Nazi Schutzstaffel (SS), designated the camp as a centre for extermination as part of the "Final Solution to the Jewish question" (Gutman 1998: 6).

In 1942, Camp Commander Rudolf Höss began construction of Auschwitz–Birkenau, in the nearby town of Brzezinka. Four crematoria and four gas chambers were constructed at the new site over the following three years. During this time nearly one million Jews throughout Europe were murdered in the gas chambers at Birkenau, and thousands of others were killed slowly through starvation and overwork. The Soviet Army liberated the camp on 27 January 1945. However, few prisoners remained since most had already been evacuated to camps in Germany proper by the SS guards ten days earlier.

Creation of the museum

Poland suffered tremendously during the war, losing over six million of its citizens (including three million Jews) (Gross 2006: 26). Many former prisoners and rising politicians of the new Communist government in Poland felt the need to establish a museum and a memorial at the Auschwitz site by making use of the remaining structures (Charlesworth *et al.* 2006).

Auschwitz was officially established as the State Museum at Oswiecim-Brzezinka on 14 June 1947. The date commemorated the seventh anniversary of the arrival of the first transport of Polish political prisoners. Over 30,000 people, almost entirely Polish, attended the opening ceremonies (Huener 2003: 32). The newly elected prime minister of the Polish Socialist Party, Jozef Cyrankiewicz, a former political prisoner at Auschwitz, spoke at the opening ceremonies and called for peace, reconstruction of the devastated Polish state and hope for the future (Huener 2003). A great emphasis was placed on Polish martyrdom and sacrifice (as opposed to the Jewish losses), which was to become a central theme at Auschwitz for the next 60 years. In fact, the 1947 directive establishing the camp museum declared that the museum was intended as "a monument to the martyrdom and struggle of the Polish and other peoples" (Smolen 1990: 261). Auschwitz was fashioned into an official state symbol that commemorated the four million people who had died there at the hands of fascism (Webber 1990: 281). The figure of four million was established by the investigations of the Soviet Commission immediately following the liberation of the camp in February 1945. This figure remained official until the fall of communism in 1989. It was later re-evaluated to 1.1 million (Piper 1994). Ceremonies concluded with a Holy Mass and the singing of 'Rota' (The Pledge), a Polish nationalist song with strong anti-German undertones. Nothing was mentioned or reserved for the Judeocide that had occurred in the nearby gas chambers of Birkenau.

The opening of the museum received little global media attention. Due to the emergence of the Cold War politics between the Eastern Communist Bloc and the West, Auschwitz was primarily accessible only to Polish visitors, and as a result, the museum's early years reflected this demographic. Unlike the Anne Frank House, advertisements to visit the site did not appear in the international press.

Auschwitz immediately became a political tool for the government of the Soviet Union in order to legitimize the triumph of communism in Poland over German fascism and Western capitalism. This aspect of memory manipulation was a battle of -isms – communism, German national socialism (fascism) and capitalism – which left an indelible impression shaping the message and organization of the site. The museum's administration, prodded by government and communist party leaders, chose to highlight particular aspects of the camp while downplaying others. The museum highlighted Auschwitz I (the main camp) and the Polish population that had been incarcerated there. While museum officials did not deny the unique treatment and awful fate of the Jews at the Auschwitz camp complex, particularly at Auschwitz–Birkenau, the information was scarcely reflected in the museum's exhibitions (Gordon 2006). The Communist regime further reinterpreted the reasons and responsibility of the concentration and death camp. Instead of blaming Nazi racial ideology and anti-Semitism, museum representations pointed the finger at fascism and Western capitalism, furthering their own communist agenda and legitimization.

The Auschwitz Museum became a site dedicated to the memory of Polish suffering at the hands of the Nazis with little attention given to Auschwitz's Jewish victims. Instead, the unique experience of the Jewish victims and their particular fate according to the Nazis' 'Final Solution' was ignored or downplayed because the Polish government and museum administrators interpreted it as a distraction from Poland's victimization (Gordon 2006: 13). The debate over Polish victimization and culpability for the Holocaust remains, and Auschwitz often ends up caught in the middle of various interest groups.

In the early years of the museum, Auschwitz's historical role was largely disregarded in favour of the government's political agenda. By choosing to ignore Birkenau and its leading role in the gruesome history of the camp, museum officials chose political favour over historical accuracy. Political propaganda and ideology shaped the message and image of the museum during its first three decades. In fact, the racial policies of the Nazis were barely touched or reflected upon. While Poles and communists received special attention as groups that suffered in Auschwitz, the number of Jewish victims was never addressed in the museum's first exhibitions. By becoming a site dedicated to the celebration of the Polish resistance and the condemnation of Western political ideology, Auschwitz became a victim itself to the politics of the era.

Changes at the museum

The mid 1950s ushered in subtle changes to the museum's design and agenda. Stalin's death in March 1953 provided a relaxation of the Soviets' tight grip on Poland's political infrastructure that carried over into the government-run museum. In 1956 Poland experienced a period of democratic reform under its new leader, Wladyslaw Gomulka (Huener 2003). Instead of being defined by its Soviet overtones as an anti-fascist and pro-communist site, Auschwitz regained its original Polish-nationalist outlook. During the first ten years of its existence approximately 1,771,300 Poles and 79,600 people from outside of Poland visited the museum (Huener 2001: 528). The camp became a required field trip for all Polish youth, and was often visited by Poles who wished to commemorate a loved one who had perished there. The museum did not, however, receive many international visitors from outside of Soviet Bloc countries due to the continuation of Cold War politics between the East and the West.

Despite its primarily nationalist agenda, the museum nevertheless had to cater to international interests. Many public events, including the tenth anniversary of the camp's liberation in 1955, the Eichmann Trial in Israel in 1961, the Frankfurt Auschwitz trials that took place a few years later, and even the rising popularity of Anne Frank's diary, drew the international press to the subject of Auschwitz. Throughout the 1960s and 1970s, interest in the Holocaust as a subject increased dramatically. A large number of memoirs were published, including some of the first comprehensive scholarly works examining the Holocaust by Gerlad Reitlinger and Raul Hilberg. Television and Hollywood followed suit, first in the widely popular television series *Holocaust* in 1978 and then in Claude Lanzmann's monumental documentary *The Shoah* in 1985, cementing Auschwitz as an identifiable place and a symbol of the Holocaust.

Today, the museum receives over one million visitors a year from across the world. The year 2007 was the first time the museum received over a million visitors (as noted earlier, the same is true for the Anne Frank House). The vast majority of visitors come from Poland, followed by the United States, Great Britain, Italy and Germany (Stanczyk 2007). In 2010, nearly 47,000 people from South Korea, 59,000 from Israel and 11,800 from Australia visited the memorial, thus truly demonstrating its global appeal (Urbaniak 2010: 20).

In 2007 it was reported "over 30 million people from over 100 countries have visited the Auschwitz Museum" (Stanczyk 2007). The number of visitors from Western Europe and the United States rose dramatically after 1989 when diplomatic relations between the East and West improved, which opened up the country's borders for tourism. Every year after this date the museum has witnessed an increase in visitors. Before this date, the majority of visitors came from communist Eastern Bloc countries, often sent by their respective governments. Poland, as well as some other Eastern Bloc countries, often absorbed the travelling costs associated with visiting the site, as well as mandating that all Polish schoolchildren take a field trip to Auschwitz (Cole 1999). It was important to the communist authorities that their populations should commemorate and be educated at the Soviets' primary site of martyrdom, Auschwitz. Tim Cole remarked that after 1989, the busloads of school children from Eastern Germany were replaced by Western tourists and the rise of the "Holocaust Industry" (Cole 1999: 116).

The 1955 permanent exhibition remains the primary focus of the museum, although some figures and vocabulary have been changed to reflect current historical research. The exhibition is housed in the former barracks of Auschwitz I and features both prisoner and perpetrator artefacts, from clandestine prisoner artwork to SS uniforms. In addition, the museum contains an extensive collection of personal possessions, which were stolen and collected from the 1.1 million victims of the Auschwitz gas chambers. Auschwitz II Birkenau remained largely untouched. Today it is a harrowing field of chimneys, barbedwire, guard towers and the dynamited ruins of the gas chambers and crematoria. While entry to the museum is free, allowing for independent learning and visitation, hiring a museum-sanctioned guided tour is strongly encouraged and is mandatory for groups. The official museum website suggests 90 minutes for Auschwitz I and 90 minutes for Birkenau with the statement that "it is essential to visit both parts in order to acquire a proper sense of the place that has become a symbol of the Holocaust as well as Nazi crimes against Poles, Romas, and other groups" (Memorial and Museum Auschwitz–Birkenau 2012). A free bus covering the three kilometers from the main camp to Birkenau is provided for visitors every hour.

The rise of Holocaust tourism

Norman Finkelstein, a historian and son of two survivors, originally coined the term 'Holocaust Industry' in his highly controversial book, *The Holocaust*

Industry: Reflections on the Exploitation of Jewish Suffering (2000). Finkelstein accused various countries and Jewish groups of exploiting the memory of the Holocaust for profit. His scathing critique built upon previous works that also expressed concern over the global exploitation of the Holocaust, notably Peter Novick's *The Holocaust in American Life* and Tim Cole's *Selling the Holocaust*, both published in 1999.

Cole illuminated the emerging differences between what he described as the "myth of the Holocaust" and the "Holocaust itself". This 'myth' was not a reference to the revisionists' theory of Auschwitz; rather, it was the mass-marketed and Hollywood-produced image of the Holocaust that had emerged through film over the previous 20 years. This image has furthermore coincided with a unique interest in a particular form of tourism. Cole offers the observation that "At the end of the twentieth century death tourism is big business... There is a fascination with the sites of 'significant' deaths." Cole labels the Auschwitz–Birkenau Museum and Memorial as "Auschwitz-land" that is "created for tourist consumption and [is] the end product of Holocaust tourism" (Cole 1999: 113–114). One outraged visitor from Israel described Auschwitz as a 'Jewish Disney' in a newspaper editorial in 2007 (Sorsby 2007). While Cole's remarks were quite harsh and cynical towards tourists' motivations for visiting Auschwitz, he nevertheless raised serious issues concerning the substantial increase in visitors and paid tours (see Figure 13.1).

Figure 13.1 A dark tour passes under the well-known gates of Auschwitz

The 'Holocaust Industry' was the result of an increased interest in the subject within Europe and abroad throughout the past 50 years. The popularity of Holocaust films released during the 1990s brought further attention, particularly via Steven Spielberg's 1993 film *Schindler's List*, Roberto Benigni's 1997 Italian Film *La Vita e Bella* (*Life Is Beautiful*) and Roman Polanski's 2002 film *The Pianist*. The tourist industry was quick to respond to Spielberg's success by establishing 'Schindler tours' that visited historical sites appearing in the movie (including Auschwitz–Birkenau). Hollywood had already had significant success with Auschwitz, most notably with *Sophie's Choice*, a William Styron novel adapted to the big screen in 1982. While the literature about Auschwitz and former inmates' experiences has consistently received a wide readership in the West since the 1960s, it is undeniable that in the visual and media-driven world of today, Hollywood has reached a far greater audience (Doneson 2002). Marshman has noted, "1993 has been described as the 'Year of the Holocaust'", referring to both the Spielberg film and the opening of the United States Holocaust Museum in Washington DC (Marshman 2005). The Holocaust had come to Hollywood, and in response, attraction and interest in the Holocaust was booming. The interest has only increased throughout the past 15 years, leading to more movies, more tours and, in general, more knowledge and awareness of the Holocaust and the horror that unfolded throughout Europe during World War II.

Holocaust sites are often incorporated into packaged tourist deals. Thus, visitors to Munich are encouraged to visit Konzentrationslager Dachau; Terezin is a half-day trip from Prague; Auschwitz is often included in a 'package deal' designed to 'save time and money' with the Wieliczka Salt Mines in the vicinity of Krakow (seekrakow.com 2011); and the Anne Frank House is a 'must see' in Amsterdam (Virtual Tourist 2011). Yet the question remains: Why do people, in increasing numbers, visit these sites? The reasons are undoubtedly numerous and impossible to isolate. Nevertheless, these sites of atrocity have become 'necessary' sites on the tourist trail. In other words, according to many travel books and brochures, when visiting Poland, "a visit to Auschwitz is a must" (Lunsche 2008). Popular travel guides, such as *Lonely Planet*, *Fodor's*, *Let's Go* and *Frommer's*, all feature popular Holocaust sites and even give 'travel tips' about visiting. Furthermore, Auschwitz has become "an obligatory place of pilgrimage for all visiting heads of state" to Poland in order to honour the Jewish and Polish victims of the Holocaust (Cole 1999: 117). Former president Gerald Ford was the first US president to visit Auschwitz in 1975 followed by the much-publicized visit by Pope John Paul II in 1979 (Szulc 1979). These visits "serve not only a symbolic purpose, but a diplomatic one" (Sanger 2003) for statesmen and countries (Smith 2005). The Anne Frank House is also an 'expected' stop on a diplomatic tour and has been visited by numerous world leaders including Hilary Clinton and Yasser Arafat.

While these 'dark' historic sites are often psychologically difficult to visit, they do offer the visitor the chance to get closer to an understanding (albeit, from a distance and from an outsider's perspective) of the horror and suffering that occurred there. People can walk through the *Arbeit Macht Frei* gate and imagine the apprehension and fear of former prisoners, or from a more sinister standpoint, the power and clout of the Nazi guards. Similarly, they can also walk through the confining rooms of the Secret Annex and try to visualize Anne's years of angst and hiding. Visiting Holocaust sites has inevitably become one way in which tourists can learn about or vicariously experience atrocities and death. In other words, these sites are available in an authentic, unadulterated form as they allow the visitor to form their own memories and interpretation of the site beyond what textbooks have explained or what Hollywood has promoted. This interpretation is then incorporated into the global memory of the site, which in turn shapes and configures the history, which, as this chapter has attempted to demonstrate, is constantly evolving.

By the 1990s, the names 'Auschwitz' and 'Anne Frank' were among the most recognized and identifiable places and names associated with the Holocaust. Auschwitz is often the only concentration camp that many people are able to name, and Anne Frank certainly stands out among, and at the same time apart from, the six million Jewish victims. Coincidentally, the images of Auschwitz and Anne Frank tend to subsume all evocations of the Holocaust. The reasons behind this movement are many and complex, and are likely the result of particular, universal events and movements such as the Eichmann trial and the overall growing curiosity and appreciation for the Holocaust and other genocides, as seen through the rise in post-Holocaust literature, national and universal educational programmes, and Hollywood. James Young, who referred to the House as a "monument to innocence", attributed this to the fact that "the Anne Frank House is the most likely introduction to the Holocaust, for it is an easy, accessible window to this period" (Young 1999: 224). In the United States, Anne Frank's Diary is often the first, and in some cases the only work associated with the Holocaust that many people have read, as the diary is 'ubiquitous' and often a mandatory part of the curriculum in middle and high school English classes (Spector and Jones 2007). Auschwitz, likewise, sustains particular attention as a dominating site of the Holocaust due to its status as the deadliest Nazi annihilation centre and the focus of many government initiatives, survivor memoirs and Hollywood movies.

Conclusion

This chapter has outlined the evolution of two Holocaust sites in Europe. It has addressed Holocaust tourism not only as a unique development within the tourism industry, but as a growing and evolving phenomenon in a post-Holocaust, post-Communist Europe that not only affects local communities, but the global community as well. It has illustrated how two sites have evolved into international tourist destinations, which now serve both a didactic and haunting experience.

The Anne Frank House and the Auschwitz Concentration Camp were originally preserved after the war as memorials for their respective victims; however, they have moved beyond mere memorials into universal symbols of the Holocaust. Despite the sites' *symbolic* power as representative of the Holocaust and of Nazi oppression, the *physical* sites are still important and sacred. The growing attention and increased visitation to the museums demonstrate that these physical sites "deeply matter to people". Thus, as Jonathan Webber has noted concerning Auschwitz:

> Even so long after the end of the war, care must be exercised to express the right meanings for the place, to preserve Auschwitz in a manner fitting to the memory of those who died there.
>
> (Webber 1990: 281)

The Anne Frank House attracts similar concern and attention, as the recent battle to preserve the large chestnut tree outside the Secret Annex demonstrates (Coughlan 2007).

Today these sites house important museums and education centres, which together welcome over two million visitors a year. They are sites of pilgrimage as well as centres of conversation and discussion. Nevertheless, controversies over the interpretation and design as well as the meaning and message of the museums continue to shape and influence the sites. While some disputes are site specific, both the Auschwitz Museum and the Anne Frank House have had to grapple with renovations to the construction and re-evaluations to outdated exhibitions. As these monuments continue to age and deteriorate, tensions have emerged between maintaining authenticity and performing reconstruction to maintain their appearance and to allow safe access for tourists.

Ultimately, these issues revolve around ownership and the ability and right to interpret and present a historical narrative. However, since these sites have emerged as universal symbols, tensions have arisen among competing interest groups, all of which have a 'claim' to the site itself. To whom do these sites belong? Are they 'owned' by their respective national governments, the European Union, Israel or perhaps the international community? Who has the authority to dictate changes? What is the overall message the sites should portray? In the case of Auschwitz, the scope is limited to the Holocaust, while the Anne Frank House has embraced a more universal appeal against intolerance and genocide. Whoever 'controls' the site exerts broad influence on creating the narrative that is to be presented and dispersed. This history will reproduce and describe not only what the past once was, but also what that past says about the present and expected future.

The importance of these places, as sites and symbols, remains. Auschwitz survivor and writer Primo Levi wrote about visiting Holocaust memorials:

> With the passing of years and decades, these remains do not lose any of their significance as a Warning Monument; rather, they gain in meaning. They teach better than any treatise or memorial how inhuman the Hitlerite regime was, even in its choices of sites and architecture.
>
> (Levi 1994: 185)

The future for these sites remains to be seen, but their importance within the understanding of the Holocaust, despite the different ways they communicate their messages, as well as their current role in the global community, is undeniable.

References

Anne Frank House (2011) Available at http://www.annefrank.org (accessed 4 December 2011).
Anne Frank House (2012) Available at http://www.annefrank.org/en/Museum/(accessed 28 November 2012).
Charlesworth, A., Stenning, A., Guzik, R. and Paszkowski, M. (2006) 'Out of Place in Auschwitz? Contested Development in Post-war and Post-socialist Oswiecim', *Ethics, Place, and Environment*, 9(2): 149–172.
Cole, T. (1999) *Selling the Holocaust*, New York: Routledge.
Coughlan, G. (2007) 'Anne Frank's Tree to Be Cut Down', *BBC News*, 10 March 2007.
De Nieuwe Dag (1954) 10 December 1954. Available at http://www.annefrank.org/en/Anne-Franks-History/From-hiding-place-to-museum/Saved-from-demolition/ (accessed 28 November 2012).
Doneson, J. (2002) *The Holocaust in American film*, New York: Syracuse University Press.
Dwork, D. and van Pelt, R. (1996) *Auschwitz*, New York: W.W. Norton & Co.
Enzer, H. and Enzer, S. (2000) *Anne Frank: Reflections on Her Life and Legacy*, Urbana: University of Illinois Press.
Gordon, R. (2006) 'Introduction to Primo Levi's *Auschwitz report*', in P. Levi (ed.) *Auschwitz Report*, London: Verso.
Gross, J. (2006) *Fear: Anti-semitism in Poland after Auschwitz*, New York: Random House.
Gutman, I. (1998) *Autonomy of the Auschwitz Death Camp*, Bloomington, IN: Indiana University Press.
Huener, J. (2001) 'Antifascist Pilgrimage and Rehabilitation at Auschwitz: The Political Tourism of Aktion Suhnezeichen and Sozialistische Jugend', *German Studies Review*, 24(3): 513–532.
Huener, J. (2003) *Auschwitz, Poland, and the Politics of Commemoration 1945–1979*, Athens, OH: Ohio University Press.
Krakow (2011) 'Auschwitz Trips'. Available at http://www.seekrakow.com/en/s/26, auschwitz_birkenau_and_wieliczka_salt_mine_on_one_day (accessed 12 December 2011).
Levi, P. (1994) 'Revisiting the Camps', in J. Young (ed.) *Art of Memory*, Munich: Prestel-Verlag.
Lunsche, S. (2008) 'Tourism: A Ride Through History', *Financial Mail*, 15 August.
Marshman, S. (2005) 'From the Margins to the Mainstream? Representations of the Holocaust in Popular Culture', University of Glasgow: *eSharp*, 6(1) *Identity and Marginality*, Vol. 1.
Memorial and Museum Auschwitz–Birkenan (2012) Available at http://en.auschwitz.org/m/ (accessed 28 November 2012).
Moger, S. (1998) *Teaching the Diary of Anne Frank: An In-depth Resource for Learning about the Holocaust through the Writings of Anne Frank*, New York: Scholastic Professional Books.
New York Times (1960) 'Anne Frank House Opened', *The New York Times*, 4 May.
New York Times (1962) 'Dutch Treat for Tourists', *The New York Times*, 28 October.
New York Times (1964) 'Where the Bookworm Turns While Traveling', *The New York Times*, 13 December.
Piper, F. (1994) 'The Number of Victims', *Anatomy of the Auschwitz Death Camp*, Bloomington, IN: Indiana University Press.

Prose, F. (2009) *Anne Frank: The Book, the Life, the Afterlife*, New York: HarperCollins.
Romein, J. (1946) 'Kinderstem', *Het Parool*, 3 April.
Sanger, D. (2003) 'The President in Europe: Death Camp; Witness to Auschwitz Evil, Bush Draws a Lesson', *The New York Times*, 1 June.
seekrakow.com (2011). Available at http://www.seekrakow.com/ (accessed 15 January 2013).
Smith, C. (2005) 'World Leaders Gather for Auschwitz Ceremony', *The New York Times*, 27 January.
Smolen, K. (1990) 'Auschwitz Today: The Auschwitz–Birkenau State Museum', *Auschwitz: A history in Photographs*, trans. J. Webber and C. Wilsack, Bloomington, IN: Indiana University Press, pp. 259–280.
Sorsby, J. (2007) 'Auschwitz Theme Park', *The Jerusalem Post*, 19 April.
Spector, K. and Jones, S. (2007) 'Constructing Anne Frank: Critical Literacy and the Holocaust in Eighth-grade English', *Journal of Adolescent and Adult Literacy*, 51(1): 36–48.
Stanczyk, A. (2007) 'Number of Visitors', *Auschwitz–Birkenau Report* (2007), pp. 26–28. Available at www.auschwitz.org.pl (accessed 15 January 2013).
Szulc, T. (1979) 'Homecoming for the Pope', *The New York Times*, 27 May.
Urbaniak M. (2010) 'Record Number of Visitors in 2010', *Memorial Auschwitz–Birkenau 2010 Report*, pp. 20–23.
Virtual Tourist (2011) 'Amsterdam Things to Do'. Available at http://www.virtualtourist.com/travel/Europe/Netherlands/Provincie_Noord_Holland/Amsterdam-463377/Things_To_Do-Amsterdam-TG-C-1.html (accessed 12 December 2011).
Webber, J. (1990) 'Personal Reflections on Auschwitz Today', *Auschwitz: A History in Photographs*, trans. J. Webber and C. Wilsack, Bloomington, IN: Indiana University Press, pp. 281–291.
Young, J. (1994) 'The Anne Frank House: Holland's Memorial "Shrine of the Book"', *The Art of Memory: Holocaust Memorials in History*, Munich: Prestel-Verlag.
Young, J. (1999) 'The Anne Frank House: Holland's Memorial Shrine of the Book', *Anne Frank: Reflections on Her Life and Legacy*, Champaign: University of Illinois Press.

14 Dark detours

Celebrity car crash deaths and trajectories of place

Gary Best

Into the darkness

Dark tourism is informed by fame, but often more informed by infamy, and a monumental infamy at that. The immense scale of the most familiar historical atrocities may begin to explain visitor interest in such destinations and sites. Without intending to diminish the inherent horror and inhumanity of such sites in any way, there can now, however, often be a sense of checking off the blockbuster events when constructing dark itineraries – the must-sees of Hitler's Germany, Pol Pot's Cambodia, mass executions and exterminations. The scale and knowledge of such horrors is widespread, as is ready access to detailed documentary material, so for the experienced or potential tourist wishing to explore the darkness, many guiding hands – of sorts – await.

There is, as Rojek (1993) and many others have indicated, another dark realm far removed not so much from the 'dark' qualifier but from large-scale historical dark tourism phenomena. This realm has as its focus a single event and, usually, a single death – the death of a celebrity in, or as the result of, a car crash or car accident. Those who have driven by an accident scene will immediately know the multiple, split-second questions that manifest almost simultaneously, such as: 'Is it anyone I know?' or the moral dilemma of: 'Should I look?' which, if a glance is undertaken, increases the risk of further personalizing the moment by having an accident of one's own. While having car accidents is not on most personal agendas, one stand-out is the character of Vaughan in J.G. Ballard's magisterially perverse auto-erotic/erotic-auto novel *Crash* (1973), who has a presumed personal apotheosis in a car crash that culminates in death and orgasm, although the latter, it would seem, was close but not realized. Most car crashes, however, are not orchestrated, but both the terrible event and the location may remain a traumatic memory.

Two significant issues worthy of consideration here are 1) the nature of recognition and 2) the moral paradigm of engagement in such contexts. On the latter, Stone (2009) writes persuasively of the necessity of acknowledging emergent and/or new moral paradigms that may begin to provide deeper understanding of, and access to, both the philosophy and operation of contemporary dark tourism phenomena within personal experiential frameworks:

individuals attempt to seek (moral) meaning on their own terms and from alternate sources... It is these morally relative individual experiences within a collective environment, namely dark tourism, which adds to a potential resurgence of moral vitality within new contemporary spaces.

(2009: 60)

Stone (2009) recognizes and validates the necessity of acknowledging alternate sources of engagement, inspiration and critical analysis as well as emphasizing the relevance and significance of individual experience as a means of energizing moribund moral frameworks.

Consequently, with regard to what must be recognized and acknowledged, the individual and the personal have never been so resonant, or so omnipresent. The rise of social media has resulted in profoundly increased opportunities for public exposure as well as public scrutiny, should the individual desire and/or permit it. Needless to say, a significant increase in the dissemination of what had been, by necessity, private in the past has resulted in a proliferation of new and frequently challenging presences, content and voices. The largely conservative and, more importantly, controlling media channels of the last century now wield much less influence and power than the voices of the current blogosphere, a still-expanding universe that astounds with its limitless diversity. The obvious corollary here is that content that in the past may have been censored or even blocked can now be found with little effort via any search engine, so those with an interest in seeing JFK's corpse on the mortuary slab or wishing to make a bid on one of Jayne Mansfield's stuffed dead Chihuahuas may immediately be more than satisfied.

Brottman (2001) offers an illuminating observation on this chapter's theme:

the car crash is the archetypal means of celebrity death – certainly the most memorable, and perhaps the most appealing, forming a dramatic closure to a life lived in public.

(2001: xv)

Four examples of celebrity car crash deaths are examined in this chapter. Three of the celebrities were major Hollywood stars of the 1950s, and one a member of the English royal family by marriage, in the 1980s and 1990s. James Dean died late on an autumn afternoon in 1955 on a California highway just as his star was beginning to rise. Jayne Mansfield died after midnight on a highway en route to New Orleans in the summer of 1967, a faded star reduced to saucy singing and dancing in shabby dinner clubs. Princess Grace of Monaco, formerly Grace Kelly of Philadelphia and an Oscar winning actress, died the day after her car crashed down a ravine above the French Riviera in September 1982. Diana, Princess of Wales, and her companion Dodi Fayed, died after their Mercedes Benz crashed in a Paris tunnel after their driver attempted to escape pursuing paparazzi in August 1997.

The victims, the car crashes, memorialization and place identity

The rebel

Newsflash – 30 September 1955

James Dean, en route to road races in Salinas, California in his Porsche 550 Spyder nicknamed 'Little Bastard', speeds towards death, and eternal fame.

While the events of Friday, 30 September 1955 have been told and retold, here is a synopsis. Dean left his Sherman Oaks (LA) home in the morning, called in to Competition Motors on Vine St for some last minute adjustments and, rather than trailer the Porsche to Salinas, decided to drive it himself to the races. Late in the afternoon (5.59 pm, according to Rojek 1993: 142), driving west on US Route 466 (now Highway 46) near Cholame, California en route to the races, a local man (Donald Turnupseed) driving a Ford turned left directly in front of Dean's Porsche, resulting in a head-on collision, with Dean dead ten minutes later (Perry 2011: 14).

At the time of his death, James Dean was known through his Broadway and television performances, and in Elia Kazan's film *East of Eden* (1955), *Rebel Without a Cause* (1955) and *Giant* (1956) had yet to be released. His three film characters were angst-ridden: two were teenagers, one seeking a mother who chose to reject him, and the other rebelling against the stifling, bourgeois constraints of middle-class, mid-50s America. These first two roles contributed to Dean's perceived public persona as a rebel as well, his life apparently echoing the scripts. In his final film *Giant* (1956) he gave a performance of depth that, while spanning a Texas lifetime, further added to the growing legend of his determination to live life distinctively on his own terms. Dean was nominated twice for the Best Actor Academy Award, the second nomination posthumous but unsuccessful. He was awarded a Golden Globe Special Achievement Award for Best Dramatic Actor – again, posthumously – by the Hollywood Foreign Press Association in 1956.

Gossip, rumours and apparent truths about Dean, particularly concerning his homo/sexuality, circulated during his lifetime but gathered a perverse momentum and grew exponentially after his death (Bast 2006). Moody, disaffected, supposedly hating the Hollywood system – and being hated by the system – Dean was unarguably a talented major player. Elia Kazan, however, observed years later:

> What I disliked was the Dean legend. He was the glorification of hatred and sickness. When he got success he was victimized by it. He was a hero to the people who saw him only as a little waif, when actually he was a pudding of hatred.
>
> (Shipman 1972: 121)

Dean's star burned out early – at 24 – and explosively in 1955, on a desolate stretch of California highway, leaving only his wrecked Porsche and his legend: celebrity and, because of his apparent contempt for the Hollywood dream factory, anti-star. Rojek (1993) wrote of 'black spots' and that on the anniversary of Dean's death:

> a procession of 1949 Mercs and 1950 Fords, driven by fans of Dean, arrive at the spot where the crash occurred in time for the exact moment of the crash. Not only do the fans visit the black spot, but they fastidiously take the same route that Dean followed from Los Angeles on his last day. Mile for mile, and moment for moment, they try to repeat the sights, sounds and experiences that their hero experienced on the journey.
>
> (1993: 142)

Rojek analyses the 'black spot' experience in terms of 1) a monument to the dead hero and 2) a touchstone to the whole way of life that has been submerged in time (1993: 142). The question now, however, is whether such devoted visitation is still undertaken more than 50 years after Dean's death and, if so, by whom? Do the rebels still have a cause? Is there still a yearning for teen gang and car crazy LA of the early 1950s? The following observation suggests that time has diminished the angst, and the attendance.

'*DEADWRITE'S DAILIES*' blog is '*A Reading Room for Time Travellers*' and the entry for 22 June 2011, titled 'Down the Road to Eternity', reflects on James Dean's fatal crash as the author and his wife drive along Highway 46:

> I expect to see dozens of Dean fans milling about... but the only people we see are two men... sitting behind several tables of James Dean memorabilia, Matthew and Glen... I ask... if we missed the crowds and he explains that there weren't any this year. He estimates that only about a dozen showed up during the whole day... If you wanted crowds, you needed to be here in 2005 on the 50th anniversary, Glen tells us. I counted 325 people that day.
>
> (22 June 2011: http://deadwrite.wordpress.com/james + dean).

What, then, *is* there to see? What is it that visitors might *expect* to see? Dean was buried in his home town of Fairmount, Indiana, where a gravestone constitutes his sole memorial. Two images of the gravestone are the only images on the Fairmount city-data.com website, indicating that the town's sole enduring claim to fame still has local resonance.

In 2002 the junction of California Highways 41 and 46 near the fatal crash site was designated the *James Dean Memorial Junction* with the marker taking the form of a highway sign reading as above. In Cholame there is an independently erected memorial beside a tree, which offers Dean's dates (1931–1955) and a quote from *The Little Prince* by Antoine de Saint-Exupery: '*What is essential is invisible to the eye*', an apt adage given the schism between the public and private Dean personae.

The critical element of these two memorials is that of providing a tangible acknowledgement of the individual in the form of "a 'permanent' site which those who wish can visit" (Lennon and Foley 2000: 4). However, neither the highway nor the Cholame memorial 'offers' Dean's corpse; that is in far-off Indiana, so proximity to his mortal remains requires a much longer journey from California to the Mid-West, where a traditional headstone over a grave can be visited. To suggest such a journey immediately evokes both the concept and the reality of pilgrimage which, in Dean's case, may have been more in evidence – in terms of formal organization and significant numbers and socio-cultural phenomena, such as a cortège of 1949 Mercs – in the years that immediately followed his death, or on each anniversary.

The Latin advice to all – *memento mori* – is 'remember you must die', and often refers to an image or object, such as a skull, intended to remind of the inevitability of death (Wilkes and Krebs 1992: 975). Needless to say, like the innumerable pieces of the 'True Cross', the souvenirs of perverse Hollywoodiana are highly prized by specialist collectors. Kenneth Anger proudly carried his car death compulsion to the extent of acquiring: "for three hundred bucks – a twisted shard of Jimmy's beloved Porsche" (Anger 2001: 6).

Anger also claims to have been one of Dean's lovers and presumably the 'twisted shard', along with his signed portrait of Dean, connect him for eternity to 'Jimmy'. Walter (2009) proposes that recent experience of dark tourism and *memento mori* indicates a diminishment of their very significant presence in medieval everyday life to being varied and uneven in reminding of mortality at contemporary dark tourism sites; for example, brochures at cemeteries mentioning every interesting activity but having no mention of death or the dead buried there.

Darius (2001) also pursues quasi-religious car-crash considerations:

> As celebrities are godlike, so their crucifixion via car crash completes this ascent. Witness James Dean, whose death by car crash created his cult. Such accidents often involve a trade in relics associated with the death, often granted supernatural powers, resembling the medieval relic cults.
>
> (2001: 310)

For the fan, discussing and sharing and reliving the celebrity death, by car crash or otherwise, has not been sequestered as suggested by Stone and Sharpley (2008), so does not comfortably fit their claim about dark tourism permitting the reintroduction of discourses of death into the public realm. Fan discourses connect the network; they always have, and now never more immediately. The primary organs of the 1950s were the familiar radio, the early television, definitely the newspapers and the dedicated fan magazines such as *Modern Screen* (1930–85) and *Photoplay* (Shine 2010), which dangled the death dramas on pages metaphorically bordered in black.

Jimmy's places – the car crash death site on Highway 46, which is commemorated by a memorial sign; the sculpture in nearby Cholame, erected by a Japanese businessman rather than local initiative (Lennon and Foley 2000); and a gravestone in his home town of Fairmount, Indiana – are modest. Jimmy's legacy: three significant cinematic performances, a profound socio-cultural impact while he lived but escalating much more so after his dramatic death, an enduring inspiration for generations of proto-rebels.

The sex bomb

Newsflash – 29 June 1967

Faded buxom blonde bombshell Jayne Mansfield dies and enters the dark movie star pantheon when her 1966 Buick Electra 225 ploughs into a trailer stopped on a murky road just outside of New Orleans.

In 1955, the year James Dean died, Jayne Mansfield made four forgettable movie flops: *Illegal*, directed by Lewis Allen; *Pete Kelly's Blues*, directed by Jack Webb; *Hell on Frisco Bay*, directed by Frank Tuttle; and *The Burglar*, directed by Paul Wendkos. Mansfield's acting prowess, limited at best, was eclipsed by her physicality, and most notably her ample bosom which, according to her, measured 44 inches in the USA and 46 inches in the UK (Liujters and Timmer 1988). The careers of Jayne and other pneumatic blondes who relied largely on cleavage – Marilyn Monroe, Mamie Van Doren, Diana Dors and Anita Ekberg – rose in the 1950s and fell out of fashion in the 1960s, all the while clinging tenaciously to their (in)glorious ample blonde pasts. Jayne maintained her media profile (of sorts) by marrying and shedding the wrong kind of men, and taking off more clothes in public. The public, however, had lost interest and Jayne appeared to have become a self-mocking parody. On the Monday evening prior to her death, and billed as 'Jayne Mansfield – Most Publicized SEX QUEEN and Movie Star' she had performed at Gus Stevens' 'On the Beach' on Highway 90 in Biloxi, Mississippi, where the dress code was '*No Need to Dress Up, Come as You Are*' and the 8oz Filet Mignon Steak wrapped in bacon cost $2.95. The same undated advertisement – on findadeath.com – has Jayne performing 'June 23 thru July 4' but an earlier departure had clearly been either negotiated, or enforced; a few hours later down Highway 90 Jayne was dead, at 36, and that's when her darker incarnation began.

Jayne Mansfield was *not* – repeat *not* – decapitated in the car crash that killed her in the very early morning of 29 June 1967 despite the following litany of erroneous claims:

> Anger, K. (2001: 6–8) – "Then there is the Jayne Mansfield Louisiana police accident investigation unit's thorough photographic coverage... Jayne's ripped-off dead head surrealistically transformed into a bloody hood ornament."
> Brandon, R. (2002: 306) – "Jayne Mansfield, though killed in her prime while driving an automobile, never made the legendary-death charts because hers was simply too gruesome – her head torn off as she leaned out of the window and met an oncoming vehicle."
> Brottman, M. (2001: xxi) – "Most accounts of the crash... describe Mansfield as being decapitated... Other... reports claim that Mansfield wasn't in fact

decapitated but scalped by the cars's roof, her blond wig thrown forward on the hood of the Buick."

Shipman, D. (1972: 312) – "she, and her new fiancé, in a sports car, were decapitated in an accident with a truck."

Despite the inaccurate reporting of vehicle and cause of death, there was always a lingering question: was Jayne Mansfield decapitated? New Orleans Times-*Picayune*'s G.E. Arnold, who took the black and white photo of the wrecked Buick, recalls the scene:

> when she went through the windshield her wig came off. It was great big wig. You remember her hair. I guess in the picture people thought it was her head. Her face was bashed in. Her skull was crushed. But her head was attached to her body. I know. I was there.
>
> (Scott 1997: 24)

The site of Jayne's car crash death on Highway 90 between Biloxi, Mississippi and New Orleans, Louisiana is a desolate stretch flanked on both sides by low scrub and swamps. It is a highway only – certainly important to those who, by necessity, must utilize it as either a point-to-point route, or as part of a tourist itinerary, but it is does not offer any formal memorial acknowledging Jayne, boyfriend/fiancé Sam Brody, or college student/driver Ronnie Harrison who all died at the site. It seems that the gruesome horror of the crash has created and maintained its own momentum but not generated any permanent memorial.

A web user self-identified as 'johnwaynebaxter' uploaded a YouTube video in which he is presumably the unidentified driver on Highway 90 heading towards New Orleans and, while in the area where Jayne Mansfield died, he 'discovers' a roadside 'memorial', which looks suspiciously new and fresh – a simple white cross with cheap necklaces draped over the horizontal of the cross, and a plaque at the bottom with the inscription: *Jayne Mansfield died here June 29, 1967 2.25am.* Maybe that is all there is as far as tangible on-site tributes to Jayne. One other vivid tribute, however, is in David Cronenberg's film adaptation of J.G. Ballard's *Crash* (1996) when the psychotic stunt-man Seagrave: "meets his end by re-eneacting, in drag, Jayne Mansfield's fatal crash of 1967, around which he has built 'an abbatoir of sexual mutilation'" (Brottman and Sharratt 2001: 209).

The grotesquerie of the physical injuries sustained by Jayne has eclipsed and all but erased Brody and Harrison from the record. Given her (albeit faded) Hollywood star status only Jayne was newsworthy but possibly more as a curiosity than deserving of sympathy. That sympathy may have been reserved for Jayne's surviving children and her former husband Mickey Hargitay, whose face, while collecting the casket containing Jayne's body at New York's JFK airport, showed the ravages of grief.

Jayne was laid to rest in Fairview Cemetery in Pen Argyl, Pennsylvania. There is also a cenotaph dedicated to her in the Hollywood Forever Memorial Park in Hollywood, California, but these two sites constitute the only formal memorials to Jayne's life and career. The Hollywood memorial offers fans a site in the home of the industry that created Jayne; far-off Pennsylvania, however, would necessitate a pilgrimage to her burial site with its heart-shaped white marble headstone.

Jayne Mansfield lives on in that larger-than-life imaginary realm of extravagant, blonde bombshell accidental deaths, and her legendary decapitation will forever be her macabre memorial of sorts.

A final wish: "We want our crash-and-burn blondes to do the decent thing and exit our lives in as ravishingly stylish a manner as they inhabited it" (Lake 2001: 62).

The cool blonde actress who became a princess

Newsflash – 13 September 1982

Her Serene Highness, Princess Grace of Monaco, driving on the Moyenne Corniche above the French Riviera, suffers a stroke, loses control of her Rover 3500 and, with her daughter Stephanie in the passenger seat, plunges down a ravine. Grace was pulled from the wreck unconscious but died the next day.

By 1955 Grace Kelly had made nine movies, and been the star of eight, winning an Academy Award for *The Country Girl* (1954). Grace starred in two more movies before marrying Prince Rainier of the Principality of Monaco, thereby becoming Her Serene Highness, Princess Grace of Monaco. Hollywood bemoaned its loss but probably not as much as director Alfred Hitchcock, who had lost his favourite cool blonde. Hitchcock announced in 1962 that Grace would return to star in his next film, *Marnie*, in the role of a frigid, compulsive thief but after Kelly withdrew, it went to Hitchcock's latest blonde discovery from *The Birds* (1962), 'Tippi' Hedren. Raymond Durgnat wrote that Hedren in *Marnie* (1964) was: "at once bland and brittle, cool and predatory, offering a plausible complexity difficult to imagine from Hitchcock's first choice for the title role, Princess Grace of Monaco" (1974: 350).

Donald Spoto offers a rather different perspective on Grace, the ice-queen: "At twenty-three, she was playful, athletic, popular and freewheeling...Her lovers (among them designer Oleg Cassini and actors Gene Lyons, Jean-Pierre Aumont and William Holden) made up an impressive platoon" (2008: 143). The year 1955 also saw a cover story on Grace Kelly in *Colliers:* 'The Key to Kelly', which observed that: "After a spell in the limelight, every celebrity acquires a 'public face'. The façade is a hodgepodge of fact, fantasy and circumstance created by a curious public and a prodding press. Grace Kelly is no exception" (Harvey 1955: 37).

Harvey recognized that there was much more to the elegant blonde that Hitchcock found so alluring but maintained a family-safe distance for the *Colliers* readership. Kissane (2012), writing on 'Grace Kelly: Style Icon', an exhibition of Kelly's clothes and accessories, cites Kelly's biographer, Gwen Robins, who reported that:

> She just adored sex. She made no bones about it. We were lying on the bed one day and I said something about sex and she said 'It's heaven'. She told someone else it 'puts lights' in her eyes. But Kelly understood that mystery was needed for mystique. She was discreet and tenaciously private about personal matters. Her active love life was a secret until after her death.
>
> (2012: 12)

Hitchcock, it appears, had recognized that those still, blonde waters ran deep, that there was, after all, the complexity that Durgnat did not sense. For Hitchcock she played threatened wife Margot Wendice in *Dial M for Murder*, flirtatiously determined girlfriend Lisa Fremont in *Rear Window* (both 1954) and equally determined but wealthy *and* flirtatious tourist Frances Stevens in *To Catch a Thief* (1955). Her final Hitchcock role had Grace driving a Sunbeam Alpine convertible high above the sparkling azure waters of the French Riviera, a view that may have been her last as, 27 years later and en route to Monaco, she suffered the stroke that caused her Rover 3500 to plunge down a ravine, resulting in her death the next day at 52 years of age.

Grace Kelly consolidated, and grew, her fashion maven status in her newest, and most sustained performance, that of Her Serene Highness, Princess Grace of Monaco. Tragically, it seems that her passion for fashion may have been a contributing factor to her death as:

> she had filled the back seat of her car with clothes she was taking to be altered for the coming season. She didn't want them crushed, so she brushed aside her normal chauffeur to take the wheel herself, with her younger daughter Stephanie by her side.
>
> (Kissane 2012: 14)

Brottman also notes: 'everyone who knew her agreed that Grace was a terrible driver' (2001: xxiii).

The irony of Grace's tragic death was it instantly recalled for so many that earlier drive – including back projections – she took with Cary Grant in Hitchcock's elegant *To Catch a Thief* (1955). The finality, however, of her last drive in 1982 counterpointed the witty optimism of that long-ago filmic imagining. The promise of Grace was tangible then – beautiful, successful, eligible – but that last descriptor was soon reconfigured by her marriage to Prince Rainier and elevation to Monégasque royalty.

The Palace first blamed the crash on a brake failure in Grace's 10-year-old, British-made Rover 3500 but two British Leyland mechanics sent to investigate were not allowed to inspect the wreck (Adler, Sullivan and Echikson 1982: 39). Aird proposed that: "Once motorists enter their car – so the theory goes – they surrender control of their movements to an imperfect machine. They become part of a compelling mechanical mythology" (1972: 201).

In this case such a mythology could disguise a strategy that the Palace hoped would distract the media from the reality of the accident. Grace had already accepted a major role in the Grimaldi mythology but that was now beginning to unravel – no amount of spin could delay the reality of the death of Princess Grace. Kroll and Sullivan (1982) wrote at the time:

> Princess Grace of Monaco maintained a feverish public interest longer than any celebrity of our time. Her death is perhaps the moment for an examination of that damnable, irresistible idea of the celebrity... It was not a career that made her such an undimming public icon, it was not even a life. It was a transfiguration, or a seeming one; the world... saw her as a creature whom destiny had transformed into something rich and strange.
>
> (1982: 36)

Grace was transfigured for again, but this time through her death. Her life of dedication to her family and Monaco immediately took the form of a memorial, but one that was shaped by a sudden, shocking tragedy.

A visit to Monaco's Cathédrale Notre-Dame-Immaculée would not be complete without visiting the tomb of Princess Grace, the formal memorial to her memory and her legacy. Another nod in the general direction of a tribute, albeit more perverse, would be to retrace Grace's final drive but without her tragic ending; that would, in any case, be illegal (but not impossible) as her Rover's plunge down the ravine was into private property. Who would even consider the thought of such a re-creation? J.G. Ballard, perhaps?

The tiny Principality of Monaco with its beautiful Mediterranean setting and history of wealth, privilege and exclusivity make it one of Europe's premiere tourist destinations. For years the Pink Palace offered visitors the possibility of a glimpse of glamorous Grace; now with both Grace and Rainier III passed on, the glamour is somewhat diminished.

The Sloane ranger who became a princess

Newsflash – 31 August 1997

Diana, Princess of Wales, and her companion Dodi Fayed, are both killed when their Mercedes Benz, being driven by drunken chauffeur Henri Paul and pursued by paparazzi, ploughs into the wall of a road tunnel under the Pont de l'Alma, Paris.

On 29 July 1982, 21-year-old Lady Diana Spencer married His Royal Highness, Charles, Prince of Wales, 32 years of age and heir to the British throne, after a two-year romance. The media frenzy that had been fully operational for the previous two years meant that there were probably few in the world within reach of a newspaper, magazine or television who did not know about the shy but well-born pre-school assistant likely to become a princess – isn't that every girl's dream? Grace Kelly, apparently, had confided just that to her sister Peggy (Kissane 2012: 12). It seems, however, that the Prince's long-standing affair with Mrs Camilla Parker-Bowles continued without losing any momentum, creating a traumatic vacuum between Charles and Diana. Despite the births of two young princes – William and Harry – the increasing number of tawdry public revelations about lovers and scandals resulted in, at the Queen's request, Diana and Charles divorcing in 1996. The media frenzy continued unabated, and no matter what Diana did, or where she went, or whose company she kept, the paparazzi persisted, following in droves. No amount of pleas to respect her privacy, or that of the princes, was heeded.

On 31 August 1997, Diana and her companion Dodi Fayed left the Hôtel Ritz in Paris shortly after midnight and were driven away by Henri Paul, a member of the hotel's security team. As always, the paparazzi were in quick pursuit but that was terminated suddenly when Paul lost control of the Mercedes Benz, which slammed into a concrete support post, then ploughed into the wall of the tunnel under the Place de l'Alma. Fayed and Paul died at the scene; Diana was treated before being cut from the wreck, then taken to the Hôpital de la Pitié Salpetrière, where she was pronounced dead at 4am. The latterly tarnished fairy tale was over; the Princess was dead at 36.

After Diana's death, Gibbs wrote of two confronting metaphors: "It is a commonplace to speak of Diana as an image consumed by the media, and through them, by us. But if she was consumed in life, she has been cannibalized in death" (1997: 75).

The frenzied consumption of both the image and the reality of Diana began as soon as rumours of her relationship with Prince Charles began to circulate, eventually becoming a tornado of harassment, intrusion and pursuit that lasted until (caused?) her death. It seemed that everything 'Diana' was newsworthy, so no detail, or opportunity, was overlooked. After her divorce the media lens shifted to each new male friend, companion or lover, with the public discourse focusing primarily on whether or not her behaviour was having a negative impact on her sons, not to mention a similar impact on the House of Windsor brand. Diana's last companion was Dodi Fayed, with both dying in a fatal car crash, their final moments captured by carrion paparazzi. According to Brandon (2002) it was:

> The crash to end all crashes, apotheosis of auto death, Princess Di obliterated in the tunnel beside the Seine, her questionable lover beside her, their driver allegedly high on drink and drugs, gory reality buried in a blur of deliciously unanswerable questions. Was it a deliberate murder cooked up by MI5 to save the future king from the shame of his mother's morganatic association with a disreputable Egyptian?...It was a paradigm of thanatic romance, a life petrified at its fragile peak of glamour and mystery...as that connoisseur of crashes J.G. Ballard observed, 'an accelerated death in both senses of the word'.
>
> (2002: 306–307)

Creating a 'Diana' itinerary may prove to be dark touristic winner but only if it includes those darker sites where she was most pestered, most harassed, most annoyed and of course, culminating in a ride in a Mercedes Benz from the Ritz into the tunnel under the Place de l'Alma. Lennon and Foley (2000) wrote that:

More recently, and to the derision of the British media, a Paris agency offers the prospect of following the final route of Diana, Princess of Wales, through the streets of the city in a black S-class Mercedes Benz, identical to that in which she died.

(2000: 164)

The derision of the British media at that time of writing may have since diminished to the point of invisibility – surely, after 14 years the wounds would have (should have?) healed. Everybody has moved on; emotional resilience manifests itself by necessity, at least after a decent mourning period. Death and loss are integrated through discourse and acknowledgement of the departed but gradually, not immediately, which can present a challenge for those who heal at a slower rate. The (Royal) family, however, being deeply pragmatic and having undertaken a respectable period of mourning, have long ago integrated Diana into its historical fabric and have just gotten on with it – the boys appear to be fine men now, with the elder famously married, the divorced husband and father has married his long-time lover, and the torrid times have, for the moment, settled.

So, where does this leave the late Princess of Wales in terms of commodification and touristic initiative? Would the Parisian last-ride recreation get the nod, or would it still be in bad taste? A report in 2008 indicated that the Parisian company that owned the Mercedes wanted it back from the British government because "It's worth a great deal of money" (*Herald Sun* 2008: 5). Going back much further, to only a year after Diana's death, Melbourne's *Herald Sun* Travel supplement had as its cover story 'In Search of Diana' and a double-page spread titled 'Desperately seeking Diana' with the caption: 'It's a year this Monday since Diana died. Matthew Pinkney reports on the travel industry the tragedy has created'. Pinkney (1998) writes of Diana "walks", which included various Diana-related residences, shops, restaurants, gym and described by one of the organizers as "tasteful and a response to public demand" and not "exploiting the memory of the Princess". Also detailed is Earl Spencer's tribute to Diana at Althorp, the family estate, which still operates in the same form:

> The award-winning exhibition is located in six rooms and depicts the life and work of Diana, The Princess of Wales. There are audiovisual displays in four of the rooms and the exhibits displayed include the famous Bridal Gown, childhood letters, school reports, and details of the Princess's work for charity.
>
> (*Pinkney* 1998: 1, 8–9)

One of the major Althorp sites is the shore of the lake, which offers a view of the island where Diana is buried in a building resembling a small classical temple of the Doric order. A black silhouette of Diana graces the front façade as well as one of her quotes, in which she offers help to society's most vulnerable.

Other memorials include the two in Harrods, London, installed by Dodi's father Mohamed al Fayed and bordering on kitsch; the Diana, Princess of Wales

Memorial Fountain in Hyde Park; and the informal memorial at the Place de l'Alma's La Flamme de La Liberté in Paris, directly above the tunnel where the crash took place.

Diana has been formally and informally memorialized. Althorp is only open to the public for a short period each year, Harrods is open every day and the memorial fountain is in a public park so also accessible all year. Response to the fountain was mixed, but Glancey (2004) insightfully observes:

> Is it by chance or design that Kathryn Gustafson and Neil Porter appear to have designed a near perfect metaphor for the life of Diana? Water ebbs, flows, gushes and chuckles round and around this prescribed oval course of beautifully cut granite slabs, before filtering out to a wider and more receptive world in the guise of the Serpentine... The cycle of a princess's life, you see, with all its ups and its downs, and their ultimate draining away.

The remains

> Nothing makes a better tabloid headline than the celebrity car crash... Nothing ends a tale of beauty, wealth and potential than blood on the tracks. The celebrity car crash is a sacred moment in time, a magic ritual, an instant constellation of tragedy, sacrifice, mass fantasy, and monumental comeuppance.
> (Brottman 2001: xv)

Brottman here is all about a perverse, quasi-religious read on deification – "the sacred moment in time" when it all becomes luminously clear, an epiphany of exultation; "a magic ritual" that transcends the quotidian, and raises the deity above the adoring throng; and that "instant constellation" where a tragic outcome is all but inevitable, sacrificing one so that others can live through the shed blood of immortality, the death that will forever obsess the mass of faithful penitents and, finally, the leaden lesson of the pride that cometh before the fall. No one will ever forget, *can* ever forget the screech of metal folding in on itself, the speeding up *and* slowing down, and even *stopping* of time, the penetration of vulnerable soft tissue, the screams, the disbelief, the horror and the final silence, which is both an end *and* a beginning.

The four crashes here – 1955, 1967, 1983 and 1997 – have all, in one sense, served the same purpose of illuminating that fateful journey from mortality to immortality, that remarkable phenomenon that blesses, metaphorically, those already so blessed. They have left the earthbound faithful, who still tend the shrines, who still run the fan clubs, who visit the crash sites, and photograph the gravestones, and celebrate the birthdays, who blog about their visits, and just will *not* let go because Jimmy and Jayne and Grace and Diana must be, and always will be, remembered and respected and revered because they deserve it, they earned it and they died for it.

This is, indisputably, dark territory, and the guides – in every sense of that term – abound. The fatal accidents discussed manifest a number of potentially dark dimensions – fame, celebrity and fandom; the allure and risk of automobility, and the finality of fatal car crashes or accidents; the forms of residual that nurture, sustain or limit, interest in such locations, sites and demises; journeys to the death sites; and the macabre embrace of those who seek something – anything – from the death sites through journeys real, virtual or imagined.

The four celebrities – Jimmy, Jayne, Grace and Diana – lived vividly, floodlit and loved by the fans who believed that they knew them. Their celebrity at its peak was like fireworks, great beauty but briefly so, brilliant bursts of light then darkness – not an intermission but a terrible, final end. The four car crashes snatched away their public personae and their private angst, their rage, their beauty and their serenity, and left a legacy of legends, misconceptions and highly sought and prized *memento mori*.

The memorials vary in form and permanence but record for the future what briefly shone so brightly in the past. Lowenthal tells us: "Relics, histories, memories suffuse human experience. Each particular trace of the past ultimately perishes but collectively they are immortal" (1985: xv).

They live.

References

Adler, J., Sullivan, S. and Echikson, W. (1982) 'A Tragic Crash, a Royal Farewell', *Newsweek*, 27 September.
Aird, A. (1972) *The Automotive Nightmare*, London: Arrow Books.
Anger, K. (2001) 'Kar Krash Karma', in M. Brottman (ed.) *Car Crash Culture*, New York: Palgrave Macmillan.
Ballard, J.G. (1973) *Crash*, London: Vintage.
Bast, W. (2006) *Surviving James Dean*, New York: Barricade Books.
Brandon, R. (2002) *Auto Mobile: How the Car Changed Life*, London: Macmillan.
Brottman, M. (2001) 'Introduction', in M. Brottman (ed.) *Car Crash Culture*, New York: Palgrave Macmillan.
Brottman, M. and Sharratt, C. (2001) 'The End of the Road: David Cronenberg's *Crash* and the Fading of the West', in M. Brottman (ed.) *Car Crash Culture*, New York: Palgrave Macmillan.
Darius, J. (2001) 'Car Crash Crucifixion Culture', in M. Brottman (ed.) *Car Crash Culture*, New York: Palgrave Macmillan.
Deadwrite's Dailies (2011) 'A Reading Room for Time Travellers', 22 June. Available at http://deadwrite.wordpress.com/james + dean (accessed 3 October 2011).
Durgnat, R. (1974) *The Strange Case of Alfred Hitchcock, or The Plain Man's Hitchcock*, London: Faber and Faber.
Fairmount, Indiana (n.d.) 'Fairmount, Indiana'. Available at http://www.city-data.com/city/Fairmount-Indiana.html (accessed 10 October 2011).
Gibbs, A. (1997) 'Eaten Alive/Dead Meat: Consumption and Modern Cannibalism', in Re:Public (ed.) *Planet Diana and Global Mourning: Cultural Studies and Global Mourning*, University of Western Sydney: Nepean, NSW: Research Centre in Intercommunal Studies.
Glancey, J. (2004) 'Diana Memorial Fountain Completed', *The Guardian*, 30 June. Available at http://www.guardian.co.uk/uk/2004/jun/30/arts.monarchy (accessed 17 January 2012).

Harvey, E. (1955) 'The Key to Kelly', *Colliers*, New York: The Crowell-Collier Publishing Company, 24 June, pp. 36–41.

Herald Sun (2008) 'Cash Bid on Di's Death Car', Melbourne, 8 September.

Kissane, K. (2012) 'Saving Grace: Guarding the Legacy of a Style Icon', *The Age, Melbourne: Life and Style*, 4 February, pp. 12–15.

Kroll, J. and Sullivan, S. (1982) 'Portrait of a Lady', *Newsweek*, 27 September.

Lake, H. (2001) 'Jump on in, You're in Safe Hands', in M. Brottman (ed.) *Car Crash Culture*, New York: Palgrave Macmillan.

Lennon, J. and Foley, M. (2000) *Dark Tourism*, London: Continuum.

Liujters, G. and Timmer, G. (1988) *The Life and Death of Jayne Mansfield*, Secaucus, NJ: Citadel Press.

Lowenthal, D. (1985) *The Past is a Foreign Country*, Cambridge: Cambridge University Press.

Perry, G. (2011) *James Dean*, Bath: Palazzo Editions Ltd.

Pinkney, M. (1998) 'Desperately Seeking Diana', *Herald Sun*, Travel, Melbourne, August, 28, pp. 1, 8–9.

Rojek, C. (1993) *Ways of Escape: Modern Transformations in Leisure and Travel*, Basingstoke: Macmillan.

Scott, L. (1997) 'Tinseled Tragedy: The Jayne Mansfield Mystery' – Chronicles of Recent History, *New Orleans Magazine*, October, *32*(1): 21–24.

Shine, A. (2010). *Inside the Hollywood Fan Magazine: A History of Star Makers, Fabricators, and Gossip Mongers*, Jackson, MS: University Press of Mississippi.

Shipman, D. (1972) *The Great Movie Stars: The International Years*, London: Angus and Robertson.

Spoto, D. (2008) *Spellbound by Beauty: Alfred Hitchcock and his Leading Ladies*, London: Hutchinson.

Stone, P. (2009) 'Dark Tourism: Morality and New Spaces', in R. Sharpley and P. Stone (eds) *The Darker Side of Travel: The Theory and Practice of Dark Tourism*, Bristol: Channel View Publications.

Stone, P. and Sharpley, R. (2008) 'Consuming Dark Tourism: A Thanatological Perspective', *Annals of Tourism Research*, *30*(2): 386–405.

Walter, T. (2009) 'Dark Tourism: Mediating Between the Dead and the Living', in R. Sharpley and P. Stone (eds) *The Darker Side of Travel: The Theory and Practice of Dark Tourism*, Bristol: Channel View.

Wilkes, G. and Krebs, W. (1992) *Collins English Dictionary*, 3rd edn, Sydney: HarperCollins Publishers.

15 Marvellous, murderous and macabre Melbourne

Taking a walk on the dark side

Leanne White

Introduction

The city of Melbourne in Victoria, Australia, offers a range of choices for those interested in more closely exploring the city's dark 'underbelly'. Three of the many tours on offer include Melbourne Crime Tours, Melbourne Cemetery Tours and the Old Melbourne Ghost Tour. This chapter will examine these three dark tours. Some of the questions that will be explored include: What places are visited? How is the tour narrated? How is the tour marketed? Along with an analysis of what takes place on the actual tour, brochures and websites will be briefly examined in order to address the above questions.

While it is possible to examine the twin phenomena of dark tourism and place identity in mutually exclusive ways, this chapter will explore the concepts with a combined approach as the dark experience is simultaneously consumed with the overall perception and experience of place in an inseparable manner. For the Melburnian or visitor seeking an escape from the more predictable Melbourne tours, the dark tourism experience is an increasingly popular option that often sheds new light on little known aspects of the city. How the destination image of 'Marvellous Melbourne', 'Murderous Melbourne' or even 'Macabre Melbourne' might be changed or enhanced by these tours will be explored.

When exploring a place such as Melbourne, we are delving deeper into our own heritage, along with that of the city and the nation. Underlying this suggestion is the proposition that heritage is a "cultural and social process" that is "ultimately intangible" (Smith 2006: 307). With this in mind, this chapter aims to demystify the ways in which the often intangible concept of heritage and thus place identity is imagined, and will examine the darker side of Melbourne's history to make that case. In particular, the meanings conveyed in the presentation of Melbourne's dark 'underbelly' will be highlighted. By focusing on dark heritage and the city of Melbourne, we can rethink our understanding and "awareness of the role" that heritage plays "in our everyday lives" (Waterton 2010: 206). Others have also argued that heritage has the ability to "guide and cement national identities" (Gammon 2007: 1).

Finally, Rojek argues that "most tourists feel they have not fully absorbed a sight until they stand before it, see it, and take a photograph to record the moment" (1997: 58). If dark tourism sites in Melbourne can help create a revised form of identity for a place, can the photographs taken at these destinations help to develop a deeper understanding of the place visited? Morgan, Pritchard and Pride argue that travel for the purpose of leisure is "a highly involving experience, extensively planned, excitedly anticipated and fondly remembered" (2004: 4). The photographs that capture the highlights of the travel occasion (dark or otherwise) constitute a vital element of both remembering the event and sharing the experience with others. Thus, relevant photographs from the three tours are included in this chapter as part of the analysis.

Marvellous Melbourne

Background

Melbourne was named in honour of the British Prime Minister Viscount Melbourne (Spicer 1992: 30). The term 'Marvellous Melbourne' was coined by George Augustus Sala – the most celebrated journalist in England (Davison 1988: 229). Some of the other words Sala used to describe the city he was so impressed with included astonishing, bustling and magnificent. Melbourne is Australia's second largest city with a population of around four million people. Melbourne is one of the world's southernmost cities and thus enjoys a temperate climate. The giant metropolis of Melbourne (one of the world's largest suburban sprawls) surrounds Port Philip Bay. To the north and west of Melbourne are suburbs built on flat basalt plains, while hillier suburbs built on sandstone and mudstone can be found to the south and east of the Melbourne Central Business District (CBD). The dividing line between the two main sides of Melbourne (both in a geographic and largely socio-economic sense) is the meandering Yarra River.

While Sydney was founded in 1788, Melbourne was founded 47 years later in 1835. As a result of the Victorian gold rush of the 1850s, the population grew rapidly and Melbourne became one of the world's wealthiest cities. During the 1880s land boom, the city became known as 'Marvellous Melbourne' – a slogan that remains in use to the present day. Another phrase that also took up some currency at the time (particularly because of the unsewered streets) was 'Marvellous Smellbourne'. Melbourne's dark side also emerged in the late 1880s as a significant number of deaths caused by typhoid helped also coin the term 'Murderous Melbourne'. Historically, Melbourne is appropriately a 'Victorian' city and represents a striking contrast to the city with which it is often compared – Sydney (Ridley 1996: 1). Melbourne today is "industrious, imaginative and creative; prolific in architecture, performance, live music and visual arts" (D'Arcy and Wheeler 2011: 7).

Successful events host

Melbourne is known as one of the world's best cities for hosting events, and the Olympic Games and the Commonwealth Games (while 50 years apart) have been the most well-known events staged. Melbourne is also home to the world famous horse race – The Melbourne Cup. The first Melbourne Cup took place at

Flemington Racecourse in 1861. With the current prize money of around $6 million to the winner, the 3,200 metre race is considered one of the most prestigious horse races in the world. The Melbourne Cup (known as 'the race that stops a nation') is considered an Australian institution and is run on the first Tuesday of November each year. On this day, most Australians stop what they are doing and watch or listen to the three minute race. 'The Cup' (as it is popularly known) attracts millions of people that do not bet at any other time during the year. On this day almost everyone in the country suddenly becomes an expert punter and the reasons for picking a winner are many and varied.

At major events such as the 1956 Olympics, the 2006 Commonwealth Games and the annual Melbourne Cup, the city of Melbourne proudly shows why it is considered one of the world's most livable cities. Melbourne's cultural diversity, friendliness and outstanding ability to organize are clearly on show to all at these times. Events such as these are important and translate into a greater share of tourists coming to Melbourne and regional Victoria. Staging significant events has well and truly reinforced Marvellous Melbourne's place on the world stage. But as outlined above and further detailed in this chapter, Melbourne has a dark side too. Melbourne, the city that was built on gold, has come a long way since the days of John Batman and John Pascoe Fawkner. Although it is argued no one or two particular individuals were responsible for the foundation of this great city (Grant and Serle 1978: 3), it is acknowledged that Batman did proclaim, "This will be the place for a village" (Newnham 1985: 52). A small plaque displaying Batman's insightful words is located on Flinders Street near William Street (McConville 1989: 19).

Murderous and macabre Melbourne

Background

Melbourne's dark past can be traced back to the early days of the settlement. As early as 1852, there were reported outbreaks of violent crime in the colony (Grant and Serle 1978: 74). The Melbourne underworld is notorious for using bullets to settle their differences. As crime reporters John Silvester and Andrew Rule point out, Melbourne gangsters "have been shot on the docks and in court buildings, dumped in the bay, stabbed in prison or have simply 'gone on the missing list'" (Silvester and Rule 2008: 416).

Some acts of crime were brought on by the excesses of the gold rush period and later, Victoria's infamous bushrangers – the most well-known of whom was Ned Kelly. At the Glenrowan Siege in 1880, five people died, and another died soon after as a result of being wounded. The story of Edward 'Ned' Kelly, who died in 1880, has been retold countless times and in a variety of textual forms including books, films, folk songs, exhibitions, advertisements, websites and Sidney Nolan's groundbreaking series of paintings. Nolan's series of 27 Kelly paintings produced in 1946 and 1947 are considered to have made a key contribution to Australian art. During the Opening Ceremony of the Sydney 2000 Olympic Games, many dancers dressed in Ned Kelly armour performed while the Sidney Nolan painting titled 'Ned Kelly' was projected onto the giant screens within Stadium Australia.

Ned Kelly has inhabited a special place in Australian history as he has been portrayed as something of a larrikin, yet a man of honour who defended himself and his gang against an incompetent police force. *The Story of the Kelly Gang* (1906) was the first feature film in Australia, and possibly the world. The legend of Ned Kelly remains popular today, more than 130 years after his death. In 2001 Peter Carey's novel, *True History of the Kelly Gang*, won the Booker Prize, and in 2003 yet another film version of the Kelly story was released in the form of a $34 million feature film. In the tradition of 'commercial nationalism' (see White 2004: 28), Ned Kelly has also been incorporated into a number of television commercials including Bushell's tea, Sunblest bread and rather ironically, an advertisement encouraging viewers to phone in and report crime to the Victoria Police.

Jane Clark argues that "Nolan's square black Kelly silhouette has become an enduring icon in the visual vocabulary of Australian identity" (Clark 1988: 213), while John Carroll argues that most Australians cite Ned Kelly as the nation's most famous hero (Carroll 1982: 211), and Don Watson claims that "You cannot live in Australia for more than a week without saying 'Ned Kelly' or something similar" (Watson 2001). Ned Kelly's suit of armour has come to be considered one of the great icons of Australia. The entire suit was reassembled in 2000 and has been displayed at exhibitions including the State Library of Victoria's 2003 exhibition, 'Kelly Culture: Reconstructing Ned Kelly'. While the entire suit of armour is imposing, it is the letterbox style helmet which has inspired the imagination of many. As Sidney Nolan captured in some of his paintings, and graphic artists since then have emulated, the space behind the helmet is left blank. The empty space is left open for the viewer of the text, or indeed Australia, to occupy.

After the bushranging era, the career criminal Joseph Leslie Theodore 'Squizzy' Taylor ruled Melbourne's streets in the 1920s and taunted police via letters to the editor when in hiding. By 1939, Melbourne had a proportionally higher crime rate for its population than London (Morton and Lobez 2011: vii). However, a particular decade that stands apart as a period when Melbourne lost its innocence was the 1980s. Four events in particular had a negative impact on the city's image – the Russell Street Bombing (1986), the Hoddle Street Massacre (1987), the Queen Street Massacre (1987) and the Walsh Street Shootings (1988). As crime journalist and writer Tom Noble argues, the perception that Melbourne is a dangerous place "probably comes down to the names of four Melbourne streets, made infamous overnight: Russell, Hoddle, Queen and Walsh" (Noble 1989: 7). All four streets feature in the Melbourne tourism experience provided by Go West Tours known as 'Melbourne Crime Tours'.

Cruising Melbourne's criminal underbelly

Melbourne Crime Tours boldly promotes itself as being "a genuinely memorable Melbourne experience" and "an entertaining and interactive guided tour that explores many of Melbourne's most fascinating criminal events" (Go West Tours

Marvellous, murderous, macabre Melbourne 221

Figure 15.1 Crime tour guide Alex explains the plaques at the Victoria Police Memorial

2012). Dressed in the orange overalls often worn by prisoners while promoting the tour company on the back of his uniform, our guide and driver for the four hour tour was Alex (see Figure 15.1). As he had worked at the Melbourne Morgue for around 20 years and had carried out countless autopsies (including some on well-known Melbourne criminals), Alex appeared aptly qualified to take us on the mini-bus tour of Melbourne's dark side – although the mortuary experience seemed just a bit too dark for some. On board that afternoon were three visitors from Brisbane, two from Hobart and six Melbourne 'locals' keen to find out more about the darker side of their backyard. The tour promised to incorporate a wide range of locations and events "from the days of bushrangers to the events of today" (Go West Tours 2012).

During the course of the afternoon, we were told stories about numerous people, places and organizations. Alex's enlightening commentary was continuous. Some of the names that passed our ears were: Russell Street, Ned Kelly, Squizzy Taylor, John Wren, Ray 'Chuck' Bennett, the morgue, Angela Taylor, Silk and Miller, Christine Nixon, Paul Mullet, the Victoria Police, the Armed Robbery Squad, Albert Park Lake, the Painters and Dockers Union, Jason Moran, Mark Moran, Carl Williams, Victor Pierce (Alex conducted the autopsy on him), Kath Pettingill, Dennis 'Mr Death' Allen and Graham 'The Munster' Kinneburgh, Pat Shannon, the Druids Hotel, Billy 'The Texan' Longley, Maria Korp, Graeme Jensen, Walsh Street, Jedd Houghton, Gary Abdullah, Peter McEvoy, Tynon and Eyre, the Turkish Consulate, Mark 'Chopper' Read, Hoddle Street, Julian Knight, La Porcella restaurant, Mick Gatto, Andrew 'Benji' Veniamin (Alex also conducted the autopsy), Lygon Street, Alfonse Gangitano, the Queen Victoria Market, Flagstaff Gardens, Queen Street and the Melbourne City Watch House. The tour started and finished on Russell Street at the front of the Old Melbourne Gaol and directly across the road from the site of the 'Russell Street Bombing'.

The event now referred to as the Russell Street Bombing took place just after 1 pm on Thursday, 27 March 1986 outside the Russell Street Police Headquarters. The main blast came from a stolen car loaded with explosives and was detonated by remote control. The bombing resulted in the death of a young police Constable by the name of Angela Taylor. With the toss of a coin a few moments earlier, Taylor had lost a bet and was given what would be the fatal undertaking of buying lunch for herself and her colleagues.

Around six explosions occurred in Melbourne on the eve of the Easter break and brought the city to a standstill as many inner city streets were closed to traffic and pedestrians. The explosions and flying debris injured 22 people and forever changed the perception of safety in Melbourne. Noble argues that the incident "threw Melbourne into a state of shock" (Noble 1989: 224). The motive for the bombing appeared to be revenge against the police over prior convictions. Reporting on the event, television newsreader David Johnston declared "Terrorism Hits Melbourne".

The Russell Street Police Headquarters was built between 1940 and 1943. The Art Deco style is reminiscent of New York's Empire State Building (see Figure 15.2). The striking building gave the police force a "modern, highly visible image" (Storey 2004: 97). The façade is so familiar to Australian television viewers as it was shown in the opening credits of the popular Australian drama *Homicide* in the 1960s and 1970s. This may have indeed made the Russell Street bombing seem just a bit too close to home for many who had grown up with the television show. The police moved out of Russell Street in the 1990s and the building has since been converted into apartments.

Another site visited on the Melbourne Crime Tour was the location where what is known as the 'Hoddle Street Massacre' took place on Sunday, 9 August 1987. Due to a stabbing incident, gunman Julian Knight had been recently discharged after a short period of training as a cadet officer with the Australian Army. Alex, our guide on the tour, summed up the 19-year-old killer as 'not Army material'. We were also told that Knight knew exactly how he wanted to die, and that was to

Figure 15.2 The Russell Street Police Headquarters and its striking Art Deco architectural style

be shot in battle. After a drinking binge earlier in the evening of 9 August Knight armed himself with two rifles, a pump-action shotgun and a combat knife.

At around 9.30 pm, Knight waited in the bushes along Hoddle Street, just a short distance from his family home (see Figure 15.3). He then began shooting indiscriminately at every car that passed him. A service station just down the road from the shootings became something of a sanctuary that night as many of the injured passengers pulled in to try to make sense of what had just happened. After more than 100 shots were fired across two kilometers in 45 minutes, Knight's ammunition supply finally came to an end and he was arrested by police.

Under the cover of darkness, the coldhearted shootings carried out by Knight resulted in seven deaths and 19 serious injuries. Victorian State Coroner Harold 'Hal' Hallenstein described the dark event as "a significant tragedy in the history

Figure 15.3 The Hoddle Street Massacre occurred near Julian Knight's home (the large building on the left)

of Australia", while Victorian Supreme Court Judge Justice George Hampel claimed it was "one of the worst massacres in Australian history". Television journalists, always keen to use alliteration, described the dark event as "Hell on Hoddle Street".

Another Melbourne shooting covered in the crime tour is known as the Queen Street Massacre. This particular dark event took place at the Australia Post headquarters located at 191 Queen Street just four months after the tragic episode at Hoddle Street. The incident resulted in nine deaths including the gunman, Frank Vitkovic. It was later found that the gun was not firing properly on the day and while 41 shots were fired, another 184 unspent cartridges were ejected from the sawn-off rifle (Creamer, Burgess, Buckingham and Pattison 1989: 8). Thus, what was Australia's worst mass killing at the time could have had an even more tragic ending.

The rampage took place on the 5th, 12th and then finally the 11th floors of the building, which has since been converted into a hotel. Former law student Vitkovic entered the Queen Street building late on the afternoon of 8 December 1987 with the aim of killing a person he had known from school, Con Margelis. The gunman died when trying to escape from office workers who had managed to tackle him to the ground and disarm him. A struggle took place and Vitkovic fell 11 floors to his death despite the fact that two workers were trying to prevent him from taking his own life. When police later searched his room, they found many newspaper clippings of the recent Hoddle Street Massacre with key words and sentences underlined in red. That the Queen Street Massacre had occurred so soon after the Hoddle Street Massacre left the people of Melbourne and Victoria with a feeling that any innocence left in their city had been forever lost. The acts of violence were widely seen as "something that happens in America, but not here in Australia" (Creamer *et al.* 1989: 4).

A further tour location where shootings had occurred was Walsh Street, South Yarra – just a short distance from Melbourne's Royal Botanic Gardens. The incident known as the 'Walsh Street Police Shootings' took place at around 4.30 am on 12 October 1988 outside 222 Walsh Street when two young policemen, Steven Tynan (22 years old) and Damien Eyre (20 years old), were ambushed and shot while checking a supposedly abandoned car. The rookie constables had been lured to the scene. Waiting just inside the block of units near the abandoned car were the killers. It was the first multiple killing of police since Ned Kelly's gang shot three officers in 1878 (Morton and Lobez 2011: 179).

In the two years prior to April 1989, there had been 11 fatal shootings carried out by police. Our tour guide Alex informed us that the criminals had vowed to kill two police for every one of their people who had been shot – and suspect Graeme Jensen was shot at 3.30 pm on 11 October. The 'Flemington Crew' led by Victor Peirce (whom Alex had worked on in the morgue) were considered the suspects.

The actual number of people who carried out the shootings is a point of contention. In court, lawyers argued that there were only two men present at the scene and witnesses also supported that argument (Noble 1991: 13). In 1991, Victorian police were devastated when a 'not guilty' verdict was handed down for the four men (Victor Peirce, Peter McEvoy, Trevor Pettingill and Anthony Farrell) who were put on trial for the Walsh Street shootings. Two other suspects (Jedd Houghton and Gary Abdullah) were killed by police before they had a chance to appear in court.

Towards the end of the four-hour Crime Tour, we passed the Flagstaff Gardens and were told that this was the site of Melbourne's first cemetery known as 'Burial Hill'. Only about half a dozen of Melbourne's first settlers were buried at the site with the first being a young boy named William Goodman in 1836. A monument to Melbourne's first deaths was eventually erected on the site in 1871 (Williams 1957: 15). Due to the many sheltered areas and proximity to the Queen Victoria Market, these particular gardens attract many of Melbourne's homeless. A year after Burial Hill was opened, a second larger cemetery was established on timbered land near the boundary of Melbourne's CBD at what is now the site of the popular Queen Victoria Market. About 10,000 people were buried at the site between 1837 and 1854 (Cooper 2011). The exact figure is not known as many of the records have been destroyed. Between 1920 and 1922 a total of 914 bodies in marked graves were exhumed and re-interred at other cemeteries around Melbourne. It is thought that more than 9,000 bodies are currently located under Melbourne's main fresh food market. A memorial to those buried at the site stands on the corner of Queen and Therry Streets. Plans to extend the market and build an underground car park have obviously been hampered by the former burial site. A site for a larger cemetery, that would be designed in the style of a public park with "a system of serpentine roadways" was chosen in 1849 (Sagazio 1992: 56). On 1 June 1853 the Melbourne General Cemetery (MGC) in the nearby suburb of Carlton opened its gates (Chambers 2003: 25). That particular location and dark tourism experience is examined in the following section.

Walking around the dead centre of Melbourne

Melbourne Cemetery Tours is promoted in a more matter-of-fact manner than the crime tour as we are told that tour guides Helen and Jan have been running the tours for more than 25 years, and that their detailed knowledge comes from "many hours of research spent in libraries and the Public Record Office" (Melbourne Cemetery Tours 2012). A range of guided walking tours with different themes are offered and the tour I chose to attend, to best fit with the theme of this chapter, was the 'Law Makers and Law Breakers' tour. Other tours run by Helen and Jan include four different 'Who was Who?' tours, The Gentle Sex, Creative Colonists, Military and Navy People, and Medicos and Misadventures. The two-hour tour took place on a Sunday afternoon, and was led by Jan, who conducted the tour for a group of about 25 people.

During the course of the afternoon, Jan read and spoke from her research. Like the crime tour, we were told stories about many people. Just some of the names that passed our ears were: Sir Robert Menzies, Harold Holt, Robert O'Hara Burke, William John Wills, Sir Samuel Gillott, William John Turner Clarke, Frederick Baker (Federici), Tommy Bent, John Wren, Julian Thomas, Amelia Gale, Frederick Deeming, Emily Mather, Edward Puckle, Emily Williams, Sir William A'beckett, William Christie, Peter Lalor, Sir Redmond Barry, Louisa Barry, Ned Kelly, Elizabeth Scott, Bradley O'Connor, Edward Thompson, Walter Rendell and Richard Sewell.

The tour began in the Prime Ministers' Memorial Garden located next to the main entrance. As the heritage listed MGC is located on a busy road across from the University of Melbourne, Jan had to compete with the highly audible noise of the traffic. In addition, being a sunny Sunday afternoon, many helicopter pilots decided to take advantage of the clear skies and conducted joy flights directly above us. Our tour guide jokingly explained that Melbourne is a very "loud cemetery" and "if you want to rest in peace, don't come here!" The origins of the MGC were explained, as was the first burial and the explanation for why people should be literally buried 'six feet under'. During the 1970s the management had allowed shallow graves to be dug and the negative consequences for the cemetery, friends and relatives and the surrounding area were unmistakable. Today, cremation memorials, vaults and graves can be purchased for either 25 years or in perpetuity. The MGC grounds now cover 107 acres with more than 500,000 burials.

The MGC opened on June 1, 1853. Being built on a water table, many of the older headstones display a distinct lopsidedness. Like the previous Melbourne cemetery, the grounds are divided in terms of religious denominations. Thus the sections Roman Catholic, Church of England, Methodist, Baptist, Lutheran, Greek Orthodox, Presbyterian, Jewish, Chinese, Other Denominations and even Undenominational can all be found in the cemetery today. Between 1861 and 1873 the Director of the Royal Botanic Gardens, Ferdinand von Mueller, supplied the cemetery with over 9,500 free plants including impressive pines, cypresses and firs (Sagazio 1992: 50). During the 1880s and 1890s, the MGC suffered from a number of problems including vandalism and poor management.

The main gates of the cemetery were moved to their current location in the 1930s (see Figure 15.4). Between the 1940s and the 1970s, a number of questionable management practices again took place, including the reselling of burial plots and removal of monuments. In 1978, all the trustees resigned and police became involved in order to stamp out corruption. Roadways were filled in with graves along the side with many new plots being sold to Melbourne's newly arrived

Figure 15.4 The main entrance of the Melbourne General Cemetery was built in the 1930s

migrant community. The result is that the striking contrast between the newer black marble graves with floral tributes and the older nineteenth-century granite graves displaying Irish and English names is a reminder that Melbourne is very much a multicultural city. The MGC is now run by the Southern Metropolitan Cemeteries Trust, which currently oversees eight cemeteries in Melbourne.

Towards the beginning of the tour, the final resting place of ill-fated explorers Burke and Wills was visited. Most Australian school children have been taught the story of Robert O'Hara Burke and William John Wills and the infamous 'Dig' tree at Coopers Creek. In 1860, an expedition of 16 men left Melbourne with the aim of heading directly north for about 2,000 miles to the Gulf of Carpentaria. For a number of reasons including poor leadership and bad luck, only one man (John King) survived the entire expedition. While there is a prominent monument to the explorers at nearby Royal Park, which marks the place where the expensive expedition commenced, at the MGC stands a "huge chunk of rough-hewn grey granite" (Chambers 2003: 52). The huge stone was mined in the town of Harcourt and weighs more than 30 tons. The monument is found at the intersection of First Avenue and Second Avenue.

Continuing along Second Avenue, we were taken to another particularly large monument – for Sir Samuel and Lady Elizabeth Gillott (see Figure 15.5). The Gillott memorial is one of the largest in the cemetery. Unlike most of the graves, it includes steps. The steps seem a little ironic as Gillott died as a result of falling down a flight of stairs at night. Gillott was President of the Law Institute, Attorney General, a member of the Legislative Assembly and the first 'Lord' Mayor of Melbourne. Gillott was the mayor when royalty visited for the Federation celebrations in 1901. His generous hosting of the event earned him and the mayoral office a knighthood.

Through his legal practice and other means, Gillott became a wealthy man and invested in a number of properties around Melbourne. His reputation was however tarnished when he was financially linked to illegal gambling (including John Wren's well-known establishment in Collingwood) and Melbourne's leading brothel. The financial connection dated back to 1877. Gillott resigned from Parliament and returned to England for a year in a bid to clear his name. He eventually died in England in 1913 and his body was returned to Melbourne. In 1922, his wife was also buried in the imposing tomb. One fifth of the Gillott estate was bequeathed to the University of Melbourne where a law prize is awarded annually in his honour.

A third impressive memorial along the same avenue is that of Australia's first millionaire, popularly known as 'Big Clarke', who died in 1874. The Clarke family had first settled in the Sunbury region in 1837. In 1850, William John Turner Clarke obtained a vast expanse of land in the area – more than 62,000 acres. Clarke was a member of the Victorian Legislative Council. The Clarke property effectively incorporated a large part of Melbourne's northern and western surrounds from what is now Campbellfield in the north to Williamstown in the southwest and across to Sunbury in the northwest. By the time of his death, the Clarke estate was worth almost £2.5 million, with freehold land in Victoria, Tasmania, South Australia and New Zealand.

Marvellous, murderous, macabre Melbourne 229

Figure 15.5 Cemetery tour guide Jan enlightens us on the life and times of Sir Samuel Gillott

Clarke's striking monument at the MGC resembles the Sunbury mansion named 'Rupertswood' that he would not live to see. Rupertswood is also known as the birthplace of cricket's coveted trophy, 'The Ashes'. Construction of the grand Italianate mansion began in 1874 with the laying of a three ton bluestone foundation. The event was marked with a half day holiday for school children and 1,200 residents from surrounding areas were invited to take part in the festivities. A significant feature of the 50-room building is the striking 100 foot tower. Well-known architect George Browne was chosen to design the building, while William Sangster was selected to landscape the impressive gardens (Clarke 1995: 77). An underground fernery was also created and the large stained glass windows at the mansion are considered to be some of the finest in the world. Clarke's first son (also named William) was given the responsibility of running much of the family empire.

Another gravesite also incorporated into the cemetery tour was that of Sir Redmond Barry. He was heavily involved in establishing the University of Melbourne (and also served as Chancellor), the Royal Melbourne Hospital and the Melbourne Public Library in the 1840s and 1850s. The State Library (as it is known today) is one of Melbourne's oldest institutions and "a magnificent building of the opulent boom period" (Lowe 1989: 85). As Chief Justice of the Supreme Court, Barry was famous for hearing the Eureka Stockade trials and for presiding over Ned Kelly's trial. Kelly's final words to Barry (that he would see him in the afterlife) came to fruition as he also died just 12 days later. Kelly was one of 178 criminals sentenced to death by hanging at the Old Melbourne Gaol (White and Newton-John 1974: 147). Our tour guide explained to the group that despite his standing in society, Barry was a womanizer who had numerous affairs, was cursed by Ned and led a scandalous private life. Although it is not revealed on the inscription of Barry's impressive monument, also buried here are his mistress and several of his children (Chambers 2003: 81).

Finally, the resting place of Melbourne's famous ghost is also found at this cemetery (see Figure 15.6). Federici is the stage name of Italian opera singer Frederick Baker who died of a heart attack at Melbourne's Princess Theatre in 1888. Somewhat ironically, Baker was playing the role of the devil when he died as he was lowered via a trap door beneath the stage. When his co-stars were told of the tragic incident, they then wondered who was standing on stage with them for the closing of the production. Thus, the legend of probably the theatrical world's most famous ghost was born.

More than 124 years later, the Princess Theatre continues to reserve an empty seat for Federici (as a good luck gesture) for every opening night performance. He is considered to be a friendly ghost and some actors have reported sightings of him over the years. Named in his honour, the Federici Bistro is located next door to the theatre. While Federici's grave could easily be passed without notice at the MGC, his story is given prominence on the 'Old Melbourne Ghost Tour' – a brief discussion of which follows.

Meandering through Melbourne's ghostly past

This ghost tour is run by Lantern Ghost Tours and operates on Friday and Saturday nights. The tour departs from Melbourne's Federation Square and is of one and a half hours duration. The company offers a range of guided walking ghost tours and even weekend trips including Ghosts of the Old City, Williamstown; Point Cook Ghost Tour; the Altona Ghost Tour and Asylums Haunted Weekend.

The tour took place on a Friday night, and was led by a young man by the name of Matt who conducted the tour for a group of about 30 people. Some of the people and places we heard about that evening were: Frederick Deeming (whom it was suggested may have also been 'Jack the Ripper'), Emily Mather, Young and Jackson's Hotel (the former Princes Bridge Hotel displaying the nude portrait 'Chloe', which caused controversy at an 1888 exhibition), Robert Hoddle, Melbourne's famous graffiti street art in Hosier Lane (see Figure 15.7), Alfred

Figure 15.6 The simple grave and repaired headstone of Melbourne's famous ghost — Federici

Place, Burke and Hare, Gun Alley, Alma Tirtschke, Pink Alley, the Melbourne Club, the Lyceum Club, Meyers Place, Parliament House, Queen Victoria, the Windsor Hotel, the Princess Theatre, Federici, Gordon Place, Her Majesty's Theatre, Dr Sun Yat Sen and China Town.

After the group met at Federation Square, Matt took us across Flinders Street to the steps of St Paul's Cathedral where he provided some background on the origins of Melbourne. We then continued to follow Matt through the laneways of Melbourne where he would occasionally stop, gather us around and tell us about the ghostly connections of where we were. The highlight of the ghost tour was possibly hearing more about the Federici story while standing outside the Princess Theatre (see Figure 15.8). The grand theatre with the world's first retractable roof was built to replace the Royal Princess Theatre (Johnston 1985: 32). It was opened

Figure 15.7 Melbourne's popular laneways such as Hosier Lane are known for creative graffiti

in time for the Queen's Jubilee celebrations in 1887 and was noteworthy as it was totally lit by electricity (Rogan 1970: 78). The Princess Theatre was built in the French Baroque style to match the flamboyance of the nearby Grand Hotel (now the Windsor Hotel) and Parliament House (Chapman and Stillman 2005: 70).

Conclusion

For the tourist visiting Melbourne, place identity becomes somehow embodied and personified by the people encountered and places visited. If we understand heritage as a process that constructs meaning about the past, then the construction of dark tourism in Melbourne is illustrative of this process. It is, essentially, a construction of place identity based upon particular places, names and past events,

Marvellous, murderous, macabre Melbourne 233

Figure 15.8 Ghost tour guide Matt tells us the story of Federici

along with reports and stories passed down. Contrary to popular notions of heritage that situate it as 'object-based', this example offers a new interpretation of heritage and place identity that builds on the work of Smith (2006), Waterton (2010), Gammon (2007) and others.

As Johnathon Culler argues, "All over the world the unsung armies of semioticians, the tourists, are fanning out in search of the signs of Frenchness, typical Italian behaviour, exemplary Oriental scenes, typical American thruways, traditional English pubs" (Culler cited in Urry 2002: 3). Equally, the search for representations of the 'Marvellous' or 'Murderous' can equally be discovered through a close examination of our cities and their key signifiers designed to reflect the core values of place.

In this chapter, narratives of dark tourism in Melbourne were presented by exploring aspects of three dark tours. Countless narratives of a place exist and will continue to be told in the years ahead. In Melbourne dark tourism plays a role in both the official and non-official discourse about place identity that is communicated to citizens and visitors. Closely examining past events, people, places, streets, buildings, monuments, memorials, cemeteries and other signifiers of the once dark provides a rich understanding as to how the destination's story can be read and understood.

Marvellous Melbourne has a dark side, which is not always evident – even to people such as myself who have lived in the city all their lives. Taking a walk on the dark side, whether it be for the Melburnian wanting to know more about their city or the keen visitor, is becoming an increasingly popular tourist option. And while the overall destination image of the city generally remains 'Marvellous', the 'Murderous Melbourne' and 'Macabre Melbourne' monikers simmer just below the surface.

References

Carroll, J. (1982) *Intruders in the Bush: The Australian Quest for Identity*, Melbourne: Oxford University Press.
Chambers, D. (2003) *The Melbourne General Cemetery*, Flemington: Hyland House Publishing.
Chapman, H. and Stillman, J. (2005) *Melbourne Then and Now*, London: Thunder Bay Press.
Clark, J. (1988) 'Convulsion and Calm: Death in the Afternoon', in D. Thomas (ed.) *Creating Australia: 200 Years of Art, 1788–1988*, Sydney: International Cultural Corporation of Australia, pp. 212–213.
Clarke, M. (1995) *Clarke of Rupertswood 1831–1897: The Life and Times of William John Clarke First Baronet of Rupertswood*. Melbourne: Australian Scholarly Publishing.
Cooper, M., (2011) 'Bodies Under Queen Vic Haunt Market Revamp', *The Age*, 11 March. Available at http://www.theage.com.au/victoria/bodies-under-queen-vic-haunt-market-revamp-20110311-1bqsp.html (accessed 15 May 2012).
Creamer, M., Burgess, P., Buckingham, W. and Pattison, P. (1989) *The Psychological Aftermath of the Queen Street Shootings*, Parkville: University of Melbourne.
D'Arcy, J. and Wheeler, D. (2011) *Melbourne Encounter*, Footscray: Lonely Planet Publications.
Davison, G. (1988) *The Rise and Fall of Marvellous Melbourne*, Carlton: Melbourne University Press.
Gammon, S. (2007) 'Introduction: Sport, Heritage and the English. An Opportunity Missed?' in S. Gammon and G. Ramshaw (eds) *Heritage, Sport and Tourism: Sporting Pasts – Tourist Futures*, Oxon: Routledge, pp. 1–8.
Go West Tours (2012) *Melbourne Crime Tours* (brochure). Northcote: Go West Tours (Vic) Pty Ltd.
Grant, J. and Serle, G. (1978) *The Melbourne Scene*, Neutral Bay: Hale and Ironmonger.
Johnston, M. (1985) *Growing Up in 'Marvellous Melbourne'*, Kenthurst: Kangaroo Press.
Lowe, D. (1989) *Walking Around Melbourne*, Port Melbourne: Leisure Press.
McConville, C. (1989) *Aird's Guide to Melbourne*, Flemington: Aird Books.
Melbourne Cemetery Tours (2012) 'Melbourne Cemetery Tours'. Available at http://helendoxfordharris.com.au/melbourne-cemetery-tours (accessed 18 May 2012).

Morgan, N., Pritchard, A. and Pride, R. (2004) *Destination Branding: Creating the Unique Destination Proposition*, Oxford: Elsevier.
Morton, J. and Lobez, S. (2011) *Gangland Melbourne*, Carlton: Melbourne University Publishing.
Newnham, W. (1985) *Melbourne: Biography of a City*, Melbourne: Hill of Content Publishing.
Noble, T. (1989) *Untold Violence: Crime in Melbourne Today*, Melbourne: Kerr Publishing.
Noble, T. (1991) *Walsh Street: The Cold-Blooded Killings that Shocked Australia*, Melbourne: Noble House.
Ridley, R. (1996) *Melbourne's Monuments*, Carlton South: Melbourne University Press.
Rogan, J. (1970) *Melbourne*, South Melbourne: Jacaranda Press.
Rojek, C. (1997) 'Indexing, Dragging, and Social Construction', in C. Rojek and J. Urry (eds) *Touring Cultures: Transformations of Travel and Theory*, London: Routledge, pp. 52–74.
Sagazio, C. (1992) 'Central Melbourne', in C. Sagazio (ed.) *Cemeteries: Our Heritage*, Melbourne: National Trust of Australia (Victoria), pp. 48–56.
Silvester, J. and Rule, A. (2008) *Underbelly: The Gangland War*, Smithfield: Floradale Productions Pty Ltd and Sly Ink Pty Ltd.
Smith, L. (2006) *The Uses of Heritage*, Oxon: Routledge.
Spicer, C. (1992) 'The First Cemeteries: Old Melbourne', in C. Sagazio (ed.) *Cemeteries: Our Heritage*, Melbourne: National Trust of Australia (Victoria), pp. 30–35.
Storey, R. (2004) *Walking Melbourne: A Guide to the Historic and Architectural Landmarks of Central Melbourne*, Melbourne: National Trust of Australia (Victoria).
Urry, J. (2002) *The Tourist Gaze*, 2nd edn, London: Sage Publications.
Waterton, E. (2010) *Politics, Policy and the Discourses of Heritage in Britain*, Hampshire: Palgrave Macmillan.
Watson, D. (2001) 'The Enduring Image of Ned Kelly', The Brisbane Institute, 14 November. Available at http://www.brisinst.org.au/papers/watson_don_kelly.html (accessed 15 May 2003).
White, L. (2004) 'The Bicentenary of Australia: Celebration of a Nation', in L.K. Fuller (ed.) *National Days/National Ways: Historical, Political and Religious Celebrations around the World*, Westport: Praeger, pp. 25–39.
White, O and Newton-John, S. (1974) *Melbourne for Everyone*, Melbourne: Wren Publishing.
Williams, W. (1957) *History Trails in Melbourne*, Sydney: Angus and Robertson.

16 War and ideological conflict

Prisoner of war camps as a tourist experience in South Korea

Eun-Jung Kang and Timothy J. Lee

Introduction

In the middle of the twentieth century, the Korean War, along with the Vietnamese War, was listed as the next most severe conflict after World War II because of its significance and its impact on the world (National Archives of Korea 2011). The Korean War was not merely an ideological conflict between the South and North, but can be regarded as an extension of the Cold War. Sixteen nations including the US were enlisted to support South Korea while China and the Soviet Union joined with North Korea (Lee 2006). The three years and one month of severe battles were finally brought to an end by the Armistice Agreement between the two sides in 1953 and resulted in the division of North and South Korea (Kim and Prideaux 2003). The war also caused enormous property damage and generated millions of casualties, refugees, widows, orphans and prisoners of war (POWs) (National Archives of Korea 2011). The Cold War still remains on the Korean Peninsula and has done for more than 60 years (The 60th Anniversary of the Korean War Commemoration Committee 2011a).

Not surprisingly, a number of sites or memorial towers associated with the Korean War inside and outside of the Republic of Korea (South Korea) were established for the purpose of remembrance, commemoration or education as with battlefield sites around the world (Baldwin and Sharpley 2009). While most of these sites present the subject of the development of the Korean War, the historic park of Geoje or Geoje POW camp is different. The park currently represents two historic events of the Korean War – the POW camp and refugees arriving from the Hungnam evacuation – which actually occurred on Geoje Island. The park is an open-air museum that consists of 25 exhibition rooms representing the development of the ideological conflicts that occurred in the small world of Geoje POW camps. It also has a large memorial tower and a shape of the SS *Meredith Victory*, which represents a successful rescue operation of refugees during the Korean War.

The historic park of Geoje is well recognized as a tourist attraction, which receives around 800,000 visitors a year. There are several factors that allow the POW camp to appeal to a variety of visitors, not only people associated with the Korean War. This chapter discusses the factors that led the POW camps of Geoje to become a popular war attraction, although they represent a serious subject, as do other Korean War attractions.

The Korean War and its prisoners

The Korean War is commonly referred to as an "offshoot of the Cold War" (Lee 2006: 158) because it was caused by ideological conflicts in Northeast Asia after World War II and resulted in the division of North and South Korea, which has persisted for over six decades. The division of the peninsula along the 38th parallel was determined by the agreement of the Allies at the Moscow Conference in 1945, in which the Allies arranged the placement of South and North Korea under the rule of the US and USSR respectively for a five-year trusteeship. The two Koreas established their own governments during the trusteeship and the South adopted capitalism and democracy following the USA, while the North adopted Stalinist communism following the Soviet Union (Kim and Prideaux 2003). The Korean War had four different stages, as outlined below.

Stage one

The North Korean troops fired on the South and crossed the 38th parallel border at 4 am on Sunday, 25 June 1950. Within four days, they had captured Seoul, the capital of South Korea, and conquered two-thirds of South Korea within a period of three months (Historic Park of Geoje POW Camp 2011; Park 2010). North Korea's surprise attack prompted American President Truman to order the US air and sea forces to support the South Korean regime, and request the assistance of United Nations (UN) members. Despite this prompt US support, South Korean troops were not able to stop the North Korean troops and retreated to the Busan Region in the southeastern corner of the peninsula, east of the Nakdong River that was considered the last stand of the South (Kirkbride 2011). During this stage, the number of North Korean prisoners of war was small and the established POW camp only accommodated 250 prisoners.

Stage two

The situation of the battle between South and North Korea changed when the UN forces arrived on the peninsula and launched a counterattack against the North. The UN forces consisted of troops from 16 countries including Great Britain, France, Canada and Australia. As the commander of the UN forces, General Douglas MacArthur carried out a surprise landing of the UN forces at Incheon on 15 September and isolated the North Korean troops in South Korea. The UN forces recaptured Seoul on 28 September 1950 and crossed the 38th parallel in pursuit of the fleeing North Korean troops. They also captured Pyongyang, the capital of North Korea and reached the Yalu River on the western front and Cheongjin on the eastern front (The 60th Anniversary of the Korean War Commemoration Committee 2011a).

During this stage, the number of North Korean prisoners increased rapidly. In particular, the Incheon surprise landing operation, which isolated the North's troops in the South, significantly increased the POWs to 11,000. By the end of October 1950, Southern and UN troops had captured around 117,000 prisoners, which far exceeded the number of prisoners they could control and treat. They had to arrange for more soldiers and equipment to guard the POWs and constructed temporary POW camps in Incheon, Seoul, Pyongyang and other cities. At the same time, the UN forces sought for suitable places to accommodate substantial numbers of prisoners and selected Geoje Island mainly because of its geographic location. As an isolated island, Geoje was convenient to control and manage. The close proximity of Geoje and Busan (the second largest city in South Korea) was convenient for the UN force when transferring prisoners from Busan. Moreover, the island provided sufficient drinking water and space to grow vegetables and crops for prisoners. With these conditions, large-scale prisoner of war camps were constructed on Geoje at the beginning of 1951 (Park 2010).

Stage three

In October 1950, over 150,000 Chinese communist troops joined the conflict. This made the UN forces withdraw troops from the North. Chinese and North Korean troops then advanced southward and captured Seoul in January 1951 (The 60th Anniversary of the Korean War Commemoration Committee 2011a). Meanwhile, the UN forces transferred 24,000 prisoners from Pyongyang prisons to Incheon and then to Busan, the final destination for POWs on the Korean Peninsula. The majority of POWs were finally transferred to Geoje Island where the total number reached 173,000 including 20,000 Chinese and 300 female prisoners. The population on Geoje including prisoners, guards and administration officers was over 300,000, or three times greater than the actual population of islanders (Park 2010).

Stage four

The UN forces counterattacked and the North Koreans retreated behind the 38th parallel. A stalemate then developed with fierce fighting between the South and the North to acquire more territory around the 38th parallel. The tide of the war gradually turned in favour of the South, and the North proposed a truce through the Soviet Union (Kirkbride 2011). As a result, the Korean Armistice Agreement was signed on 27 July 1953 and the demilitarized zone (DMZ) was established on the Korean Peninsula (Yoon and Park 2010). During this stage, POW camps in Geoje experienced an atrocious battle between communist prisoners, anti-communist prisoners and guards (Park 2010).

The prison camps of Geoje

The former POW camps of the Korean War were almost all destroyed after the armistice agreement in 1953 and subsequent economic development of Geoje. Only a small number of POW camps were restored and turned into the historic park of Geoje in 1999. The site represents the atrocity of the ideological conflict between prisoners. Moreover, Geoje Island was also related to the Hungnam evacuation – the largest humanitarian rescue operation carried out by UN forces. Thus, the historic park of Geoje currently presents the two historic events of the Korean War.

Incidents in the POW camps

South Korean and UN troops had a reputation for treating North Korean and Chinese prisoners reasonably well. They strictly followed the Third Geneva Convention of 1949 that stipulated the humane treatment of POWs (International Committee of the Red Cross 2011). The POW camps in Geoje were constantly under the scrutiny of the public; the International Committee of the Red Cross also frequently checked the treatment of prisoners, and the media from Western countries also reported on the treatment of POWs on Geoje Island. As a result, North Korean and Chinese prisoners at the camps had a relatively comfortable life compared to the refugees, islanders and some South Korean troops. Despite wartime, they were offered the necessities of life such as three meals per day, along with warm clothes and shelter in the colder months. They did not have to worry about their safety or returning to the battlefield. Moreover, the prisoners could engage in a wide range of educational and recreation activities offered by the Civil Information and Education Section of the UN. The educational programmes for the prisoners included an orientation programme, literacy classes, hygiene and a variety of job training, for example to become a smith, a carpenter, a barber, a shoe repairer or a tailor. Other educational content included the value of life in a democratic society. The recreational activities for the prisoners included watching 20–30 movies per month and listening to radio news and music for 21 hours in Korean and seven hours in Chinese per week. These activities influenced the prisoners' ideology and led to disputes between prisoners (Park 2010).

The POW camps in Geoje were peaceful in the beginning, with only a few conflicts between prisoners and South Korean camp guards. At that time the conflicts were not planned and not caused by ideological differences. However, the peaceful mood at the camps gradually changed after the final transfer of prisoners from Busan to Geoje in June 1951. After that the camp had communist prisoners, anti-communist prisoners and guards. The first fierce fighting between guards and prisoners occurred after several North Korean high-ranking officers were interned. North Korean officer prisoners led collective actions such as refusing meals and throwing stones at the guards. Several guards and eight prisoners were injured and three prisoners were killed by gunshot (Park 2010).

Such collective actions of prisoners began in the summer of 1951 when the truce talks between representatives of North and South Korea opened. The truce talks implied the end of war on the peninsula and repatriation of all prisoners. However, a substantial number of prisoners refused to go back to North Korea and China, which led to a separation of prisoners according to their ideology – communist and anti-communist. At the same time the North was aware of anti-communist prisoners in Geoje and sent spies to support them and induce conflicts in the camps. On the other hand, anti-communist prisoners were also united against the communist cause. In the prison camps, therefore, severe violence causing death was frequent among prisoners, which led to lack of control by the prison guards. One severe conflict occurred on 17 September 1951 and lasted for three days. Around 300 anti-communist prisoners were killed and their bodies were either buried or placed in rubbish bins and thrown outside the camp (Park 2010).

One of the main issues in the truce talks was the repatriation of prisoners of war. The UN forces and the North had to examine the number of prisoners who refused repatriation. When the UN forces entered the camp to check the number of prisoners who refused repatriation, around 1,000 to 1,500 communist prisoners attacked the UN forces using swords, axes, bamboo spears and so on. During this riot, 77 prisoners and one US soldier were killed and 140 prisoners and 36 prison guards were injured. The riot led to a change in the commander of the POW camp and Brigadier General Francis Dodd took control. Meanwhile, the anti-communist prisoners who refused repatriation were killed by communist prisoners. The guards could not control the violence inside the camp although it caused more than 100 prisoner deaths. General Dodd entered the camp to meet communist officer prisoners on 7 May 1952 and was kidnapped by prisoners. After rescuing Dodd, the UN forces decided to separate prisoners for their own safety. The UN forces transferred 82,000 anti-communist prisoners to other camps outside of Geoje. They also separated communist prisoners and transferred 32,000 communists and 5,600 Chinese prisoners to other prison camps. Only 48,000 communist prisoners were left in Geoje prison camps. The anti-communist prisoners were released in 1953 before the armistice agreement in July 1953 and the other prisoners were returned to the North or China, while some chose to settle in other countries (Park 2010).

Geoje as a last destination for refugees from Hungnam

The Hungnam evacuation occurred during the third stage of the Korean War when Chinese communist troops crossed the 38th parallel and the UN had to withdraw their troops by sea while other retreat paths were blocked (Jeong 2010). The UN forces implemented the evacuation from the North Korean port of Hungnam between 15 and 24 December 1950. The Hungnam evacuation was a large-scale operation involving the Army, Navy and Air Force, and included the transfer of men, supplies, equipment and civilian refugees (Vargesko 1991). The operation withdrew 105,000 soldiers, 18,422 cars and 35,000 tons of supplies from the Hungnam port.

The Hungnam evacuation is frequently described as a 'miracle' (Ahn 2006; The 60th Anniversary of the Korean War Commemoration Committee 2011b) because the SS *Meredith Victory* transported 14,000 refugees from the Hungnam port to the southern port of Busan. The SS *Meredith Victory* as a cargo vessel was deployed to transport supplies and equipment for the Korean War. The ship arrived at the Hungnam port on 22 December to perform the evacuation. On that day, the port was full of refugees who heard the news of evacuation and fled from the communists. Captain Leonard LaRue of the SS *Meredith Victory* decided to unload all weapons and supplies from the ship in order to transport all remaining refugees at the port. As a result, the ship could hold more than 14,000 refugees, despite the ship normally only accommodating just 12 passengers. According to Officer Lunney, the SS *Meredith Victory* was fully packed with refugees in the cargo hold and on deck (Ahn 2006). The majority of the refugees had to remain standing up, shoulder-to-shoulder in freezing conditions. There was very little food and water available on the ship and the refugees in the cargo hold could not get fresh air or enough room to move. Lunney also stated that his crew delivered five babies during the three-day passage to safety (Ahn 2006). On Christmas Day the SS *Meredith Victory* arrived at Geoje Island and miraculously no casualties were discovered (Kirk 2003). Consequently, the Hungnam evacuation was described as an example of outstanding success by the US Army (Vargesko 1991). The SS *Meredith Victory* was also described as a *Ship of Miracle* (Gilbert 2000).

How do POW camps become tourist attractions?

The Korean War clearly had a significant impact on all Koreans. It resulted in enormous property damage and more than two million casualties in South Korea including South Korean and UN troops, and South Korean civilians. The North also had more than two million casualties including North Korean and Chinese troops and civilians. It generated 3.2 million refugees, 300,000 war widows, 100,000 war orphans and 132,027 prisoners of war (National Archives of Korea 2011). Despite the significance of the war in Korean contemporary history and current Korean life, only a small number of Koreans associated with the war such as veterans or family or relatives of victims are interested in or visit sites associated with the conflict. However, POW camps in Geoje are different from other war memorial sites in terms of the number of visitors, interpretation and authenticity. The Geoje POW camps receive around 800,000 visitors per year, which is relatively large given its isolated location and that visitors need to travel more than 40 minutes by ferry from the mainland port of Busan.

Accessibility to the site

One of the factors for the successful development of tourist attractions in a remote region is the improvement of physical and political accessibility (Hall and Boyd 2004; Khadaroo and Seetanah 2008; Prideaux 2000). Many dark tourism and battlefield sites around the world are remote or distant shrines where the actual tragic events occurred (Lennon and Foley 2000) and it is often difficult to access such sites. As a result, these sites receive fewer visitors than otherwise might be the case and are difficult to turn into successful and well-known tourist attractions.

Visiting dark tourism sites is often regarded as a side trip or excursion within a bigger trip. Few visitors use an entire holiday to visit a dark tourism site and few return to these sites (Walter 2009). In this respect, the physical accessibility to the site is the most important factor to increase the number of visitors. Typical examples are Ground Zero in New York and the US Holocaust Memorial Museum in

Washington DC. Both are located in large cities and attract millions of visitors per year (Blair 2002; Lennon and Foley 2000). Political accessibility refers to the conditions that allow entry into a destination (Weaver and Oppermann 2000). This type of accessibility can be a constraint factor for the number of visitors to dark tourism sites. A typical example is the DMZ between North and South Korea where all visitors are requested to provide identification or passport numbers before the actual visit. The ID check takes at least ten days for foreigners and at least one month for domestic visitors. Some domestic visitors are not allowed to visit the DMZ.

In terms of the historic park of Geoje, physical and political accessibility is relatively convenient compared with some other sites associated with the Korean War such as the DMZ. First of all, the historic park is located in Gohyeon, in the centre of Geoje on the southern part of the Korean Peninsula and 40 minutes away from the port of Busan. Visitors often select the POW camp as part of their internal itinerary for their Geoje Island tour and stay only a few hours there. The park is not a major draw card for visitors to Geoje but is an adequate site for a side trip or a few hours' excursion within a Geoje Island tour because of convenient physical accessibility to the site. Moreover, since the bridge between Geoje Island and the mainland was completed on 14 December 2010, management of the park reported that the number of visitors to the site increased markedly in 2011. With regard to political accessibility, the POW camp does not have strong restraints or a dress code for visitors. The USS Arizona Memorial Museum and some Holocaust sites including Auschwitz request appropriate dress code for visitors. Thus, the POW camp is regarded as an appropriate stopover site and frequently included in itineraries of Geoje Island.

Interpretation of the site

One crucial factor in the development of dark tourism or battlefield sites is interpretation. Interpretation is defined as "a set of information – focused communication activities, designed to facilitate a rewarding visitor experience" (Moscardo and Ballantyne 2008: 239) and often regarded as the primary means of communication between the attraction and visitors (Sharpley and Stone 2009; Wight and Lennon 2007). It is noted that without interpretation, dark tourism or battlefield sites may be meaningless to visitors. Many dark tourism sites or attractions make serious efforts to present the site effectively to enhance visitor understanding of the theme of the site (Sharpley and Stone 2009). However, war sites or some dark tourism attractions face a series of challenges in terms of interpretation because the main subject involves controversy (Henderson 2000). In particular, war sites such as World War II attractions should include information about both perpetrators and victims. In this respect, some dark tourism sites caused by ideological conflict or governments employ selective interpretation, given the impact of the subject matter on society (Wight and Lennon 2007).

The interpretation policy of war sites or attractions is classified into three categories: victim strategies, perpetrator strategies and spectator strategies (Ashworth and Hartmann 2005). Victim interpretation strategies focus on the victim of the atrocity or war. In contrast, perpetrator interpretation strategy is often denial of the occurrence of, or responsibility for, the seriousness of the tragedy. The third category, spectator interpretation strategy, is less sensitive than victim or perpetrator interpretation strategies because it is not directly involved in the atrocity. It is commonly employed to provide more general lessons to local contemporary societies who may not be directly involved in the original atrocity (Ashworth and Hartmann 2005).

The spectator interpretation strategy applies to the POW camp of Geoje because only a few South Koreans may be directly associated with the ideological conflict in the POW camp of Geoje and the purpose of the site is to inform visitors about the atrocity. The camp presents the daily life of prisoners and the series of conflicts between communist and anti-communist prisoners. It can satisfy visitor curiosity about the life of POWs and their ideological conflict. Moreover, the tragedy inside the POW camp seems now far in the past and may not deeply affect South Koreans in general, despite dealing with the outcomes caused by an ideological conflict. In this respect, visitors may not have serious emotional involvement, which means the site can become an important educational tourist site.

The POW camp of Geoje also employs 'hot interpretation' as an effective way to deliver its messages (Uzzell 1989). It evokes visitors' negative emotions by presenting both the brutality of the cruel fighting between communist and anti-communist POWs, and the gruelling three-day journey of the SS *Meredith Victory*. The former may not deeply affect individuals, given that the tragedy in the camp does not seem relevant to individuals. On the other hand, the latter, that involves the carving of the names of heroes and survivors who arrived at Geoje Island on the SS *Meredith Victory*, may deeply touch the heart. It evokes the sympathy or empathy of individuals; given that over 10 million people are the immediate family or relatives of refugees from North Korea during the Korean War (Boo 2000).

Authenticity of the POW camp

Authenticity, the meaning of "traditional culture and origin, a sense of the genuine, the real or the unique" (Sharpley 1999: 189), is also an essential factor to enhance visitor experience at dark tourism or battlefield sites. The importance of authenticity at dark tourism sites is emphasized by Miles (2002), who applied the dark and darker paradigm to two Holocaust sites – the concentration camp of Auschwitz–Birkenau and the US Holocaust Memorial Museum. The former is described as a darker site because it is an actual holocaust site and enhances visitor experience despite relatively undeveloped museum facilities. The latter is described as 'dark' because the site is associated with the holocaust but is not the site where the atrocity took place.

The POW camp of Geoje can be regarded as an authentic and representative site of the Korean War. South Korea has a relatively small number of authentic war sites because the armistice agreement between South and North Korea in 1953 and the subsequent economic development in South Korea have removed most authentic battlefields. The large-scale original POW camps were also destroyed and only small remains of POW camps were designated as a cultural treasure of Gyeongsang Province in 1983. The present POW camp is the reproduction of the former POW camp and includes 1,300 photographs, documents and exhibits. Without the authenticity of the site and the remains, the Geoje POW camp would not perform its role as an educational space dedicated to the Korean War. However, the authentic POW camp is meaningful and is able to educate about the history of the Korean War.

Management of the site and visitors

Geoje POW camp has the characteristics of a museum. As a war park, the camp performs some commercial activities such as charging four US dollars as an entrance and parking fee to visitors (Sharpley and Stone 2009). It also operates a small snack bar and cafeteria, a souvenir shop and several vending machines for visitor convenience and to obtain an operating fund for the park. These necessary commercializing activities can be claimed to be inappropriate, given that the site represents a part of the Korean War. However, the limited commercial activities of the park can be somewhat acceptable in terms of the purpose of visiting and the type of visitors. The park was constructed to educate visitors about the history of the Korean War, not to provide a memorial service for those who were killed. Moreover, the park as a historic war museum is currently comprised of around 25 exhibition rooms and settings for visitor experiences. Exhibition rooms present the relics of the Korean War and the POW camps with clear descriptions. Free guided tours and other educational services are also provided to visitors.

With regard to visitors, the historic park of Geoje is distant from battlefields or battlefield pilgrimages despite being representative of the Korean War. The battlefield pilgrimage is defined as "travelling for remembrance with the focus on the spiritual and emotional experience of visiting graves and memorials" (Baldwin and Sharpley 2009: 194), and attracts visitors such as veterans, widows or immediate families or relatives. However, the POW camps may not appeal to these types of visitors who are the main visitors or repeat visitors at other war attractions (Baldwin and Sharpley 2009). It attracts tourists or leisure travellers who are interested in war and searching for some extraordinary experiences.

The Geoje POW camp may inspire patriotism in visitors like other POW museums. However, the source of patriotism visitors may feel is significantly different from other sites. Boyles (2005) notes that patriotism was a strong motivator for POWs in their survival of the most difficult circumstances and visitors can feel a sense of love for their country by watching the POW story in the Andersonville National Historic Site in the US. In contrast, this kind of patriotism may not be experienced in the Geoje POW camp that focuses more on the atrocity of ideological conflict. The Geoje POW camp presents a warning that strong ideology can cause man's inhumanity to man. However, it provides the experience of patriotism with the appreciation of present life, the country they live in and the ideology the country selected.

Conclusion

Dark tourism or battlefield sites play an important role in our society by continuously reminding us about the outcome of disasters, war and other atrocities. However, most of these sites or attractions receive a limited number of visitors because the subject matter is associated with the dark side of human nature (Sharpley and Stone 2009). The locations tend to be remote (Lennon and Foley 2000); nevertheless, some dark tourism attractions or battlefield sites have performed their role successfully through identifying and developing effective ways to deliver their messages to visitors. Moreover, these sites often receive a large number of visitors every year and are listed as famous attractions.

This chapter discussed several factors that have led the historic park of Geoje to become a successful heritage tourist attraction on Geoje Island and a representative site of the Korean War. One of the factors is the significance of the tragic event the site presents. The Korean War was the most significant event for Korea in the middle of the twentieth century and the outcome of the Korean War, the division of South and North Korea, continuously impacts on Koreans in all aspects of their lives. In this respect, the tragic events in the POW camps of Geoje can easily evoke sympathy from visitors about the reality or atrocity of ideological conflict.

The physical and political accessibility and interpretation of the site are also considered important factors to the development of the dark tourism site. The convenient location of Geoje POW camps attracts a large number of visitors as a side trip or excursion while visiting the southern region of the country. In terms of interpretation, the POW camps of Geoje adopted a spectator interpretation strategy (Ashworth and Hartmann 2005) in which South Koreans are directly associated with the ideological conflict inside the camp during the Korean War. Visitors to the park may not have strong emotional involvement as a perpetrator or victim, which visitors may experience in some other dark tourism or battlefield sites. In this respect, visitors can absorb the important educational messages the park presents throughout all exhibition rooms.

As Miles (2002) argues, authenticity in dark tourism attractions is important. The authenticity of the POW camps is regarded as a key pull factor for visitors, given that South Korea has a relatively small number of authentic war sites as a result of poor economic development. A visitor's experience can be enhanced by emphasizing the sad reality of tragic events. Consequently, the way in which the park is managed is a vital factor in determining the success of the dark tourism destination. The ability of management to deliver effective services to visitors is the basic foundation in the development of this dark tourism attraction.

References

Ahn, J. (2006) 'At that Night Hungnam Evacuation', *The Chosun Ilbo*, 24 February, p. 19.

Ashworth, G. and Hartmann, R. (2005) 'Introduction: Managing Atrocity for Tourism', in G. Ashworth and R. Hartmann (eds) *Horror and Human Tragedy Revisited: The Management of Sites of Atrocities for Tourism*, Sydney: Cognizant Communication Corporation, pp. 1–14.

Baldwin, F. and Sharpley, R. (2009) 'Battlefield Tourism: Bringing Organised Violence', in R. Sharpley and P. Stone (eds) *The Darker Side of Travel*, Bristol: Channel View, pp. 186–206.

Blair, J. (2002) 'Tragedy Turns to Tourism at Ground Zero', *The New York Times*, 29 June.

Boo, H. (2000) 'Do Not Know Exact Number of the Seperated Family, but Around 7.67 Milion People in South Korea', *The Donga Ilbo*, 15 August.

Boyles, F. (2005) 'Andersonville: A Site Steeped in Controversy', in G. Ashworth and R. Hartmann (eds) *Horror and Human Tragedy Revisited: The Management of Sites of Atrocities for Tourism*, Sydney: Cognizant Communication Corporation, pp. 73–85.

Gilbert, B. (2000) *Ship of Miracles*, Chicago, IL: Triumph Books.

Hall, C.M. and Boyd, S. (2004) 'Nature-based Tourism in Peripheral Areas', in C.M. Hall and S. Boyd (eds) *Nature-based Tourism in Peripheral Areas: Development or Disaster?* Clevedon: Channel View, pp. 3–20.

Henderson, J.C. (2000) 'War as a Tourist Attraction: The Case of Vietnam', *International Journal of Tourism Research*, 2(4): 269–280.

Historic Park of Geoje POW Camp (2011) 'Museum Report'. Available at http://www.geojeimc.or.kr (accessed 31 March 2011).

International Committee of the Red Cross (2011) 'Geneva Convention Relative to the Treatment of Prisoners of War'. Available at http://www.icrc.org (accessed 21 November 2011).

Jeong, J. (2010) 'Chinese Troops' Participation in the Korean War and Hungnam Evacuation', *The Kyounghyang Shinmun*, 3 May, p. 11.

Khadaroo, J. and Seetanah, B. (2008) 'The Role of Transport Infrastructure in International Tourism Development: A Gravity Model Approach', *Tourism Management*, 29(5): 831–840.

Kim, S.S. and Prideaux, B. (2003) 'Tourism, Peace, Politics and Ideology: Impacts of the Mt. Gumgang Tour Project in the Korean Peninsula', *Tourism Management*, 24(6): 675–685.

Kirk, J. (2003) 'Book on Wartime Evacuation aboard the SS *Meredith Korean*', *The Stars and Stripes*, 27 October.

Kirkbride, W.A. (2011) *Panmunjeom*. Seoul: Hollym.

Lee, Y.S. (2006) 'The Korean War and Tourism: Legacy of the War on the Development of the Tourism Industry in South Korea', *International Journal of Tourism Research*, 8(3): 157–170.

Lennon, J. and Foley, M. (2000) *Dark Tourism*, London: Continuum.

Miles, W.F.S. (2002) 'Auschwitz: Museum Interpretation and Darker Tourism', *Annals of Tourism Research*, 29(4): 1175–1178.

Moscardo, G.M. and Ballantyne, R. (2008) 'Interpretation and Attractions', in A. Fyall, B. Garrod, A. Leask and S. Wanhill (eds) *Managing Visitor Attractions: New Directions*, Oxford: Butterworth-Heinemann, pp. 237–252.

National Archives of Korea (2011) 'Statistics of Korean War Damage'. Available at http://www.archives.go.kr/next/main.do (accessed 20 November 2011).

Park, T.M. (2010) *Geojedo POW Camp*, Geoje City, Korea: Geoje City Office Publication.

Prideaux, B. (2000) 'The Role of the Transport System in Destination Development', *Tourism Management*, 21(1): 53–63.

Sharpley, R. (1999) *Tourism, Tourists and Society*, Huntingdon: ELM Publications.

Sharpley, R. and Stone, P. (2009) '(Re)presenting the Macabre: Interpretation, Kitschification and Authenticity', in R. Sharpley and P. Stone (eds) *The Darker Side of Travel*, Bristol: Channel View, pp. 110–128.

The 60th Anniversary of the Korean War Commemoration Committee (2011a) 'Korean War'. Available at http://eng.koreanwar60.go.kr (accessed 25 November 2011).

The 60th Anniversary of the Korean War Commemoration Committee (2011b) 'Hungnam Evacuation'. Available at http://eng.koreanwar60.go.kr (accessed 25 November 2011).

The Memorial Hall for Incheon Landing Operation (2011) 'Korean War'. Available at http://www.landing915.com/htmls/data02.htm (accessed 25 November 2011).

Uzzell, D.L. (1989) 'The Hot Interpretation of War and Conflict', in D.L. Uzzell (ed.) *Heritage Interpretation*, Bristol: Belhaven Press, pp. 33–47.

Vargesko, A.M. (1991) 'An Analysis of the Hungnam Evacuation Based on Current and Emerging Joint Doctrine', PhD thesis, Indiana University of Pennsylvania, Fort Leavenworth, Kansas.

Walter, T. (2009) 'Dark Tourism: Mediating between the Dead and the Living', in R. Sharpley and P. Stone (eds) *The Darker Side of Travel*, Bristol: Channel View pp. 39–55.

Weaver, D. and Oppermann, M. (2000) *Tourism Management*, Brisbane: John Wiley & Sons Australia.

Wight, A.C. and Lennon, J. (2007) 'Selective Interpretation and Eclectic Human Heritage in Lithuania', *Tourism Management*, 28(2): 519–529.

Yoon, J. and Park, J.H. (2010) *Peaceful Area DMZ*, Seoul: Yeseong.

17 Dark tourism in the Top End

Commemorating the bombing of Darwin

Elspeth Frew

Introduction

The war-time air attack on Darwin by the Japanese in February 1942 led to the worst death toll from any event in Australia, with over 290 people killed (Grose 2009). At the 70th Anniversary commemoration service in February 2012, Australian Prime Minister Julia Gillard described the 1942 attack as 'Australia's Pearl Harbor' in terms of the impact on the nation, the hundreds who died at the scene and the fact that Australians did not believe they would be attacked and, she lamented, its forgotten place in Australian history. She said Australia had learnt the lessons of the past and the attack still informed the country's military preparations (Murphy 2012). This chapter explores the ways in which a tragic World War II event in Darwin, Australia has been commemorated and interpreted within the context of dark tourism. In particular, the chapter considers how the bombing of Darwin is depicted in the permanent exhibits of the Darwin Aviation Heritage Centre, the Darwin Military Museum, which incorporates the Defence of Darwin Experience, and at several outdoor locations in the Darwin city centre.

Interpretation is the process of explaining to people the significance of the place or culture they are visiting but the practice is under-represented in academic enquiries in tourism studies. However, interpretation is important because it is often the key process that influences the conceptions visitors hold and negotiate with others as they experience the site (Pearce 2005). To ensure the quality of the tourism experience, successful interpretation is critical both for the effective management and conservation of built heritage sites and for sustainable tourism (Moscardo 1996). Interpretation is now a well-integrated management practice in both public and commercial settings and warrants detailed research attention in tourism (Pearce 2005). Indeed, the grandfather of interpretation, Tilden (1977) believed that through guided tours, exhibits and signs, visitors receive a very special kind of education through the interpretation of informative materials. In addition, planners and destination managers need to develop a better understanding of the most appropriate way to commemorate events associated with incidents of accidental or violent death. This is particularly important since the respectful development and interpretation of sites associated with death and atrocity will encourage site managers to create places where family, friends and interested visitors can pay respect to the dead, allow visitors to understand the tragedy and to value the site (Frew 2012).

An observational visit to two museums and four commemorative sites in Darwin was conducted in mid 2012 to investigate the interpretation of the wartime bombings of Darwin. The researcher made field notes, photographed the sites and examined the commemoration of the 1942 air raids by the Japanese military. The visit was designed to answer the questions: What imagery, text and language is used to depict the Darwin bombings? and, How are the victims commemorated and which aspects of the bombings are interpreted?

Bombing raids on Darwin, 1942–3

During the late 1930s and early 1940s, Darwin had become a strategic staging base for the defence forces, with hospitals, an increased naval presence and Royal Australian Air Force (RAAF) squadrons based in Darwin. So when Japan entered the war on 7 December 1941 the Australian Federal government recognized the implications for the town. Prior to the first Japanese air raids the government issued a General Evacuation Order on 12 December 1941 and around 1,500 women, children, the aged and infirm were evacuated from Darwin from 16 December to 18 February 1942. On 19 February 1942, a Japanese military force attacked Darwin during two air raids. A total of 188 Japanese aircraft flew from four aircraft carriers located between Timor and Darwin. The air raids on Darwin resulted in at least 292 fatalities. This figure has been described as a minimum figure and only includes those deaths that were recorded at the time and can now be verified. In addition, eight ships were sunk in Darwin harbour, many buildings were damaged, 23 aircraft were destroyed, communications were cut and the township was badly damaged. The Darwin Post Office was the first building hit in the initial raid and nine of the staff were killed as they sheltered in a slit trench. The Japanese raids continued across the Top End of the Northern Territory for a further 20 months and represented 64 air raids. It was not until late February 1946 that civilians were allowed to return to Darwin. However, many who had been evacuated chose not to return (Grose 2009; Powell 2009; Rechniewski 2010).

Darwin Military Museum and the Defence of Darwin Experience

The Darwin Military Museum (DMM) is a traditional museum set in extensive grounds and features tanks and guns from World War II, in addition to some traditional exhibits such as firearms, medals and uniforms. It was founded in the mid 1960s by Lieutenant Colonel Jack Haydon and members of the Northern Territory branch of the Royal Australian Artillery Association. The museum features a range of military related memorabilia including a 9.2 inch gun emplacement; military vehicles; uniforms, medals, models, and firearms and artillery pieces – several of which are recorded as being used to defend Darwin in Wold War II. The Museum handbook describes the Darwin Military museum as "a unique combination of Australian military heritage and modern tropical garden and surrounds" (Northern Territory Government 2012).

On the same site as the traditional style Darwin Military Museum is the newly developed Defence of Darwin Experience (DDE), which is located in a purpose-built building and uses extensive modern technology to interpret the bombing of Darwin. The site was developed by the Northern Territory Government at a cost of $10 million and was opened on 18 February 2012 to commemorate the 70th Anniversary of the Bombing of Darwin. The museum handbook describes the site as providing the story of Darwin's role in World War II and concentrates on the period 1932–45, described as "a very important time in Territory history". The handbook explains that the DDE provides visitors with the opportunity to understand the impact of the war on Darwin on its civilian and military inhabitants, through the use of "iconic objects, images, firsthand accounts and multimedia presentations. It acknowledges the sacrifice of those who lost their lives, and the courage of all who served in the defence of the Northern Territory" (Northern Territory Government 2012).

The DDE comprises five main interpretive areas; one provides a short video explaining the expansion of Japan (see Figure 17.1); another depicts the air raids and the impact of the bombing; one provides a series of black and white photographs of Darwin depicting before and after the bombing; and a final room doubles

Figure 17.1 Depiction of the expansion of the Japanese Empire at the Defence of Darwin Experience

as a theatre for an audio-visual show, which runs regularly throughout the day. In the area that depicts the bombing there is an interactive table. When a visitor presses the screen on the outside of the table, the Japanese bombing aircraft are depicted as flying over an aerial map of Darwin and the areas bombed are depicted by animated explosions (see Figure 17.2). Visitors can follow up on various aspects of the bombing by listening to a voice-over describe in detail the impact of the bombing on a particular building or groups of people. The most poignant of the stories involves a young girl working in the post office, since the words of a friend explain that one minute she was planning a night out at the local cinema, the next she was dead in a trench.

Every 20 minutes an air-raid siren sounds and a yellow light flashes. The doors of an adjacent room open automatically and visitors enter the area, which is encircled with glass cases containing various artefacts from the Darwin air raids. After a few minutes another air-raid siren sounds and the doors slowly close as if the visitors have entered an air-raid shelter. The room becomes a theatre when a film is projected onto one of the walls and an impressive sound and light show runs for 12 minutes, using original black and white images and voice-overs from actors reading out original transcripts of conversations among soldiers and civilians. This is a very powerful audio-visual experience and is described as providing the visitor

Figure 17.2 The interactive table depicting the bombing of Darwin at the Defence of Darwin Experience

with a "real sense of the shock and horror experienced in Darwin that day through multi-sensory elements" (Northern Territory Government 2012).

The DDE also provides a video recording kiosk for visitors to record their own experiences. The notice outside the recording kiosk states:

> Share Your Story. Do you have a story to tell about yourself or a family member who was in Darwin during World War II? If the answer is 'yes' then this is your chance to share your story in the StoryShare kiosk.

The DDE then explains that all stories will be moderated and those approved for public viewing will be placed on the StoryShare touch screens, located opposite the recording kiosk. The visitor can then watch and listen to the video created by the visiting public. Interestingly, although the exhibit had been opened for several months at the time of the author's visit, there was no evidence of new stories being recorded or shared in the viewing area – perhaps because of the newness of the exhibit, perhaps the ones recorded were not appropriate or perhaps those people with first- or second-hand memories of the bombing have not yet visited and recorded a story. However, the existence of the recording kiosk reinforces the belief that many people have personal stories to tell about the bombing, which are as important as official histories of the event.

Darwin Aviation Heritage Centre

The Darwin Aviation Heritage Centre (DAHC), on the outskirts of Darwin on the Stuart Highway, is located in a large aircraft hangar and the majority of exhibits are military aircraft such as the Spitfire, jet fighters, a military helicopter and the Boeing B-52 bomber, which dominates the building. The massive B-52 bomber is on permanent loan from the United States Air Force and is described as being one of only two on public display in the world outside the USA. The Centre was opened in 1990 in a purpose built facility constructed by the Northern Territory Government and is described as being the largest single span building in the Northern Territory (DAHC 2012).

Along with displaying military aircraft there are also displays concerning the epic long-distance flights of 1919 and 1934. In one area of the museum there is a display about the bombing of Darwin. The museum also contains the wreckage of a Japanese Zero Fighter aircraft, which was shot down in the first air raid on Darwin in 1942. The centre also contains an area where visitors can view a video entitled the 'Battle of Australia'. This video provides a graphic insight into the war against the Japanese in North Australia in World War II and contains video footage from the first air raid on Darwin and original footage from Japanese archives (DAHC 2012). The video is repeated every 15 minutes and rows of seats are provided for the visitors to sit down and view it. The centre also contains a shop, which stocks a range of books about the bombing of Darwin and Australia's involvement in World War II as well as Northern Territory related souvenirs.

Other bombing commemorative sites in Darwin

Within the city of Darwin there are four other sites that provide commemoration of the bombing of Darwin. The Survivors Lookout was developed in 2001 and provides information on the first air raids via six static interpretive panels located high up in a covered wooden shelter, which explain in detail the first air raids of Darwin. There is also a commemorative plaque located close to Government House. The plaque has been embedded in a large rock and includes a map of the damaged areas of Darwin and two images, one of an anti-aircraft gun being used and one of a Japanese bomber over the Darwin wharf. The panel contains three long paragraphs of textual information and then a summary list of the number of casualties. It also mentions the destruction of Government House as it is near to that location. There is a similar commemorative plaque located in Darwin's main shopping mall. The difference between the two plaques is that the one in the shopping mall explains the impact of the raids on the civilians and includes images of civilians in air raid shelters and civilians being evacuated from Darwin (see Figure 17.3). It also provides a couple of paragraphs entitled "Civilians in Darwin". At Darwin's cenotaph there is a low lying wall labelled "Defence of Darwin, 19 February 1942 – 15 August 1945". The other low lying wall is labelled "Defence of Australia, 3 Sep 1939 – 15 Aug 1945". Along both walls are listed the

Figure 17.3 Depiction of the impact of air raids on Darwin civilians

names of countries where Australian defence forces were stationed. Thus, these outdoor commemorative sites in the city centre provide several places for quiet reflection about the bombing raids on Darwin and indeed, the Darwin Military Museum recently published a brochure listing all of the bombing sites in the Top End as a guide for visitors.

Interpretation themes

Use of original photographs and artefacts

The DMM, the DDE and the DAHC use black and white photographs of the impact of the bombing and of civilians and members of the armed forces before and after the bombing. For example, the DAHC displays a photograph of six defence force personnel standing arm in arm, three wearing naval uniforms and three in khaki shorts. The caption reads, "US Navy personnel under Australian care following the raids". Below that photograph another one is displayed of five bare-chested men standing among some rubble. The caption reads, "American servicemen cleaning up after the raids". In the DAHC section entitled "After the War" a photograph is displayed of an armed forces man marrying a nurse. The bride and groom are both wearing their respective uniforms and are walking arm in arm between two lines of uniformed nurses throwing confetti at them. The caption reads, "and life carried on. A military wedding at Adelaide River, 1944". The use of such photographs allows visitors to see hundreds of faces of men and women engaged in day-to-day activities before, during and after the war, which reinforces the fact that hundreds of people were impacted because of the bombing.

At the DMM there is an area dedicated to armed forces uniforms, which includes an interesting comparison between the uniform of the Australian soldier designed for living in the tropics with khaki shorts and long sleeved shirt to "combat the heat and insects" in contrast to the Japanese pilot's uniform, which was designed to keep the wearer warm in the aircraft while flying. This highlights the foreign nature of the Japanese raids, since the Japanese were flying from the cold, northern hemisphere winter to the height of the tropical summer in Darwin in February (see Figure 17.4).

In the DAHC an original wartime bicycle is displayed. The caption beside it reads: "It was said that, following the 19 Feb 1942 raids, one cyclist rode from Darwin to Adelaide River, discovering... for the first time, that both tyres were flat". This original artefact is one that all visitors should be able to relate to since many people have ridden a bicycle with a flat tyre and know how uncomfortable and difficult it is to ride. As such, this artefact and description highlights the feelings of fear, panic and perseverance experienced by the rider following the bombing raids.

The DMM, the DDE and the DAHC each utilize headlines of newspapers to impart important information about key events following the bombing of Darwin. For example, at the DAHC the front page of the *Courier Mail* newspaper from Friday, 20 February 1942 is displayed with the headline: "Darwin bombed heavily in two day raid: 93 Enemy Planes in First Swoop; 4 Brought down". Similarly, the

Dark tourism in the Top End 255

Figure 17.4 Contrasting Australian and Japanese uniforms at the Darwin Military Museum

DMM displays two yellowing original newspapers of the day in a glass case announcing the end of the war. The front page of the *Courier Mail* has the headline: "Atomic Bomb Blasted 480,000 Japs. 200,000 were hit; 280,000 left with no home". Use of such headlines from newspapers records and displays the events as civilians would have experienced them at the time. This allows visitors to reflect on the impact of seeing such headlines during traumatic times, reinforces the important role of newspapers to record historic events and highlights the role of newspapers as the major form of communication during this time.

Use of direct quotes by civilians and the Allied and Japanese military

There are many examples provided at the DMM, the DDE and the DAHC of direct quotes from people living through the Darwin bombings. Use of direct quotes from both soldiers and civilians makes the story come alive as the visitor can more readily relate to what is being said, particularly if informal language is used (including swear words). This reflects more accurately how people actually speak rather than conveying the story using much more formal language via formal texts. At the DAHC there were several direct quotes that highlight an Australian sense of humour. For example, one interpretive panel provided an account of the reported exchange between Captain H. Brown at 23rd Brigade HQ and Sergeant W.J.F. McDonald of the 19th Machine Gun Battalion at Casuarina Beach, 19 February 1942 (which also reflected the soldiers' knowledge of the Japanese flag): "Mac, I'm busy; don't play games with me. How do you know they're Japs?" "They've got bloody great red spots on 'em!'" Another example of Australian humour was illustrated in the reported reaction to the bombing by Bombardier Jack Mulholland of the 14th Heavy Anti-Aircraft Battery at the Darwin Oval, 19 February 1942:

> some alarms had lasted up to an hour or ninety minutes. Not to be caught out...I had with me a fifty packet of Cravan A cigarettes...a paperback cowboy yarn entitled *Gun Whipped* in my hip pocket. I didn't open either the cigarettes or the book.

The use of humour reinforces that these were ordinary people living through extra-ordinary times.

At the DAHC there were several mentions of the role of indigenous people in rescuing American pilots and tracking downed Japanese air pilots and handing them in to the armed forces. For example, one panel describes how Jack Mulberry of Delissaville rescued a downed American fighter pilot Lt. Clarence Johnson, after five days in the mangroves of Byrone Harbour, June 1942:

> We bin hearem one fellow white man singing out...we bin go a long way amonga mangrove. We bin find im...up alonga tree...him close up bugger up...we fella bin lift him outa tree, alright...want to carry him. He says, 'No, I guess I can make it alright'...we cook tucker. That one American man him properly hungry bugger.

Indeed, instructions were given out to Allied pilots regarding how to survive if they had to make a forced landing on the northwest coast of Australia: "Your nomad Abo [*sic*] mightn't smell like a garden of roses, he mightn't have an aristocratic profile but don't lose sight of the fact that he means more to you than an Angel with wings."

Such quotes reinforce that all civilians were involved in some way with the raids, and all played a role in supporting each other. It also reflects the remoteness, terrain, climate and distances involved in the Top End whereby a downed serviceman would find it difficult to survive without local support.

When describing the rise of Japan and the Japanese Imperial Army, the DDE aims to achieve a balance between remaining respectful towards the Japanese but at the same time hinting at some of the negative feelings towards the Japanese at the time. In the multi-media experience there is only one audio clip of an

Australian soldier saying something derogatory about the Japanese: "Get him in the arse, get him in the arse. And I got him – the bastard." Similarly, in one display there is a quote from an American airman who had been brought in severely injured and who was very restless and semi-conscious. He is quoted as saying: "I got one of those little yellow devils I did, but as I was getting away another... came out of the clouds and got me on the tail. But I got one."

Therefore, some effort has been made to minimize any racist and offensive material being included in the exhibits but even so, such outbursts hint at the strength of feeling that must have existed among the soldiers and civilians against the Japanese.

Several times in the exhibit the DAHC has provided translated quotes from Japanese airmen about their experiences of bombing Darwin. This is a very interesting technique as it allows the visitors to hear another series of voices alongside those of the Australian soldiers and civilians, providing a more balanced account of the event and revealing the reality of being in the Japanese military. For example, the Japanese Sub Lieutenant Sadao Yamamoto, who was an observer in a Nakajima B5N 'Kate' from the carrier Soryu during the 19 February 1942 raid on Darwin, is reported as saying, "Of course, I could see the damage to the building... But I did not really think about whether there were people inside. I had been concentrating on just hitting the target." Similarly, another Japanese observer Lieutenant Takayoshi Morinaga said:

> Bombing Darwin was different from Pearl Harbor. We felt bad about it. Pearl Harbor was a military target but we know our attack on Darwin might have killed civilians. I was carrying an 8000 kg bomb, just like at Pearl Harbor. I picked a building, dropped the bomb and I saw a huge explosion... The building had disappeared.

Another quote reinforces the size of the raids on Darwin, when the leader of the air raids on Pearl Harbor and Darwin, Commander Mitsuo Fuchida is quoted as saying, "It seemed hardly worthy of us. If ever a sledgehammer was used to crack an egg it was then." Similarly, when the Japanese Admiral Nagumo wanted to launch a second attack against Darwin, the same Commander Mitsuo Fuchida is reported to have said, "It isn't necessary to repeat the attack. There are no enemy forces. It isn't worth it... Don't swing such a long sword... (recent victories have)... amounted to no more than snatching a fan from a geisha." Such quotes reinforce the fact that the Japanese were also members of the military and were experiencing a range of emotions, similar to those of the Allied Forces.

The evacuation of Darwin residents was a theme that is addressed in both the DDE and the DAHC. The DDE uses the stories of individuals to highlight the feelings of displacement and loss experienced when separated from home and loved ones, with actors quoting residents about their experiences. A variation on the direct quotes of people on the day occurs with reference to the Evacuation Order notices placed around the town to announce the evacuation of Darwin and published in *The Northern Standard* newspaper on 16 December 1941. The notice explains the arrangements that had been made to evacuate the sick in hospital, expectant mothers, the aged and infirm and women carrying infants:

> Darwin citizens will greatly assist the war effort by cheerfully carrying out all requests. There will be hardship and sacrifice, but the war situation demands these and I am sure Darwin will set the rest of Australia a magnificent example to follow.

It is interesting to reflect on the fact that residents were asked to carry out these requests "cheerfully" and to provide a good example for the rest of Australia.

Bombing of Darwin Post Office

At both the DDE and the DAHC attention has been given to the destruction of Darwin Post Office during the bombing raids and the associated deaths of the Postmaster, his daughter and seven other postal staff. The exhibit provides eerie details of messages exchanged before, during and after the bombing and associated photographs and artefacts (such as stonework salvaged from the ruins of the Post Office and a brass air mail postal slot and coin tray) (see Figure 17.5). The

Figure 17.5 The original brass air mail postal slot from the bombed Darwin Post Office at the Darwin Aviation Heritage Centre

photographs show the destroyed Post Office and residence from various angles and the road in front of the building contains a large crater.

By focusing on the civilian deaths at the Darwin Post Office, which represent only about 3.1 per cent of the overall deaths (nine out of 292), perhaps makes their deaths more meaningful and poignant as visitors are given insights into their last moments. For example, the DAHC reports on the last morse transmission from Archibald Halls, who was killed at the Darwin Post Office, to transmission engineer, Francis O'Grady, in Adelaide: "The Japanese are attacking us...I cannot stay any longer. I'll see you shortly." Indeed, 45 minutes after the raid ended Harry Hawke and William Due communicated the following to Francis O'Grady in Adelaide:

> Advise have just had bombing raid... several officers' lives lost number cannot be stated at present... many injured... postmaster not located but bodies seen which appear to be postmaster's daughter and telephonists. Will confirm loss life when wardens ascertain... Postmaster's family and telephonists in shelter which received direct hit bombing commenced before air raid alert had ceased sounding most officers caught at their posts stop... Raid lasted forty minutes.

One particularly poignant quote is provided from Reverend C.T.F. Goy after having his suggestion on identity cards for all civilians rejected by authorities, who is recorded as saying: "As I know personally and intimately the entire Post Office staff, I had the sad task of identifying nine bodies as they lay outside the hospital and pinning on each its first and last identification card."

The emphasis on these particular deaths reinforces that the very heart of the town had been hit, namely the Post Office. This was particularly painful for Darwin residents as the Post Office represented effective communication, with the place often perceived as being at the centre of any town in Australia where good communication over long distances is crucial for survival. The emphasis of these civilian deaths makes the event more real. However, interestingly, on that day there were also 170 American servicemen killed on board a ship anchored in Darwin Harbour, only a couple of kilometres offshore from the Post Office, but very little interpretation is provided to this in any of the commemorations.

Japanese pilot

At the DAHC, visitors are able to follow the story of the Japanese pilot Petty Officer Hajime Toyoshima. Visitors are first introduced to him via a photograph of him as a young airman, then two direct quotes are provided from local indigenous Australians who captured him. The second quote from local Aboriginal man Matthias Ulungura on 20 February 1942 states:

> I see that Jap... through the bushes... and then I sneak up quick and wait behind a tree. He walk close past me. I walked after him and grab his wrist

near gun. He got proper big fright. I take revolver... I say 'Stick 'em up, right up: two hands...' Then I call Barney, Paddy the Liar and Three Feller and told them to take clothes off pilot but to leave underpants on him... I took from him a camera, map and blue cloth... Morning time we start to take him to the mission.

The exhibit then displays a photograph of the prisoner standing to attention with a bandage on his face under guard beside two Australian soldiers. The quote from Sergeant Les Powell, of the 23rd Field Company RAE, recalls the Japanese pilot, and allows the reader to start to build up a picture of a proud man:

I... disarmed him of a .32' automatic which had seven bullets in the magazine (found out later). We took him round to our quarters... fixed his wounds... fed him and removed his boots and overalls. A message was sent to Darwin informing them and requesting an aircraft which came two days later... at night time we used to sit around the table interrogating him in Pidgin English. Quite a nice fellow.

However, as a means of explaining what happens to the pilot subsequently, the following quote is provided by a former Japanese prisoner of war at Cowra NSW, Sergeant Major Akira Kanazawa, which emphasizes the disgrace for Japanese airmen of being captured by the enemy:

The shame of capture was just about unbearable... Our conventions, our histories are different... we received no mail as prisoners, and we wanted none. We were dead men. We had been dishonoured, and we felt our lives as Japanese were over. I frankly felt I could never face my family again.

The display notes how Hajime Toyoshima was taken from Darwin and was interned at the prisoner of war camp at Cowra in New South Wales. Two years later he was one of the camp leaders who blew the bugle to start the attempted breakout on 5 August 1944. The reader then discovers his fate following the breakout of Cowra prison by Japanese prisoners via the following quote:

The longest-serving prisoner of all... went down in a hail of fire... He was losing a lot of blood... Sometime between 3 and 4 am... he took a cigarette from his pocket and lit it. He managed one puff... put the cigarette down... borrowed a carving knife from an unwounded comrade, and sawed into his throat.

The exhibit notes that Hajime Toyoshima is buried in the Japanese Cemetery at Cowra under his alias name Todao Minami. The original crashed aircraft Zero used by this pilot is available to view in a damaged state as if it had just crashed. Since the story of one Japanese pilot follows him from his discovery in the bush in 1942 to his suicide in 1944, the story is particularly poignant and quite shocking.

Dark tourism in the Top End 261

Depiction of death

At the DDE there was very little evidence of sensationalism or the gruesome side of war, except for an American 'Mae West' inflatable life jacket, which still shows dried blood from the events of the day. The display notes that the wearer of the life jacket, Lieutenant John Glover, was shot down by the Japanese over the RAAF Base in Darwin. When Glover arrived aboard the HMAHS *Manunda* with extensive facial wounds he was still wearing his blood-soaked government-issued life jacket. He gave it to a colleague, Major George Allen Whitely, who passed it to his son-in-law, who stored it for 50 years before donating it to the Museum and Art Gallery of the Northern Territory in 1992 (see Figure 17.6).

At the DAHC there is a photograph of a destroyed aircraft and nearby the viewer can see the leg and booted foot of a dead Japanese pilot who died as a result of the crash. The caption beside the photograph reads: "The fate of many Japanese

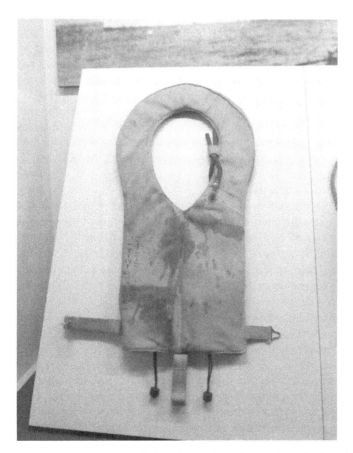

Figure 17.6 Blood-soaked life jacket at the Defence of Darwin Experience

raiders. A 'Betty' bomber shot down over Darwin". Another unsettling type of photograph depicted the smiling Australian and American pilots who had just killed the Japanese pilots. One colour photograph depicts a uniformed pilot sitting in the cockpit, smiling into the camera, with two red dots painted on the plane under his name. The caption reads: "Lieutenant Clyde Barnett Junior in his P-40 at Strauss Airstrip 1942. He has two kills to his credit". The use of present tense in the caption makes the event have some immediacy. Similarly, a black and white photograph is provided of a uniformed pilot leaning against the cockpit of his aircraft. He is looking relaxed and smoking a cigarette. The caption reads: "Sergeant Rex Watson of No 457 Squadron RAAF after his first 'kill'. 15 March 1943".

However, apart from these examples, from a dark tourism perspective very few gruesome images of death are provided, which is particularly interesting given the more than two hundred deaths that occurred due to the bombing.

Conclusion

The aim of this chapter was to consider the commemoration of the bombing of Darwin at several sites around the city. The question was raised as to what imagery, text and language were used in the commemoration. This discussion has demonstrated that the sites provide many examples of the use of informal language via direct quotes, formal language in the texts, and the imagery provided via artefacts and photographs of the people involved in various activities before, during and after the bombing. To address the second question about how victims were commemorated, the sites ensure civilian victims are acknowledged via first-hand accounts, original quotes and individualized stories about the fate of many of these people. In addition, the evacuation of Darwin was recognized in the DDE and the DAHC by using the stories of individuals to explain the feelings of displacement and being separated from loved ones.

The examination of the indoor and outdoor interpretive sites in Darwin also revealed several themes in the interpretation and commemoration of the bombing of Darwin. First, the use of original photos from the period creates authentic images for the visitor of the lives of both civilians and the armed forces before and after the bombing. The use of uniforms in photos and in glass cases reinforces that this was a military event and occurred during war, and highlights the similarities and differences between the warring nations.

The use of the original crashed Japanese aircraft illustrates some of the destruction experienced during the raid. The focus on human-interest stories at both the DDE and the DAHC, particularly via the examination of the destruction of the Post Office and the Japanese prisoner of war, is very powerful. The use of the translated material from the Japanese military personnel is effective as it revealed what they were thinking, providing an alternative perspective. Some use of humour helps break up the serious nature of most of the exhibits, which are intepreting death and destruction. There are some similarities in the images used at the sites with frequent images provided of civilians being evacuated or sitting in shelters or among the rubble. However, very little is mentioned of the American personnel who lost their lives in the raids with more attention given to the deaths of civilians. Perhaps this reflects that the military were killed 'in the line of duty' but the locals were accidental victims of war.

At the DAHC centre there were several mentions of the role of indigenous people in the bombing including the tracking of Japanese downed pilots and taking them to the Allied defence forces. However, this aspect of the bombing of Darwin is not highlighted in the DDE. Each site has steered away from showing gruesome images – apart from one leg of a dead Japanese pilot and blood on the life jacket. However, the photographs of the smiling pilots who had just killed Japanese pilots were challenging, as was the graphic description of how the Japanese pilot committed suicide. This was particularly powerful as the visitor became acquainted with the pilot through the displays and could read about his politeness towards his captors and his pride. However, the non-sensationalist aspect of the majority of the exhibits allows the visitor to visit the sites and experience quiet reflectiveness and contemplation, which in turn encourages respectfulness. As there are several sites situated at various locations throughout the Darwin area, this reinforces the large geographical area that was bombed and the impact of the raids.

References

Darwin Aviation Heritage Centre (2012) 'The Australian Aviation Heritage Centre'. Available at http://www.darwinsairwar.com.au/index.html (accessed 23 April 2012).

Frew, E.A. (2012) 'Interpretation of a Sensitive Heritage Site: The Port Arthur Memorial Garden, Tasmania', *International Journal of Heritage Studies*, *18*(1): 33–48.

Grose, P. (2009) *Awkward Truth: The Bombing of Darwin, February 1942*, Crows Nest, NSW: Allen & Unwin.

Moscardo, G. (1996) 'Mindful Visitors: Heritage and Tourism', *Annals of Tourism Research*, *23*(2): 376–397.

Murphy, P. (2012) 'Our Pearl Harbour 70 Years on, Survivors Mark Darwin Bombing', *Herald Sun*, 20 February, p. 15.

Northern Territory Government (2012) 'Defence of Darwin Experience: Self Guide to World War II Military Heritage Sites'. Available at http://www.nt.gov.au/defenceofdarwin. (accessed 23 April 2012).

Pearce, P.L. (2005) *Tourism Behaviour: Themes and Conceptual Schemes*, Clevedon: Channel View Publications.

Powell, A. (2009) *Far Country: A Short History of the Northern Territory*, Darwin: Charles Darwin University Press.

Rechniewski, E. (2010) 'Remembering the Battle for Australia', *PORTAL Journal of Multidisciplinary International Studies*, *7*(1), Fields of Remembrance, special issue, guest edited by Matthew Graves and Elizabeth Rechniewski.

Tilden, F. (1977) *Interpreting Our Heritage*, 3rd edn, Chapel Hill: University of North Carolina Press.

18 Darkness beyond memory
The battlefields at Culloden and Little Bighorn

Paul Willard, Clare Lade and Warwick Frost

Introduction

Battlefields are dark, disturbed and disputed. They are poignant cultural landscapes whereby physical geography is transformed into a symbolic space through pilgrimage, memorialization and tourism (Bull and Panton 2000). Battlefield sites, especially those continuing to attract ongoing tourist interest, are marked in a variety of ways including visitor centres, interpretive signage and trails, on-site museums, costumed re-enactments and the ambiguity of marked and unmarked graves. McLean, Garden and Urquhart (2007) believe this 'marking' is important as the preservation of battlefield sites play an important role in memory making and place identity. For tourists, the visiting of battlefields allows both reflection on war and sacrifice, and the reinforcement (even imagination) of their own identities.

Cutler and Carmichael (2010) believe the experience of 'place' or 'self in place' is arguably what an individual seeks. Battlefields represent important heritage sites, which continue to attract visitors seeking profound, transformative or numinous experiences. Lacquer (1996) considers wars the 'time-markers' of society, with their cultural effects covertly invading society's beliefs and behaviour. The linkage with notions of national identities is vital to the significance and appeal of battlefields. As Linenthal argues, battlefields are "ceremonial centers where various forms of veneration reflect the belief that the contemporary power and relevance of the 'lessons' of the battle are crucial for the continued life of the nations" (1991: 1). Commemorative events, media coverage and the range of commercial tourism products are influenced by, as well as influence, the depth and scale of tourist interest. Ravio (2007) argues that both the name and history related to 'place' must awaken visitors' imagination in developing their interest in, and understanding of, the battle and its consequences. Accordingly, visitors expect a more engaging encounter that draws their attention, and in doing so, stimulates their minds as well. Battlefield sites designed with the tourist experience in mind assist visitors in making sense of 'place' with site interpretation and supporting infrastructure providing for memorable tourist experiences.

As interest in battlefields and other forms of dark tourism rises, there is commercial pressure to develop packaged experiences for visitors. The concept of the 'experience economy' formulated by Pine and Gilmore (1999) advocates that attraction managers provide special staged experiences as the key to competitiveness and increased revenue flow. Whether such an approach is appropriate or viable for battlefields and other forms of heritage tourism is increasingly a topic of debate (Chan 2009; Richards 2001).

The nature of battlefield tourism is complex. While it is a form of heritage tourism, Prideaux (2007: 17) believes not only that people are motivated by a search for knowledge, but that the rise of battlefield tourism:

> has much to do with the human urge to visit battlefields – to remember comrades, to rekindle memories of loved ones who fell in battle, to ponder on the feats of those who they will never know; and/or gloat on victory or lament over defeat.

Increasingly, the vast number of monuments and military cemeteries dotting the international landscape provide a constant reminder of the level of human sacrifice. This is often associated with an intense degree of emotional engagement. Part of that engagement arises from the 'heritage dissonance' associated with battlefields. As conceptualized by Tunbridge and Ashworth (1996), heritage is dissonant as different people hold different and contested interpretations of the meaning and relevance of past events. Battles, by definition, are contested and old wounds in societies and nations run deep.

Warfare is prominent in the literature of dark tourism. In particular, there is an emphasis on modern warfare. Lennon and Foley (2007) specifically argue that dark tourism is a function and product of modernity. While acknowledging that many battlefields attract tourists, they contend that only those from World War I onwards qualify for inclusion within dark tourism. This, they argue, is because they are within recent memory and continue to pose questions and create anxiety for modern societies. Such an argument is intriguing, for it sets up a sharp division of battlefields and tourism. On the one hand we have post-1914 battlefields, which are firmly in the dark tourism camp, while on the other we have pre-1914 sites deemed as having a different level of significance and meaning.

In this context, can older battlefields still qualify as dark sites? Can they still have a profound place in our collective memories, stir up modern anxieties and challenge our identities? In this chapter we explore two older battlefields. These are Culloden (1746) in Scotland and Little Bighorn (1876) in the USA. Both have the dual functions of visitor attractions and memorials. Both battles are well beyond contemporary memory. Our interest is in how they are interpreted, how they continue to stimulate debate and controversy and what they contribute to modern society and identity.

Culloden

Culloden, on the isolated and windy Drumossie Moor, is situated 8 kilometres southeast of Inverness in the Highlands of northern Scotland. The battle, fought on

16 April 1746, was destined to be the final clash in the Jacobite Rebellion. The Jacobites were attempting to restore the Stuarts to the throne, and with French support had recruited heavily among the Highland clans. Culloden was the last land battle to be fought on mainland Britain (Pfeifer, Savage and Robinson 2009). Led by Prince Charles Edward Stuart (popularly known as Bonnie Prince Charlie), the Jacobites faced the equally determined Hanoverian government and the royal army of King George II under the command of his son, Prince William Augustus, Duke of Cumberland. In less than an hour, Culloden brought the Jacobite cause to a decisive defeat. Between 1,250 and 1,500 Jacobites died, a similar number wounded and 376 taken prisoner. By contrast, the government forces suffered only around 50 fatalities with fewer than 300 wounded (Bowditch, Mackillop and Pollard n.d.). The aftermath of the battle was brutal and earned the victorious general the name 'Butcher' Cumberland (Pfeifer *et al.* 2009). The repression launched by the Royal Army was savage and sustained in punishing Jacobite Scotland and in particular the Highland clans who had fiercely supported the rebellion. Government legislation was introduced suppressing the Highland way of life, banning such iconic cultural symbols as the kilt, tartan and bagpipes. Other legislative measures deprived clan chiefs of their legal powers, while all Jacobite estates were forcibly forfeited to the Crown (Bowditch *et al.* n.d.).

A number of sites associated with the battles and events of the rebellion are important in contemporary Scotland, both in attracting tourists and in the building of Scottish national identity. Many of the sites deemed to be of national importance in Scotland are associated with the commemoration of battles or wars relating to the national fight for self-determination. Knox (2006) acknowledges that most of the work on landscape in cultural geography and archaeology highlights the symbolic and iconographic nature of landscape representation and interpretation. Culloden sits within the concept of iconic landscape as specific memories of the 1746 battle, while general memories of the Highland culture of Scotland are also attached (Knox 2006). Such interpretations have influenced both collective memory and associated narratives. Smith (1998) states that shared mythology and historical memory are essential to national identity. McLean *et al.* (2007) considers Culloden both a battleground and a burial site, with evidence suggesting the site is instilled with sacred qualities. In that respect, Culloden has come to be regarded as a hallowed place for both locals and visitors. The vivid imagery of battlefields, cemeteries, memorials and monuments has impressed on society's historical consciousness, as well as the cultural memory of war (Lacquer 1994; 1996). Culloden is considered a highly sensitive site, and is a focal point for the Scottish diaspora worldwide (Pfeifer *et al.* 2009).

Today both the battle site and interpretive facilities at Culloden are managed by the National Trust for Scotland (NTS). Officially opened on 16 April 2008, at a cost of more than £7 million, a new state-of-the-art visitor centre (including gift shop, cafeteria, rooftop view, car parking facilities and information desk) was opened alongside the reinterpreted battlefield (Bowditch *et al.* n.d.; Gold and Gold 2007; Pollard 2009a). Our fieldwork was undertaken in 2010. The visitor centre has been carefully designed to reflect aspects of the story it tells. This is partly achieved through the choice of materials. Stone and wood reflect the landscape and traditions that surround Culloden; many of the graphic panels are printed on wood, and elements are carved into stone. Inside the exhibit, the wall at the first point of the government story is composed of jumbled planks, which reflect the confused response of the government in the early part of the Jacobites' campaign. This gradually changes as the government army gets organized, and by the time of the Night March (which saw the Jacobites fail in their planned ambush of government forces the night prior to Culloden due to fatigue, darkness and terrible terrain), the Jacobites' wall becomes confused and fragmented. The physical turning points in the exhibition come at key decision points in the story.

The visitor centre incorporates three important elements in its interpretation including audio-visual and interactive displays that engage the emotions by immersing visitors in the sights and sounds of battle, an emphasis on the personal stories and eyewitness accounts of those who participated and a balanced telling of both sides of the story. A key aim of the interpretation is providing both meaning and an understanding of the circumstances surrounding the conflict (Gold and Gold 2003; 2007). In discussing interpretive tools commonly used at battlefield sites, Piekarz (2007) lists a number of options for revealing the meaning and significance of 'place', all of which are used at Culloden to facilitate the visitor experience. These include a dedicated visitor centre hosting a range of interpretive approaches and techniques, which provide a balanced view from the standpoint of both the Hanoverian government and the Jacobites. In assisting visitors exploring the battlefield, several information panels situated at various points along the main interpretive pathway display not only a detailed map showing the location of the visitor centre, but also the Leanach and Culwhiniac enclosures, as well as the position of flag poles representing the Royal Army (red flags) and the Jacobite (blue flags) front lines. Each of these 'front lines' are spaced approximately 500 metres apart. A map legend is included, together with brief information associated with that specific point of interest.

In addition to the visitor centre and information panels, Culloden is marked by a memorial cairn, which acts as a physical reminder of the events that took place in 1746. Erected more than a century later in 1881 by Duncan Forbes 10th of Culloden (the last laird, or landed gentry, to live at Culloden House), the memorial reads: "The battle of Culloden was fought on this moor 16th April 1746. The graves of the gallant highlanders who fought for Scotland and Prince Charlie are marked by the names of their clans".

Several mass graves situated on the battlefield are each identified by a number of simple headstones listing the names of those Highland clans who fought and died that fateful day. These were placed as markers by Duncan Forbes around the same time that he built the memorial cairn. At this point, a small plaque has been positioned near the headstones reminding visitors not only to be quiet but also to stay on the defined (interpretive) pathway as a mark of respect; given the site's formal recognition as a war grave.

An important part of the visitor experience is the narrative with the exhibition being broadly chronological – starting off with the years prior to 1745 and finishing with a look at the long-term aftermath of the battle. Upon entering the exhibit, visitors can follow the story of the conflict from its origins, culminating in its climax and its eventual consequences. The left-hand wall tells the story from the government point of view, while the right-hand wall reveals the Jacobite perspective. The two stories told on opposing walls use a mixture of text panels, pictures and object displays, interspersed with audio-visual material. Each new section of the exhibition is introduced by a free-standing Threshold Panel, positioned in the middle of each display. These summarize the theme of the section and include a contemporary quotation in English or in Gaelic (with translations). The gaining of knowledge is a major attraction of visitation to battlefields. There is widespread visitor expectation that the past will be presented as accurately as possible. Any visitor assessment of heritage sites is normally based on a comparison between the efforts of curators to offer the history of the site and visitor perception of what the 'actual' event was (Chronis and Hampton 2008). The Culloden narrative includes firsthand accounts of the battle, biographies of major characters, archaeological artefacts, a wall commemorating the names of known casualties and a 'Battlefield Immersive Theatre' showing a surround-screen video display, which invites visitors to experience a filmed reconstruction of the battle that fully engages the emotions through the sights and sounds of conflict, hence the immersive effect.

In addition to the visitor centre, the site has employed the use of global positioning system (GPS) technology in developing the visitor experience by providing visitors with a personal guidance device together with a headset when exploring the battlefield. The NTS wanted to use technology to enhance the visitor experience, while also allowing for a better understanding of events surrounding the battle (Pfeifer *et al.* 2009). The guidance device is collected by visitors at a customer service desk situated to the rear of the complex before walking out onto the actual site. Visitors can access a range of media comprising maps (such as the master site plan, zoom-in and/or animated artwork), textual information, audio (including narration, voice-overs, sound effects and/or music) as well as still images (such as illustrations and photographs) and videos. At specific locations, the GPS technology activates the guidance device providing visitors with an audio narration concerning a point of interest and its significance during the battle. Depending on the level of interest, additional location-related information can be explored by using the guidance device in 'metal-detector mode', which provides for 'surprise' discoveries along the way. Visitors can also listen to historically accurate yet engaging character-based stories. This content, recorded at the BBC with professional actors, ensures all content has the required timbre (tone) to engage the user, thereby enabling the technology to bring the story to life by delivering relevant content at exact locations (Pfeifer *et al.* 2009). Use of the guidance device also provides the opportunity for visitors to tailor their experience. Battlefield enthusiasts can 'dig deeper' in search of further background information, while novice visitors may choose not to fully engage these features, but focus instead on site interpretation requiring a more passive approach.

The memorial cairn, clan headstones, the Leanach and Culwhiniac enclosures, as well as the respective flagpoles signifying the front lines of the opposing forces are permanent markers at Culloden. Each of these tells the story of the battle and its aftermath. The visible markers of historical landscapes assist with remembrance as artefacts related to war situated on former battlefields confirm that the place was (and is) real. To this end, archaeology plays an important role in developing the battlefield narrative. Battle debris found at a site makes an important contribution towards its historical visibility, with Culloden having on display recovered artefacts providing a direct link to the fighting, killing and dying that created the hallowed ground beside the visitor complex (Pollard 2009a: 3). Not only this, but archaeological surveys help provide a better understanding of the battlefield itself by allowing revised on-site reinterpretation. In 2000, an investigation by Pollard (2009b: 143) recovered archaeological evidence that helped identify three specific elements of the battle. These included grapeshot (consisting of lead balls with a diameter of around 2.8 centimetres, similar to the size of a squash ball, with a weight of around 100 grams) and canister shot (small lead balls debouched from a tin canister once fired from the muzzle of a 3-pound canon), that had been fired into the charging Jacobites, helping reveal the fierceness of the barrage, but also showing the determination of the Royal Army to repel the frontal assault.

Second, debris including buttons, musket and pistol balls, as well as the ball-impacted trigger guard strap from a Brown Bess musket, was found 80–100 metres further south than Barrell's Regiment, which was situated on the far left of the Royal Army's front line. Not only did this suggest the intensity of the hand-to-hand fighting on the government left, which was hit by the Jacobite right and centre at the end of its charge across the moor, but it also allowed this reinterpretation to be reflected in the redisplay of the site as opposed to what was shown by the NTS display board at the time of the investigation. Finally, British .75 calibre and French .69 calibre musket balls found immediately to the west of the Leanach enclosure, as well as just inside it, suggest there was a fire-fight between the Campbells (Royal Scots Fusiliers) positioned behind the stone walls at the Culwhiniac enclosures, and the retiring elements of the Jacobite assault. This incident involving French muskets, which has been recorded in historic accounts of the battle, suggests the Royal Ecossois regiment (Scots in French service) also fought at Culloden. They were brought forward by Lord George Murray (Jacobite general) to support the failing attack by the Jacobite right, but finding that all was lost made a disciplined withdrawal, returning fire when they received fire in their own flank from Royal troops in the second line of defence. It was the discovery of this scatter in 2000 that clearly demonstrated that the Jacobite line, as delineated by the red flags at the time (as opposed to the blue flags now used), was much too far forward. This information was subsequently used to inform the relocation of that front line in the recent redisplay of the site (Pollard 2009b: 143).

Landscape markings, archaeological remains, museum-style exhibits, as well as multimedia and GPS navigation technology combine to create the visitor experience at Culloden. The use of various media in dramatizing the historical narrative of the landscape gives a sense of the experience economy. The concerted efforts of management in presenting and interpreting the site not only provide for a clear and balanced perspective of events, but the combined approach gives visitors the opportunity to more actively engage with the history of the conflict, as well as the battle site. As conceptualized in the experience economy model, visitors at Culloden can experience a mixture of entertainment and educational elements in relation to site interpretation in the visitor centre while also exploring the battlefield. From an aesthetics (visual) perspective, visitors can enjoy the landscape, its markers and associated museum-style exhibits, while elements of escapism (nostalgia) focus on romanticized aspects of the conflict including honour, bravery and heroism.

Little Bighorn

In 1876, General George Armstrong Custer led an attack of the US 7th Cavalry against a large force of Lakota (Sioux) and other Indian tribes camped along the Little Bighorn River. Custer hoped to repeat the success of his 1868 dawn attack on the Cheyenne at Washita. At that time Custer had reflected that this was probably the last time that hostile Indians would ever congregate in such large numbers. The Indian Wars now seemed over, as Custer ironically prophesized, "nor is it probable that anything more serious than occasional acts of horse-stealing will occur hereafter" (Custer 1874: 245). Little Bighorn was an unexpected opportunity for Custer and he was worried that the Indians might scatter at his appearance. Instead, strong resistance led by Crazy Horse and Sitting Bull resulted in Custer's column being cut off and surrounded. In desperation, Custer made a last stand on a small hill where he and all 225 soldiers in his command were killed. Though the Indians were victors, retribution by a vengeful US government was swift and brutal and within a few years their nomadic lifestyle had been replaced by reservations.

Little Bighorn is located in a remote part of Montana. Yellowstone is 300 kilometres to the west, Mount Rushmore 500 kilometres east and there is little in between. The site is managed by the US National Parks Service (NPS) as one of its extensive National Monuments series. Until 1991 it was designated as the Custer Battlefield National Monument, though colloquially known as Custer's Last Stand. Its current official designation as Little Bighorn Battlefield National Monument reflects the NPS policy of using geographical names for battlefields, rather than partisan honouring of just one protagonist (Buchholtz 2005; Frost and Hall 2009). Our fieldwork was undertaken in 2008.

Little Bighorn has been the subject of much controversy over its naming, control and how the battle is commemorated (Buchholtz 2005; Elliott 2007; Frost and Hall 2009; Linenthal 1991). The battlefield site is federal property, its use subject to the policies and conventions of the centralized NPS. The surrounding land is part of a Crow Reservation Agency, for after the Sioux were defeated, the land was given to the Crow who had fought as scouts with Custer. The region is one of the poorest in the USA and attempts at tourism development have been limited by its isolation (Elliott 2007).

Little Bighorn is the site of regular commemorative events. At the 50th Anniversary in 1926, about 70,000 people attended. In contrast, in 1976 disputes with Native Americans and the shadow of the Vietnam War discouraged attendance and only 800 were present. Up to 1940, the site was managed by the War Department, which allowed reenactments of the battle. However, since the NPS took over, their policy (also applied at other battlefields such as Gettysburg) prevents these from being staged on the actual battlefield (Linenthal 1991). This contrasts with elsewhere, for example the annual re-enactment of the Battle of Hastings is held on the battle site in England and is staged by the land manager, the government agency English Heritage. Two annual re-enactments of Little Bighorn are staged by enthusiasts on nearby private land (Battle of the Little Bighorn n.d.; Custer's Last Stand n.d.).

This is a highly contested site and the conflicting interpretations of Little Bighorn may be understood in a number of different ways. It is a rare example of modern Western troops unexpectedly defeated by indigenous tribesmen. The idea of heroic 'Last Stands' and of military martyrdom may be drawn from across history and function as universally engaging stories (Rosenberg 1992). That there were no survivors of Custer's command to explain the disaster generated a "mystery and tragedy [that]... immediately captured the nation's imagination" and has become an enduring myth (Hutton 1992: 398). Interpretations of the enigmatic Custer have varied widely over time. A heroic cavalier up until World War II, he became widely regarded as either a bloodthirsty monster or buffoon in the 1960s and 1970s. In recent years (reflecting America's current military situation), he has been reimagined as a patriotic soldier just following orders (Elliott 2007; Hutton 1992; Laing and Frost 2012). His chief antagonists – Crazy Horse and Sitting Bull – are also the subject of substantial interest. Sympathy for the Indians, both their historic experience and current plight, is an important element in touristic interest (Buchholtz 2005; Elliott 2007). Indeed, for many foreign tourists, the fascination is with the Indians and this being the one battle they emphatically won (Laing and Frost 2012).

Little Bighorn is dominated by a series of monuments (and apart from them there are no other structures on the battlefield). Most prominent, in chronology and height, is the Custer monument on Last Stand Hill. Built in 1881 (coincidentally the same year as the main Culloden monument), it has long been the focal point of commemorative events and tourist visits. Surrounding it are nearly 200 white markers erected in 1890. These represent where the individual cavalry troopers are thought to have died (Linenthal 1991). Dramatically, they are mainly clustered around the top of the hill, clearly depicting a pattern of the Last Stand.

Notably this monument honours the defeated. For years there were attempts to remember the other side and promote their point of view. At the 1988 anniversary, protestors unveiled the following plaque (Elliott 2007: 41): "In honor of our Indian patriots who fought and defeated the U.S. Calvary [*sic*]. In order to save our women and children from mass murder. In doing so, preserving rights to our Homelands, Treaties and Sovereignty".

In 2003 an official memorial to the Indians was opened, also on the anniversary date. Not as high as the Custer Monument, it covered a larger area. In shape and conception it is similar to the Vietnam War Memorial Wall in Washington DC (National Parks Service n.d.). This new memorial honours all the Indians who died in the battle, including those Crow scouts who fought with Custer. Paralleling the white markers for dead soldiers, a series of red stone markers have recently been erected to show where Indians died. As an example, one such red marker reads (Frost and Hall 2009: 76): "Hahpehe'Onahe, Closed Hand, A Cheyenne Warrior fell here on June 25, 1876 while defending the Cheyenne way of life".

There is a small interpretation centre at Little Bighorn. It is conventional, even old fashioned, in its design. Displays are static and video presentations are shown on standard television sets. Its main function, as in most NPS operations, is to act as a gateway for the collection of entry fees. Such an approach delegates staff to revenue collectors rather than interpreters. This widespread problem of the equation of visitor centres with fee collection blights the NPS and Little Bighorn is no exception.

A series of interpretive panels is strung for three kilometres across the battlefield. While these follow the path of Custer's attack and defeat, they are back to front in that the visitor centre is situated near where the battle culminated rather than where it started further up the valley. This problem has been recognized by the NPS since 1986, though there is a lack of funding to reposition the visitor centre and site entry (Linenthal 1991). Given the contested nature of battlefields, the interpretive panels are well written and designed in their attempts to tell multiple stories and highlight areas of debate about what actually happened. As with the visitor centre, they are conventional and restrained. They encourage visitors to reflect, switching their gaze between the text and line illustrations and the contemporary landscape. Here, there is little sense of the experience economy in their planning and execution.

What is outstanding at Little Bighorn is that visitors can walk the battlefield and experience its physical topography and how that influenced the battle. The only structures are monuments. With few visitors, the battlefield can be experienced in profound silence. Critical points in the battle are highlighted by the interpretive panels, inviting visitors to stop and use their imagination and analytical faculties. Particularly poignant is Medicine Tail Coulee, where early in the battle Custer attempted to cross the river and strike his enemy in the rear. Either as a result of fierce resistance or swampy land, he abandoned his advance and fell back to higher ground. If he had retreated eastwards towards his reserve column on a high hill, he would probably have survived. For reasons unknown (and unknowable), he turned westwards, away from his reserve and his command was wiped out.

Conclusion

Are Culloden and Little Bighorn dark tourism experiences? Our argument is that they most certainly are. Both were tragic, one-sided battles. Their aftermaths were ruthless, sustained retribution visited upon pre-modern peoples by modern societies. Temporally, they are beyond our individual memories, which, if we follow Lennon and Foley (2007), disqualify them as dark tourism. However, the consequences of these two battles remain vitally relevant today. They both symbolize the savage repression of the culture and lifestyles of the Highland Scottish clans and the Plains Indian tribes. Even today, these are unresolved issues. Indeed, they are vivid scars within modern societies. That makes these battles just as much dark tourism as more recent conflicts. They are like other touristic representations of one-sided encounters between modern and traditional societies, such as festivals celebrating 'discovery' and 'explorers' (Gapps 2009; Witz 2009), they encourage debate over how contemporary societies should deal with the darker aspects of their history.

The sustained and bloody retribution that followed the battles are among the most important factors in the modern identities of Native Americans and the Highland Scots. The aftermaths of these two battles were strategic and ruthless attempts to destroy those identities. Despite those attempts, these identities did survive (though modified) and the battlefields serve as crucial physical testaments to this cultural resilience.

Little Bighorn still holds an important place in US identity. Late in the twentieth century it came to be overlooked by mainstream America, a reminder of imperialism and militarism. In the last decade or two, that interpretation has changed dramatically. Influenced by 9/11 and conflict in the Middle East, the soldiers who died at Little Bighorn are honoured and remembered for doing their duty. Even Custer has been rehabilitated along these lines. Interestingly, while honouring the soldiers for doing their duty, there is an increasing recognition that the US policy towards the Native Americans was wrong. Accordingly, Little Bighorn is increasingly a site of reconciliation. In contrast, Culloden seems to have little part in identity formation for the English.

In regards to Culloden and Scottish identity, while there are other related sites connected with the Jacobite Rebellion, each having their own special significance, including Glenfinnan Monument (29 kilometres west of Fort William), marking the spot where Prince Charles Edward Stuart began his campaign to restore the Stuarts to the throne, or the Battle of Killiecrankie (situated five kilometers north of Pitlochry, Perthshire), where the first shots were fired in the Jacobite cause as early as July 1689 (Bowditch *et al.* n.d.), it is Culloden that remains the most well-known, especially given its status as the last mainland battle fought on British soil. Over time, Culloden came to be affiliated with the ongoing Scottish struggle against English rule in the fight for self-determination and religious freedom. However, until the memorial cairn was erected in the latter half of the nineteenth century, the site at Culloden was largely unmarked.

Culloden is the defining moment of the rebellion, the final outcome originating from the plot to overthrow King George II and restore the deposed Stuart monarchy; an ambitious attempt ending in bloody retribution at the hands of the Royal Army, and their commanding officer, the Duke of Cumberland. Nowadays, Culloden has come to represent the Scots' perseverance in the face of oppression; the emergence of Highland culture from the shadow of persecution; and the rise of Scottish national identity on the world stage. Films including *Bonnie Prince Charles* (1948), Peter Watkins' drama-documentary *Culloden* (1964) and the costumed drama *Chasing the Deer* (1994) (Gold and Gold 2002), as well as more recent television episodes in programmes including *Two Men in a Trench* (2002–2004) and *Battlefield Britain* (2004), have all provided a new means with which to interpret the conflict, and in doing so, helped raise public awareness and tourist interest in the site's historical and cultural significance.

Finally, we must recognize that dark tourism is not only about place and national identity. For example, none of the writers of this chapter who visited these battlefields identify as Lakota, Highlanders, Americans or English. Similarly, there are many visitors to these battlefields without these national connections. What are they seeking from their tourist experience? Do they have collective memories or anxieties that are being challenged? Our suggestion is that in addition to personal connections and identity-shaping, visitors may also be drawn by a general human interest in sacrifice, bravery and tragedy.

References

Battle of the Little Bighorn (n.d.) *Battle of the Little Bighorn Reenactment*. Available at http://www.littlebighornreenactment.com (accessed February 2012).

Bowditch, L., Mackillop, A. and Pollard, T. (n.d.) *[Guidebook to] Cuil Lodair/Culloden*, Edinburgh: Stewarts.

Buchholtz, D. (2005) 'Cultural Politics of Critical Public History? Battling on the Little Bighorn', *Journal of Tourism and Cultural Change*, 3: 18–35.

Bull, N. and Panton, D. (2000) 'Drafting the Vimy Ridge Charter for Conservation of Battlefield Terrain', *Managing Cultural Landscapes*, 31: 5–11.

Chan, J.K.L. (2009) 'The Consumption of Museum Service Experiences: Benefits and Value of Museum Experiences', *Journal of Hospitality Marketing & Management*, 18: 273–296.

Chronis, A. and Hampton, R.D. (2008) 'Consuming the Authentic Gettysburg: How a Tourist Landscape Becomes an Authentic Experience', *Journal of Consumer Behaviour*, 7: 111–126.

Custer, G.A. ([1874] 1963) *My Life on the Plains*, London: The Folio Society.

Custer's Last Stand (n.d.) *Custer's Last Stand Reenactment*. Available at http://www.custerslaststand.org/ (accessed February 2012).

Cutler, S.Q. and Carmichael, B.A. (2010) 'The Dimensions of the Tourist Experience', in M. Morgan, P. Lugosi and J.R.B. Ritchie (eds) *The Tourism and Leisure Experience: Consumer and Managerial Perspectives*, Bristol: Channel View Publications.

Elliott, M. (2007) *Custerology: The Enduring Legacy of the Indian Wars and George Armstrong Custer*, Chicago, IL: Chicago University Press.

Frost, W. and Hall, C.M. (2009) 'National Parks, National Identity and Tourism', in W. Frost and C.M. Hall (eds) *Tourism and National Parks: International Perspectives on Development, Histories and Change*, London: Routledge.

Gapps, S. (2009) '"Blacking Up" for the Explorers of 1951', in V. Agnew and J. Lamb (eds) *Settler and Creole Reenactment*, Basingstoke: Palgrave Macmillan.

Gold J.R. and Gold, M.M. (2002) 'Understanding Narratives of Nationhood: Film-makers and Culloden', *Journal of Geography*, 101: 261–270.

Gold, J.R. and Gold, M.M. (2003) 'Representing Culloden: Social Memory, Battlefield Heritage, and Landscape of Regret', in S.P. Hanna and V.J. Del Casino (eds) *Mapping Tourism*, Minneapolis, MN: University of Minnesota Press.

Gold, J.R. and Gold, M.M. (2007) '"The Graves of the Gallant Highlanders": Memory, Interpretation and Narratives of Culloden', *History and Memory*, 19: 5–38.

Hutton P.A. (1992) 'From Little Bighorn to Little Big Man: The Changing Image of a Western Hero in Popular Culture', in P.A. Hutton (ed.) *The Custer Reader*, Lincoln, NE: University of Nebraska Press.

Knox, D. (2006) 'The Sacralised Landscapes of Glencoe: From Massacre to Mass Tourism, and Back Again', *International Journal of Tourism Research*, 8: 185–197.

Lacquer, T.W. (1994) 'Memory and Naming in the Great War', in J.R. Gillis (ed.) *Commemorations: The Politics of National Identity*, Princeton, NJ: Princeton University Press.

Lacquer, T.W. (1996) 'Names, Bodies and the Anxiety of Erasure', in T.R. Schatzki and W. Natter (eds) *The Social and Political Body*, New York, NY: Guilford.

Laing, J. and Frost, W. (2012) *Books and Travel: Inspirations, Quests, and Transformations*, Bristol: Channel View Publications.

Lennon, J. and Foley, M. (2007) *Dark Tourism*, London: Thomson.

Linenthal, E.T. (1991) *Sacred Ground: Americans and their Battlefields*, Chicago, IL: University of Illinois Press.

McLean, F., Garden, M.C. and Urquhart, G. (2007) 'Romanticising Tragedy: Culloden Battle Site in Scotland', in C. Ryan (ed.) *Battlefield Tourism: History, Place and Interpretation*, Oxford: Elsevier.

National Parks Service (n.d.) *Vietnam Veterans Memorial – National Parks Service*. Available at http://www.nps.gov/vive/ (accessed February 2012).

National Trust for Scotland (n.d.) *Culloden: Using the Visitor Centre*. Available at http://www.nts.org.uk/Culloden/Learning/ (accessed January 2012).

Pfeifer T., Savage P. and Robinson, B. (2009) 'Managing the Culloden Battlefield Invisible Mobile Guidance Experience', paper presented at *Management of Ubiquitous Communications and Services conference*, Barcelona, 15 June.

Piekarz, M. (2007) 'It's Just a Bloody Field! Approaches, Opportunities and Dilemmas of Interpreting English Battlefields', in C. Ryan (ed.) *Battlefield Tourism: History, Place and Interpretation*, Oxford: Elsevier.

Pine, B.J. and Gilmore, J.H. (1999) *The Experience Economy: Work Is Theatre and Every Business a Stage*, Boston, MA: Harvard Business School Press.

Pollard, T. (2009a) 'The Battle of Culloden: More than a Difference of Opinion', in T. Pollard (ed.) *Culloden: The History and Archaeology of the Last Clan Battle*, South Yorkshire: Pen & Sword.

Pollard, T. (2009b) 'Capturing the Moment: The Archaeology of Culloden Battlefield', in T. Pollard (ed.) *Culloden: The History and Archaeology of the Last Clan Battle*, South Yorkshire: Pen & Sword.

Prideaux, B. (2007) 'Echoes of War: Battlefield Tourism', in C. Ryan (ed.) *Battlefield Tourism: History, Place and Interpretation*, Oxford: Elsevier.

Ravio, P.J. (2007) 'In This Very Place: War Memorials and Landscapes as an Experienced Heritage', *The Thingmount Working Paper Series on the Philosophy of Conversation*, Lancashire: Lancaster University.

Richards, G. (2001) 'The Experience Industry and the Creation of Attractions', in G. Richards (ed.) *Cultural Attractions and European Tourism*, Oxford: CABI Publishing.

Rosenberg, B.A. (1992) 'The Legend of the Martyred Hero in America', in P.A. Hutton (ed.) *The Custer Reader*, Lincoln, NE: University of Nebraska Press.

Smith, A. (1991) *National Identity*, London: Penguin.

Tunbridge, J.E. and Ashworth, G.J. (1996) *Dissonant Heritage: The Management of the Past as a Resource in Conflict*, Chichester: Wiley.

Witz, L. (2009) 'History Below the Water Line: The Making of Apartheid's Last Festival', in V. Agnew and J. Lamb (eds) *Settler and Creole Reenactment*, Basingstoke: Palgrave Macmillan.

19 Beyond the dark side

Research directions for dark tourism

Leanne White and Elspeth Frew

Dark tourism and the place identities: a conclusion

When we announced the call for chapter abstracts in 2011, we welcomed a broad range of topics from contributors around the world. The chapters in this book were selected from more than 50 abstracts. The book announcement took place a few months after we had presented a working paper entitled 'Popularising and Politicising Place: Dark Tourism and the Politics of Place Identity in Australia', at the New Zealand Tourism and Hospitality Research Conference in November 2010. Shortly after the call for papers was released, we presented a further working paper entitled 'Place Perception and National Identity: Exploring Dark Tourism Sites in Australia' at the Council for Australasian Tourism and Hospitality Education (CAUTHE) Conference in South Australia. Some of the contributors in this book attended those presentations and became involved in a healthy dark tourism/place dialogue beyond the conferences.

This collection has considered what happens when dark tourism and place identity meet. The three main themes of Visitor Motivation, Destination Management and Place Interpretation were addressed from both a demand and supply perspective by examining a variety of case studies from around the world. Many of the chapters in this book take the dark tourism discussion to another level. They reinforce the critical intersecting domains of dark tourism and place identity and, in particular, highlight the importance of understanding this connection for visitors and destination managers. This book builds upon our earlier Routledge volume: *Tourism and National Identities: An International Perspective* (Frew and White 2011) by narrowing the focus of study to dark tourism (yet acknowledging that the definition of dark is wide-ranging) while, at the same time, broadening the discussion of identity to encompass the wider notion of place.

This book is a reference text aimed principally at the academic market. It is designed to address the void that currently exists in the discursive space where dark tourism and place identity meet. This stimulating volume of 19 chapters could become a prescribed text for postgraduate coursework units or a recommended reading for advanced undergraduate and postgraduate students in a number of discipline areas. It will be of interest to the many academics around the world and other interested stakeholders including those in the tourism industry, government bodies and community groups.

The sections and the chapters of the book

While the focus of this book was on dark tourism and place identity/ies, some of the connected terms that have also been discussed include: battlefield tourism, heritage tourism, cultural tourism, thanatourism, atrocity tourism, morbid tourism, grief tourism, doomsday tourism, dissonant heritage, conflict heritage, undesirable heritage, negative heritage, dark events, dark exhibitions, dark shrines, dark conflict sites, dark camps of genocide, place perception, place branding and destination marketing. This book is unique in that it incorporates a broad understanding of dark tourism and place identity and exposes these areas to both a multidisciplinary and an international approach. As discussed in Chapter 1, the book was divided into three themed sections: visitor motivation, destination management and place interpretation.

Visitor motivation

In the first section of the book on 'visitor motivation' each of the five chapters demonstrated why visitors are attracted to particular dark sites. The authors in this section discussed case studies in France, the United States, China, Ireland and the Ukraine and demonstrated the particular attractions of these sites for the dark tourist.

In Chapter 2, Touissaint and Decrop examined the relationship between dark tourism and sacred consumption in the context of the famous Père-Lachaise Cemetery in Paris, France. They suggested that the place is a heterotopia (Foucault 1967), as it meets its basic principles and provides a valuable background in the study of the blurred sacred–profane dialectic. The authors argued that cemeteries can address the postmodern concern for re-sacralization and are continuously triggering consumers' interest. Touissaint and Decrop's argument was that with its historical, cultural and commemorative ethos, the cemetery fulfils an 'edutainment' function. Its artistic and aesthetical characteristics have contributed to make it a quintessential place, preserving the sacred in a secular era.

In Chapter 3, Lelo and Jamal explored the African Burial Ground National Monument (ABG), a former cemetery for enslaved Africans who lived in New York (New Amsterdam) during the seventeenth and eighteenth centuries. They argued that the ABG is a site of cultural and heritage significance for African Americans. It is effectively a 'third space' in which diasporic visitors may explore identities and relationships with place and past. Lelo and Jamal claimed that the site offers an opportunity to provide understanding of the scale and scope of slavery: its local as well as its regional, national and global manifestations.

Continuing with the theme of 'visitor motivation', Du, Litteljohn and Lennon (Chapter 4) examined the site of the Nanjing Massacre – an atrocity that took place from December 1937 until the end of January 1938 in Nanking (now Nanjing) where up to 300,000 Chinese civilians and military personnel were killed by Japanese soldiers. The authors argued that three dimensions of place identity are relevant to the site of the Nanjing Massacre – the physical, the chronological and the social layers. Du, Litteljohn and Lennon also illustrated that place is a valuable tool in exposing the dynamic influences of the political, historical, social and cultural. These four persuasive influences are critical in gaining a deeper understanding of dark tourism sites. The authors argued that sites such as Nanjing are important in developing the collective memory at a national level, and that the interpretation of sites such as these is a major factor in the construction of what it means to be Chinese.

In Chapter 5, Simone-Charteris, Boyd and Burns explored the contribution dark tourism has made to place identity in Northern Ireland. They investigated the visitor motivations of dark tourism attractions, and the views of tourism organizations on the management, interpretation and promotion of such sites. The authors argued that by understanding dark tourism sites and events linked to the Province's turbulent past, visitors develop a deeper appreciation of the destination's identity. Simone-Charteris, Boyd and Burns argued that while the authorities might wish to distance themselves from the past, the dark history of Northern Ireland continues to shape place identity. Furthermore, they claimed that dark tourism is allowing the diverse communities to overcome years of mistrust and suspicion due to cooperative tourism projects.

The final chapter in the first section of this book explored how Chernobyl has become a tourist product. In Chapter 6, Stone examined how a place of industrial disaster can convey broader narratives about politics and identity. The author suggested that Chernobyl can be viewed as a heterotopia (Foucault 1967) – a ritual space that exists outside of time – in which time is not only arrested but also notions of 'Otherness' are consumed in a post-apocalyptic place. Stone argued that Chernobyl allows us to gaze on a post-apocalyptic world, in which the familiar and uncanny collide. Yet, Chernobyl and its dead zone is a surreal space that reflects the reality of our contemporary world – a world exposed by dark tourism.

Destination management

In the second section of this volume on 'destination management' each of the six chapters demonstrated how dark sites might be effectively managed and marketed. The authors in this section discussed case studies in England, the Baltic States (in particular Estonia, Latvia and Lithuania), New Zealand, Rwanda, French Guiana and Canada.

In Chapter 7, Laws explored pagan engagement with sacred sites and ancient places within the context of dark tourism. The author paid particular attention to the process of meaning-making and place identity formation, and considered the implications for site management in light of modern heritage industry policies. Laws argued that dark tourism is linked by its preoccupation with evoking 'otherness' in the present context, and that mediation, interpretation and (re)imagining play a key role in understanding place. The author contended that organizations such as the Cornish Ancient Sites Protection Network (CASPN) have a positive future due to their collaborative heritage site management approaches.

In Chapter 8, McKenzie examined the difference between remembrance tourism and nostalgia tourism within the context of dark tourism in Estonia, Latvia and Lithuania. The author argued that rightly or wrongly, the Soviet period remains a defining characteristic of the history of each of these countries. Under the guise of either remembrance or nostalgia, there continues to be an opportunity to develop and support various aspects of dark tourism. McKenzie suggested that as the breadth of offerings in this tourism niche has continued to grow in all three countries, future research in this field would benefit from longitudinal studies of how tourist providers and tourists react to this dark tourism niche.

The third chapter in the Destination Management section examined dark tourism in New Zealand. In Chapter 9, Morales examined the 2008 murder case of Scottish backpacker Karen Aim, and the impact the tragic incident had on New Zealand. Aim's family and the local community in Taupo were left with many unanswered questions when the backpacker was murdered. However, Morales discovered that the Taupo community managed to work together to prove that their small town was not a dangerous place. They wanted to change the negative place perception and portray a positive tourist image. Consequently, the community created a special place to remember the area's dark event as a way of moving forward.

In Chapter 10, Hohenhaus explored the forms of place identity that dark tourists find themselves in at memorials in Rwanda. The author argued that their experience is influenced by a certain awkwardness, which derives from an uneasy feeling of sharing the collective guilt that the international community bore for not having prevented the genocide. Hohenhaus argued that as a result, the tourist's own national identity collides with the identity of the locals, which can lead to uncomfortable feelings of being a voyeuristic intruder. In terms of site management, this is reflected in recent changes in policies such as English language provision and restrictions on tourist behaviour. The author concluded that the shocking display of bodily remains is defended in Rwanda as a necessary measure to prevent genocide denial. He argued that the Rwandan case is about the darkest form of tourism available in the world.

In Chapter 11, Dehoorne and Jolliffe examined the case of French Guiana (Guyanne) and found that dark tourism developments have been random. Some former prison locations are open to tourism, but they are not integrated into the overall process of tourism development in the country. Despite this, tourism demand is constant and it is inconceivable for a visitor to travel to French Guiana without becoming aware of some remains of the former prison system during their stay. The authors argued that this painful past tarnishes the country's image. Their research found that the prevailing public sentiment hinders effective dark tourism development in the country.

The final chapter of the 'destination management' section examined the relationship between remembrance and tourism in Normandy, where Canadians fought in World War II. In Chapter 12, Bird examined five sites of war with each site evoking a different dimension of Canada's cultural memory of war. The chapter demonstrated the complexity of the context, conflicts and contributions of the tourism–remembrance relationship. It revealed the central role of tourism and the tourist in the construction of meaning and engagement in remembrance, and underlines the power of a memorialized landscape of war in evoking a connectedness with memories of war. The author's research identified the politics of remembrance in Canadian war heritage at a time when living memory is fading, and tourism grows in prominence as a guardian of that vital memory.

Place interpretation

In the final section of this book on 'place interpretation' each of the six chapters examines dark sites from the perspective of the visitor. The authors in this section discussed case studies in the Netherlands, Poland, the United States, France, Australia, South Korea and Scotland.

In Chapter 13, Partee Allar examined two places that represented different extremes in Holocaust tourism. One place focused on an individual's story while the other memorialized the suffering of over a million victims. The author explained that these two places were also the most visited Holocaust sites in Europe. The Anne Frank House approaches the Holocaust from an individual level, while Auschwitz–Birkenau is a dark site where over one million were killed. Partee Allar argued that these two sites house important museums and education centres which together welcome over two million visitors a year. They are sites of pilgrimage as well as centres of discussion. Nevertheless, controversies over the interpretation and design continue to influence the two dark places.

In Chapter 14, Best took us on the dark journey of four celebrity car crash deaths over a period of just over four decades. The author discussed the tragic death of James Dean in 1955, Jayne Mansfield in 1967, Grace Kelly in 1982 and Diana, Princess of Wales in 1997. Best argued that the four crashes served the purpose of illuminating that fateful journey from mortality to immortality and left the earthbound faithful to tend the shrines, run the fan clubs, visit the crash sites, photograph the gravestones and celebrate the birthdays. While the memorials vary in form and permanence, they all record for the future what briefly shone so brightly in the past.

In Chapter 15, White examined the city of Melbourne's dark 'underbelly'. The three tours that were the focus of this chapter were Melbourne Crime Tours, Melbourne Cemetery Tours and the Old Melbourne Ghost Tour. The author found that dark tourism has a role to play in both the official and non-official discourse about place identity. White found that examining past events, people, places, streets, buildings, monuments, memorials, cemeteries and other signifiers of the once dark provides a rich understanding as to how the destination's story can be read and understood. The author contended that while the overall destination image of the city generally remains 'Marvellous', the 'Murderous' side simmers just below the surface.

Chapter 16 examined the historic park and former prisoner of war (POW) camp of Geoje in South Korea. The chapter discussed several factors that helped the historic park of Geoje to become a successful heritage tourist attraction. Kang and Lee argued that one of the factors was the significance of the tragic event, and how the Korean War continuously affects all Koreans in all parts of their lives. The authors also claimed that the physical and political accessibility of the site enable it to attract a large number of visitors as a side trip or excursion while visiting the southern region of the country.

In the penultimate chapter of the 'place interpretation' section, Frew explored the ways in which a tragic World War II event in Darwin, Australia was commemorated and interpreted within the context of dark tourism. In Chapter 17, the author considered how the bombing of Darwin has come to be depicted at the Darwin Aviation Heritage Centre, the Darwin Military Museum and at several outdoor locations in the city centre. The chapter considered the imagery, text and language used in commemorating the bombing. Frew demonstrated that first-hand accounts and original quotes were used to explain the deep feelings of displacement in Australia's Top End.

Finally, in Chapter 18, Willard, Lade and Frost asked whether or not older battlefields qualify as dark sites. The authors explored two older battlefields – Culloden (1746) in Scotland and Little Bighorn (1876) in the USA – battles well beyond contemporary memory, yet most certainly dark. They argued that Little Bighorn still holds an important place in US identity, and that with regard to Culloden and Scottish identity, Culloden remains the most well-known and has come to be affiliated with the ongoing Scottish struggle against English rule in the fight for self-determination and religious freedom.

Finally

This edited volume has explored the numerous ways in which aspects of dark tourism and place identity intersect and overlap. Dark tourism as it has been discussed in this book has increasingly broad appeal due to the opportunity to become involved in new and sometimes confronting experiences. With this form of tourism, individuals and groups travel to a variety of destination types, partake in different experiences and often reflect upon their own identity and the perception of the place visited.

We trust that you have been inspired and energized by the diverse international cases of dark tourism and place identity that were explored in this volume. As the editors of this collaborative international body of work, we are delighted that from the tremendous collegial work of scholars around the globe, we have produced a volume that advances the academic debate surrounding dark tourism and place identity. The 27 contributors have truly combined an applied approach with solid academic and critical analysis.

References

Foucault, M. (1967) 'Dits et Écrits 1984: Des Espaces Autres', Conference at the Cercle d'études architecturales, March 1967, in *Architecture, Mouvement, Continuité* (1984), 5: 46–49.

Frew, E. and White, L. (eds) (2011) *Tourism and National Identities: An International Perspective*, Oxon: Routledge.

Index

Abbaye d'Ardenne, Normandy 177–9, 181
Abdullah, Gary 225
Aegis Trust 144, 146, 148, 151
African Americans, slavery tourism 5, 28, 42–5, 277: African Burial Ground National Monument 5, 34–42, 277; diasporic travels 28–9; Ghana 29–32; USA 32–42
African Burial Ground National Monument (ABG), New York 5, 28, 29, 32, 42, 277: conflicted beginnings 35–6; differing interpretations 36–7; emancipatory journeys and pedagogic opportunities 41–2; history 34–5; homecoming 40–1; participatory engagement and production of pride 37–9; secular and sacred meanings of place 39–40
ages of tourists to Northern Ireland 69
Aim, Brian 135–6
Aim, Karen 129, 130, 131, 134–8, 279
Aird, A. 210
Alcatraz, California 156
Alexievich, S. 86
Althorp estate, exhibition 213, 214
Ambrose, Stephen 169
American tourists: Auschwitz–Birkenau 195; Normandy battlefields 169, 171; Northern Ireland 69; Rwanda 145; *see also* African Americans, slavery tourism
ancient historic sites 97, 103, 110–11: Cornwall 6, 97, 104–10, 278–9; Culloden battlefield 8–9, 265–70, 272–4, 281; Little Bighorn battlefield 8–9, 265, 270–4, 281
Anderson National Historic Site, USA 244
Anger, Kenneth 206, 207
Annamites Prison of Eel Creek (la Crique des Anguilles), French Guiana 161

Anne Frank House, Amsterdam 7–8, 189–92, 193, 197–9, 280
Antaalnis Cemetery, Vilnius 117
Apprentice Boys of Derry Memorial Hall, Northern Ireland 67
Arafat, Yasser 197
archaeological surveys, Culloden battlefield 269
Areas of Outstanding Natural Beauty 6, 98, 107
Arnold, G.E. 208
art gallery, African Burial Ground National Memorial 35, 38
Arusha Accords 143
Ashworth, G.J. 31, 46, 101, 102, 265
Asia-Pacific War 50: *see also* Nanjing Massacre Memorial
atrocity tourism 63: Nanjing Massacre Memorial 49; *see also* undesirable heritage
audio-guides: Culloden battlefield 268; Rwandan genocide memorial sites 146, 149
auratic quality of a site 169: Normandy battlefields 171, 177, 181
Auschwitz–Birkenau, Poland 7–8, 189, 192, 198–9, 280: authenticity 198, 199, 243; changes at the museum 194–5; creation of the museum 192–4; dress code 242; rise of Holocaust tourism 196, 197–8
Australia: Darwin bombing 8, 248–63, 281; Melbourne 8, 217–34, 280–1
Australian tourists: Auschwitz–Birkenau 195; Gallipoli 47, 64; Melbourne 221, 234; Northern Ireland 47, 64, 69
authenticity: Anne Frank House 192, 198, 199; Auschwitz–Birkenau 198, 199, 243; cemeteries 15, 22, 23; Chernobyl 88–9; Darwin bombing commemorative sites

262; Geoje POW camp 243–4, 245; Nanjing Massacre Memorial 50; Père-Lachaise Cemetery 21, 22, 23–4; Rwandan genocide memorial sites 149, 152; 'shades' of dark tourism 102; spiritual tourism 100, 110
Avebury, England 97

Bachelor, P. 176, 178
Bagnall, G. 174
Bain, Wallace 136
Baker, Frederick (Federici) 230, 231, 233
Baldacchino, G. 171
Baldwin, F. 244
Ballantyne, R. 242
Ballard, J.G., *Crash* 202, 208, 211, 212
Baltic States *see* Estonia; Latvia; Lithuania
Band of Brothers (TV show) 169
Barry, Sir Redmond 230
Basly village, Normandy 172–4, 181
Basque tourists to Northern Ireland 67
Bastable, J. 171
Batman, John 219
Battle of Hastings 271
Battle of Killiecrankie 273
Battle of Sedgemoor 170
Battle of the Boyne 67
battle reenactments 271
Battlefield Britain (TV show) 273
battlefield tourism 63, 245, 264–5: accessibility issues 241; Culloden 8–9, 265–70, 272–4, 281; Gallipoli 47, 64, 170; interpretation of sites 242; Little Big Horn 8–9, 265, 270–4, 281; Nanjing Massacre 57; Normandy 7, 167–82, 279–80; pilgrimages 244, 264
Baum, T. 64
Beech, John 150, 152
Beirman, D. 130
Belarussia, Chernobyl-related deaths 82
Belfast 61, 66, 67–9, 72–3
Belgium, and the Rwandan genocide 143
Bell, M.M. 177
Beloved (film) 30
Benediktsson, K. 170
Benigni, Roberto 197
Beny-sur-Mer, Normandy 174–7, 178, 181
Beres, M., *Chernobyl Murders* 83
Birds, The (film) 209
Bisesero Memorial, Rwanda 148, 149
black-spot tourism 46, 63
Blain, J. 97, 101, 109, 111
blogs, Chernobyl 84

Blom, T. 14, 19, 24–5
Bloody Sunday Monument, Londonderry/Derry 66
Bonnie Prince Charles (film) 273
Booker T. Washington National Monument, Virginia 41
Borg, A. 169
Boscastle, Cornwall 105
Boswarthen chapel, Cornwall 107–8
Bowman, M. 100, 103
Boyd, S.W. 64
Boyles, F. 244
Boym, S. 174
branding, Baltic States 116, 118, 122, 126
Brandon, R. 207, 212
Brazil, tourism partnership with French Guiana 162
Brezhnev, Leonid 82, 119
British tourists: Auschwitz–Birkenau 195; Normandy battlefields 169; Northern Ireland 64, 65, 69; Rwanda 145
Brody, Sam 208
Brottman, M. 203, 207–8, 210, 214
Broughton, Jahche 135, 136
Browne, George 229
Bruner, E.M. 31
Brunsden, V. 83
burial grounds *see* cemeteries, graves and burial grounds
Burial Hill, Melbourne 225, 226
Burke, Robert O'Hara 228
Burundi 143
Butler, D.L. 33, 42

Caen, Normandy 181
Canadian Battle Monuments Foundation 181
Canadian tourists: Normandy battlefields 7, 167–82, 279–80; Northern Ireland 69
Cane River Creole National Historical Park, Louisiana 32, 41
Cape Coast Castle, Ghana 29
car crash deaths *see* celebrity car crash deaths
Carey, Peter, *True Story of the Kelly Gang* (novel) 220
Carmichael, B.A. 264
Carpiquet, Normandy 181
Carroll, John 220
Carter, P.L. 33, 42
Cartier, C. 171
Catalonian tourists to Northern Ireland 67, 69, 74

Caton, K. 115
Causevic, S. 72
celebrity car crash deaths 8, 202–3, 214–15, 280: Dean, James 204–7; Diana, Princess of Wales 211–14; Kelly, Grace 209–11; Mansfield, Jayne 207–9
Celtic spirituality 100, 103, 104, 105
cemeteries, graves and burial grounds 63: African Burial Ground National Monument 5, 28, 29, 32, 34–42, 277; Antaalnis Cemetery 117; battlefield tourism 265; celebrity car crash deaths 205–6, 207, 208–9, 210; Culloden battlefield 266, 267; Estonian Defence Forces Cemetery 118; as heterotopias 86; Melbourne 225–30, 231; Nanjing Massacre Memorial 49, 53, 55; Normandy battlefields 169, 174–7, 181; Northern Ireland 67; Père-Lachaise Cemetery 4, 13–27, 277; Pokrov Cemetery, Riga 119; Rwandan genocide 146, 146
Central/Eastern Europe, political tourism 62
Charles Edward Stuart, Prince (Bonnie Prince Charlie) 266, 273
Charles, Prince of Wales 211–12, 213
Charriere, Henri, *Papillon* (novel) 157
Chasing the Deer (TV show) 273
Chernobyl 6, 79–80, 90–1, 278: dead zone 81–91; as heterotopia 79, 80–1, 84–90; touristification 83–4
Chernobyl Diaries (film) 83
Chernobyl Murders (novel) 83
China: Korean War 236, 238, 239, 240, 241; Nanjing Massacre Memorial 5, 46–58, 277–8
China–Japan Society 55
Chronis, A. 62, 69, 181
civil rights movement, USA 32–3
Clark, Jane 220
Clarke, William John Turner ('Big Clarke') 228–9
Clinton, Hillary 197
Coiste na nIarchimí Political Tours 72–3
Cole, Tim 168, 195, 196
Coles, T. 99
collective effervescence 21, 25
collective memory, and the Nanjing Massacre 57
Collins, P. 170
Colliers (magazine) 209
colonialism 156, 157

commercial issues: Geoje POW camp 244; Père-Lachaise Cemetery 23–4; Rwandan genocide memorial sites 149
Commission Nationale de Lutte contre le Génocide (CNLG) 144, 146, 150
Commonwealth Games (Melbourne, 2006) 218, 219
Commonwealth War Graves Commission 175
Communist Party, China (Gongchandang) 49–50, 54
comunitas 103: Père-Lachaise Cemetery 21, 25
Confucius 54
Congo 144
Conover, P.J. 100
consumption, postmodern 24: sacred and profane 16–17, 25
contamination of the sacred 21, 23
contemplation of death 3, 47, 63
Cook, Susan E. 153
Cooper, M. 73
Cooper, Rick 136, 137
Cornwall, England 6, 97–9, 104, 110–11, 278–9: Cornish Ancient Sites Protection Network 6, 98, 105, 107, 108–10, 111, 279; Cornwall Tourist Board (CTB) 104; Cornwall and West Devon Mining Landscape 104; heritage site management, paganisms and dark place identity 101–4; New Age and pagan tourism 100–1; spiritual heritage landscape 105–8; spiritual tourism 100, 104–5
Country Girl, The (film) 209
Craik, J. 62, 70
Crash (novel) 202
Crazy Horse (American Indian tribe) 270, 271
Creamer, M. 225
crime: avoiding the glorification of criminals 3; media reporting of 130, 131; Melbourne 219–25; New Zealand 6–7, 129, 132–8, 297; and tourism 132; *see also* jails and penal colonies
Cronenberg, David 208
cruise-ship tourists, Baltic States 122, 125
Crumlin Road Gaol, Belfast 68
Culler, Johnathon 233
Culloden (TV show) 273
Culloden battlefield, Scotland 8–9, 265–70, 272–4, 281
cultural tourism 60, 102–3: Soviet Union 121

Index 285

Cumberland, Duke of (Prince William Augustus) 266, 273
Currie, Major David 181
Custer, General George Armstrong 270, 271, 272, 273
customs officials, Soviet Union 120
Cutler, S.Q. 264
Cyrankiewicz, Jozef 193
Czech Republic 50, 67, 197

D-Day and commemorations 7, 167, 169, 171–82
Danish tourists to Northern Ireland 69
Dann, G.M.S. 33, 47
Darius, J. 206
Darwin bombing 8, 248–9, 262–3, 281: cenotaph 253–4; commemorative plaques 253; Darwin Aviation Heritage Centre (DAHC) 252, 254–5, 256, 257, 258–60, 261–2, 263; Darwin Military Museum (DMM) 249–50, 254, 255, 257; Darwin Post Office 249, 251, 258–9, 262; Defence of Darwin Experience (DDE) 250–2, 254, 255, 256–8, 261, 262, 263; interpretation themes 254–8; Survivors Lookout 253
Dean, James 203, 204–7, 214–15, 280
death: contemplation 3, 47, 63; sequestration 151, 154
decontextualization 17
Defence of Darwin Experience (DDE) 250–2, 254, 255, 256–8, 261, 262, 263
Deng Xiaoping 51, 52
denial of events: Nanjing Massacre 46, 50, 52; Rwandan genocide 151, 154, 279
Department of Conservation, New Zealand 133
Departmental Museum (Musée Departmental), French Guiana 161, 163
Derry/Londonderry 61, 66–9, 72–3
destination management 6–7, 278–80: Cornwall 97–114; French Guiana 156–66; Normandy 167–85; Rwanda 142–55; Soviet tourism in the Baltic States 115–28; Taupo 129–41
destination marketing: Baltic States 116, 126; Père-Lachaise Cemetery 13, 25
deviant leisure 85–6
Devil's Island (Île du Diable), French Guiana 159, 160, 161, 163
Diamond, Jared 143
Dial M for Murder (film) 210
Diana, Princess of Wales 203, 211–15, 280

Diana, Princess of Wales Memorial Fountain, London 213–14
diasporic travels 28–9: African Americans 29–32, 41, 42
Digance, J. 100
Diller, E. 169, 171
Dimanche, F. 132
disaster tourism 63: Chernobyl 6, 79–91, 278
dissonant heritage 3, 46; *see also* undesirable heritage
Dobraszczyk, P. 87, 89
documentary films: African Burial Ground National Monument 35, 37, 38; Culloden battlefield 268; Darwin Aviation Heritage Centre 252; Defence of Darwin Experience 250, 251–2; Little Bighorn battlefield 272
Dodd, Brigadier General Francis 240
donations at Rwandan genocide memorial sites 149
doomsday tourism 63
Dracula Tourism 62
dress codes 242
Dreyfus, Captain Alfred 159, 160
Dunkley, R.A. 170
Durgnat, Raymond 209, 210
Durkheim, Émile 21, 25
Duval, D.T. 130
Dwyer, O.J. 33, 42

earth mysteries 106
Eastern/Central Europe, political tourism 62
Echtern, C.M. 130
economic importance of tourism 4: Chernobyl 84; Cornwall 104, 105; French Guiana 161, 162; Ghana 30; New Zealand 132; Northern Ireland 65, 66, 72, 73; Soviet Union 121
economic issues *see* commercial issues
ecotourism: French Guiana 162, 164; Latvia 122; Rwanda 145
ecstasy, and the Père-Lachaise Cemetery 21
Edelheim, J.R. 131
Eden Project, Cornwall 104
Edensor, T. 87, 168
education *see* pedagogy and education
Edwards, S. 169
effervescence, collective 21, 25
Eichmann trial 198
Eliade, M. 16, 17
Elmina Castle, Ghana 29, 30–1, 40

English Heritage 271
Estonia: branding 118, 122, 126; Estonian Defence Forces Cemetery, Tallinn 118; Soviet tourism 6, 115–26, 279
Euromoniter 163
European Space Program 161
European Union: Amazonia technical assistance programme 162; Baltic States 122
exhibits: African Burial Ground National Memorial 35, 37, 38–9; Althorp estate (Diana, Princess of Wales) 213; Anne Frank House 192; Auschwitz–Birkenau 195; Baltic States museums 116–17, 119; Culloden battlefield 267–8, 269, 270; Darwin bombing commemorative sites 251, 252, 254–63; Geoje POW camp 244; Juno Beach Centre, Normandy 179; Little Bighorn battlefield 272; Nanjing Massacre Memorial 49, 52–3; Rwandan genocide memorial sites 146, 147, 148, 149, 154
experience economy 265: Culloden battlefield 269, 270; Little Bighorn battlefield 272
Eyre, Damien 225

Fairview Cemetery, Pen Argyl, Pennsylvania 208–9
Farmer, S.B. 174
Farrell, Anthony 225
Fawkner, John Pascoe 219
Fayed, Dodi 203, 211, 212, 213
Fayed, Mohamed al 213
feature films: Chernobyl 83; Dean, James 204, 207; Jacobite Rebellion 273–4; Kelly, Grace 209, 210; Kelly, Ned 220; Mansfield, Jayne 207, 208; World War II 169, 197, 198
Federici (Frederick Baker) 230, 231, 233
ferry service, Tallinn–Helsinki 121
Filippucci, P. 168
films *see* documentary films; feature films
Finkelstein, Norman 195–6
Finnish tourists to Baltic States 121, 122
First World War *see* World War I
First World War Museum, Péronne 180
flow experiences, Père-Lachaise Cemetery 21
Foley, M. 46, 63, 99, 102, 129, 169, 212–13, 265, 272
Footitt, H. 174
Forbes, Duncan 267

Ford, Gerald 197
Fordist tourism industry 102
Forsmark Nuclear Power Plant, Sweden 82
Fossey, Dian 142
France: Diana, Princess of Wales 211, 212–13, 214; French Guiana 157, 158–9, 163; Kelly, Grace 209, 210; Lourdes Miracles 17; Normandy battlefields 7, 167–82, 279–80; Père-Lachaise Cemetery 4, 13–27, 277
Frank, Anne 7–8, 189–92, 193, 194, 197–9
Frank, Otto 189–90, 191
Free Derry Tours 73
French Guiana 7, 156–7, 164-5, 279: dark history 157–60; French Guiana Tourism Committee 157, 160, 162, 164; sites of dark tourism 157, 158; tourism context 160–4
French tourists: to French Guiana 161, 162, 163; to Northern Ireland 69; to Suriname 162
Frew, E. 74
Fuchida, Commander Mitsuo 257
Fukushima Daiichi nuclear power plant, Japan 81
future tourism 24–5

Gallipoli battlefields 47, 64, 170
gaols *see* jails and penal colonies
Garden, M.C. 264
Geertz, C. 177
genealogy tourism 62: Northern Ireland 69, 74
genocide tourism *see* Rwandan genocide
Geoje Island POW camps 8, 236–41, 245, 281: accessibility 241–2; authenticity 243–4; interpretation 242–3; management of the site and visitors 244
George II, King 266, 273
German tourists: Auschwitz–Birkenau 195; Northern Ireland 69, 74; pagan tourism 109
Germany, Konzentrationslager Dachau 197
Gettysburg 62, 64, 271
Ghana, roots tourism 29–32, 39, 40, 42
ghost tourism 63: Melbourne 230–2, 233
Gibbs, A. 212
Gibson, D.C. 137
gift shops: African Burial Ground National Monument 35; Darwin Aviation Heritage Centre 252; Geoje POW camp 244; Rwandan genocide memorial sites 146, 149

gifts *see* tributes, offerings and gifts
Gillard, Julia 248
Gillott, Sir Samuel and Lady Elizabeth 228, 229
Gilmore, J.H. 265
Gisozi Genocide Memorial, Kigali 142, 145, 146, 147, 148, 149–50, 151, 153, 154
Glancey, J. 214
Glastonbury, England 97
Glenfinnan Monument, Scotland 273
global positioning system (GPS) devices, Culloden battlefield 268, 269
globalization and cultural homogenization 74
Goatcher, J. 83
Gomulka, Wladyslaw 194
Gongchandang (Communist Party, China) 49–50, 54
Goodman, William 225
Goodrich, J.N. 30
Gorbachev, Mikhail 121
Gough, P. 170
Graham, B.J. 31
graves and graveyards *see* cemeteries, graves and burial grounds
Great Siege of Derry 67, 68
Greenpeace 82
grief tourism 63
Ground Zero, New York 3, 241–2
Grutas Park ('Stalin World'), Lithuania 117, 119
Guiana Space Centre 161, 162, 164
guidance devices, Culloden battlefield 268, 269
guides and guided tours: African Burial Grand National Monument 38; audio-guides *see* audio-guides; Auschwitz–Birkenau 195, 196; Baltic States 116–17, 121, 123–4; Chernobyl 79, 84; Cornwall 109; French Guiana 160; Geoje POW camp 244; Juno Beach Centre 180; Melbourne 221–32, 233; Nanjing Massacre Memorial 49, 52, 53, 55, 56–7; Northern Ireland 69, 72–3, 74; Père-Lachaise Cemetery 15, 23, 24; Rwandan genocide memorial sites 146, 147, 148, 149, 150, 153; Soviet Union 120–1
Guomindang (Nationalist party, China) 49–50
Gustafson, Kathryn 214
Guyana *see* French Guiana

Habyarimana, Juvénal 143
Hague Declaration on Tourism 132
Hailey, Alex 30
Halbwachs, M. 47
Hale, A. 105
Hall, C.M. 130
Hallenstein, Harold 'Hal' 223
Hampel, George 223–4
Hands Across the Divide Monument, Londonderry/Derry 67
Hanks, Tom 169
Hargitay, Mickey 208
Harrison, Ronnie 208
Harrods, London 213, 214
Harry, Prince 212, 213
Harvey, D.C. 101
Harvey, E. 209
Hawkes, Jacquetta 103
Haydon, Lieutenant Colonel Jack 249
Hedges, C. 174
Hedren, 'Tippi' 209
Helsinki, Finland 121
Henderson, J.C. 60
heritage 3: dissonant 3, 46, 265; Melbourne 217, 232–3; undesirable 5, 60–74; World Heritage Sites 4, 29, 30–2, 103, 104
heritage site management, pagan tourism 101–4
heritage tourism 2, 62, 110: African Americans 5, 32, 36, 39–41, 42–3; and community peace building 66; Cornwall 105, 110; dark tourism as development of 47; experience economy 265; French Guiana 162, 163; Nanjing Massacre Memorial 46, 52
Hertz, R. 170
heterochronism 87–8
heterotopias: Chernobyl 79, 80–1, 84, 85–90, 278; of chronology 87–8, 90; of crisis and deviation 85–6, 90; of (de)valorization 88–9, 90; framework 85–90; of functionality 86, 90; of illusion and compensation 89, 90; of juxtaposition 86–7, 90; Père-Lachaise Cemetery 14, 15–16, 19, 21–5
Hetherington, K. 106, 110
Heynen, H. 81
Hickton, George 131
hierophany 17: Père-Lachaise Cemetery 19, 23, 24, 25
Hilberg, Raul 194
Himmler, Heinrich 192
Hiroshima 50, 55

Hitchcock, Alfred 209, 210
Hoddle Street Massacre (1987), Melbourne 220, 222–4, 225
Hollywood Forever Memorial Park, California 208–9
Holocaust (TV show) 194
Holocaust tourism 7–8, 63, 189, 198–9, 280: Auschwitz–Birkenau 192–5, 196; dress codes at dark sites 242; Frank, Anne 189–92; rise of 195–8; selectivity of attention 50
Holt, T. 169
Holt, V. 169
homecoming, roots tourism 40–1
Höss, Rudolf 192
Houghton, Jed 225
Howard, P. 157
Howell, John 136–7
Huigen, P.P.P. 55–6
humiliation, Nanjing Massacre as site of 52–4
Hungarian tourist industry 120
Hungnam evacuation (Korean War) 236, 239, 240–1
Hunt, S.J. 103
Hutus 142–4, 148, 150–1, 153

Iles, J. 181
illegal tourism at Chernobyl 79, 84
Indian Wars 270–3
industrial disaster, Chernobyl 6, 79–91, 278
Interahamwe militia 143
International Committee of the Red Cross 239
International Council for Monuments and Sites (ICOMOS) 6, 98
International Nuclear and Radiological Event Scale 81
International Shelter Implementation Plan, Chernobyl 82
Intourist (Soviet tourist agency) 120
Irish Famine 69
Irish Republican Army (IRA) 64, 65
Ishihara Shintaro 50
Israeli tourists to Auschwitz–Birkenau 195, 196
Italian tourists: Auschwitz–Birkenau 195; Northern Ireland 69

Jackson, Jesse 66
Jacobite Rebellion 266–70, 273
jails and penal colonies 63: Alcatraz 156; Belfast 68; French Guiana 156, 157–61, 163–4, 165; Karosta Military Prison 117; Robben Island 67, 156
Japan: Darwin bombing 248–63; Fukushima Daiichi nuclear power plant 81; Hiroshima and Nagasaki attacks 50, 55; Nanjing Massacre 5, 46, 49–55, 58
Jensen, Graeme 225
Jewish Holocaust *see* Holocaust tourism
John Paul II, Pope 197
Joly, Marc 180
Juno Beach, Normandy 167, 171–2, 180, 181
Juno Beach Centre, Normandy 178–81
Jurmala, Latvia 119

Kanazawa, Sergeant Major Akira 260
Karen Aim Memorial Working Group 136–7
Karosta Military Prison, Latvia 117
Kawamura, Takashi 46
Kazan, Elia 204
Keegan, J. 167
Kelly, Grace 204, 209–11, 214–15, 280
Kelly, Ned 219–20, 225, 230
Kelly, S. 73
KGB 120
Kigali, Rwanda 142, 143, 144, 145, 146, 147, 148, 149–50, 151, 153, 154
King, John 228
King, Martin Luther, Jr. 33
Kissane, K. 209, 210
kitsch 17
Knight, Julian 222–4
Knox, D. 266
Koenker, D.P. 120
Konzentrationslager Dachau, Munich 197
Kopitoff, I. 25
Korean War 8, 236–45, 281
Kourou Space Centre, French Guiana 161, 162, 164
Krakow, Wieliczka Salt Mines 197
kratophany 21, 22–3
Kuomingtang (Nationalist party, China) 49–50

Lacquer, T.W. 264
Lake, H. 209
landscape 167: ritual 104, 105; spiritual heritage 105–8; of war 168–82
Lanfant, M. 61
language issues: French Guiana guided tours 160; Rwandan genocide memorial sites 150, 154
Lanzmann, Claude 194

LaRue, Captain Leonard 241
Latvia: branding 118, 122, 126; Latvian People's Front Museum 116–17; Soviet tourism 6, 115–26, 279
Laura Plantation, Vacherie, Louisiana 33
Lefebvre, H. 171
leisure, deviant 85–6
Lenin, Vladimir Ilyich 88, 116
Lennon, J. 46, 47, 50, 63, 72, 99, 102, 129, 134, 137, 169, 212–13, 265, 272
Lepetic, A. 132
Letcher, A. 103, 104, 111
Lety, Czech Republic 50
Levi, Primo 199
Levinson, C. 121
Lew, A. 171
Lexow, M. 131
library, African Burial Ground National Monument 35
Lightbody, R. 71
Linenthal, E.T. 32, 179, 264
Lithuania: branding 118, 122, 126; Holocaust 50; Soviet tourism 6, 115–26, 279
Little Big Horn battlefield 8–9, 265, 270–4, 281
Lombardi, R. 130
London: Diana, Princess of Wales memorials 213–14
Londonderry/Derry 61, 66–9, 72–3
Londres, Albert 159
Lonely Planet (travel guides), Baltic States 116–17
Lourdes Miracles 17
Lowenthal, D. 50, 102, 215
Lund, K.A. 170
Lunney, Officer 241
Lynch, P. 72

MacArthur, General Douglas 237
MacCannell, D. 101, 168–9
McClarty, David 72
McEvoy, Peter 225
McGeer, E. 175
McLean, F. 61, 264, 266
Madron Holy Well, Cornwall 107–8, 109
Magnolia Plantation, Vacherie, Louisiana 32
Maihi-Carrolls, Chattrice 131
Mansfield, Jayne 203, 207–9, 214–15, 280
Mansfield, Y. 132
Mao Zedong 50
Māoris 133–4, 138

Margelis, Con 224
markers of battlefields 168–81
marketing *see* destination marketing
Marnie (film) 209
Marshman, Sophia 197
Martin Luther King, Jr., National Historic Site, George 32, 33
Marxism–Leninism 88
Maskey, Paul 72
mass media *see* media
Maze Prison/Long Kesh, Belfast 68
media: celebrity car crash deaths 210, 211, 213, 214; crime coverage 130, 131, 132, 135–6; Darwin bombing 254–5; Diana, Princess of Wales 211, 212, 213; Kelly, Grace 210; Korean War 239; portrayals of tourist destinations 129–31; Rwandan genocide 151
Medvedev, Z. 82
Meierhenrich, Jens 145
Meijering, L. 55–6
Melbourne, Australia 8, 217–18, 232–4, 280–1: background 218; cemetery tours 226–30; crime tours 220–6; ghost tours 230–2, 233; as host of successful events 218–19; Melbourne Cup 218–19; Melbourne General Cemetery (MGC) 226–30, 231; murderous 219–32
Mels, T. 170
memento mori (Latin expression), celebrity car crash deaths 206, 215
memorials and monuments 2, 3: African Burial Ground National Monument 5, 28, 29, 32, 34–42, 277; Aim, Karen 136, 137; Anne Frank House 191, 198, 199; Auschwitz–Birkenau 193, 195, 196, 198, 199; Baltic States 117, 118, 119, 121; battlefield tourism 265; celebrity car crash deaths 205–6, 208–9, 210, 213–14, 215; Cornwall 98, 106–7, 108, 109; Culloden 266, 267, 273; Darwin bombings 253–4; Dean, James 205–6; Diana, Princess of Wales 213–14; Kelly, Grace 210; Korean War 236, 241, 244; Little Bighorn 271–2; Mansfield, Jayne 208–9; Melbourne 221, 225, 227, 228; Nanjing Massacre Memorial 5, 46–58, 277–8; Normandy battlefields 169, 172, 179, 180, 181; Northern Ireland 66, 67; Rwandan genocide 142, 144–51, 152–3, 154
Mên an Tol monument, Cornwall 106–7, 109

Michalski, S. 169
Miles, W.F.S. 64, 243, 245
Milltown Cemetery, Belfast 67
Miracles, Lourdes 17
Mironko, Charles 143
Monaco 211
monuments *see* memorials and monuments
morbid tourism 63
Morgan, N. 218
Morrison, Toni 30
mortality, contemplation of 3, 47, 63
Moscardo, G.M. 242
Mosse, G.L. 174
Mueller, Ferdinand von 227
murals, Northern Ireland 66, 67, 68, 69, 73
Murambi Memorial, Rwanda 147–8, 149, 150, 151, 152–3, 154
Murray, Lord George 269
museums: Anne Frank House 191–2, 199; Auschwitz–Birkenau 192–5, 196, 199; Darwin Military Museum 249–50, 254, 255, 257; First World War Museum, Péronne 180; French Guiana 161, 163, 164; Geoje POW camp 236, 244; Museum of Free Derry 66–7, 68; Museum of Genocide, Lithuania 117, 119; Museum of Occupation of Estonia, Tallinn 118, 123; Museum of Occupation of Latvia, Riga 118–19; Père-Lachaise Cemetery 18; Robben Island Museum 67; Rwandan genocide 146, 148, 149, 153, 154; sacredness 17; United States Holocaust Museum, Washington DC 197, 241–2, 243; USS Arizona Memorial Museum 242; World War 180
Mutanguha, Freddy 151
mystery, Père-Lachaise Cemetery 23
myths 174: Père-Lachaise Cemetery 21, 23

Nagasaki 50, 55
Nanjing Massacre Memorial, China 5, 46–9, 55–8, 277–8: context 49–52; national humiliation site 52–4; place identities 52; war resistance site 54–5
National Civil Rights Museum, Tennessee 32
National Commission for the Fight against Genocide (CNLG) 144, 146, 150
National Geographic (magazine) 121
national humiliation, Nanjing Massacre as site of 52–4
national identity and place identity 2, 61, 63

National Monuments, USA 270
National Parks Service (NPS), USA 270, 271, 272
National Tourist Organization (NTO), Northern Ireland 60
National Trust for Scotland (NTS) 266, 268, 269
neo-pagan tourism 100–1, 109
Netherlands, Anne Frank House 7–8, 189–92, 193, 197–9, 280
New Age tourism 97–8, 100–1, 103: Cornwall 105, 109
New Zealand: crime 132–4; New Zealand Institute 133; Taupo 6–7, 129–38, 279; tourists to Gallipoli battlefields 47, 64
Nielsen, C. 129, 130
Nkrumah, Kwame 30
Noble, Tom 220, 222
Nolan, Sidney 219, 220
Normandy battlefields 7, 167–71, 177, 178, 181–2, 279–80: Abbaye d'Ardenne 177–9; Basley village 172–4; Beny-sur-Mer 175–7; Juno Beach 171–2; Juno Beach Centre 179–81
North Korea 236–41, 242, 243, 245
Northern Ireland tourism 5, 60–8, 73–4, 278: demand perspective 68–71; Northern Ireland Tourist Board (NITB) 60, 65, 69, 71–2, 73; supply perspective 71–3
nostalgia tourism 115: Baltic States 116–17, 119, 122–3, 125, 126, 279
Noukagude Eesti (travel book) 121
Novelli, M. 99, 102–3
novels and Chernobyl 82, 83
novelty, search for 102
Novick, Peter 196
Ntarama Memorial, Rwanda 147, 149, 150, 152
nuclear accidents 81: Chernobyl 6, 79–91, 278
Nyamata Memorial, Rwanda 146–7, 149, 154
Nyarubuye Memorial, Rwanda 148, 149, 151

Oakland Plantation, Vacherie, Louisiana 32
Obama, Barack 29
objectification: Père-Lachaise Cemetery 21–2; sacredness 17
offerings *see* tributes, offerings and gifts
Official District, French Guiana 160
Olsen, D.H. 97, 100

Olympic Games: Melbourne (1956) 218, 219; Sydney (2000) 219–20
Omaha Beach, Normandy 169, 171
Orange Order Parade, Northern Ireland 67
Orbasli, A. 115

pagan tourism 97, 98, 100–1, 103, 104, 110–11: Cornwall 6, 104–10, 278–9
Palestine and Northern Ireland, links between 67, 68, 74
Pan-African Movement 30
Papillon (novel) 157
Paris: Diana, Princess of Wales 211, 212–13, 214; Père-Lachaise Cemetery 4, 13–27, 277
Park, H.Y. 177, 178
Parker-Bowles, Camilla 211, 213
patriotism and prisoners of war 244
Paul, Henri 211, 212
Pearl Harbor bombing 257
Pearson, J. 100
pedagogy and education: African Burial Ground National Monument 41–2; Cornish Ancient Sites Protection Network 108; Culloden 267, 268, 270; Geoje POW camp 244, 245; Northern Ireland 70, 71; remembrance tourism 115
Peirce, Victor 225
penal colonies *see* jails and penal colonies
Pension Līgatne Nuclear Bomb shelter, Latvia 117
Père-Lachaise Cemetery, Paris 4, 13–14, 24–7, 277: commitment, sacrifices and rituals 19–21; *communitas*, ecstasy and flow experiences 21; contamination and objectification 21–2; ethnographic study methodology 17–18; heterotopia 15–16; heterotopias and temporal hierophany 19; myths, mystery and kratophany 22–3; opposition of sacred and profane 23–4; place identity and attachment 14–15; sacred and profane in postmodern consumption 16–17; visitors' motives and sacred properties 18–19
perpetrator interpretation strategies 243
Pettingill, Trevor 225
Phillips, C. 105
photographic galleries and exhibitions: Chernobyl 84; Darwin bombing commemorative sites 250, 254–5, 258–9, 261–2, 263

photography by tourists: Chernobyl 89; Melbourne 217–18; Rwandan genocide memorial sites 146, 149, 150
Pianist, The (film) 197
Pierkarz, M. 170, 267
pilgrimages 99: Anne Frank House 190, 191, 199; Auschwitz–Birkenau 197, 199; battlefields 244, 264; celebrity car crash deaths 206, 209; cemeteries 13, 18, 21; *communitas* 21; Cornwall 105, 108; Normandy battlefields 174; Père-Lachaise Cemetery 18, 21; religious 97, 100; Rwanda 142, 145, 152, 154; sacredness 17; slavery tourism 31
Pine, B.J. 265
Pinkney, Matthew 213
Pitchford, S. 61
Pizam, A. 132
place attachment, Père-Lachaise Cemetery 14
place interpretation 7–9, 280–1: celebrity car crash deaths 202–16; Culloden and Little Bighorn 264–75; Darwin 248–63; Holocaust tourism 189–201; Melbourne 217–35; South Korean POW camps 236–47
plantation tourism 29, 33, 63
Pointe-du Hoc, Normandy 169
Pokrov Cemetery, Riga 119
Poland: Auschwitz–Birkenau 7–8, 189, 192–9, 242, 280; Museum of Free Derry (Northern Ireland) 67; tourist industry 120
Polanski, Roman 197
political tourism 62: Northern Ireland 72
Pollard, T. 269
Port Arthur Historic Site, Tasmania 64
Porter, Neil 214
post-colonial tourism 156, 157
postmodernity 24: novelty, search for 102; sacred and profane 16–17, 25
Powell, Sergeant Les 260
prayer: African Burial Ground National Monument 39, 40; Père-Lachaise Cemetery 19, 21, 23
Pride, R. 218
Prideaux, B. 265
Pripyat, Ukraine 79, 82–90
prisoner of war (POW) camps, Geoje Island, South Korea 8, 236–41, 245, 281: accessibility 241–2; authenticity 243–4; interpretation 242–3; management of the site and visitors 244

prisons *see* jails and penal colonies
Pritchard, A. 218
profane, Père-Lachaise Cemetery 16–17, 21, 23–4, 25
purification rites at Chernobyl 88

Queen Street Massacre (1987), Melbourne 220, 224–5

Rainier, Prince 209, 210, 211
Ravio, P.J. 264
Rear Window (film) 210
reconciliation after the Rwandan genocide 144, 152, 153
recording kiosk, Defence of Darwin Experience 252
regulation of travel and tourism: Korean demilitarized zone 242; Rwandan genocide memorial sites 150, 154; Soviet Union 120–1
Reitlinger, Gerlad 194
religion and religious tourism 97, 100, 102–3: sacred 16; *see also* pagan tourism; spiritual tourism
Remembrance Day (Commonwealth countries) 168
remembrance tourism 115: accidental sites 134; Baltic States 117, 119, 122–3, 125, 126, 279; Canadian tourists to Normandy battlefields 7, 167–82, 279–80
Republic of Ireland 65, 69
research area, African Burial Ground National Monument 35
Richter, L.K. 62, 70
Riga, Latvia 118–19, 124
Ritchie, J.R.B. 130
rites and rituals: heterotopias 16; Normandy battlefields 177, 178; pagan tourism 104, 107; Père-Lachaise Cemetery 20–1, 25; sacredness 16, 17, 20–1
ritual landscape 104: Cornwall 105
Roadside Picnic (novel) 83
Robb, J.G. 105–6, 110
Robben Island, South Africa 67, 156
Robins, Gwen 209–10
Rojek, C. 46, 102, 202, 205, 217
Roma mass extermination, Czech Republic 50
Romania, Dracula Tourism 62
Romein, J. 190
Roots (film, novel, TV series) 30, 39
roots tourism, African Americans 5, 28, 29–32, 40, 42

Royal Australian Air Force (RAAF) 249
Royal Australian Artillery Association 249
Royal Island (Île Royal), French Guiana 159, 160, 161, 163
Rule, Andrew 219
Russell Street Bombing (1986), Melbourne 220, 222, 223
Russia, Chernobyl-related deaths 82
Rwandan genocide 7, 142, 153–4, 279: aftermath, commemoration, politics and place identity 144–5; dimensions of place identity 152–3; historical background 142–4; memorial sites 145–51
Rwandan Patriotic Front (RPF) 143, 144, 151
Ryan, C. 169

S.T.A.L.K.E.R.: Call of Pripyat (video game) 83
S.T.A.L.K.E.R.: Shadow of Chernobyl (video game) 83
sacred: African Burial Ground National Monument 35, 37, 39–40; Holocaust tourism 198; pagan tourism 6, 97–8, 104, 278; Père-Lachaise Cemetery 14, 16–17, 18–24, 25; religious tourism 100; spiritual tourism 101
St Columb's Cathedral, Londonderry/Derry 67–9
St Jean du Maroni, French Guiana 161
Saint Joseph Island (Île Saint-Joseph), French Guiana 160, 161, 163
St Lambert sur Dives, Normandy 181
St Michael's Church, Krasnoe, Ukraine 84
Sala, George Augustus 218
Salvation Islands (Île du Salut), French Guiana 160
Sands, Bobby 67
Sanger, D. 197
Sangster, William 229
Santos, C. 115
Saving Private Ryan (film) 169
Scates, B. 168, 170
Schadenfreude (German expression) 47
Schindler's List (film) 197
Scofidio, R. 169, 171
Seaton, A.V. 33, 46, 47, 63, 98, 99, 101, 103, 169, 174, 175
Seaton, T. 29
Second World War *see* World War II
secularization of the sacred 17
Sennett, R. 89

sequestration of death 151, 154
Shackley, M. 97, 100
Sharp, Jeb 151
Sharpley, Richard 99, 102, 103, 126, 145, 150, 156, 206, 243, 244
Shipman, D. 208
Shiranshi Shinichiro 57–8
Shoah, The (TV show) 195
shops *see* gift shops
Siege of Londonderry/Derry 67, 68
Silverstone, R. 130
Silvester, John 219
Singer, A. 42
Sinn Fein 65, 72
Sitting Bull (American Indian tribe) 270, 271
Sivan, E. 168, 174
Slade, P. 47
slavery tourism, African Americans 5, 28, 42–5, 277: African Burial Ground National Monument 5, 34–42, 277; diasporic travels 28–9; Ghana 29–32; United States of America 32–42
Smith, A. 266
Smith, D. 50
Smith, L. 101, 111
Smith, William 73
social media 203
solar eclipse (1997, Cornwall) 98, 105, 109
Solo, Mano 20
Somme 170, 174
Sophie's Choice (film) 197
South Africa, Robben Island 67, 156
South Korea: POW camps 8, 236–45, 281; tourists to Auschwitz–Birkenau 195
South West Tourism (SWT), England 104
souvenirs: celebrity car crash deaths 206; Darwin Aviation Heritage Centre 252; Geoje POW camp 244; Père-Lachaise Cemetery 21, 22, 23–4; Rwandan genocide memorial sites 146; sacredness 17; *see also* gift shops
Soviet Experience tours, Estonia 123–4
Soviet Life (magazine) 121
Soviet tourism in the Baltic States 6, 115–26, 279
Soviet Union: Auschwitz–Birkenau 193, 194, 195; Chernobyl 6, 79–91, 278; Korean War 236, 237, 238
Spanish tourists to Northern Ireland 69
spectator interpretation strategies 243: Geoje POW camp 243, 245

Spencer, Earl Charles 213
Spielberg, Steven 169, 197
spiritual tourism 97, 98, 100, 101, 110–11: African Burial Ground National Monument 39–40; Cornwall 104–10; Père-Lachaise Cemetery 17–18; *see also* pagan tourism; religion and religious tourism
Spoto, Donald 209
SS *Meredith Victory* 236, 240–1, 243
SS *Tallinn* 121
staff: African Burial Ground National Memorial 40–1; Cornish Ancient Sites Protection Network 108; Nanjing Massacre Memorial 49, 55; *see also* guides and guided tours
Stalin, Joseph 120, 194
'Stalin World' (Grutas Park), Lithuania 117, 119
Stalker (film) 83
State Library of Victoria, 'Kelly Culture' exhibition 220
Stephanie, Princess 209, 210
Stone, Philip R. 64, 99, 102, 103, 111, 126, 134, 145, 156, 157, 202–3, 206
Stonehenge, England 97
Story of the Kelly Gang, The (film) 220
Straffon, Cheryl 109, 110
Strugatsky, Boris and Arkady, *Roadside Picnic* 83
Styron, William 197
suicide tourism 63
Suriname tourism development plan 162
Survivors Lookout, Darwin 253
Sydney, Australia 218, 219

Tallinn, Estonia 116, 118, 121, 122, 123, 124
Tanaka Masaaki 50
Tarkovsky, Andrei 83
Tarlow, P. 47, 63, 102, 103
Tasmania, Port Arthur Historic Site 64
Tate St Ives, Cornwall 104
Taupo, New Zealand 6–7, 129, 137–8, 279: accidental place of remembrance 134; crime and tourism 132; crime in New Zealand 132–4; media 129–31; murder of Karen Aim 134–7
Taylor, Angela 222
Taylor, Joseph Leslie Theodore 'Squizzy' 220
temporal hierophany, Père-Lachaise Cemetery 19

Terezin, Czech Republic 50, 197
thanatourism 3, 29, 46, 63, 99, 169: definition 47; Normandy battlefields 177; pagan tourism 98, 101, 103; Père-Lachaise Cemetery 13–27
Tilden, F. 248
Tilley, C.Y. 167
Timothy, D.J. 97, 100, 130
Tintagel, Cornwall 105
To Catch a Thief (film) 210
Torgovnick, M. 173
Tourism New Zealand 133
tours *see* guides and guided tours
Toyoshima, Petty Officer Hajime 259–60
Transportation Camp (Camp de la Transportation), French Guiana 160, 161, 163
tributes, offerings and gifts: African Burial Ground National Monument 40; Normandy battlefields 178, 179; pagan tourism 108; Père-Lachaise Cemetery 19–20, 25
Trintignant, Marie 21
True Story of the Kelly Gang (novel) 220
Truman, Harry S. 237
Tuan, Y.-F. 17, 170
Tully, Jim 131
Tunbridge, J.E. 31, 46, 101, 102, 265
Turner, V.W. 21, 25, 175
Tutsis 142–4, 148, 150–1, 153
Two Men in a Trench (TV show) 273
Tynan, Steven 225

Uganda 143
Ukraine 6, 79–91, 278
Ulster Unionist Party (UUP) 72
Ulungura, Matthias 259–60
undesirable heritage 60: Northern Ireland 5, 60–74; *see also* atrocity tourism; dissonant heritage
UNESCO 30
Union of Soviet Socialist Republics *see* Soviet Union
United Kingdom: Battle of Hastings 271; Cornwall 6, 97–111, 278–9; Culloden battlefield 8–9, 265–70, 272–4, 281; Northern Ireland tourism 5, 60–74, 278; pagan tourism 97–8; World War II 169; *see also* British tourists
United Nations: International Council for Monuments and Sites 6, 98; Korean War 237, 238, 239, 240, 241; Rwanda 143; UNESCO 30

United States of America: accessibility of dark tourism sites 241–2; African Burial Ground National Monument 5, 28, 29, 32, 34–42, 277; Air Force 252; Anderson National Historic Site 244; celebrity car crash deaths 204, 205–9; China's foreign policy 51; civil rights movement 32–3; economic power 52; Frank, Anne 198; Gettysburg 62, 64, 271; Hiroshima and Nagasaki attacks 50; Korean War 236, 237; Little Big Horn battlefield 8–9, 265, 270–4, 281; Memorial Day 168; National Monuments 270; National Parks Service 270, 271, 272; and Northern Ireland 69; paganism 100, 109; World War II 50, 168, 169, 256, 257, 262–3; *see also* American tourists
United States Holocaust Museum, Washington DC 197, 241–2, 243
Urquhart, G. 264
USS Arizona Memorial Museum 242

Vallen, J.J. 121
Vance, J.F.W. 174
Vernon, Phil 148
Verrières Ridge, Normandy 181
victim interpretation strategies 242–3
victims, respect for 3, 4: Aim, Karen 136–7
Victoria Police Memorial, Melbourne 221
video games and Chernobyl 83
video recording kiosk, Defence of Darwin Experience 252
Vilnius, Lithuania 117, 119, 125
violent crime: media reporting of 130, 131; Melbourne 219–25; New Zealand 6–7, 129, 132, 133, 134–8, 279; public perceptions of 131
Viru Hotel, Tallinn 121
visas, Soviet Union 120
visitor motivation 4–6, 277–8: Chernobyl 79–93; Nanjing Massacre Memorial 46–59; Northern Ireland 60–78; Père-Lachaise Cemetery 13–27; slavery tourism 28–45
Vita e Bella, La (*Life is Beautiful*) (film) 197
Vitkovic, Frank 224
vodka tourism 121
volunteers: African Burial Ground National Memorial 40–1; Cornish Ancient Sites Protection Network 108

Wallis, R.J. 97, 101, 109, 111
Walsh Street Shootings (1988), Melbourne 220, 225
Walter, Tony 145, 206
war resistance, Nanjing Massacre as site of 54–5
Watkins, Peter, *Culloden* (film) 273
Watson, Don 220
Webb, Garth 180
Webber, Jonathan 199
websites: Cornish Ancient Sites Protection Network 108; memorial 137; Nanjing Massacre Memorial 49
West Penwith, Cornwall 6, 98, 104–8, 109, 110
White, G. 172
White, L. 74
Wieliczka Salt Mines, Krakow 197
Wight, A.C. 50, 99, 101, 102
William, Prince 212, 213
Williams, Paul 151, 152
Wills, William John 228
Wilson, J.Z. 72, 73
Winter, J.M. 168, 174, 175–6, 177
Woodward, S. 115

World Heritage Sites 4, 103: Cornwall and West Devon Mining Landscape 104; Elmina Castle 29, 30–2
World War I: battlefield tourism 265; Gallipoli battlefields 47, 64, 170; myth 174; Somme 170, 174
World War II Memorials: Antaalnis Cemetery, Vilnius 117; Estonian Defence Forces Cemetery 118; Pokrov Cemetery, Riga 119
World War II: D-Day and commemorations 7, 167, 169, 171–82; Darwin bombings 8, 248–63, 281; interpretation of dark sites 242; Normandy battlefields 7, 167–82, 279–80; Pearl Harbor bombing 257; Soviet tourism in Baltic States 119; *see also* Holocaust tourism; World War II Memorials
Wren, John 228

Yin, R.K. 157
Yoshida, T. 50
Young, James 198

Zaire 144

CPSIA information can be obtained
at www.ICGtesting.com
Printed in the USA
BVHW04*1456070718
520804BV00007B/189/P